P9-DXZ-257

THE REGIONAL IMPERATIVE

THE REGIONAL IMPERATIVE

The Administration of U.S. Foreign Policy
Towards South Asian States
Under Presidents Johnson and Nixon

LLOYD I. RUDOLPH
SUSANNE HOEBER RUDOLPH
AND OTHERS

With an Epilogue by
CHRISTOPHER VAN HOLLEN

HUMANITIES PRESS, INC.
ATLANTIC HIGHLANDS, NEW JERSEY

© Lloyd I. Rudolph and Susanne Hoeber Rudolph 1980

First published in 1980 in the U.S.A.
by Humanities Press Inc.
Atlantic Highlands, N.J. 07716

Library of Congress Cataloging in Publication Data

Rudolph, Lloyd I
    The regional imperative.

    Originally published in 1975 as appendix 5 of v. 7
of the U.S. Commission on the Organization of the
Government for the Conduct of Foreign Policy's Report.
    Includes index.
    1. South Asia—Relations (general) with the United
States.   2. United States—Relations (general) with
South Asia.   3. Johnson, Lyndon Baines, Pres. U.S.,
1908-1973.   4. Nixon, Richard Milhous, 1913-
I. Rudolph, Susanne Hoeber, joint author. II. Title.
DS 341. 3.U6R83   327.73054   80-21815
ISBN 0-391-02178-8

First published in 1980 in India by
Concept Publishing Company
New Delhi-110015

Printed in India by

Sunil Composing Co.
at S.P. Printers, New Delhi 110028

Introduction

The Regional Imperative first appeared in 1975 as one of twenty-four studies prepared by consulting scholars for the national Commission on the Organization of the Government for the Conduct of Foreign Policy. The Commission was created in 1973 on the initiative of the U.S. Senate's Foreign Relations Committee by an act of Congress. Chaired by Robert Murphy, the Commission was composed of twelve members equally chosen by the Senate, the House of Representatives and the President. It included the vice-president, senators, congressmen, educationists, businessmen and professionals. The Commission's mandate was "to submit findings and recommendations to provide a more effective system for the formulation and implementation of the nation's foreign policy."

In March, 1974, the Commission authorized a study program. We were asked at the time to prepare a study responsive to one of the program's objectives, i.e. to evaluate "the capacity of the U.S. to maintain coordination between a large number of policies impinging on a . . . region." It was published along with the Commission's *Report*, and six additional volumes of appendices in June, 1975 as Appendix V of Volume 7 by the Superintendent of Documents, U.S. Government Printing Office, Washington D.C. and is published here as *The Regional Imperative : The Administration of U.S. Foreign Policy towards South Asian States under Presidents Johnson and Nixon.* We are pleased that Concept Publishing Company in India and Humanities Press in the United States are making it available to wider publics by bringing out trade editions.

The Commission was created at a time when the imperial presidency had reached its apogee with the beginning of Richard Nixon's second administration in January, 1972. It carried on its work during the presidency's most serious crisis, the president's unprecedented resignation in August, 1974, and the incumbencies of an unelected president and vice-president, Gerald Ford and Nelson Rockefeller. The Commission concluded its efforts in 1975 under the influence of primaries for the 1976 presidential election. It was during this period too that Henry Kissinger, as the president's assistant for national security affairs, invoked executive privilege to declare himself immune to Congressional inquiries or accountability and became simultaneously secretary of state, again unprecedented situations that influenced the creation of the Commission and its work.

The conduct of U.S. foreign policy towards the states of South Asia in the high noon of the imperial presidency under Presidents Johnson and Nixon reflected their personal and strategic predispositions and concerns. The result detailed in our overview and in the case studies by Oldenburg, Bjorkman and Moulton, was the confusion of presidential with national interest, global over-determination in the assessment of other states' intentions and actions, and poorly informed and managed imperative coordination of policy. Henry Kissinger's after-the-fact justification of the Nixon administration's response to the Bangladesh independence crisis in *White House Years* (1979) rationalizes its failure to deal effectively with Pakistan's genocidal civil war and the Indo-Pakistan war that followed. Kissinger's retrospective rationalizations of 1979 continue to reflect the conceptual and organizational inadequacies of the Nixon-Kissinger era. Happily, we have been able to append Christopher Van Hollen's telling and informed critique of Kissinger's interpretation of these events, "The Tilt Policy Revisited: Nixon-Kissinger Geo-Politics and South Asia," which appeared in the April, 1980 number of *Asian Survey*. Van Hollen, Deputy Assistant Secretary of State for South Asia at the time of the Bangladesh crisis, deals particularly well with the effects of global over-determination on national objectives and on the intentions and capabilities of global as against regional actors.

The Regional Imperative is the result of extensive research carried out in 1974 under our direction. It examines the capacity of the U.S. government to maintain coordination among a large number of policies affecting the states of South Asia over the ten years (1965-1974) spanned by the Johnson and Nixon administrations. Our overview and the ten case studies examine the difficulties of coordinating policies across several divides : from crises to more routine situations; from one function to another; from one state to another within the region ; from one region to other regions ; and from regional and functional to global or strategic considerations.

Of the ten case studies three (Cohen, Oldenburg and Rubin) deal with national security ; four (Bjorkman, Hadden, Kochanek, and Moulton) with economic policy; and two (Andersen and Lenth) with people-to-people aspects of American policy making and execution as they related to South Asian states. Our overview, *inter alia*, comments on these cases and proposes organizational modifications to improve the policy process. We argue that regional considerations often were given less consideration than they require and propose conceptual, normative and organizational changes designed to promote better approximations of the national interest. We have kept the recommendations of the original report because they are an integral part of its analysis and explanation.

The studies in this volume were written under the influence of the literature on bureaucratic politics, particularly Graham Allison's study of the Cuban missile crisis, *The Essence of Decision*. Its influence was negative as much as positive, i.e. the concepts and explanations used here were as much in tension as in accord with a bureaucratic politics framework. Other conceptual dimensions such as world views encompassing ideological predispositions and national character stereotypes; cognitive categories that select and organize knowledge about international politics; and psychological processes that affect organizational, particularly small group, relationships, are among the additional determinants that shaped our analysis and recommendations.

Perhaps the least familiar of these determinants are the psychological processes that affect organizational relationships among those who formulate and manage policy, relationships we designated with the contrasting concepts imperative and deliberative coordination. We were less concerned with minimizing the irrationality that can result from "group think" and "effectiveness traps" than with maximizing the rationality that can result from deliberative coordination among knowledgeable and experienced colleagues. We recognize that administrative hierarchies, particularly those affected by presidential attention, are meant to produce results more desired by those higher than by those lower in the hierarchy. We also recognize that deliberation among colleagues across vertical and lateral differences can result in better informed and more rational decision making and policy management. Organizational arrangements that promote collegiality and deliberation at the expense of hierarchy and command most of the time produce better approximations of the national interest.

The contradictions between hierarchy and collegiality will remain powerful as long as president's men seeking to promote the president's interest resist incorporating in their understanding of the national interest the knowledge and judgment independent career professionals can provide. Two years is a long time in a president's term. He needs results sooner rather than later. The opening to China (July, 1971) was well timed for the November election but the South Asia crisis with which it coincided was an unwanted irritant and embarrassment.

The mechanics of mounting and coordinating the studies in this volume were fairly straight forward. The project was funded by a grant from the Commission to us, the principal investigators. We in turn recruited knowledgeable and experienced academic colleagues, research assistants and clerical staff. A preliminary conference of participants formulated an agreed framework of analysis, division of labor and schedule of work. At a second conference draft studies were critiqued and subsequently revised. The revised papers were read and criticized by us and by the Commission study directors, who also critiqued our draft overview paper. At a final conference, this time in Washington rather than Chicago, the re-written papers, which had been circulated beforehand, were critically discussed by outside experts, mostly academic but some governmental, and Commission representatives. The papers were then put in their final form.

Under the terms of the legislation creating the Commission, consulting scholars with security clearance were given access to classified material on the understanding that it would be used only to inform judgments and make evaluations. Serving officials were expected to be forthcoming in the many interviews conducted in Washington and in South Asia. These arrangements, as might be expected, were only moderately successful.

A wide range of interviews were conducted, not only on diplomatic activities (State) but also on strategic (Department of Defense, Central Intelligence Agency and the White House's own state department, the National Security Council), economic (Treasury, Agricultural, Commerce) and people-to-people (United States Information Agency, Bureau of Educational and Cultural Affairs, now combined in the International Communication Agency). Information is a source of power as well as knowledge. Scholars and officials have overlapping but divergent interests with respect to information and this difference affected what we and our colleagues could learn. Kissinger loyalists for example, may have left some things unsaid not only because it was convenient to do so but also because they shared his world view.

The Commission's study directors, Peter Szanton and William I. Bacchus, were helpful throughout. Bacchus, who had primary responsibility for our study, greatly facilitated access to records and arrangements for interviews in Washington and made many valuable substantive and analytic suggestions to us and our colleagues. Over all, the Commission framework provided a unique opportunity to do research on foreign policy.

Chronology, the order of events, in fact orders events. It too is an important determinant of foreign policy. Reading Joan Landy Erdman's "A Chronology of Events in South Asia Bearing on the Conduct of Foreign Policy," which appears as an Annex, makes this abundantly clear.

Philip Oldenburg managed the flow of people and papers with aplomb and made important contributions to editing manuscripts.

Susan Lenth, who managed the office and finances with

finesse, remained calm and charming throughout the hectic
months of 1974 and 1975 that it took to complete the project.

"Fernworth"   LLOYD I. RUDOLPH
Landour Cantonment   SUSANNE HOEBER RUDOLPH
Mussoorie, Uttar Pradesh

21 April 1980.

Contents

CASE STUDIES

List of Contributors

Walter Andersen,
    Analyst for India and Indian Ocean, Bureau of Intelligence and Research, Department of State.

James W. Bjorkman,
    Assistant Professor of Preventive Medicine and Political Science, University of Wisconsin, Madison, Wisconsin.

Stephen Philip Cohen,
    Professor of Political Science and Asian Studies, University of Illinois, Urbana, Illinois.

Joan L. Erdman
    Outreach Coordinator, South Asia Language and Area Center, University of Chicago and Adjunct Assistant Professor, Department of Criminal Justice, University of Illinois at Chicago Circle.

Susan G. Hadden,
    Assistant Professor, Lyndon Baines Johnson School of Public Affairs, University of Texas, Austin, Texas.

Gerald A. Heeger,
    Dean of University College, Associate Professor of Political Studies, Adelphi University, Garden City, New York.

Stanley A. Kochanek,
    Professor of Political Science, Pennsylvania State University, State College, Pennsylvania.

Charles S. Lenth,

  Policy Analyst, Illinois Economic and Fiscal Commission, State of Illinois, Springfield, Illinois, Ph. D. Candidate, Department of Political Science, University of Chicago.

Anthony D. Moulton,

  Assistant Director for State Planning, State of Missouri, Columbia, Missouri.

Philip Oldenburg,

  Assistant Professor of Political Science, Columbia University, New York.

Barnett R. Rubin,

  Ph.D. Candidate, Department of Political Science University of Chicago.

Lloyd I. Rudolph,

  Professor of Political Science, University of Chicago.

Susanne Hoeber Rudolph,

  Professor of Political Science, University of Chicago.

Christopher Van Hollen,

  Senior Associate, Carnegie Endowment for International Peace, Washington, D.C. ; formerly Deputy Assistant Secretary of State for Near Eastern and South Asian Affairs (1969-1972); and Ambassador to Sri Lanka (1972-1976).

The Coordination of Complexity in South Asia

Lloyd I. Rudolph and Susanne Hoeber Rudolph

1. What was Done, and Why

THIS report is based on an analysis of the conduct of foreign policy in South Asia during the decade that encompasses the Johnson and Nixon administrations, 1965-1975. Its methodology deploys inductive and deductive modes of analysis, drawing upon case studies on the one hand and reasoning from concepts, assumptions and findings from the literature on organization and foreign policy on the other. The cases* were chosen with an eye to illuminating three broad policy areas in the conduct of foreign policy : diplomatic, economic and people to people. They were also selected with an eye to representing "normal" and crisis activity. Finally, our interviews were in part designed to provide an ethnography of bureaucratic subcultures.

Prescriptions for organizational reform seem to have a

---

* In addition to the case studies printed here, the project benefited from a number of background papers, not printed :

United States Foreign Aid to India : An Overview, by Stephen J. Blake

Impact of U.S. Military and Economic Aid to Pakistan 1954-1969, by Muzammel Huq

The Power of Information in the Conduct of U.S. Foreign Policy : Examples from South Asia, by Robert Rich

United States Military Aid to the Ayub Khan Regime, by Roger E. Sack

The Devaluation of the Indian Rupee in 1966 : A Case Study of the World Bank and the United States in India, by Harinder Shourie.

cyclical quality; yesterday's pathologies become today's cures only to become, again, tomorrow's pathologies. But the recurrence in organizational change of various principles and strategies should not be dismissed as mere re-inventions of the wheel by those who never got the word. Organizational principles change with historical context. The cyclical nature of organizational reform reflects applications to changed circumstances of a limited repertoire of organizational possibilities. We find, for example, that excessive centralization and isolation of power and the layering of control mechanisms associated with it call for a return to a decentralization more finely tuned to the diversities of complex and differentiated circumstances and capable of protecting long term goals from depredation; that excessive presidential domination of the direction of foreign policy generates good reasons to restore a modified State Department centered system; that policy planning and management dominated by staffs encapsulated in the meta-realities of global strategy and the balance of power engenders justifications for increasing the participation and influence of line officials whose operating responsibilities bring them in contact with events and people on the ground; that the imperium of non-career policy intellectuals deploying strategic and generalist knowledge on behalf of the president enhances an appreciation for the experience and expert knowledge of departmental professionals; and that the costs of hierarchically patterned relationships highlight the benefits of collegiality. Most if not all of these "new" directions have been tried before in one form or another and, under different circumstances and for a variety of reasons, found wanting. But as circumstances and leading personalities change and as organizational medicines administered to cure pathologies come to generate new ailments, reformers return again to older remedies from the organizational repertoire.

The principal investigators and contributors, all of whom have had extensive research experience in South Asia, met in Chicago early in June, 1974, to discuss and coordinate the research designs of case studies jointly selected in the light of the principal investigators' proposal to the Commission and of on-going discussions designed to relate the knowledge and interests of the contributors to the requirements of a regionally based study of the conduct of foreign policy. Background material designed to provide a common conceptual language for the meeting included some of the Commission's early papers on organizational reform, three books on the organizational dimensions of the conduct of foreign policy,[1] and a book on the substance of US policy toward South Asia in the post-war era.[2]

From June to September, the principal investigators and contributors pursued their research, interviewing extensively in Washington and South Asia. Preliminary drafts were presented and criticized at a second conference in early September and the case studies were revised throughout September and October in the light of written and oral criticism by the principal investigators. On November 20, the report was discussed at the Commission headquarters in Washington by Commission staff and senior officials and scholars with South Asia experience. These scholars and officials, and several others that did not attend the conference, provided general and specific comments on the report. On the basis of the conference discussion and the comments, the introductory essay was again revised, culminating in the present report.[3]

II. The Present Context of Organizational Change

A. Administrative Reform and Presidential Aggrandizement
The conduct of foreign policy in South Asia and elsewhere during the decade encompassed by the Johnson and Nixon administrations did not occur in historical isolation. The

1. Graham Allison, *The Essence of Decision* : *Explaining the Cuban Missile Crisis* (Boston, 1971); I. M. Destler, *Presidents, Bureaucrats and Foreign Policy*; (Princeton, 1972) and Morton Halperin, *Bureaucratic Politics and Foreign Policy* (Washington, D.C., 1974).
2. William Barnds, *India, Pakistan and the Great Powers* (New York, 1972).
3. We are grateful to all those who allowed themselves to be interviewed, or who participated in reviewing the cases and summary report at various points in the life of the project. Their insights and comments were most helpful. Naturally, the opinions and conclusions expressed in this paper are those of the authors, and not necessarily of those interviewed, who participated in the review process, of the Commission, or of any agency of the governments of the United States or of South Asian countries.

presidency as an institution and executive organization for the
conduct of foreign policy were shaped by the political contexts
and administrative reforms that preceded and followed World
War II. The reforms of the 1947-1949 period creating the
National Security Council, the Department of Defense, the
Central Intelligence Agency, etc., are frequently cited and
commented upon in studies of administrative reform dealing
with the conduct of foreign policy; but these arise out of the
earlier reforms of 1939 proposed by the President's Committee
on Administrative Management. Both periods are important in
promoting and accelerating a process of presidential aggran-
dizement that peaked at the beginning of President Nixon's
second term. It is this historical experience, particularly its
administrative origins in the recommendations of the
President's Committee on Administrative Management (the
Brownlow Committee), that orient our argument.

Clark Clifford has observed that the executive branch is
like a chameleon, taking its color from the character and
personality of the president.[4] The "color" of the presidency
makes a difference to some some of the time but it is the nature
of the institution, whatever its color, that matters to everybody
all of the time. When the Brownlow Committee adopted as its
slogan and strategy, "The president needs help," and provided
help in the form of presidential assistants and a White House
office, it prepared the way for fundamental change in the
presidency. The Brownlow Committee believed itself to be
making the president a more efficient executive. But its reform
proposals, once implemented, also made him more powerful
within the executive branch and in relation to the congress.
President Roosevelt, transmitting his version of the Brownlow
Committee recommendations to the congress, depicted them as
providing "the tools of management and authority to distribute
work" and insisted that they were "not a request for more
power."[5] What began in 1939 as an effort to promote adminis-

4. "The Presidency as I Have Seen It," in Emmet Hughes, *The Living
   Presidency* (New York, 1973), page 315.
5. See Edward S. Corwin, *The President, Office and Powers* (New York,
   1940), page 97ff., and Barry D. Karl, *Executive Reorganization and
   Reform in the New Deal; The Genesis of Administrative Reform*
   (Cambridge, Massachusetts, 1963).

trative reform was continued and enhanced by the legislation of 1947-1949, particularly the legislation creating the National Security Council. The intention, again, was to help the president with the formulation and execution of policy by giving him more and better access to advice and information. The practice and precedents of the "cold" and Vietnamese wars accelerated and deepened the process by further "liberating" the president from executive branch and congressional constraints.

The ambiguities buried in the technocratic populism of Louis Brownlow, Charles E. Merriam and Luther Gulick were not evident in 1937 when Brownlow said of his committee's recommendations : "There is but one grand purpose, namely to make democracy work today in our National Government; that is, to make our Government up-to-date, an efficient, effective instrument for carrying out the will of the Nation."[6] But the latent thrust of these ambiguities became more manifest in the post-war period and in the policy literature, notably of the bureaucratic politics school, it produced.[7] Writers in this post-war tradition continue to found their hopes for greater efficiency, coherence and "rationality" in the president. As one writer put it after rehearsing the personal and partisan limitations and biases that flawed the motives and actions of actual incumbents, "There is no other choice."[8]

Presidential expansion was not solely or merely a product of administrative reform; it was more fundamentally a product of hopes and aspirations for the presidency on the part of those seeking in the pre-war period social justice at home and after World War II national security abroad. From the Brownlow Committee onward, intellectuals and professionals in the neutral garb of management or policy science have collaborated

6. Barry Karl, *Executive Reorganization and Reform in the New Deal*, page 229.
7. For a systematic account of the first and second wave and their differences see Robert J. Art, "Bureaucratic Politics and American Foreign Policy; A Critique," *Policy Sciences* (1973), pages 467-490. The first generation includes Warner Schilling, Paul Hammond, Samuel P. Huntington and Richard Neustadt, the second Graham Allison, Morton Halperin and I.M. Destler among others.
8. I.M. Destler, *Presidents, Bureaucrats and Foreign Policy* (Princeton, 1972), p. 89.

with presidents in the essentially political task of expanding and strengthening the presidency. Doing so seemed wholly justified; who else could represent the national constituency and purpose? What other institution or office could create and lead a welfare state to social justice at home and insure national security and international order abroad? The congress, the states and, later, the cities, were seen as representing narrow constituencies and interests and, in any case, lacked the capacity and will to secure needed change.

Proposals since Brownlow have argued that the president must be strengthened, not only because he must efficiently manage a continuously increasing volume and range of responsibilities but also because he should be able to direct and control the vulnerable and amorphous executive branch of government and to protect it from congressional and interest group rivalry for power and control over policies and bureaucracies. The president is the best hope for policy and administration directed to national goals and purposes; he represents the people, particularly the weak and powerless against vested and partial interests, and the nation, especially its national interest and security.

Richard Neustadt captured the mood and goals of this school of administrative reform when he invoked Harry Truman's bemused reflection on the surprise he believed was in store for the military man who was to follow : "He'll sit there, and he'll say, 'Do this, do that,' and nothing will happen."[9] Neustadt elaborated on this image by contrasting a president in sneakers and a president in boots and spurs, the first the president as he was, the second a phantasy of what he was thought to be. The president in sneakers figuratively pads about the corridors of power in search of leverage, trying to persuade or cajole his putative administrative or political subordinates that what is in his interest is in theirs too.[10]

The organizational and procedural prescriptions that flow from an image of a president in sneakers seek to amplify his influence, enhance and tighten his control, improve the quality

9. Richard Neustadt, *Presidential Power* (New York, 1960), page 9.
10. Richard Neustadt, "White House and White Hall," *The Public Interest*, 1966, No. 2 page 64.

and quantity of advice and information and provide the means to counter resistance and sabotage. This model of the problems and needs of presidential power no doubt provided a more valid empirical account of the president in action than did conceptions which credited the idea that presidents could automatically command the organizational behavior they required. This model of the presidency also directly countered conceptions that celebrated or tolerated a pluralism that left the public interest in the hands of congressional committees, bureaucracies and private interests.

Writing at a different historical moment we take a less sanguine view of presidential power. We do not question the existence or the costs of bureaucratic politics, organizational dysfunctions or interest group liberalism, but we also recognize the limitations and costs of presidential power. Those limitations and costs are visible in the conduct of foreign policy toward South Asia and elsewhere, as well as in the conduct of domestic politics, and they have been with us for some time.

The problem is how to reconcile a Hamiltonian with a Madisonian presidency, i.e. how to reconcile a presidency of energy and initiative with a presidency that is constrained by forms of representation, debate and advice that are at once independent of presidential power but subject to its influence. Among the means to hand, given an understanding of their desirability and the will to act on that understanding, is the institutionalization in policy planning and management of the professional and expert knowledge available in the bureaucracy and the routine and systematic involvement of Congress in the foreign policy government. The deleterious effects of presidential power can be contained and turned in positive directions by recognizing and legitimizing an autonomous but coordinated role for the bureaucracy and the congress in the foreign policy government. Giving them more autonomy and authority will involve, within the executive branch, more collegiality, multiple advocacy, dissent, insulation of policy arenas and, in relationship to congress, fixed means to consult with and account to a congress willing and equipped to maintain an independent but cooperative role in the making and conduct of foreign policy.

B. The Relevance of the South Asian Region for Administrative Reform

The focus of this study is the coordination of complexity in South Asia. We address ourselves, therefore, to the value of comparative inquiry by examining why and how the analysis of a particular region provides organizational lessons for the conduct of foreign policy generally.

We start with the assumption that each region can be profitably dealt with as a separate policy arena with a distinguishable "government", composed of United States Government bureaucratic actors concerned with that region. The range and type of USG, foreign governmental, international agency and "private" actors and the norms and patterns that govern their activity and relationships vary significantly by region. So too do the presenting problems and the proximate and distant "causes" of conditions, events and policies.

Among the more salient variables that affect the conduct of foreign policy toward regions are (1) the level and continuity of USG interest and attention; (2) the amount and quality of knowledge available at various levels of the USG; (3) constraints in the USG and in the region on USG intervention; and (4) the type, influence and number of private US actors with interest in the region. For example, US government for South Asia has been characterized by sporadic but forceful high level (presidential) attention; like Japan, by little knowledge of high quality at the presidential level and considerable knowledge of good quality at the bureau level; by relatively low levels of constraint within the USG and from the region on USG actions; and by few, relatively uninfluential private actors. (As Ambassador Saxbe put it, to the consternation of some Indians, America's interest in India was largely humanitarian and cultural.) The US government for Inter-American Affairs shares some of these characteristics, but not others. USG attention to Latin America has been similar but not precisely like that toward South Asia. There has been even less of it, but when it has come, it has been sporadic, high level, and sometimes violent. Again, like South Asia, knowledge at the presidential level has been low in quantity and quality. An important contrast between the two regions can be found in the constraints dimension. Constraints on action in Latin America arise not so much from powerful actors within the executive branch or in the region but from the existence of a plentiful supply of private actors and their congressional allies. According to a recent study, the regional bureau is subject to pressure from a wide range of powerful private interests and has had to face them "alone, without the backing of a counter-constituency" or a president.[11]

The US government for Europe has very different characteristics from those associated with South Asia and Latin America. Relative to other regions, it attracts continuous high level attention. Goodly amounts of high quality knowledge about Western and Eastern Europe are available not only at the presidential and bureau levels but also, and this is distinctive for the European region, on the seventh floor of the State Department among deputy and under secretaries and policy planners. USG intervention in Europe is more constrained than in any other region by competition and conflict among governmental agencies, not least of which are the military and intelligence bureaucracies, and by the existence in Europe of powerful foreign governmental actors, including political personalities who are sufficiently familiar in their culture and style to matter to presidents and other senior officials. Finally, the plethora of private actors concerned with European-US relations—a result of immigration, trade, investments, and culture—creates constituencies and publics that cannot, taken together, be equalled by any other region.

Differences and similarities among regions imply that certain organizational strategies may be relevant across regions, others not. Organizational proposals should be explicitly examined in this comparative light. Several of our organizational proposals which are designed to strengthen the articulation of policy planning at the regional level, such as the Assistant Secretary Policy Planning Council and the Regional Conference, speak to the problems of other areas as well.

11. Abraham F. Lowenthal, " 'Bureaucratic Politics' and the United States Policy Toward Latin America : An Interim Research Report." Delivered at the American Political Association Annual Meeting, September, 1974.

III. Defining Coordination

A. Imperative and Deliberative Coordination of Complexity

Complexity generates the need for coordination. Scale and diversity compounded by continuous change in conditions and goals characterize the organizational life of governments. Coordination without complexity is easy; if all are alike, they can share the same questions and answers, the same ends and means. Alternatively, coordination is easy if all can be made to be or think alike, an induced form of simplicity captured by the German term Gleichschaltung, all on the same wave length. But these are the conditions of simplicity, not complexity and they are not easily achieved in modern governments. The conduct of foreign policy engages a world of multifarious activities, domains and time frames that do not ordinarily lend themselves to this kind of direction and control, nor should they.

We have organized the discussion of coordination around two terms, imperative and deliberative, that approximate what can and should be done. Imperative coordination relies upon the mystique of high office, hierarchy in organizational and personal relationships, and will as the source of policy and of compliance. Deliberative coordination involves the knowledge and judgment of officials, collegiality in formal and informal relationships and reasoned argument and bargaining as the source of policy and compliance. Like all models, these models of two types of coordination simplifiy and exaggerate in order to generate concepts for analysis.

Our argument is counter-cyclical and tends to highlight the costs of imperative coordination and the benefits of deliberative coordination. Yet we are under no illusion that the world with which the conduct of foreign policy is engaged can do without the benefits of imperative coordination or can be made free from the costs associated with deliberative coordination. Indeed, during the period when this report was being researched and written, the presenting problems for the conduct of foreign policy in the United States may have begun to change in ways that will generate in the not too distant future a need to emphasize in doctrine and practice the virtues of imperative coordination. Even if this proves to be the case, it in no way lessens the importance of learning from the experience of the past decade in South Asia. That experience supports the need to develop the counter-cyclical position argued here.

We take as our text for exploring imperative coordination Henry Kissinger's statement to the WSAG meeting of December 3, 1971 : "The President is under the 'illusion' that he is giving instructions . . ."[12] The president is invoked. He has been elected by a national constituency, represents the national will and purpose, commands the largest, most comprehensive view of the national interest, has constitutional responsibility for the direction of foreign policy and command of the armed forces, and, as the head of state as well as the head of government, commands the authority, respect and reverence which a secular state in a secular age invests in the highest office of the land. He can generate the majesty associated with a sovereign power and the mystique associated with the attitudes that develop around those thought to possess the esoteric knowledge and skills associated with a unique calling.

When Henry Kissinger told the assembled WSAG members that the President was under the "illusion" that he was giving instructions he was, of course, mocking them. The implication was clear; some or all of them were not following the president's instructions. The presidential will was being thwarted. The man at the top had declared his policy but it was not being implemented. At best, there was a withdrawal of affect and efficiency, at worst subversion and sabotage.

The instruments of the president's will are the president's men organized in staffs in the White House, elsewhere in the Executive Office and, hopefully, in the bureaucracies engaged in the conduct of foreign policy. In the imperative mode of coordination, an essential component of effectiveness is to be close to the president and the most recent recipient of his views. President's men are, for the most part, "can-do" policy intellectuals, in-and-outers drawn from the academy, the law, investment houses, business firms, and journalism, whose knowledge of foreign affairs is usually of a general kind. Their appointment arises out of the president's confidence that they share his preferences and their continuance in service depends upon the president's pleasure.

12. The *New York Times*, January 6, 1972, p. 16.

Under imperative coordination, coherence is introduced by the president and the president's men who are depicted as the bearers of the public interest in domestic affairs and of the national interest in foreign affairs. This depiction made considerable sense in the days of Harry Truman, when, a relatively weak president confronted great baronies which controlled large blocks of power. If presidential power and direction were to replace bargaining equilibriums with coherence, a relatively symmetrical distribution of power had to be replaced by a more asymmetrical one favoring the president, and this began to happen.

As Truman gave way to Eisenhower and Eisenhower gave way to Kennedy, presidents became, relatively, more powerful and barons less. "Bargaining advantages" were, increasingly, held by the president and his men. In the policy arena of foreign affairs particularly, Congress and its leadership surrendered the bargaining advantages that lay at the roots of their power. In the federal bureaucracy, officials who offered non-presidential alternatives, or more commonly, suggested the costs and dangers associated with presidential decisions and strategies, became increasingly suspect.

Presidents came to live in a world of asymmetrical power relations, isolated from the kind of peership and collegiality that sustain argument and rational discourse and free from the restraints that competition and bargaining among actors in a political market provide.

Relying on the president for coherence made certain assumptions about him : his voice spoke for the people; his will expressed the national interest. But these assumptions proved at best only partially true. The president had his own political interests. The search for "immediate gains visible during the current term,"[13] the personal desire for honor and historical immortality, and the need to prove himself politically and personally too often lead to an activism divorced from the national purpose and interest.[14] Proponents of presidential

13. I. M. Destler, *Presidents, Bureaucrats, and Foreign Policy*, (Princeton, Princeton University Press, 1972), p. 87.
14. Morton Halperin, *Bureaucratic Politics and Foreign Policy*, (Washington, The Brookings Institution, 1974), Chapter 4, "The Presidential Interest."

power lament the fact that presidents are deeply engaged in partisan and personal politics but see no alternative to imperative coordination by the president and the president's men in the conduct of foreign policy. "One may argue against enhancing Presidential influence because of mistrust of a particular Oval Office occupant, or a more general belief that the potential dangers of executive power outweigh the benefits it can bring. But to do so would, for all practical purposes, be to renounce the aim of coherent policy altogether."[15] The argument for deliberative coordination below takes the dangers of executive power seriously but establishes a framework in which coherent policy is possible.

Deliberative coordination is the product of informed argument, rational persuasion and bargaining among professionals representing diverse interests in a context mandated to consider common problems and recommend joint solutions. In invoking the word deliberative we mean to emphasize organizational arrangements and procedures that are characterized by careful and thorough consideration of the matter at hand, a concern for consequences, and attention to the reasons offered for and against proposed measures. A necessary condition for deliberation is collegiality and the peership it generates. There is a direct relationship between the quality and effectiveness of deliberation and the degree of equality that characterizes those engaged in it. Governments are, of course, organized as hierarchies and appointed officials are and ought to be subordinate to elected officials. In the executive branch, the only elected official is the president. At the same time we are concerned to mitigate the costs associated with administrative hierarchy and presidential power and to gain some of the benefits associated with deliberation among professionals. If presidents are able to practice imperative coordination without any attention to the benefits of deliberative coordination, the conduct of foreign policy will be devoid of the kind of knowledge and accountability available to lawyers, legislators, politicians, academics, many professionals other than lawyers, and, in some measure, to participants in formal organizations such as businesses, labor unions, churches, etc. While it may be true that there is

15. Destler, *Presidents*, pp. 89-90.

no other office like the President of the United States and that
this uniqueness is enhanced with respect to his responsibility
for the national security, it is also true that the conduct of
foreign policy involves the use of knowledge, skills, experience
and judgment that are not the special or unique possession of
the president.

The benefits of deliberation in professional life are needed
in the conduct of foreign policy. Lawyers are licensed professionals who carry on their work in the context of judicial processes
that require adversary procedures. They must write briefs and
make arguments that are disciplined by the precedents the law
provides and the arguments of their opponents. It is a process
that involves deliberation in the sense that we have described it.
Legislators engage in the rational examination of proposals in
committee, in reports and, to an extent, on the floor through
debates and conference procedures. Politicians produce and
debate platforms and defend their own record and attack their
opponent's record. Legal, legislative and electoral processes
require licensed or qualified practitioners to engage in deliberation. In academic life, the work of scholars is scrutinized by
other scholars; scholars debate the validity of the arguments
and findings of their colleagues and are held accountable by a
deliberative process for the knowledge they produce or transmit. Doctors are held accountable by specialized medical
boards and by malpractice suits brought by patients in courts.
By contrast, presidents in their conduct of foreign policy have
been relatively unconstrained by deliberative processes found in
professional and organizational life. Yet the conduct of foreign
policy requires knowledge, experience, skills and judgment
comparable to those found in professional and organizational
life outside the foreign affairs government. Such knowledge and
experience is available in the foreign policy bureaucracy. Our
arguments for deliberative coordination and our prescriptions
for organizational and procedural means to realize it are
designed to make their benefits available.

There are family resemblances and differences between the
"governmental pluralism" relevant for foreign policy and the
interest group pluralism relevant for domestic politics. These
comparisons have important implications for our discussion of
deliberative coordination. Interest group pluralism in the

domestic policy arena powerfully counteracts the hierarchical authority and asymmetrical power relations of the presidentially dominated executive branch. Our recommendations are designed to institutionalize in foreign policy the relative equality of bargaining that characterizes interest group pluralism in domestic politics. Interest group pluralism in the making of domestic policy involves an interaction of groups and their congressional allies in the decision making process designed to foster outcomes favorable to their interests. Groups with more resources and effective leadership do better than groups with less; those without resources and leadership remain unrepresented. Groups bargain to produce compromise settlements. Losers, groups that find compromise settlements unsatisfactory, can attempt to expand the scope of conflict, bring other groups into the arena of those immediately concerned and establish a coalition with a better prospect of "winning".

But there are important differences that distinguish interest group pluralism characteristic of domestic policy formation and governmental pluralism characteristic of foreign policy formation. One is the nature of the groups constituting the pluralist universe. Another is the nature of the process shaping policy outcomes. The groups active in interest group pluralism "represent" domestic producer and consumer interests capable of mobilizing electoral and other forms of support. The groups active in governmental pluralism are bureaucratic actors within the executive branch who "represent" expert knowledge and experience on the one hand and bureaucratic interest on the other. Organized interests outside the federal bureaucracy play some part in foreign policy formation but, relative to the domestic policy arena, their influence is marginal and their participation sporadic.

It is this difference that makes it possible to distinguish between interest group pluralism in domestic policy formation and governmental pluralism in foreign policy. This difference profoundly affects the nature of bargaining. Whereas in domestic policy, bargaining occurs among relatively equal actors, in foreign policy formation the actors, in so far as they are affected by administrative hierarchy and operate in the shadow of presidential power, are relatively unequal. The kind of informed argument and rational persuasion that can occur under conditions of relative equality is more difficult to realize in the context of governmental pluralism when asymmetrical power and authority relationships inhibit or vitiate deliberative coordination.

A second difference that distinguishes interest group pluralism in domestic policy formation and governmental pluralism in foreign policy is the relatively greater importance of professional knowledge, judgment and accountability for foreign policy formulation, choice and management. This is not to say that professional knowledge and judgment are not an important component in the formulation and implementation of domestic policy. The difference lies in the relative weight accorded in domestic policy to bargaining shaped by trade-offs; compromises and coalitions based on interests and the weight accorded in foreign policy to bargaining shaped by professional knowledge and experience. It is this difference that establishes the resemblance between the conduct of foreign affairs and the modes of deliberation characteristic of the professions and of scholarship.

If deliberative coordination is to occur within the context of the governmental pluralism that characterizes foreign policy conditions comparable to those that prevail in private professional domains are required. Institutional means and a psychological climate must be found that enable actors to "coordinate" on the basis of informed argument, rational persuasion, and organizational accountability. Our prescriptions and recommendations are designed to strengthen such conditions. If governmental pluralism is to avoid the costs depicted in our discussion of imperative coordination and is to benefit from the advantages of deliberative coordination, organizational and procedural arrangements that allow relatively equal professional actors to deliberate are necessary.

It should be clear from the discussion so far that coordination, whatever its characteristics, is not an unmixed blessing. There are costs associated with coordination and these can be understood in terms of the relative success or failure of efforts to coordinate policy formulation and management. "Costs" is a neutral term that implies more or less and is associated with benefits. Costs can also be understood in terms of pathologies of administration, particularly those associated with

THE COORDINATION OF COMPLEXITY IN SOUTH ASIA

coordination. For example, clearance, formally designed to foster coordination by informing or involving relevant actors, becomes a pathology when it fosters delays and excessive caution, takes the edge off good proposals, muddies priorities and blocks timely action. As pathology, clearance feeds the propensity of presidential actors to practice imperative coordination, to move the action up and out of the State Department to the Executive Office or White House level. In order to insure timely action and to block those with stakes in the issue from mounting counter-mobilizations and widening the conflict to gain added support, presidents and president's men practice counter pathologies such as non-consultation with informed officials close to the problem, the creation of "closely held" or "tightly held" decision contexts, and secrecy directed against other governmental actors. Other pathologies follow. Bypassing clearance and deliberative modes of coordination generates an underground form of clearance and deliberation in the form of leaks which introduce new or suppressed information and generate advocacy and argument.

Decision making for the abortive Bay of Pigs operation in Cuba provides a striking example of the pathology associated with imperatively coordinated closely held decisions. Roger Hillsman, then the Director of Intelligence and Research at State knew nothing of the planned Cuban invasion. Overhearing a remark by the then Director of the CIA, Allen Dulles, he asked Secretary of State Dean Rusk about it. Rusk told him not to inquire further because "this is being too tightly held". State's Cuba Desk Officer, Robert Hurwitch, was equally in the dark. "There was, in my judgment," Hurwitch says, "a divorce between the people who daily or minute by minute had access to information, to what was going on, and the people who were making plans and policy decisions."[16]

The Bay of Pigs paradigm points to a more general pathology associated with secrecy and imperative coordination, the growth and operation of a "them and us" division of the world. President's men in the context of the bureaucratic struggle often regard actors in the non-presiden-

16. Quoted in Henry Raymont, "Kennedy Library Documents, Opened to Two Scholars, Illuminate Policies on Cuba and Berlin," The *New York Times*, August 17, 1970, p. 16.

tial domain as "natural enemies" of the president,[17] identify the president's political interests with the national interest,[18] and believe that foreign policy officials, however expert, are cautious, *status quo* oriented and concerned to maintain good relations with clients of the moment.[19] The operating rule seems to be that the more we know and the less they know the better. In this context, information and advocacy, instead of promoting deliberative coordination, become weapons in a political struggle within the federal executive.[20]

B. An Evaluation of Operational Means for Coordination

Our discussion of coordination in terms of imperative versus deliberative has been at a fairly general level. There are operational means associated with particular forms of organization and procedure that require evaluation in the context of our typology.[21] Among the operational means advanced for insuring coordination is good management either in the form of a single high level official charged with "management" or a programming system designed to relate the allocation of resources to the realization of tasks and objectives, or both. The well documented history of the relative failure of management strategies to

17. Richard Neustadt in *Presidential Power* argued that to some extent the executive departments, and their heads, are by the very nature of their functions, "natural enemies" of the president.

18. Morton H. Halperin, *Bureaucratic Politics and Foreign Policy*, p. 63 and, more generally, the facts and arguments adduced in Chapter 4, "Presidential Interests."

19. See I.M. Destler, "Country Expertise and U.S. Foreign Policy Making : The Case of Japan," The Brookings Institution, General Series Reprint 298 ; Destler, who credits the characterization, is surprised that the experts did so well in arranging Okinawa's "reversion" to Japan, and prescribes strengthening the president's hand further even while recognizing that the State Department has "the organizational depth and breadth to bring coherence to a wide range of U.S. foreign policy" If presidents, who "do not feel the Department is their own," would stop feeling that way and provide support. p. 551.

20. See also Leon V. Sigal, *Reporters and Officials* ; *The Organization and Politics of Newsmaking* (Lexington, 1973).

21. For two different perspectives on the problem that inform our view see Destler, *President Bureaucrats and Foreign Policy*, Chapter Seven, and John F. Campbell, *The Foreign Affairs Fudge Factory* (Basic Books, 1971), Part 2.

produce better coordination provides ample reason to doubt their efficacy. Among the lessons is the impossibility in the conduct of foreign policy of separating management from policy. Formal rationality, i.e. the effort to establish the most efficient relationship between means and ends, makes most sense when the goals of an organization are relatively clear and its tasks can be routinized. Put another way, the manipulation of organizational roles, tasks, and resources with a view to maximizing output and minimizing input can be most efficiently accomplished when outputs are tangible, simple, and predictable. The conduct of foreign policy is at the opposite extreme from the routine and repetitive production of a known product. It involves goals and actions that are, relatively, non-repetitive and therefore not easily subject to routine procedures and solutions and it is directed to an environment which is subject to frequent and often radical transformations, including those produced by the feedback effects of policies pursued and actions taken.

Another operating level procedure designed to foster coordination is comprehensive formal policy guidance. From the Eisenhower administration's BNSTs (Basic and National Security Policy Document) through the Nixon administration's NSSMs (National Security Memorandums) and, for a time, including foreign policy messages to Congress, formal policy guidance has constituted an important part of the effort to coordinate foreign policy. The record has not been encouraging. Such documents are too often overrun by events and cannot take account of or anticipate those particulars of a situation decisive for decision or action. Foreign policy messages in particular are often euphemistic, less than frank, or deliberately misleading in their effort to influence external or internal publics and actors. A great deal of effort has been invested over the past fifteen years in preparing such documents. More can be gained, we argue, from line officials close to operations directly and continuously exchanging views.

Standing inter-departmental committees constitute yet another attempt to coordinate foreign policy. Because they constitute an effort to capture the advantages of deliberative coordination by establishing collegial contexts for discussion and decision, we find the idea and the practice of the inter-departmental committee attractive. At the same time, the history of interdepartmental committees in the decade under review reveals problems and tendencies which require change in doctrine and practice. Unfortunately, the more serious the issue and the higher the level at which it is discussed, the less likely is it that appropriate interests and spokesmen capable of collegial interaction and deliberative coordination will be represented. When the fundamental purpose of an inter-departmental committee is to serve the president's will and preferences, then hierarchical behavior will govern discussion, procedure and outcomes, and membership will reflect presidential pleasure. If, on the other hand, committees are designed to foster deliberation among knowledgeable and interested actors, there is some prospect that collegiality will orient the norms governing discussion and decision.

The inter-departmental committee as a means to broadcast presidential preferences and to gain compliance with them is captured by Henry Kissinger's remark, previously cited, at the meeting of a leading inter-departmental committee, the WSAG of December, 3, 1971: "The President is under the 'illusion' that he is giving instructions . . . " The record as far as it is known of decision making in connection with the Cambodian invasion of 1970 suggests an even more dramatic conclusion, that interdepartmental committees can be fictional constructs that misleadingly imply consultation : The president sat with himself totting up pluses and minuses on yellow pads and preparing a speech for television without serious consultation with responsible advisors. He told the nation on April 30, 1970, that the Cambodian action was directed at "the headquarters for the entire Communist military operation in South Vietnam." No such communist headquarters was found by the attacking forces, an embarrassment the president might have been spared if he had consulted with almost any State Department official with southeast Asia experience.

What is constructive about the inter-departmental committee is its potential for deliberative coordination. What is problematic about it is its susceptibility to exploitation by those willing and able to practice imperative coordination. So long as the interdepartmental committee system is dominated by the presidentially oriented National Security Council it remains too susceptible to presidential influence and manipulation. Insofar as it does coordinate deliberatively as well as imperatively, it is often over-weighted with representatives of the Department of Defense interests, particularly those of the services and the joint chiefs. If the conduct of foreign policy is to be political in the best and most comprehensive sense and to be coordinated by deliberative means, a high level committee dominated by State and drawing its membership mostly from within State is required. This leads us to the final practical means of coordination, organizational integration.

The proliferation of mini-state departments throughout the executive branch has created the most serious problem for the coordination of foreign policy. An observation of the Jackson Subcommittee captures what is at stake here : "The National Security Council was chiefly the inspiration of James Forrestal, who wanted to enhance the defense role in peace time policy making. . ."[22] The domestic departments, Treasury, Agriculture, Commerce, and Labor, with major overseas operations also have succeeded in establishing organizational enclaves and procedural requirements to represent their interests in the conduct of foreign policy. The military services and the Department of Defense argue that because they have enormous stakes in the conduct of foreign policy their interest and outlooks should be represented organizationally and procedurally. Many domestic departments and agencies argue that their responsibilities and constituencies generate or involve major U.S. international objectives. These are clear instances of the tail wagging the dog. However elusive a term the national interest is and however contingent and problematic the relationship between domestic and foreign policy, the conduct of foreign policy should aim at something other and greater than the interests of particular federal bureaucracies.

The organization of the government for the conduct of foreign policy has proliferated in ways and to a degree that have, on the one hand, dwarfed the State Department and on the other created problems of scale and complexity of an unnecessary and counterproductive kind. State Department primacy

---

22. Jackson Subcommittee, "Basic Issues'" in *Administration*, Staff Reports, p. 9, quoted in Destler. *Presidents*, pp. 84-85.

in the conduct of foreign policy and the radical reduction or elimination of non-State units now engaged in foreign policy activity can be achieved by a strategy of modified organizational integration. What is entailed by such a strategy includes making representation overseas a State Department function with the needs of other departments and agencies met by international travel and the deputation of State Department personnel; making routine gathering and evaluation of intelligence a State Department function; eliminating non-mission connected intelligence activities by the military services and the Defense Intelligence Agency; dismantling of the USIA; furthering the movement of development assistance activities into multilateral agencies; dismantling the Office of the Assistant Secretary of Defense for International Security Affairs and providing the Secretary of Defense with a high level political advisor seconded from the State Department; cutting back the number of personnel serving in the Office of the Secretary of Defense, the Joint Chiefs of Staff and the headquarters staffs of the Army, Navy and Air Force departments; and dismantling the Bureau of Political Military Affairs in the Department of State. In these and other ways the objective should be to reduce the scale and complexity of the foreign affairs government throughout the executive branch and to restore to a leaner State Department primacy for the formulation and the conduct of foreign policy. In such a context, an Assistant Secretary Policy Planning Council, which will be discussed further in the recommendations section, may be able to make deliberative coordination work.

Our preference for organizational integration as a practical means for furthering coordination is not unqualified. As we will make clear elsewhere in this report and in the recommendations, we recognize the need for insulation of policies with long run time frames and of programs dealing with activities that require autonomy. Specifically, certain economic policies and programs and activities associated with education and culture should be insulated from the usual pressures associated with the political struggle and the need for leverage.

IV. A Closer Look at Complexity

Differences in the manifestation of complexity can be specified in terms of (1) organizational levels; (2) variations in time-

frames; (3) functions expressed in policies and programs; and
(4) regional contexts including variation within and among
them. Each manifestation of complexity dynamically intersects
with the others in continuously varying contexts. We conclude
our discussion of complexity with an examination of variations
in the types of diplomacy used by officials to manage complexity, i.e. normal diplomacy, crisis management, and strategic
diplomacy.

A. Levels

We categorize the complexity of levels in terms of global,
regional, and bilateral. The categories capture and organize
discernable differences in organization, procedure, and action in
the conduct of foreign policy. Global perspectives and activity
are associated with roles in presidential organizations (e.g. White
House assistants and staffs, National Security Council, etc.)
and with roles at the highest departmental levels, such as the
"Seventh Floor" at State and the Office of the Secretary of
Defense. Regional perspectives command fewer roles and organizational resources than global and bilateral. The regional
bureaus in State and mini-regional units in other departments
such as DOD's ISA capture the regional category but in a form
diluted by the location of responsibilities at the bilateral level.
The bilateral category is organized in the country director
system in Washington and in embassies abroad.

The presenting problem for complexity manifested in levels
is the parochialism associated with each level. How can each
level be given its due in the face of differences of priorities
agendas and claims on resources ?

Conventionally "parochialism" is a term of opprobrium
that designates a narrow or exclusive attention to local
concerns. Parochial officials are thought of as those who confine
their attention to a country and have difficulty looking beyond
bilateral relations and the needs of clientelism. They are
thought of as parochial because they fail to relate their
"client's" concerns to the broad framework of U.S. national
interest.

Client parochialism is not the only form of parochialism.
Global parochialism is another. The wide-angle vision of the
global perspective loses particular information and detail. Its

lens focus blurrs intra-regional linkages and country issues. This loss of information about proximate causes and presenting issues detracts from the adequacy with which foreign policy is conducted. The "mere" details seen by the bilateral and regionally oriented observer have critical implications for the global perspective even as the global vision indicates judgments and actions that regional or country perspectives may ignore or discount.

Parochialisms are theories about the world of foreign policy. As more or less articulated and systematized theories, they furnish the minds of key actors by identifying for them entities, processes, and relationships and by shaping the way they know and explain what happens. Parochialisms as thories generate an observational language that establishes what counts as a fact and as a mistake and supply criteria for proof and validation. For example, when the "structure of peace" is defined in terms of "balance" among the super powers and in terms of "linkage" that relates regional and lesser states to them in subordinate and reflexive relationships, those who conduct foreign policy are constrained to perceive and explain what they are doing and why they are doing it in these terms. As Gerald Heeger and Stephen Cohen suggest in their studies, such a definition of the structure of peace constitutes global parochialism. It creates a frame of mind among middle level actors in Washington and the field that lowers the salience and relevance of countries not essential to the hypothesized "global system," invites selectivity in reporting the facts and skews recommendations to fit the theory.

Too exclusive reliance on any one perspective, global, regional or client parochialism, is likely to jeopardize the conduct of foreign policy by divorcing it from "reality." As the Secretary of State, in an interview with James Reston, put it : "In the Bureaus—in the geographic bureaus—the relationship between a more conceptual approach and a more operational approach has not yet been fully balanced."[3] The cure for giving undue weight to any one parochialism is not to give undue weight to another. What is needed theoretically and institutionally are middle range concepts and organizational arrangements that mutually engage global, regional and

23. The *New York Times*, Sunday, October 13, 1974.

country perspectives in the formulation of the national interest. Deliberative coordination as we have defined it above and as we operationalize it below provides a context and a process for involving the regional bureaus and the embassies in policy planning and management in ways intended to give each level its due.

B. Time

The time dimension of complexity is characterized by the critical contrast between simultaneous events and relationships on the one hand and sequential events and relationships on the other. Simultaneous or synchronic time conceptualizes complex events and relationships in a limited time frame and ignores historical antecedents. Diachronic or sequential time conceptualizes complex events and relationships as they occur or change over a period of time, i.e. historically. The fact that things happen all at once, that they happen together, is a very important and problematic condition for the conduct of foreign policy. Simultaneity creates opportunities on the one hand and difficulties on the other. Opportunities have to do with positive forms of coordination such as creating complementary and reinforcing relationships within and among functional arenas and transferring or translating resources to provide leverage. Simultaneity creates difficulties because the finite nature of human and organizational capacities cannot respond to and process an infinite number of claims. Which claims should be given priority in the allocation of attention, resources, and action ? Simultaneity requires simplification. It is achieved by theories (world views) and concepts on the one hand and priorities, agendas, and routines on the other that structure perception, organization and action.

Diachronic time or the sequential occurrence of events and relationships over a period of time poses equally difficult challenges for the conduct of foreign policy. The "half-life" (by anology from a technical term in atomic physics that refers to the time required for half of the atoms of a radioactive substance present to become disintegrated) of the events and processes that constitute the substance of international politics varies enormously. The visitations of world statesmen, international kidnappings and border skirmishes have short half-lives, the development of weapon systems and the consumption of world resources have longer ones. The challenge here is how to order priorities among policies and programs with different half-lives, short term (one month to one year), medium term (one year to five years), and long term (five years and more). The great problem that diachronic time poses for the conduct of foreign policy is the propensity for high level actors to concentrate attention and resources on problems of the short term and the expense of policies and programs directed to the medium of long term. Known as leverage, it concentrates all available means on the solution of an immediate problem.

The durability of the half-life of presenting problems and the policies directed to meet them creates an opposite kind of complexity. Long run policies and programs such as those associated with global strategies, weapon systems and "facilities", because they are thought to entail particular commitments and arrangements with other states, inhibit or preclude short run or medium run responses sensitive to the facts and requirements of the moment.

Coordination of the complexity associated with diachronic time is most problematic in relationship to balancing the claims of the short run against the medium and long run. Because presidents and presidents' men are peculiarly sensitive to the timing of elections, the vagaries of poll support and the current state of the domestic political struggle, their sense of time gravitates to the short run with consequences that are often problematic for the generation or selection of information and the range of policy options actually considered. Presidents, of course, must be sensitive to elections, to polls and to maintaining their political ascendancy if their conduct of foreign policy is to be accountable to public opinion and the voter. At the same time, the coordination of complexity associated with variability in the nature and consequences of time can be strengthened by heightened consciousness of the risks and costs of sacrificing the medium and long term to the short term and by efforts to devise policies and construct programs that insulate medium and long term objectives from the political struggle at home and abroad.

C. Functional Complexity

Another dimension of complexity is to be found in the variety of activities pursued by the USG in a region. Complexity of governmental functions in a region is distinguished from regional complexity (discussed below) expressed in the variety of circumstances that characterize regions and the states that compose them and from the intra-organizational complexity that characterizes the missions and country teams in the region. Here we are concerned to explore within a regional framework the complexity that arises from the pursuit of a variety of functions and the programs and policies associated with them. The functional arenas to be considered here, primarily in a field context, are military, economic, intelligence, information and culture.

The U.S. foreign policy "government" for South Asia and its environment have undergone considerable change during the decade under review. The decade reveals major changes in players, motives and plot, such as the appearance of Bangladesh and changes of regime, leadership or governments in Pakistan, India and Sri Lanka. Even so, there have been some enduring and critically important characteristics. Among them are the relatively low level of U.S. private investment and commercial activity. Investment in South Asia represents a small fraction of total U.S. investment abroad and the states of South Asia are not among America's major trading partners. Nor are there, with some important exceptions, major natural or scientific and technological resources located in South Asia that are vital to U.S. economic or security interests. As a result of these circumstances, Treasury, Commerce, and Labor have not had important stakes in the region, nor have firms, industries and organized economic interests and their allied Congressional committees played an active role in the regional government. In the heyday of bilateral and multilateral development assistance, particularly with respect to consortium and IDA loans managed by the World Bank, Treasury, was, of course, actively involved, but such activities have tapered off sharply in recent years. Such circumstances contrast markedly with, for example, the circumstances associated with the regional government for Latin America.

The major problems associated with the coordination of

functional complexity in South Asia over the 1965-1975 decade
have involved policies and programs related to security and
economic relations. By the end of the decade both types of programs had markedly declined. DOD, CIA, AID, and USDA,
at the beginning of the decade, had important stakes in the
region; by its end they no longer did, or at least not stakes of
the kind that existed in the 1960s. The Sino-Soviet split followed by polycentrism and then detente with the major communist
powers led to the dissolution of the containment policy and,
de facto, put an end to accompanying treaty arrangements that
affected South Asia, CENTO and SEATO. At the opening
of the decade AID was engaged in administering large
scale development assistance programs but by its end it
had closed up shop in Delhi, for a time its largest recipient, and
was doing business elsewhere in the region within the framework of a much reduced U.S. aid budget. USDA which, in the
1960s, in the context of agricultural surpluses served producer
interests by sending billions of dollars and millions of tons of
concessional food aid to the subcontinent, in the 1970s, in the
context of scarcity, serves the same interests through high price
commercial sales. USDA's interest in sales for hard currency
reduced its stakes in South Asia compared to those it held in
the days of domestic and world surpluses.

With the closing of the U-2 base in Peshawar and other
facilities in Pakistan the CIA and DOD no longer had the kinds
of vital stakes they once did. The conflict between the interests
of the military and intelligence bureaucracies, which required
good relations with Pakistan, and the aid and food bureaucracies which, while not indifferent to good relations with
Pakistan, required good relations with their principal client,
India, had subsided, fueled at best by the legacies and
memories of the earlier era. For example, the resumption
of military sales to Pakistan in 1975, while in part arising
from the legacies of the earlier era, was argued and promoted
by a rather different constellation of actors and done for a
different reason (having to do primarily with domestic
politics in Pakistan) than the large scale military aid programs
of the period prior to 1965.

Changed world views, captured in strategies and slogans,
have affected the content and structure of functional complexity

in South Asia. The romance and promise of third world development, the humanitarian concern to help the needy and the efforts to insure peace in the long run by a more equitable distribution of world resources, like the strategies of containment or counterinsurgency to promote U.S. security, are now challenged by doctrines of "triage" and "life-boat," detente with Russia and China, and threats to counter "strangulation" with force. In South Asia the presenting problems of the 1970s are defined by the geopolitics of the Indian Ocean, particularly its relation to Middle East oil, and by nuclear proliferation. Also present but of lesser concern is the fate of agricultural and industrial development in third world countries faced with quadrupled oil prices. Under these new circumstances the DOD, particularly the Navy, and ACDA have developed major stakes in the region. U.S. agencies active in formulating policy and funding for multilateral efforts to assist South Asian states to finance the import of critical resources, such as Treasury and State's Bureau of Economic and Business Affairs (EB), or those active in food policy, such as USDA, AID, and, not least, the Secretary of State and his staffs, also are among the actors that constitute the new dimensions of functional complexity in the South Asian government.

The process of decline and transformation is also apparent with respect to information and cultural functions. The USIA "presence" varies somewhat by country but its influence and impact are well below that which prevailed at the beginning of the decade. How much the decline in demand for library services, speakers, and performing arts is related to the decline in supply and quality resulting from severe budget cuts and how much from indifference and hostility to American cultural products is hard to determine precisely. But there can be little doubt that the decline in the influence and impact of USIA programs is related to negative public responses to U.S. policies and consequently to America's reputation and appeal. A similar fate has affected State Department programs such as those that deal with Fulbright and Visitor Exchange. The 1967 revelation concerning indirect CIA funding of labor, student, research, and cultural organizations did considerable damage to them and, more serious, contributed to a climate of opinion which makes it possible to accuse with impunity any

U.S. citizen or organization of CIA connections. The decline in America's reputation and appeal also affected the Peace Corps, whose program in India in the mid-60s was once its largest. GOI policies, reflecting a growing tendency towards cultural nationalism, exacerbated the decline of U.S. people to people programs. They forced the closing of U.S. (and other) libraries-cum-cultural centers and, for a time, cut the flow of U.S. (and other) visitors, academic programs, and scholars to a trickle. The nadir for U.S. cultural policy and programs was probably reached in 1971, when USG policies and actions alienated Indian, Pakistan and Bangladesh governments and public opinion. The Joint Commissions for trade and commerce, science, and technology and education and culture established at the time of the Secretary of State's October, 1974 visit to India reflect an upturn in the prospects for people to people diplomacy and promise further reconstruction of cultural relations.

The record of functional complexity in South Asia makes clear the difficulty of reconciling the divergent interests of USG actors in the region. The "government" for South Asia in Washington as well as in the region, lacks the means to coordinate functional complexity. Its reconstruction should include organizational integration focused on the State Department, particularly the scaling down or elimination of policies, programs, and operations outside State's direct control. The creation of contexts for deliberative coordination in the field and in Washington will also be helpful. Finally, insulation of medium and long term interests in multilateral economic agencies and autonomous governmental units or quasi private organizations for cultural and educational programs and for the Peace Corps can inhibit if not prevent the kind of precipitous declines in receptivity for such programs that occurred in South Asia over the past decade.

D. Regional Complexity

A presenting problem for the consideration of regional complexity is that regions as policy arenas are not adequately recognized nor organizationally articulated in the bureaucratic structure of the USG. Regions require organizational articulation because they are the most frequent source of international crisis. Present policy mechanisms are oriented to bilateral or global rather than regional policy formulation and management.

"Regional governments", particularly in their field dimension, are the least articulated and organized interests among those represented in governmental pluralism. By regional governments we mean the network of U.S. bureaucratic interests and actors that deal with the South Asia policy arena. Organizational actors are physically divided between those in the field and those in Washington, and each set is normatively "divided" by the claims of other orientations and roles. In Washington, the authority and bargaining advantages of bilateral and global actors and, in the field, the authority and bargaining advantages associated with ambassadors, country teams and specialist roles tend to be superior to the authority and bargaining advantages of actors concerned to articulate regional problems and policies. Among the states of the region, regional identities and institutions are, relative to national, also weakly articulated and organized.

Another presenting problem for regional complexity is the diversity of field environments within regions. The States of South Asia are complex in a variety of dimensions : regimes with different ideologies, governments with different policies, cultures with different ways of life, and economies with somewhat different needs and possibilities.

In Washington, South Asia is officially defined by two country directorates in a regional bureau of eight country directorates. One deals with Pakistan, Afghanistan Bangladesh (NEA/PAB); another with Bhutan, Nepal, India, Maldive, and Sri Lanka (NEA/INS). This composite regional bureau encompassed six additional Near East country directorates (including the North African Arab states); three deputy assistant secretaries, only one of whom, usually, is responsible for territorially defined South Asian affairs, and a regional affairs unit (NEA/RA) responsible for a variety of functional policy arenas.[24] A number of other actors can be located within the loosely defined boundary of South Asia regional government : actors at the

24. For the country directorate system generally, see William I. Bacchus, *Foreign Policy and the Bureaucratic Process; The State Department's Country Director System* (Princeton, Princeton University Press, 1974).

Under Secretary level and other seventh floor units such as the Policy Planning Staff (in the Department of State); the Office of South Asian Affairs in AID's Bureau for Near East and South Asia (AA/NESA) and a variety of other AID functional units at various levels; and territorially defined South Asia units or functional units with South Asia concerns in the Executive Office of the president, including the White House, the National Security Council, the Central Intelligence Agency and the Office of Management and Budget; the Arms Control and Disarmament Agency; the United States Department of Agriculture; the Department of Commerce; the Treasury Department; and a variety of statutory, administrative and *ad hoc* interdepartmental committees.[25] Especially important in the environment of Washington USG actors dealing with South Asia Policy are the ambassadors and embassy officials of South Asian states.[26]

These field, environmental and Washington characteristics of regional complexity are obstacles to the articulation of the regional idea and reality in organizational and policy terms. The coordination of regional complexity involves in the first instance improved institutionalization of the regional dimension. Several of our recommendations are designed to meet this necessary condition.

Most of the troubles with which the conduct of foreign policy has to deal arise in the relations among neighboring states. Distance under the technological conditions of modern warfare is a decisive deterrent to war among non-neighbors. Only the two super powers can easily and readily fight wars against non-neighbors, or make it possible for others to do so. But the weak and amorphous nature of regional government limits its capacity to deal with crises of this kind, those that arise regionally from tensions and conflicts among neighboring states

25. Interdepartmental committees active in the South Asia policy arena are depicted in the case studies printed elsewhere in this volume, particularly those by Bjorkman, Kochanek, and Moulton.
26. For a study of the role of ambassadors and embassy officials in the Washington environment see Roger Sack and Donald L. Wyman, "Latin American Diplomacy and the United States Foreign Policy Making Process," study for the Commission on the Organization of the Government for the Conduct of Foreign Policy, December, 1974, printed in Appendix I to the Commission's Report.

Policies and programs too are rarely formulated and implemented in regional frameworks yet policy needs and problems, like crises, are often region specific. Variations among regions are greater for the most part than variations within regions; data that measure and organize regional characteristics and problems are often a better guide for policy formulation than aggregative world data designed to capture and define policy needs in arenas such as population, food, resources, trade, and science and technology. More important, regional needs and problems, unlike world needs and problems expressed in disembodied and abstract terms, can be connected to political forces and actors, to people on the ground with ideologies, policies and interests.

Our formulation of the nature of regional complexity and the problems for the conduct of foreign policy associated with it point to the need for conceptual, organizational and procedural reforms designed to strengthen regional government.

E. Complexity Management

Like policy, complexity has to be managed if it is to be coordinated. In this section, we distinguish, characterize and evaluate three types of complexity management, normal diplomacy, crisis management and strategic diplomacy.

By normal diplomacy we refer to those activities and tasks (e.g. political reporting; lateral clearance) which recur on a fairly regular and predictable basis even though their substantive content may be subject to rather large variations. By crisis management we refer to responses to events which threaten peace and security, particularly those that have a high saliency for U.S. interests. Unlike normal diplomacy, crises are unpredictable (although, of course, some can be anticipated). Strategic diplomacy deals with the relationships among the great powers including the rare but significant occasions when fundamental realignments occur. It is exemplified by the opening to China and the deepening of detente with the Soviet Union. Strategic diplomacy involves, then, the orientation and reorientation of great power relationships in the attempt to shape and manipulate the balance of power at the global level.

There are certain organizational implications that follow

from these analytic distinctions. In the repertoire of organizational resources available for the conduct of foreign policy, some organizations are more suitable for one or several types of diplomacy and less suitable for others. Clearly, normal diplomacy is in the first instance the responsibility of the Department of State and U.S. embassies abroad. Strategic tends to be "presidential." The White House offices, including particularly the assistant to the president for national security affairs and the National Security Council (which, *inter alia* engages the attention of the secretaries of state and defense, the chairman of the Joint Chiefs of Staff, the director of the Central Intelligence Agency, etc.) have been the home of strategic diplomacy. In between normal diplomacy and strategic diplomacy lies crisis management. While we are not aware of any quantitative studies that use these or like terms to establish a distribution of activity or resources as among these three modes of conducting foreign policy, crisis management probably occupies the largest single proportion of time for higher level ("White House") personnel in organizations concerned with the conduct of foreign policy.

Because one of the characteristics of normal diplomacy is the relatively high degree to which activities recur, regularity and predictability make it possible to subject tasks and activities to organizational routines. On a scale bounded by predictability at one end and randomness at the other, crisis management is the least stable, normal diplomacy the most. Strategic diplomacy is ordinarily fairly stable although subject to occasional abrupt change. What concerns us here is the suitability of organizational capacity to the type of activity involved in the conduct of foreign policy. Crisis management involves the most difficult and problematic area. Yet it is precisely here that shifts in the location of action tend to occur, i.e. there is a certain instability in the organizational responsibility for crisis management. Conversely, there is a certain stability in the relationship between organizations and the management of normal and strategic diplomacy.

When crises occur there is a general tendency for the action to move up and out of those levels of the state department that are country and regionally informed. Action moves from roughly the embassy and country director level beyond the assistant secretary to the seventh floor policy planning levels and out to the White House and National Security Council. Efforts have been made to stabilize these relatively unstable organizational responses by creating such entities as senior review groups (SRGs) and Washington special action groups (WSAGs), arrangements designed to unite White House generalists with State Department professionals. But these have been not entirely satisfactory; they have not operated, in South Asia, to overcome several important undesirable effects which follow the movement of action up and out under crisis conditions.

One is the separation of professional from generalist knowledge, another the conflict between professional authority and presidential power. People who know most about the bilateral and regional relations involved in a crisis tend to lose control of the action; people who know most about strategic diplomacy and the global balance of power and least about bilateral and regional relations gain control. The result is not only that different organizational actors become dominant but also that they impose on the understanding and the analysis of the situation a different vocabulary and a different world view. It is in this sense that there is a separation of knowledge and power. Crisis management as it has been practiced also distorts or disrupts the coordination of time and functional complexity by subordinating longer term policies and programs to an often undiscriminating use of leverage directed toward "winning" in the short run and by subordinating political goals and means to military.

V. Findings

A. Crisis Diplomacy and Imperative Coordination

The findings of the case studies in this report and our interviews in South Asia and Washington provide the bases for the organizational and procedural changes we recommend. Other often more detailed findings and additional recommendations can be found in the case studies. Here we present and analyze findings relevant for certain large issues in organizational change, drawing, where appropriate, on the cases for evidence and arguments.

Among our principal findings are : (1) Coordinating organizations and procedures of the Johnson and Nixon administrations failed to sustain compatible policies at the global,
regional and bilateral levels. By unnecessarily subordinating
regional and bilateral to global considerations, gratuitous losses
were suffered in regional and bilateral relations. (2) The
substantive failure of coordination among levels was related to
the absence of organizational arrangements and of norms that
adequately enlisted professional knowledge, experience and
judgment. (3) Coordination under conditions of crisis
diplomacy was effective but not successful because presidential
initiatives, direction and control narrowed the scope of
consultation and/or constrained deliberation in ways that
blocked the appreciation of available information and options.
The formulation and coordination of policy was relatively
effective and successful under conditions of normal diplomacy
because more collegial conditions supported deliberation and
engaged bureaucratic interest and their professional knowledge. (4) Policies designed to further interests or achieve goals
with longer run time-frames were less easily understood and
justified than policies with short run objectives and more
immediate benefits. Because the need for leverage to solve
crises in the short run was especially suited to presidential
needs for political effectiveness and success, policies and
programs directed to the longer term were sacrificed to the
requirements of leverage.[27] (5) Presidential preferences for
closely held decisions and/or personal control of plans and
operations blocked non-presidential, line officials from knowledge of operative assumptions relevant for related policy
arenas and, in turn, cut off presidential level actors from
information, arguments and options relevant to the closely
held decisions or operations.

27. Evidence for this finding can be found not only in the case studies of
     this report but also in the study by Joan Hochman, "The Suspension
     of Economic Assistance to India" in *Cases on a Decade of United
     States Foreign Economic Policy : 1965-1974*, a report submitted to the
     Commission on the Organization of the Government for the Conduct
     of Foreign Policy by Griffenhagen-Kroeger, Inc., Edward Hamilton,
     Principal Investigator, printed in Appendix H to the Commission's
     Report

We have categorized the studies of the conduct of foreign policy in South Asia over the past decade under two of the terms drawn from our discussion of the management of complexity : (1) crisis management and (2) normal diplomacy. (The third term, strategic diplomacy, plays an important but indirect role in the crisis management cases.) Two cases fall under the first category, eight under the second. The crisis management cases, Johnson's food aid policy of 1965-66 and the formation of Bangladesh in 1971, exhibit two characteristics : (1) the strongest possible presidential level involvement, assertion of presidential preference and will, and use of imperative coordination and (2) the absence of deliberative coordination in dealing with complexity (e.g. the absence of a balance between generalist and professional knowledge to promote the mutual appreciation of information, informed discussion and the representation of bureaucratic interests; between global, regional and bilateral levels of policy; and between longer and shorter run time-frames).

1. Food Aid and the Primacy of the Presidential Will
The first crisis management case, (see James Bjorkman, "Public Law 480 and the Policies of Self-Help and Short-Tether : Indo-American Relations, 1965-1968") deals with President Johnson's food aid policy. In it, the president personally intervened to secure the aid and later, to control, in considerable detail, the amount and timing of its allocation. Johnson's food aid policy was a composite of many features. Partly in response to the efforts of the Ford and Rockefeller Foundations and to Chester Bowles' conversations with Nehru, the GOI from about 1963 had begun to shift its development strategy from a heavy emphasis on industrialization to an increased attention to agriculture. Its interest in agricultural self-sufficiency was strengthened by the food aid cut-offs that followed the Indo-Pakistan war of 1965, and was accelerated by the severe food shortages that followed the monsoon failures of 1965 and 1966. In 1964, Ambassador Chester Bowles had begun a massive effort to relate U.S. aid to positive Indian initiatives in the agriculture sector.[28] This emphasis, in turn,

28. Chester Bowles, *Promises to Keep, My Years in Public Life, 1941-1969*, (New York : Harper & Row, 1971), p. 552.

was to be coordinated with policies and programs for industry, export promotion, and population control. In the spring of 1965, these proposals under the direction of John Lewis, Director of AID, India, were translated into a detailed agenda for American aid over a five year period. The strategy was predicated on Indian responses leading to food self-sufficiency in five years.[29] The World Bank, which was coordinating efforts and perspectives with those of the United States, joined these efforts in 1965 by coupling bank assistance with relaxation of licensing, devaluation, and self-help in agriculture.

All of these efforts began to acquire urgency after the monsoon failure of 1965. In Fall, 1965, India requested and began to receive food aid. President Johnson ordered that the aid be put on stream on a short term basis, in order, he said, to "judge requirements month by month," and assure that "India changed its farm policy."[30] Chester Bowles, citing American press commentaries, believed the reasons were different. "By this time a delay in granting economic assistance to India. . . was interpreted (often correctly) as an attempt by the administration to force the recipient nation to change its position on Vietnam," he wrote Bill Moyers on August 26, adding that such tactics would damage the good name of the president and of the United States.[31] In 1966, President Johnson promised additional food aid to Mrs. Gandhi during her March visit to the United States, and undertook a massive, successful effort to mobilize the House and Senate on behalf of food aid. This effort resulted in the joint congressional resolution of April 19. Once again he proceeded to put food shipments on a short tether, and took personal charge of the dispatch of grain shipments. "I became an expert on the ton by ton movement of grain from the wheat fields of Kansas to ports like Calcutta. I described myself as 'a kind of country agricultural agent with intercontinental clients'."[32]

Ambassador Bowles saw the matter differently: "[President Johnson] embarked on a foot dragging performance that I still

29. Chester Bowles, *Promises to Keep*, p. 557.
30. Lyndon Johnson, *The Vantage Point, Perspectives of the Presidency, 1963-1969*, New York, Holt, Rinehart and Winston, 1961), p. 225.
31. Bowles, *Promises*, p. 559.
32. Johnson, *The Vantage Point*, p. 226.

fail to understand. Assuming personal charge of a program, he adopted what was referred to in Washington as a 'short tether approach' holding up authorization for new shipments until the very last moment . . . This placed the Indian rationing system under almost impossible strain. India's needs could be met only by an uninterrupted stream of grain shipments. . . ."[33]

President Johnson's expressed motives for the strategy were to enlist other countries in the food effort, to shock India into a more expeditious approach to agricultural reforms, and to persuade Congress that he was hard-headed about food, not a rat-hole-man, and would insist on self-help and early self-sufficiency. It is also true that the interruption of food aid, from August to December, followed Mrs. Gandhi's joint communique with the Soviet government condemning the Vietnam War, and accompanied repeated similar provocations—such as birthday greetings to Ho Chi Minh.

The August to December *de facto* food aid cut off followed by less than two months India's decision of June 6, 1966, to devalue the rupee in the face of enormous pressure by the USG and World Bank. Coinciding with a second massive failure of the monsoon, it wrought havoc with an Indian food policy premised on American commitments. The anticipated food and development assistance aid needed to cushion the consequences on food prices of the devaluation was delayed for six months and anticipated large-scale consortium aid for subsequent years did not materialize.

The President believed the policy was a success. He related the self-help efforts of 1966-67 in India to it, as well as the $ 200 [of $ 725] million contributed to food aid by other foreign donors. Again, Chester Bowles saw the matter differently : "It is a cruel performance. The Indians must conform; they must be made to fawn; their pride must be cracked. Pressure to improve India's performance was sensible, but. . . in this way . . . distrust and hatred are born among people who want to be our friends."[34] In retrospect, it seems evident that the August to December "delay" in food shipments played an important part in vitiating India's effort to keep its economy

33. Bowles, *Promises*, p. 525.
34. Cited from his Journal of February 6, 1966. Bowles, *Promises*, p. 534.

stable in the face of the consequences of the 1966 summer
monsoon failure, the consequences of the rupee devaluation,
and the delay and subsequent unavailability of consortium aid.
President Johnson's pressure operated to weaken the influence
of those Indians who advocated a more liberal economic strategy, including devaluation and de-controls, by emphasizing
the link among food and development assistance, adherence to
American economic advice, and silence with respect to President Johnson's Southeast Asia policy.

From the point of view of organizational prescriptions, the
notable features of the case are President Johnson's personal
and direct involvement and his isolation from professional
advisors on Asia. Bowles notes that here, as in other cases,
Johnson frightened advisors out of their willingness to take
initiatives : "Even the senior officials in our government dealing
with India's food problem became so intimidated that they
refused to make even those decisions which they could have
made for themselves."[35]

The President explicitly saw himself as opposed in his
actions by the professionals concerned with South Asia, and
was confident he was right : "I stood almost alone, with only a
few concurring advisors, in this fight to slow the pace of U.S.
assistance, to persuade the Indians to do more for themselves,
and to induce other nations to lend a helping hand. This was
one of the most difficult and lonely struggles of my
Presidency."[36]

The food aid case has in common with the Bangladesh case
the element of unnecessary cost. If President Johnson hoped to
exact silence from the GOI on Southeast Asia, which he does
not acknowledge in *The Vantage Point* as a goal, but which the
press and other observers of his administration assure us was
a goal, Dulles' failure to influence Nehru under similar
circumstances might have warned him off. Further, it seems
unlikely that the self-help efforts of 1966-67 were speeded by
the short tether policy. Such efforts were agreed upon and

35. Bowles, *Promises*, p. 525.
36. Johnson, *The Vantage Point*, p. 225.

set in motion by 1965.[37] And it is unlikely that the Congress required the short tether as proof of hard-headedness. When it passed a supporting resolution in 1966 before the August hold up, the most significant factor in its doing so was the Congressional mission to India in late 1966, headed by Congressman Poage, chairman of the House Agricultare Committee. It seems unlikely too that short tether influenced U.S. allies to help with food aid as much as the mission of Under Secretary of State Engene D. Rostow and direct appeals to them by the GOI. If these goals were won by means other than the short tether, and GOI silence with respect to United States Government policy in Southeast Asia could not be exacted by it, for reasons relatedt o internal Indian politics, it is apparent that the policy resulted in unnecessary costs—the discrediting of liberal economists and policy makers in India; the loss of Indian goodwill and harm to America's reputation for relatively disinterested humanitarian and development assistance—while garnering few benefits.

However tenuous counter-factual arguments, are there is good reason to believe that a more routine handling of food aid policy for India in this period, i.e., greater reliance on normal diplomacy, at least would have avoided such costs and might have secured some of the short run and long run benefits contemplated by key actors such as Ambassador Bowles.

2. Bangladesh and the Dominance of the Global View

The Bangladesh case of 1971 (see Philip Oldenburg, "The Breakup of Pakistan") illustrates how, despite organizational and procedural arrangements designed to engage generalists and professionals with each other in crisis management, a global policy orientation and imperative coordination exclude or

37. See, for example, V.K.R.V. Rao, economic advisor to the GOI, who wrote at the time : "Our immediate task is to rid the country of stultifying and nationally dangerous dependence on imports for our food supplies" [GOI, *The Meaning of Self-Reliance*, November, 1965], and of course C. Subramaniam, India's Food Minister, had gained parliamentary approval for a comprehensive "self-help" policy in December, 1965.

devalue the regional and bilateral perspectives of professionals. As one former senior official put it, "Our policy [in 1971] . . . seems to me to have been a classic case of doing the wrong thing in a regional situation for the sake of wider relationships . . ."[38]

The case depicts an extreme instance of the lack of engagement between global and regionally oriented policy makers, between generalists and professionals. It is important, in judging the lessons of the case, to recognize the difference between communication and engagement among administrative layers. Oldenburg's account establishes that information flows to the top were plentiful, continuous, informed and accurate. There is no question that those at the top were formally informed and presented with alternative evaluations and courses of action. When we say there was no engagement, we mean that there was no "appreciation" of the information supplied, no attempt to reason together, to jointly assess meaning or judge implications. The obverse of Henry Kissinger's remark at the WSAG meeting of December 3, 1971—"The President is under the 'illusion' that he is giving instructions . . . "[39] was that officials of the South Asia establishment and other high-level officials outside the Department of State were under the illusion that they were providing information and policy guidance to the President. Much of the conflict took the form of Henry Kissinger and the President against everybody else. As one senior official observed, nobody saw it their way.

There were at least four areas in which actors with global and actors with regional roles "saw" different facts and made different judgments : (1) Was the crisis primarily global or regional ? (2) What counts as the use of force in international politics? (3) What counts as a political settlement and were prospects for a political settlement promising ? (4) Did India intend to "dismember" West Pakistan ?

38. William Bundy, "International Security Today," *Foreign Affairs*, Vol. 53, No. 1, October, 1974, p. 38. Bundy argues for priorities that recognize that "the regions of the world have reasserted a life of their own . . ." and against "pernicious abstractions" and using "universal principles as a guide."

39. The *New York Times*, January 6, 1972, p. 16. All quotations of government officials addressing themselves to the Bangladesh problem are from this report, unless otherwise noted.

The main conflict of viewpoint, which governed all other differences, concerned whether the Bangladesh crisis should be regarded as global or regional. In part, this appeared to be beyond the reach of organizational arrangements to change but only in part. Whether only one policy level, global or regional, could be operative, or whether both might be accommodated, was a matter of options perceived, and has to do with who and what was heard and appreciated. This is an appropriate question for organizational and procedural reform.

The President's view of the crisis was stated after the fact in the State of the World Message of February 9, 1972 :

> It was our view that the war in South Asia was bound to have serious implications for the evolution of our policy with the People's Republic of China. That country's attitude toward the global system was certain to be profoundly influenced by its assessment of the principles by which the system was governed . . .

In WSAG discussions Henry Kissinger generally read events in South Asia to show that their primary significance was their effect on America's relations with the Soviet Union and China. He also read actions by states in South Asia as reflexive of global power strategies. In his 1972 State of the World Message, President Nixon interpreted the December War in South Asia in terms of the Soviet Union "projecting a political and military presence without precedence into many new regions of the globe;" warned that detente must not be "interpreted as an opportunity for the strategic expansion of Soviet power," pictured America's stand as discouraging such Soviet aspirations and efforts ; and deplored the Soviet Union's failure to prevent "the Pakistani conflict from being turned into an international war."

The questions that Mr. Kissinger's shop asked throughout the crisis turn on how China and the Soviet Union were involved with South Asia and how their involvement in turn affected the security of South Asia. South Asia was important to China, on this reading, because China feared Soviet penetration and influence in the subcontinent. Would the Soviet Union succeed in encircling China from that direction ? Since the United States as a superpower was at that time concerned with establishing relationships with China, it needed to assure China that it was prepared to strengthen its ally Pakistan against Russia's ally India and thus limit or deter the encirclement. Furthermore, the United States was concerned to show its prospective ally, China, how it treated allies (such as Pakistan) generally. As one official familiar with the reasoning of the Kissinger group put it : "If the Chinese were looking to the United States as an ally, what kind of an ally would the United States be ? They might learn something from how the United States treated its ally Pakistan . . . How we treated our ally Pakistan and how we stood up to India, the Soviet Union's ally, would indicate how we would act with respect to our allies generally. The United States did not go in for a pro-Pakistan tilt per se but rather engaged in behavior consistent with these kinds of concerns."

Officials close to Mr. Kissinger stressed the fact that the Soviet Union had decided to "back the Indians" in the Bangladesh crisis. "The Soviets dropped their earlier efforts to restrain India. They signalled the Indians that they could go ahead." Reports in October that the Soviet Union was willing to allow India to go ahead contrasted with reports on Soviet policy and intentions in July when it was thought that the Soviet Union wanted India to avoid war and wanted to preserve its influence and good relations with Pakistan. By this account, some time late in August it became apparent that the Soviets stopped urging India to avoid war. The global and reflexive interpretations reached their apogee when Henry Kissinger, returning on December 14, 1971 with President Nixon from the Azores where they had conferred with President Pompidou of France, signalled the Russians in a backgrounder that unless they restrained India "very soon" the "entire U.S. Soviet relationship might well be reexamined" including the up-coming summit scheduled for May, 1972."[40]

This view is composed of two elements, one having to do with policy choices and one having to do with perceptions of facts. The first element, the emphasis on a global conceptualization, selects global actors (China, Russia, United States) as the most significant element and the lever to affect action.

40. Marvin Kalb and Bernard Kalb, *Kissinger* (Boston, 1974), p. 262.

The second element, related to the first, is a factual supposition about motives; nonglobal powers' actions are mainly reflexive of the needs and strategies of global powers, a supposition that influences perceptions of regional powers' behavior.

Regional officials read events in South Asia differently. India had interests and capabilities. Her decision about the use of force was a result, they thought, of the burdens that ten million refugees imposed and the progressively unlikely possibility that a political settlement would relieve them. There were gains for India; an independent Bangladesh meant a weakened and discredited Pakistan. Nor did they ignore Soviet interests and influence. It was, they held, one among a number of factors that shaped Indian action, not the overriding one. One official, noting that Mrs. Gandhi had gone to Moscow after her abortive November visit to the United States, characterized her conversation there more in terms of bargaining interdependence than reflexive subordination when he said : "She told the Russians she was going ahead and they said okay, if you must."

On can imagine another sort of report on Mrs. Gandhi's visit to Moscow that would interpret her conversations there in terms of them telling her what to do. Because the Kissinger shop was confident that Moscow was telling her, responding to India became much less important than signalling the Russians —as the *Enterprise* and backgrounder on the way back from the Azores did.

Does all of this mean that the China opening was, indeed, the real rationale for tilt ? Many of our interviewees thought it was. Otherwise they found the tilt inexplicable. But some did not. One thought that the China factor made for good retrospective rationalization of American policy by providing a good reason as against bad reasons for the bad policies pursued. He argued that on balance the China factor was not the overriding reason for U.S. policy. More important in his view were Mr. Nixon's prejudices and the need for striking initiatives in time for the elections.

Line officials concerned with the region entertained different assumptions about actors' motives than did global generalists on presidential staffs. Professionals credited the influence on regional actors of what they thought Russia's and

China's and the U.S.' goals and actions might be but they were also deeply influenced by factors in the region : the economic and political problem of the refugees for India; the standing of the Awami League in the Pakistan political equation; the potential strategic gains for India of an independent Bangladesh. These judgments led to different conclusions about what signals and actions—the *Enterprise*, negotiations with Mujib—would generate desirable outcomes.

Global generalists and regional professionals differed on what counts as the use of force in international politics. In part this question relates to the "facts" about who starts a war and they in turn relate to the kind of events that count for starting war.

For the secretary of state the facts that counted were, who bore the "major responsibility" for "broader hostilities" and what was meant by broader hostilities. Charles Bray III, the State Department spokesman, stated on December 4 that "India bears major responsibility for the broader hostilities." George Bush over the next few days at the U.N. and on television referred to India's action as aggression, and Henry Kissinger, in WSAG meetings, after wondering whether the facts of the Pakistan attack on India's airfields might have been misperceived (December 3 : "Is it possible the Indians attacked first that day and the Paks simply did what they could before dark?") stated on December 6 that the President "is not inclined to let the Paks be defeated" and on December 8 that "the President believes that India is the attacker." Richard Helms, the Director of the CIA, at the WSAG of December 4, gives a different interpretation : "We do not know who started the current action (in East Pakistan), nor do we know why the Paks hit . . . Indian airfields yesterday." After the fact, CIA analysts wondered whether Pakistan escalated hostilities from the local to the international level to save a deteriorating situation by bringing in third powers or to win a decisive military victory from which to bargain.

By December 7, when Henry Kissinger held the backgrounder briefing that Senator Goldwater introduced into the *Congressional Record* of December 9, he had abandoned his question of December 3 about who had attacked first that day. Instead, he told the reporters that "On November 22nd, military action started in East Bengal." (The Indians acknowledge a "local" attack on the border town of Bovra on November 20 to end, as they put it, Pakistan shelling of Indian "villages.") He then went on to say that "international anarchy" would result if "the right of military attack is determined by arithmetic." India's population was 500 million and Pakistan's 100 million. The issue was, he said, should the United States "always be on the side of the numerically stronger ?" and the answer was, of course, no.

Other kinds of facts were counted by professional middle-level officials as relevant to judgments about the use of force in international relations. For most of them the Pakistan government's violent repressions, confirmed by AID, U.S. consular and World Bank reports, counted as the use of force. They saw it directed against the Awami League leadership, middle-class professionals and the civilian population in order to put down protests against the abrogation of the results of the general election that brought the Awami League to power in the center and in the East. They doubted whether a state's internal use of force properly extended to Islamabad's abrogation of the results of the recent (December, 1970) constitutionally conducted election. They also doubted whether killing and repression on a scale that generated 8 to 10 million refugees could be encompassed by the doctrine of a sovereign state's legitimate monopoly of force.

Another central question was what would count as a political solution to the Bangladesh crisis and what were the prospects for one ? What was required and, in the light of what was required, what was being done with what effect when ?

Before March 25, 1971, when Islamabad began its attempt to suppress the Awami League by force, some of those outside the President and National Security Advisor's immediate circle saw advantages for the United States in a Sheikh Mujib-led Pakistan government; it would be, they held, constitutional and would pursue a moderate foreign policy. Others cautioned against any suggestion of U.S. encouragement to Sheikh Mujib because it would feed West Pakistani fears about the steadfastness of U.S. support. After March, 1971, when Islamabad began what most professionals thought highly unlikely because of the improbability that it could succeed and because of the risk of Indian intervention—the use of violence to hold East Pakistan and to crush the Awami League and its supporters—many officials saw U.S. interests lying with measures designed to stop civil violence and restore peace even though such measures might displease the West Pakistanis.

Once Sheikh Mujib was arrested and imprisoned in West Pakistan there was fundamental disagreement over what should be done to secure a political solution. Those outside the presidential circle held that some form of negotiation with the imprisoned Sheikh Mujib, the leader of the Awami League which had won a majority of assembly seats in the national election of 1970, spokesman for greater autonomy within a loose federal system, and prime minister elect of Pakistan, was essential. Whether he was "released" by Pakistan or direct or indirect talks arranged were open and difficult questions, but to most of those outside the immediate presidential circle Sheikh Mujib was seen as the *sine qua non* of a political settlement.

To those who believed negotiations with Mujib were essential, the appropriate path was pressure by the U.S. government on President Yahya Khan of Pakistan, and other key actors, such as Z.A. Bhutto and leaders of army factions, to accept the possibility of autonomy and to negotiate with the majority party leader. The Kissinger proposal of December 7, for civilian government and autonomy for East Pakistan, was not viable, they thought, because it assumed that even a loosely federated Pakistan could be governed without the participation of the Awami League, whose elected leaders, declared traitors by the Pakistan government, were dead, under arrest, or in exile. The President's approach to a peaceful solution was stated during the heat of the crisis in the Kissinger backgrounder of December 7 that appeared in the *Congressional Record* of December 9 and was repeated after the crisis, in the President's State of the World Message of February 9, 1972 :

> Return to civilian rule was pledged for the end of December (1971) and could have increased the chances for a political settlement and the release of Sheikh Mujib. Meanwhile, in August, we established contact with Bengali representatives in Calcutta. By early November, President Yahya told us

he was prepared to begin negotiation with any representative of this group not charged with high crimes in Pakistan. In mid-November, we informed India that we were prepared to promote discussion of an explicit timetable for East Pakistani autonomy.

The President and his advisors did not believe that Pakistan either could or should be pushed on release of Mujib. "We will go along," Henry Kissinger told the December 4 WSAG, with reference to political accommodation in East Pakistan, "but we will certainly not imply or suggest . . . the release of Mujib." On only one issue were the President and his immediate advisors prepared to bring pressure on President Yahya Khan, sparing Sheikh Mujib's life. President Yahya Khan was advised that Sheikh Mujib was more dangerous dead than alive and the President obtained an assurance from President Yahya that Sheikh Mujib Rahman would not be executed.

A fourth area where facts were in dispute and judgements differed markedly was India's intentions with respect to West Pakistan. Henry Kissinger warned at the December 8 WSAG that "what we may be witnessing is a situation where a country [India] equipped and supported by the Soviets may be turning half of Pakistan into an impotent state and the other half into a vassal." The theme of dismemberment, of the intolerability of the "complete disintegration by force" of Pakistan referred to by President Nixon in his February, 1972, State of the World Message, was based on the "convincing evidence" received during the week of December 6, 1971, "that India was seriously contemplating the . . . destruction of Pakistan's military forces in the West." At the December 8 WSAG CIA Director Helms stated that Mrs. Gandhi "intends to attempt to straighten out the southern border of Azad Kashmir" and that "it is reported . . . [that] she intends to attempt to eliminate Pakistan's armor and air force capabilities." Mr. Kissinger commented that if the Indians do so, "we would have a deliberate Indian attempt to force the disintegration of Pakistan . . . It would turn Pakistan into a client state . . . Can we allow a U.S. ally to go down . . . Can we allow the Indians to scare us off . . . with a blockade ?"

Later, in the context of the dispute over India's intentions in the West, an intelligence report was leaked to show that the Indian cabinet had discussed action in the West in ways that indicated an intention to dismember Pakistan. The publicly known hawkish proclivities of Defense Minister Jagjiwan Ram were reported in the leaked version, but Mrs. Gandhi's view that a major effort in the West was unwise and would not be attempted was not. The dispatch of the aircraft carrier *Enterprise*, the move which was probably most damaging to American relations with India and Bangladesh, was related to these estimates, as well as to the belief that the critical actor in the South Asia drama was the Soviet Union. In a move that some have characterized as gun-boat diplomacy and others as a dangerous bluff, the *Enterprise* was dispatched to the Bay of Bengal to signal the Soviet Union and India that America meant business on the sub-continent. "If we had not taken the stand against the war," the President argued in his 1972 State of the World Message "it would have been prolonged and a likely attack in the West greatly increased."

On the other hand, there is a trend in the WSAG discussions, coming mainly from the regional professionals but also from others, including the CIA, that India did not have aggressive intentions in the West. CIA Director Helms on December 6 reported that Indian activity in the West "is essentially limited to air attacks." Assistant Secretary Sisco and Deputy Assistant Secretary Van Hollen agreed that the Indians would pull their troops out of East Bengal once the Pakistan forces were disarmed, and AID Deputy Administrator Maurice Williams argued that the Indians, who may "have to give ground in Kashmir" were attacking from Rajasthan into Sind in the South to gain real estate to ward off parliamentary criticism. General John Ryan (representing the Office of the Joint Chiefs of Staff) "indicated that he did not see the Indians pushing too hard at this time [in the West], rather they seemed content with a holding action," and Joseph Sisco "doubted ... that the Indians had the disintegration of Pakistan as their objective."[41]

41. Kalb and Kalb in *Kissinger* depict Kissinger and Assistant Secretary of State for the Near East and South Asia, Joseph Sisco as engaged in "a rip-roaring battle" over the direction of American policy. Sisco, the Kalbs report, expressed the State Department's best judgment when he argued that "India had limited ambitions in the war"

The Bangladesh case represents a failure of understanding and judgement which improved organizational arrangements and procedures could reach if there were presidential appreciation of their value and the will to use them. Coordination did not succeed in harmonizing global, regional, and bilateral interests; it did not harmonize the perspective of policy intellectuals at the presidential level with the professional knowledge of State Department officials in Washington and the field. It is not always possible to do so; not all goals are mutually compatible. But it is an essential element of the case that little effort was made to reason and bargain; to inquire whether China's reasons for agreeing to an opening were compatible with a regional formulation of U.S. interests in South Asia; to consider how much and what kind of support could be given to Bangladesh and to India without tearing relations with Pakistan; to explore realistically what was necessary to restore peace; in short, to establish to what extent and how global, regional and bilateral objectives could be simultaneously realized.

B. Normal Diplomacy and Deliberative Coordination

Normal diplomacy provides more fertile ground than does crisis management for deliberative coordination. However, less desirable attitudes and practices can and do grow in the same soil. The stereotype of the principal practitioners of normal diplomacy, the FSOs, depicts them as the prisoners of low risk routine, unwilling, even unable, to initiate; without imagination or breadth of vision; conventional conformists wedded to the safety and security of the *status quo*. Some of this image is an artifact of the conflict of interest and the struggle for influence between policy intellectuals oriented to presidential interests and favor and career officials oriented to professional knowledge and experience; some is the result of observable attitudes and behavior. Our research for this study and the normal diplomacy cases included in this report do not for the most part support the negative stereotype.

---

and "did not want to extend the war into West Pakistan;" saw little chance of intervention by the Soviet Union or China; and advocated "a policy of cool rhetoric and calm behavior," but "Sisco lost the battle." p. 259.

Five of the seven normal diplomacy cases, those by Moulton, Cohen, Kochanek, Hadden and Rubin, depict career officials responding to changed conditions and the need for policy with imagination, flexibility and skill. Lenth's study too, by showing how over time an organization can learn from failure and adapt its ideology and practice to organizational and environmental operating conditions, supports a positive view of normal diplomacy and its practitioners. The findings of Andersen's paper, to be discussed in the context of the need for insulation, are more problematic.

Stephen Cohen's paper on "South Asia and U.S. Military Policy" analyzes three policy contexts, the reformulation of weapons policy in 1966-67, the "one-time" exception to that policy in 1970, and the proposed expansion of the facility on Diego Garcia. The first is of primary interest here because it illustrates how and why deliberative coordination in the context of normal diplomacy works. The second and third, the result of *ad hoc* and isolated high level intervention, dramatize and illustrate the contrast between deliberative and imperative coordination.

Between 1954 and 1965 the USG supplied Pakistan with $750 million worth of arms and in 1962 it supplied India with $90 million worth. At the peak of the programs American equipment amounted to over 80 per cent of Pakistan's weapons. For years there was a "gigantic"[42] Military Assistance Advisory Group (MAAG) in Pakistan and, for a few years after 1962 a "huge" U.S. Military Supply Mission to India (USMMI) in India administering the flow of equipment for six mountain divisions, road building and air defense.

The 1965 war between India and Pakistan revealed the "dismal results" of American arms policy in South Asia to career officials in Washington and the field. Without U.S. equipment "Pakistan would not have become a serious military power" but the consequences were not those intended. The 1965 war crystallized opinion. By 1965, Cohen finds. there was "remarkable agreement" among FSOs dealing with South Asia about the strategic and military situation in South Asia, an agreement that included the realization that Pakistan could not

---

42. Unless otherwise indicated, all quotations are from the Cohen paper.

establish strategic superiority on the subcontinent and that a continuation of USG arms supply would continue to de-stabilize the regional balance. "This shared perception of local conditions and American interests" was a necessary condition for the reformulation of arms supply policy.

After fighting broke out in 1965 the USG began a policy of treating India and Pakistan identically, first by establishing an embargo on military shipments, then, in 1966, by allowing cash sales of "non-lethal" items. At the same time, the India and Pakistan desks were searching for an arms policy that "would maximize what they perceived to be American interests in the region," including recognition of China's new role as Pakistan's major arms supplier, of the Soviet Union's major role in supplying India's military needs, and of the findings of a major DOD study of military assistance, completed in 1965, that held that most current programs were obsolete.[43] The result, announced on September 23, 1967, was a "willingness to consider on a case-by-case basis the cash sale of spare parts for previously supplied lethal equipment." Grant assistance was terminated and the MAAG and U.S. Military Supply Mission were withdrawn. The policy, by removing the USG from its role as a major arms supplier in South Asia while maintaining limited military-to-military contact and some leverage over Pakistan via decisions over spare parts, reduced the USG's strategic involvement in South Asia.

The USG arms supply policy to South Asia did not, ostensibly, arise from an intention to affect the strategic balance in South Asia but it did effect it. Programs begun in the name of containment became self-justifying and self-perpetuating interests which involved the USG in fueling both sides of an arms race whose consequence, regional conflict, served neither the USG's nor India's or Pakistan's interest. Career officials in Washington and the field, recognizing that changed global conditions (polycentrism, detente and the Vietnam build-up) and unintended and counter-productive regional consequences

43. The reappraisal of military assistance programs was under the general supervision of Assistant Secretary of Defense for International Security Affairs, John T. McNaughton and directed by Townshend Hoopes. See Roger Sack, "United States Military Aid to the Ayub Khan Regime," a background paper for this report.

required action, successfully initiated and coordinated a new policy.

The organizational and procedural characteristics of the "one time exception" of 1970 and the creeping commitment to a facility on Diego Garcia stand in marked contrast to those of the 1967 arms supply. The one time exception to the carefully prepared 1967 decisions foreshadowed some of the difficulties that surfaced in the decision making and coordination associated with the break-up of Pakistan in 1971. Global (or at least extra-regional) objectives were pursued at the expense of U.S. regional interests in South Asia and imperative coordination practiced in ways that isolated presidential level actors from the knowledge and goals of departmental professionals and cut off the professionals, in turn, from formulation of or knowledge about presidential objectives and plans. Earlier, isolated, *ad hoc* presidential intervention had almost upset the carefully orchestrated 1967 arms policy. President Johnson, on an around the world junket, conversed at the Karachi airport with Pakistan President Ayub Khan. Ayub made a statement on Vietnam and President Johnson, in contradiction to his recent support of the new arms policy, made conversational reference to the desirability of supplying tanks to Pakistan via USG pressure on Turkey.[44]

Richard Nixon too, soon after his election in 1968, took a trip around the world. With Henry Kissinger as "mentor and executor," he fashioned "a global foreign policy" that "relegated the Third World to a subservient position ... important only as individual countries had a special relationship with one of the major power centers." Cohen surmises that Pakistan, "which had stubbornly pursued close ties with China," was one such country. When Nixon visited Pakistan in 1969 he probably "initiated discussions about future U.S. Chinese relations" and as a *quid pro quo* undertook to modify the 1967 arms policy. Like the Johnson intervention, the commitment was made in an "off hand and casual" way; those in the President's party heard that he wanted to "do something for Pakistan" but no specific

---

44. Ambassador to India Chester Bowles refers, in *Promises to Keep*, to USG encouragement of third country sales of tanks to Pakistan. Ensuing publicity, he believes, forced a retreat. Page 521.

policy guidance was forthcoming until mid-1970 when President
Nixon, after being reminded by the Pakistan Ambassador of
his 1969 pledge and told that no action had followed, demanded immediate action from State Department officials who, in
response to NSC requests, had for months been "blindly
offering up suggestions without a clear understanding of the
reasons for making an exception to the 1966-67 policy." The
result was the one-time exception of 1970. More symbolic than
substantive (no really offensive weapons were provided), the
public justification (offsetting Pakistan's growing dependence
on Chinese arms) in retrospect seems "almost comical" in view
of Pakistan's intermediary role between the USG and the PRC.
The Pakistanis were, at best, disappointed, but cooperated in
the hope, no doubt, of better things to come. Whether the
Chinese in any way indicated that a condition or price of an
opening included sharing the burden of arming its ally Pakistan
seems, particularly at this early stage, extraordinarily doubtful.
We are left to conclude that the president and his national
security advisor, in the face of a variety of other means to
establish communication with the Chinese leadership, chose to
disturb the South Asian regional balance in ways that, then
and later, produced undesirable and unnecessary consequences.

Cohen concludes that, from a regional perspective, the one
time exception was "calamitous." He also finds that "had a
broader circle of participants been involved in the actual
policy decisions during the 1970-71 period it is quite probable
that a way could have been found to minimize the harmful
impact on U.S.-Indian relations and still bring off the China
visit." Inadequacies in the form and quality of coordination,
led to the unnecessary sacrifice of bilateral relations to extra-
regional considerations, a result that can be mitigated by
"periodic consultation between relevant Country Directors
(most urgently, the India, China and Soviet CD's)" and by
more frequent consultation among Assistant Secretaries "on
issue that cut across their geographic boundaries."

The creeping commitment to a facility on Diego Garcia too
is marked by isolated, *ad hoc* presidential-cum-secretarial level
intervention. Although Diego Garcia had been an object of
naval planning for over thirty years, deliberative coordination
in the context of governmental pluralism had, until the mid-

1960s, confined action to just that. Cohen reports that until 1973 "the Navy was the only agency which wanted to expand Diego Garcia, and they were successfully neutralized by civilian DOD officials in ISA working in collaboration with regional and functional bureaus (Political-Military Affairs) of the State Department."[45]

The Middle East war in 1973 gave the Navy case a new lease on life. Its ship movements in and around the Indian Ocean, it claimed, were "artificially constrained" for lack of a facility in the Indian Ocean. An alleged Soviet naval build-up in the Indian Ocean required a bigger balancing force. "Before these issues could be fully discussed within the bureaucracy," Cohen reports, secretaries Henry Kissinger and James Schlesinger "took Washington by surprise" when their decision, made "over breakfast," to raise Diego Garcia to the level of a significant support facility was made public. "Diego was to be expanded, and then the expansion would be properly justified in and out of the U.S. government " But by mid-1973, the Washington climate for the conduct of foreign policy had changed significantly; the constraints of governmental pluralism had revived and with them the strengths and weaknesses of deliberative coordination. A "full fledged political battle began to shape up" over Diego Garcia. On June 18, 1973, it became publicly known that the Navy had, on March 20, commissioned (i.e. put into operation) a communication station on Diego Garcia, making the U.S. the first major power to establish a base on foreign territory in the Indian Ocean area. But further expansion, despite President Ford's endorsement at his first news conference, will depend, in the new Washington climate, on something more closely approximating deliberative coordination.

Anthony Moulton's study of "The U.S., the International

---

45. Further, ISA/DOD "pointed out that refueling could be done more efficiently and cheaply in the Persian Gulf, that developing a U.S. facility would anger littoral states without yielding any particular benefit, and that even a small facility might be the prelude for a larger and unnecessary establishment" whose vulnerability could be used to justify additional costly aircraft carriers and might result in trapping an undue portion of the American fleet on the wrong side of the Suez Canal.

Development Association and South Asia" documents a dramatic though little known effort to extend the leverage and imperative coordination of the 1971 tilt toward Pakistan to the World Bank[46] affiliate, the IDA. Created in 1960 to make concessional development loans (termed credits) to countries whose per capita GNP is less than $ 375, the IDA is funded by periodic, non-reimbursable contributions from twenty donor countries. Its governing structure is identical with the World Bank's, which means that Robert McNamara, the President of the WB, is an important actor in the case, as is the U.S. Secretary of the Treasury (then John B. Connally) who, with nineteen other finance ministers, serves as one of the WB's Governors, and instructs the vote of the U.S. appointed Executive Director (simultaneously a paid WB employee and an unpaid special assistant to the Secretary of the Treasury) who, again, is one of twenty Executive Directors.[47] The key agencies dealing with multilateral economic aid, i.e. State, Treasury, the NSC and AID, Moulton finds, apply somewhat different perspectives. State is "enthusiastic,"[48] rarely objecting to IDA projects, concerned to use multilateral aid as a resource in promoting U.S. national interests. South Asia officials in particular "virtually always approve proposed projects." Treasury emphasizes close financial monitoring, as do the Federal Reserve, Commerce and the Exim bank. "In normal times," the NSC staff shares State's view. AID

46. The World Bank's official designation is the International Bank for Reconstruction and Development or IBRD. Hereafter we refer to the World Bank as WB.
47. The Secretary of the Treasury is advised by the National Advisory Council on International Monetary and Financial Policies (NAC), an interdepartmental committee with five voting units, Treasury (which has the chair), State, Commerce, the Federal Reserve Board, and the Exim bank, and a number of "participating" non-voting units including USDA, AID, OMB, DOD, the Council of Economic Advisors (CEA) and the Council on International Economic Policy (CIEP). NAC has two "policy" levels (Secretaries as Principals and Assistant Secretaries as Alternates) and a technically oriented operating level which meets weekly to discuss agency positions on, *inter alia*, IDA proposals and to recommend positions to their respective Principals who vote on the IDA Board
48. Unless otherwise indicated, all references are to the text of Moulton's study.

consistently and strongly supports multilateral economic aid
from a long term economic and political perspective.

Moulton examines between December, 1971 and March,
1972 the adequacy of USG organizational and procedural
arrangements to deal with two successive issues, IDA credits to
India following suspension of bilateral aid to India on
December 6, 1971 and an IDA credit to India in March, 1972
for purchase of four crude oil tankers. Policy formulation and
implementation occurred in the context of "a pronounced antagonism" toward India that "not only exacerbated Indo-
American relations but also seriously jeopardized the U.S.-IDA
relationship."

One key factor that constrained U.S. policy in the face of
rapidly changing circumstances between December, 1971, and
March, 1972, was IDA's structure and decisional rules. The
USG, with approximately 25 per cent of total shares, holds the
largest portion but by no means a majority of the votes required to decide questions brought before the twenty member
Board of Executive Directors. (The minimal winning coalition
needed, given the distribution of votes for the required simple
majority, is six members.) Important conventions also
constrained USG policy and action : Most important, "the
WB president never has been defeated on a Board vote; if he
were, it is understood he would resign;" IDA credits are
usually approved by a consensus rather than by a formal vote
of the Board; abstentions and votes against IDA credits are
"extremely rare."

(The U.S. has never abstained and voted against only once,
on the credit for Indian tankers in March, 1972.)

NSC studies and WSAG meetings in October and
November on how to use economic aid as leverage in the
context of the crisis in South Asia culminated, in late
November, 1971, in a decision to request the WB management
to defer action on two Indian credits scheduled for Board
action on December 21. Henry Kissinger and John Connally
"probably made direct contact with the Bank President
[Robert McNamara] by early December." McNamara, after
discussions with Bank management in early December,
"decided against it [deferral] reportedly in order to avoid
charges that the Bank was a tool of U.S. foreign policy. The

outbreak of war on December 3 altered the situation by strengthening the USG's hand. On NSC directions, USG representatives successfully negotiated provisos, unprecedented in IDA history, requiring that the projects be unrelated to military operations and unimpaired by the war. Justification for "a non-routine stance on IDA credits to India were articulated to few of the participants" but most of them believed that it was meant to punish India in ways consistent with the December, 6, 1971, cut-off of bilateral economic aid. The argument was phrased in terms of bilateral-multilateral "parallelism."

The issue in the USG during the critical period when the war was in progress (December 3-16) was whether the provisos sufficed or whether the more severe options of abstention, deferral or opposition should be adopted or pursued. The White House and the NSC pressed for "an emphatic U.S. stance" while State (particularly NEA/INS and EB) and AID (NESA), in a joint memo to the Secretary of State, argued for treating the projects (now with the provisos) "routinely" at the up-coming December 21 Board meeting. The memo, which its drafters recommended be communicated to Henry Kissinger and John Connally, noted precedents for Bank lending to countries at war and pointed out that "U.S opposition or abstention would neither 'penalize' India (since the credits would be approved anyway) nor further our longer run foreign policy interests, either in India or in the World Bank." Kissinger and Connally, who were in frequent contact about the USG stand at the December 21 Board meeting, found the memo orientation and recommendation unsatisfactory. The ensuing policy debate proceeded at two levels, the Secretarial (Kissinger, Connally and Rogers) and the Assistant Secretarial, but inter-level coordination lacked collegiality and an attendant appreciation of views. At the lower level, Assistant and Deputy Assistant Secretaries in State, Treasury and AID consulted with each other and with the NSC and WB staffs to ascertain agency and Bank positions and to attempt to find a mutually satisfactory policy. "Those daily consultations," Moulton observes, "involved contacts with friends and acquaintances and were conducted in informal but well-esta-

blished channels, primarily by telephone . . . Participants dealt
with each other on equal or near-equal terms . . ."

Somewhere between December 16 and 20, between, that is
the day the war ended and three days after it ended, Kissinger
and the NSC decided on an abstention policy ; " . . . the end
of the war undoubtedly being the most important consideration militating against a harder line".[49]

Between the January 11, 1972 and February 29, 1972
meetings of the IDA Board, at which additional credits for
India were to be decided, Kissinger "presumably" decided
to drop the abstention policy. Treasury had cooled in its
support for provisos and for abstention, insisting that the NEA-
drafted instructions to the USG Executive Director be appropriately revised at the NSC level, and Robert McNamara in
a visit to South Asia in late January, 1972, had made clear his
strong support for IDA programs in that region by committing
40 per cent of all IDA credits to India. As the crisis rapidly
dissipated, so too did the bargaining advantages required
for imperative coordination and the reasons for punishing
India, an action that entailed jeopardizing USG relations with
the WB and WB autonomy.

The USG's unprecedented decision on March 7, 1972 to
vote against an Indian credit for the purchase of crude oil
tankers to ply the Persian Gulf route stands in marked contrast
to the earlier decisions and provides a different and important
lesson for the South Asia policy arena. The international
crisis in South Asia was no longer an important consideration.
The tanker credit was opposed by U.S. shipping and oil
companies and within the USG, by Treasury, the Exim bank
and the Federal Reserve. NAC, which advised the Secretary of
the Treasury on how to instruct the U.S. Executive Director
at IDA, rather than the NSC or WSAG, provided the context
for coordination and decision. In the end, after support in
NEA (but not EB) for the tanker credit collapsed only AID

---

49. Moulton adduces a number of other reasons including "the friendly
and respectful relationship obtaining between McNamara and
Kissinger" which may have "diluted" the tilt policy when applied in
IDA's direction. Kissinger allegedly had intervened earlier to dissuade Nixon from attempting to dislodge McNamara from the Bank
presidency.

advocated supporting it. AID systematically rebutted arguments advanced for voting against, particularly the "major" argument that the tankers would hurt U.S. shipping, and recommended to NEA/INS that Robert McNamara should be urged to pre-empt negative USG action by making a USG vote against, much less a negative decision by the Board, a cause for his resignation, On March 3 or 4 "in an unknown forum" it was decided that the U.S. would vote against the tanker credit, an action that stands alone in the annals of USG-IDA relationships. The relationship survived, the credit was approved, and those responsible for the South Asia policy arena learned how vulnerable the arena was to powerful private interest.

The two decisions illustrate how the deliberative coordination of normal diplomacy, particularly when reinforced by the insulation that a multilateral agency can provide, may be able to give longer run interest their due even when they are confronted with the short run need for leverage or the powerful influence of vested interests.

Stanley Kochanek's study, "United States Expropriation Policy and South Asia," illustrates the capacity of deliberative coordination to make compatible seemingly incompatible objectives by delay, "slicing" and reconciliation. In 1972, the governments of India, Pakistan and Bangladesh nationalized the subsidiaries of two American insurance groups, the American Foreign Insurance Association (AFIA) and the American International Underwriters (AIU). U.S. policy towards commercial issues outside the communist bloc, Kochanek observes "tends to be global rather than oriented toward a particular region or country."[50] On January 19, 1972 President Nixon's statement on "Economic Assistance and Investment Security in Developing Nations" laid down that in future expropriation of U.S. assets, failure to pay prompt, adequate and effective compensation would result in withholding of new bilateral economic aid and a refusal to support loans from multilateral development banks unless over-riding considerations of national interest required the USG to act

---

50 All subsequent references, unless otherwise indicated, are to the Kochanek paper.

otherwise. "Within a few months this policy was being tested" in South Asia.

The vehicle established by the president to implement the policy declaration of January 19, 1972 was the Expro Group, a special sub-committee of the Council on International Economic Policy (CIEP). Chaired by the Assistant Secretary of State for Economic and Business Affairs (EB), its members included representatives from State, Treasury, Defense and Commerce.[51] Day to day monitoring, however, was the responsibility of the India, Pakistan, and Bangladesh country desks in the Bureau of Near East and South Asian Affairs (NEA) which prepared reports and recommendations for the Expro Group, advised the U.S. companies on strategy, coordinated inputs from the White House, other executive agencies, the companies, and Congress, and drafted and cleared all major instructions to appropriate embassies.

The president's policy of January 19, 1972 allowed for flexibility in responding to expropriations in the light of national interest considerations, but this flexibility was constrained by the Hickenlooper[52] and Gonzalez[53] amendments. The first requires suspension of bilateral assistance if suitable steps, including arbitration, have not been initiated within a reasonable time (defined as six months) to provide adequate compensation. The second requires a negative vote by U.S. Executive Directors on mutilateral agency loans unless prompt compensation has been paid, the dispute has been submitted to arbitration under the rules of the Convention for the Settlement of Investment Disputes, or good faith negotiations are in progress.

Responding to expropriation in three South Asia states with very different political conditions involved a variety of complex problems such as defining terms (e.g. what constitutes expropriation ? how does a capital gains tax relate to

51. See Kochanek, footnotes, for personnel with office designations as of April 2, 1972. Its functions were to review and compile information relevant to potential and actual expropriation cases; to make specific findings about compensation; to recommend courses of action; and to coordinate and implement policy

52. Section 620(e) of the Foreign Assistance Act of 1961.

53. Section 12 of the International Development Association Act.

expropriation? what about the exchange rate, "financial practices," and revaluation of assets?); the reliability of evidence (e.g. the value of property, the existence of good faith negotiations); and determining whether remedies, including internal remedies, have been exhausted. But "the most important problem . . . was conflicting U.S. interests." State and AID wanted good relations with countries of South Asia. Commerce, realizing that U.S. insurance interests totalled only $8 million, feared overreaction might jeopardize larger pharmaceutical and petroleum interests, both prime targets for nationalization. DOD, with minor stakes, supported the goal of good relations over support for private interests. Treasury, although the most active supporter of the insurance companies, did not challenge Expro Group decisions by taking them up to the CIEP. The basic strategy of State and the Expro Group was to secure negotiated settlements that freed the USG from a finding that expropriation without compensation had occurred. "Both Country Directorates and the Expro Group made special efforts to ward off triggering the Hickenlooper and Gonzalez Amendments . . ." They succeeded. Frequent efforts by the insurance companies " to force actions through repeated appeals to the White House, the Congress and other executive agencies considered to be more sympathetic" were marginally effective at best in the face of State's effort to avoid official action. Nor did they succeed in transforming the disputes between the insurance companies and particular host countries into direct confrontations with the USG on terms of settlement or as a result of sanctions associated with a finding of expropriation without compensation. Skilful maneuvering and negotiations by the companies, sometimes in collaboration with British firms and the British Government which were faced with parallel problems, led by the end of 1973 to settlements which if less than the companies' view of adequate, were, in the circumstances, acceptable. Kochanek concludes that because decisions within the USG did not go beyond the Expro Group and were based on consensus, "the case of insurance nationalization in South Asia . . . represents an excellent example of the type of significant foreign policy decisions which never reach the top levels of the United States Government decision making system." The result succeeded in reconciling long run U.S. bilateral and regional interests; the interests of the insurance firms, and the domestic policies of South Asian states by accommodating to a substantial measure the interests of the various actors.

Barnett Rubin's study of "The U.S. Response to the JVP Insurgency in Sri Lanka, 1971," portrays how a crisis of relatively minor proportions can be successfully handled by normal diplomacy. Confronted with an unanticipated emergency, the attack on the night of April 5-6, 1971, by the Janata Vimuki Peramuna (or People's Liberation Front) on administrative offices and police posts throughout Ceylon, and Prime Minister Bandaranaike's appeal for military aid, the U.S. (along with India, Pakistan, Britain, the USSR, Yugoslavia and Egypt) responded with a timeliness and finesse that transformed poor into good relations, including the restoration of permission for U.S. naval ships to call, without a non-nuclear declaration on behalf of those ships. The successful handling of policy and action within the State Department, primarily at the regional bureau and country director level, supports the view not only that "the State Department be given a greater role as against the NSC in foreign policy planning, but that within State itself policy planning should more deeply involve the line officers."[54] Rubin recognizes that special circumstances, such as the spill-over effect of the parallel crisis in Pakistan, which attracted higher level attention that benefitted those dealing with Sri Lanka, the fact that the JVP insurgency in effect failed, thereby obviating the possibility that foreign troops (e.g. Indian) might have intervened, and the lack of strong bureaucratic or national interest in Sri Lanka, contributed to the "normal" management of a crisis situation. Even so, the organizational and procedural means employed provide suitable prescriptions for comparable problems of policy formulation and management.

"The emergency was handled mainly in State," where the regional bureau had the action, and policy making within it "was centered around the country director." NEA provided leadership and coordination for other actors such as Political Military Affairs (PM) and Intelligence and Research (INR)

---

54. Unless otherwise indicated, all references are to the Rubin paper.

Bureaus in State, as well as for DOD's Office for International Security Affairs (ISA) and effectively utilized at the White House level the Senior Review Group (SRG) of the NSC to obtain, *inter alia*, a legally mandated presidential decision. Within NEA, the country director did almost all of the drafting of policy documents and hence most of the coordination of information and policy. Evaluation of options took place in the daily meetings in Secretary Rogers' office (an extraneous "benefit" of the Pakistan crisis) rather than in the NSC-presidential context. The NSC and its SRG provided "quick clearances and . . . communications" of presidential decisions to NEA officials working on the problem. ISA and the military services were "content to act as support for State; they provided information on 'nuts and bolts' questions without pushing for greater authority or special military interests."

"It seems apparent," Rubin concludes, "that constant contact with high level officials and increased responsibility for policy lead working line officers to see issues in broader perspective. 'Clientelism' may not be built into their roles *per se*, but into the organizational structure which isolates line officers from decision making and planning." In short, "this case gives an idea of the conditions under which a State Department, regional bureau centered foreign policy system can work, and what its limitations might be."

Charles Lenth's examination of "The Role of the Peace Corps in U.S. Relations with South Asia" also contributes insight into the strength of normal diplomacy, in part by offering a contrast to the model. The Peace Corps captured the 1960's optimistic interventionism so characteristic of the Kennedy administration. Its volunteers were suspicious of bureaucracy, whether in the U.S. State Department or among officials of South Asian governments, because such officials were crippled by routine and weighted down by conventional knowledge. The Peace Corps prided itself on its exclusion from normal diplomatic channels and activities, an exclusion expressed through its organizational detachment from State both in Washington and the field. The excessive optimism of the mid-sixties, and its organizational and political innocence, led to rebuffs in Sri Lanka and Pakistan, and to an over expansion in India that exposed and discredited the Peace Corps' technical claims.

The Peace Corps learned from its set-backs, but in ways that did not lead Peace Corps volunteers and administrators to embrace careerism, bureaucratic caution or conventional thinking. The Corps assumed a more modest self-conception and developed a greater respect at home and abroad for coordination with other agencies. Its experience in South Asia illustrates how a people-to-people program with long term interests cannot do without the sheltering framework of normal diplomacy, but at the same time requires sufficient autonomy to pursue its unconventional mission and preserve an identity separate from the USG.

Together, these normal diplomacy cases do not sustain the stereotype view of career officials. Using "routine" organizational and procedural means the officials proved capable o imaginative, flexible and purposeful action in pursuit of the national interest. The positive features of normal diplomacy—the significance of professionalism and professionals in policy formulation and management; the integration of policy planning with operations; the importance of collegiality and deliberative coordination; the representation of multiple interests, levels and perspectives—can be promoted, we believe, by mechanisms suggested below, the assistant secretary policy planning council and the regional conference.

C. Coordination Among Time Frames

1. The Case For Insulation

Several case studies highlight the conflict between long run policy goals and the short run requirements of crisis management. Organizational interests as well as public support are more frequently on the side of the short than the long run. Operating officials in Washington and the field tend to focus on the most recent cable or on the need for leverage now. The President's need for immediate gains and the constraints of the next election push him too toward short run solutions. Lyndon Johnson had to "solve" Vietnam in time for 1968, and Richard Nixon needed the opening to China in time for 1972. The media's concern for news leads them disproportionately to attend to today's crisis rather than to next year's solution; they are less likely to feature a President's or secretary's long range goals.

In our discussion of the time dimension of complexity we argued that the half life of some programs required a medium or long term framework because they addressed values and dimensions of the national interest incompatible with short run competition for influence and power. Policies and programs designed to promote security and welfare through economic growth or the redistribution of wealth require time and autonomy from the vicissitudes of short run political conflicts. Culture, knowledge and science stand apart from the ebb and flow of political relations; they cannot serve the national interest in the short or long run unless they maintain their autonomy. There are no short run solutions to the food, population, resource and pollution problems. Yet because they vitally affect security and welfare, they help define the national interest. In times of conflict insulated programs not only sustain medium and long term interests but also help to preserve those lines of communication and relationships without which the inevitable restoration of "normal" relations is much more difficult.

The principle of insulation has been recognized in the relative autonomy given to some agencies such as AID, the Peace Corps, and USIA and in the increasing use of multilateral agencies. Their (limited) autonomy recognizes that some programs profit by distance from the ordinary flow of policy. But organizational forms cannot, alone, assure insulation; a concept of insulation needs to be recognized and practiced by policy makers. Our cases suggest that AID, the Peace Corps, and multilateral agencies were drawn into the pervasive quest for leverage despite their organizational location.

Insulation makes it possible to pursue multiple interests or finely graduated strategies concurrently. The national interest is often complex and includes mutually conflicting goals. The insulation of programs and activities makes it possible when needed to speak with several voices and to pursue simultaneously different objectives.

2. The Case Against Insulation

The notion of insulation made some of our respondents

profoundly uneasy. (That a number of them understood us to be saying isolation is not quite accidental.) Essentially they saw isolation as a threat to political clout on the one hand, and to political protection on the other. It diminished, for example, their capacity to go to the ambassador for help or support. In Washington and the field officials feared being separated from the political definitions of national interest particularly as it was being articulated and applied at high levels by persons whose estimate of them could affect their careers. Nor did the officials we interviewed feel comfortable with the notion that the instrumentalities and resources available for them or others when leverage was needed should be reduced or constrained by the doctrine or practice of insulation. They argued that insulation or autonomy would not be understood or, if understood, not accepted. In South Asia, political officials or public actors could not or would not, we were told, accept a distinction between the U.S. government and a U.S. government agency. India's unfriendly cultural policy in 1971-2, and Sri Lanka's hostility to the Peace Corps in the mid-sixties, confirm this estimate. (Charles Lenth's examples of continuing requests from Indian states for a Peace Corps presence during the difficult post-1971 period in U.S.-Indian relations suggest the opposite possibility.)

Officials in Washington and ambassadors in the region argued that they needed control over programs and resources to direct and manage policy. AID officials in Pakistan and Bangladesh, for example, argued that more insulation would deprive them of the means to tie aid to what they believed were demonstrated means of development and self help. Insulation, in any case, would not protect you when the chips were down from the consequences of political conflict.

3. Insulation in Practice : Multilateral Agencies
Multilateral agencies in the last ten years have represented the most successful expression of insulation. Their specific political form has been a response to the belief in receiving countries that aid created less dependency when offered in internationalized form. In so far as the USG supports multilateral agencies, its formulation of national interest includes a commitment to trading off losses in the short run context of

crisis management for the gains attending growth and justice. The specific distance of multilateral agencies from American influence has varied over time. In the early and middle 1960s, many Indians alleged that the parallelism between U.S. and World Bank policies was too close to be accidental and that it arose more from American political influence than from objective economic reasons. More recently, the Bank has been accused by U.S. officials of being "too soft" on LDCs, a charge which may signify more distance between the Bank and the USG in the McNamara era. The World Bank's policies and programs do not bear out the fear that insulation obstructs the means to impose "conditions" on aid. Constraints imposed by multilateral agencies such as the World Bank are more likely to be perceived by recipients of aid as legitimate demands for performance than as objectionable political conditions.

The Bjorkman and Moulton studies cast light on the extent to which multilateral agencies have or have not acted independently of U.S. policies and interests, and on the reasons and mechanisms involved. James Bjorkman's study, Harinder Shourie's background paper, and our interviews in Washington suggest that in the 1966-67 period, when consortium aid under World Bank auspices was associated with devaluation and the liberalization of economic policy in India, World Bank and USG policies were at least parallel. On the other hand, the degree of agreement among American and some Indian economists concerning the nature of India's problems in 1964-67 and the steps needed to remedy them, lend some credence to the World Bank's claim that its policies and programs were independent of the USG's. Moulton's study of IDA suggests that multilateralism insulated IDA decisions on credits for India from USG efforts to use IDA programs to gain leverage for its "tilt" policy during the Indo-Pakistan war of 1971. The two examples suggest that, given the large U.S. contributions to multilateral agencies, those agencies are likely to be both responsive to but somewhat insulated from current U.S. political objectives and policies. It would, no doubt, be more difficult for a fairly autonomous USG economic aid agency to achieve a similar degree of insulation, but this may not be so for other functions and their policy arenas.

4. Insulation in Practice : *Cultural and Informational Agencies*
Walter Andersen's study of "United States Educational and
Cultural Exchange Programs in India" reviews the severe
difficulties that U.S. educational and cultural programs encountered in India in the years surrounding the 1971 tilt toward
Pakistan, examines the policy and administrative relationships
between informational and cultural (including educational)
programs, and makes recommendations in light of his
evidence and findings. Our interest here is primarily those
aspects of his analysis that illuminate the need for and the
means to insulate educational and cultural programs.

In Washington, the principal agencies concerned with
educational programs are State's Bureau of Educational and
Cultural Affairs (CU) and the Institute of International Studies
housed in HEW's Office of Education. In the field the United
States Information Agency [whose parent agency in Washington
is the semi-autonomous United States Information Service
(USIS)] supervises educational and cultural programs through
the Country Public Affairs Officer (CPAO). The Cultural
Affairs Officer (CAO), appointed by USIA with the approval of
CU, is responsible for CU's programs that involve scholars and
books, including USIA libraries.

This is an unsatisfactory state of affairs. The USIA
principal goals are "to create support for U.S. foreign policy
objectives and to develop a favorable image of American
society."[55] The CAO, who reports back to the area desks of
both CU and USIA, is administratively subordinate to the
CPAO and is "located within USIA's promotional system."
"The major limitation on the CAO's ability to aggressively
pursue educational goals," Andersen finds, "is the environment
in which he must work." Not only is USIA's orientation
"promotional" but also its means are informational with
"emphasis on the 'fast' media such as radio, television and press
releases." Under such circumstances educational and cultural
activities are subsumed to informational goals. The linkage of
education to a propaganda agency creates the impression that
U.S. scholarship and culture are related to propaganda.

Andersen proposes the creation of a single semiautonomous
foundation analogous to the National Endowment for the

55. Unless otherwise indicated, all references are to the Andersen paper.

Humanities to deal with the basic problems of insulating educational and cultural programs from the effects of USG and host country political leverage and separating them from promotional and information objectives and means. Like NEH, its governing board would include both public and private representatives and it would draw financial support from both public and private sources. It would have a full time staff whose members would periodically serve in the field. Like the British Council, which provides an effective example of an autonomous cultural agency, it should not, in the words of the Duncan Commission of 1969, "be regarded in any way as a mouth piece of Government policy." Even though ninety per cent of the British Council's funding is governmental it has over the years succeeded in creating a reputation for recognizing in its programs and operations cultural and intellectual standards and competency rather than national political objectives of the moment. Its director, not a foreign service officer, distinguished his organization from the foreign service hierarchy and fought for his agency's independent standing and reputation. The considerable respect and success which the British Council, like the BBC. commands in many countries, including those in South Asia, are in large part related to successful insulation.

A semi-autonomous agency could deal more effectively with a number of other troublesome organizational and procedural problems that now plague educational and cultural administrative arrangements and programs. It could gather the presently dispersed and segmented organizations and programs into a common home. It could make possible longer term programing and budgeting. It could solve structural and operating problems in the field. It could provide, in the case of India, that single point of contact the GOI seeks (without, we are quick to add, jeopardizing the diversity and pluralism that characterize American cultural and educational life). It could mesh effectively with the newly constituted[56] Indo-U.S. Sub-Commission on Education and Culture by having its U.S. members appointed by and responsible to the foundation's governing board. It could give internationally oriented edu-

56. As per the Agreement between the United States and India of
    October, 1974.

cational and cultural policy and programs visibility at home
and abroad, including with the Congress and philanthropic-
cum-international interested publics.

D. Coordination in South Asia

We identify four types of coordination in South Asia :
(1) Regional coordination involving relations among U.S. embassies in the region; (2) cross-sovereignty barrier coordination
involving relations between U.S. government agencies and
agencies of the host country; (3) South Asia-Washington coordination involving relations between U.S. government
agencies and agencies of the host country; and (4) mission or
in-country coordination among various embassy functions and
goals. We shall focus mainly on regional and cross-sovereignty
barrier coordination, where both our findings and our recommendations are more substantial.

1. Regional Coordination

One form of complexity associated with policy making in South
Asia arises from the need to devise policies appropriate to each
country in the region even while dealing with their consequences for regional relations. It is in this context that we
explore systematically the possibilities of regional coordination.
Regional coordination relates to a number of processes, from
sharing information, through systematic exchange and confrontation of perspectives on common problems and shared policies,
to efforts to identify and to formulate policies suitable for the
region. Both in the field and in Washington, we inquired into
present actualities of regional coordination. How is it understood and how is it practiced ? We have also considered means
to improve coordination and their costs and benefits.

The region has traditions of conflictual relations between the
ambassadors to India and Pakistan. One senior observer commented that ambassadors had sometimes fought more sharply
than their respective clients and, at times, even egged them on.
Such conflicts reflect more than the envoys' clientelist orientations. Different types of men are characteristically chosen for
the two posts. The image of India as "the world's largest
democracy" has contributed to ambassadorial appointments of
men with public reputations and standing, executive and

legislative connections, and an interest in communicating outside official channels. In Pakistan, where strong men have
ruled in much of the post-independence period, a more conservative perspective was valued, leading to more appointments
of envoys with military and business connections. That the
selection process has produced ambassadors with different
styles and views strengthened the propensities to conflict for
which clientelism might have laid a base. Ambassadors Byroade
and Moynihan have talked about this legacy rather self-
consciously as part of an effort to do better. Appointments to
Sri Lanka and Bangladesh have not exhibited similar
differences.

Good ambassadorial intentions may have difficulty over-
coming conflictual traditions in situations where their clients
are pitted against each other. On defense matters, where the
interests of the regional clients have indeed been in conflict,
there has not been very close coordination among embassies
since the fifties; the consensus represented by the 1967 arms
policy was more the product of State-Defense and desk officer
and CD coordination in Washington than it was of coordination
in the region. There has been some talk among embassies of
sharing cables to the Department of Defense, but the Delhi
embassy appears to learn after the fact and from the Department of State about Islamabad initiatives. Senior actors on
both sides tend to believe that regional coordination is exceptionally difficult in situations where the ambassadors are
fundamentally opposed. Then, instead of compromising, they
attempt to win the contest at the next highest level—in
Washington. One official thought that where ambassadors have
had previous assistant secretarial experience, and thus recognize
the appropriate higher constraints on clientelism, coordination
even in crisis situations might be easier. The observation
suggests a strategy of rotating ambassadors and assistant
secretaries through each other's slots.

Ambassadors and their staffs at Islamabad, Delhi, Dacca
and Kathmandu have encouraged some regional exchanges. In
recent times, Ambassador Moynihan visited Islamabad.
Ambassador Boster from Bangladesh has consulted at Delhi;
Ambassador Byroade was scheduled to visit Delhi when we
were interviewing in August, 1974. These visitations appear

to promote some sense of common problems and habits of discourse concerning differences. We were told that there is a rather brisk "back channel" traffic between the ambassadors to explore questions in a preliminary way, although reports differ concerning the frequency and importance of this communication link. While these efforts indicate some of the ways that coordination might be improved, their sporadic and irregular nature has not resulted in durable and significant coordination.

The South Asia specialists in Washington and in South Asia have a high degree of common consciousness, with respect to the facts and judgments they command and the common experiences between them. This common cadre feeling has an important if hard to specify effect on regional coordination. The actors who are communicating are mutually known, as are their styles and previous roles. Officers who have served in Islamabad are posted to Delhi, Dacca or Kathmandu; those who have served on a country desk in Washington are sent to Delhi, Islamabad, and Colombo. A political officer who has served in Islamabad may become political officer in India or country director for INS. An excessive enthusiasm for GLOPping could well run counter to this infra-structure of regional coordination.

Throughout our interviews, whenever we pressed the possibilities of regional coordination, we encountered variations on a bilateral frame of mind. Actors see the lines of communications running to Washington, not across the subcontinent. The idea that a conflictual situation might be explored in the region instead of in Washington is generally not recognized and if recognized rejected. We discussed at length arms, food, the Indian Ocean, and development assistance, and encountered resistance to the idea of a regional interest and strategy with respect to all of them. In fact, potentially difficult or conflictual issues are routinely referred to as issues that have to be handled in Washington. Washington actors in turn viewed the prospect of regional collaboration among embassies as a threat to their initiative and control over policy formulation, decision and management.

Embassy officers often believe that they do not have enough information to make recommendations, or even develop views, about matters that fall outside their own narrowly defined responsibilities. There is circularity in this reasoning : because there are no habits of regional coordination, country actors are not aware of information concerning other countries in the region that bears on their own situation. Often lack of information, in the areas of economic development or political costs, is a matter of not asking questions, or of choosing to collect information only on a country and bilateral basis. Since bilateral frames of mind follow from bilateral channels of communication, regional frames of mind would require more organizations and/or procedures emphasizing regional channels of communication.

Some of the policy areas where more and better regional coordination seems possible are food ; economic aid and development assistance; cultural and scientific activity, relations and programs ; arms supply ; and crisis management, notably the settling of regional disputes. While officials on the whole resisted the notion of coordination in any of these areas, they considered the prospects better for the first two than for the last two. We investigated the possibilities for coordination in the areas of food, economic development and arms supplies in some depth.

The bilateral conception that subcontinental actors have of their roles militates against regional coordination with respect to food. People in the region felt, "We must trust those in Washington"; they believed that coordination was simply not their task. In only one of the three embassies was there any support for the idea by a high level official : "The embassies should be communicating with each other but they aren't. Everyone is going their own way. I assume that in Washington it will be put together and that some sort of strategy and set of priorities will be worked out."

One justification for regional coordination is to develop, at maximum, a reasonable and coordinated South Asia policy; at minimum, a clearer view of the costs and benefits of different allocations. It is obvious that the countries in this area (notably India, Pakistan and Bangladesh) have similar food needs and problems and that together they represent a substantial proportion of world food needs. The needs of the region are large enough to come in serious competition with food requirements in other nations, for example, Egypt, China and Russia. As this report is written, decisions about U.S. food shipments abroad are dominated by the Department of Agriculture's "market" orientation, an approach that leaves "policy" in buyers' hands as the Russian purchases in 1972 and 1974 make clear, and by the struggle over humanitarian as against political food aid, a struggle that, under current circumstances, pits Secretary of State Kissinger against key congressional leaders and AID. Neither the states of South Asia nor the U.S. embassies have taken steps to shape the policy process, much less policy decisions, in ways that confront and deal with the region's food needs. The international allocation of food involves political, developmental and humanitarian objectives as much as it does market forces of dominance. Formulating a regional interest and relating it to the world production and allocation of food would provide the Department of State with policy inputs that it could use to assess foreign relations implications of food.

Food and guns do not appear on the same agenda in the South Asian region. The notion that food aid and arms supplies are subject to trade offs or that a shift to an emphasis on food (and economic development) could affect the salience or priority of security concerns in the region was not on anybody's mind or agenda. Clearly, a regional framework is required if South Asia is to shift its concerns and priorities from arms to food.

Development assistance too may be an appropriate area for regional coordination because certain problems, notably agricultural production, are common across the region, e.g. wheat in Pakistan and North India; rice in Bangladesh, Bengal, Madras, Sri Lanka. Regional coordination among U.S. officials concerned with common problems and challenges could help to promote sharing of resources and the development of common policies for development and regional cooperation and security. The use of subcontinental planning and coordination in the areas not only of food and development assistance but also trade and investment is likely to spill over in ways that affect the frame of mind and lines of connection between the countries of the region.

There may be obstacles to regional coordination. Officials in several of the embassies thought that regional coordination of food policy would unleash a struggle among them over relative proportions in the light of policy needs, political relations, etc. (should the ratio be 2 : 1 :1, 4 : 2 : 1, etc.) In at least one case a regional policy for food was opposed because the embassy could do better not coordinating than coordinating its country requirements with those of other countries in the region

While such a struggle is not unlikely, it could also lead to the search for "objective" and political grounds to resolve it. To use an example drawn from the subcontinent, the fact that Bengal and Madras argued about the financial allocations that should go to each area before the sixth finance commission has helped produce the principles by which the finance commission makes its allocation. Conflict may, and often does, contribute to coordination. Brokering the conflicting demands of different interests goes on in Washington in any case. Instituting a parallel process in the field would inaugurate the process earlier and, in the context of agreed criteria, shift it downward.

While we realize that regional coordination is no panacea, we do argue that it could produce better staffed options and a more comprehensive and comparative view than is now available of policy needs and choices. At a maximum, it would produce more thoughtful and weighty policy proposals and enhance the viability and autonomy of regions in the policy process.

Regional coordination of arms supply seemed exceptionally difficult to embassy officials because it approached the ground on which the two major countries and embassies in the area have been most deeply divided. Yet the possibilities for meaningful regional coordination seemed much better in 1974 than in 1964. As Stephen Cohen's paper emphasizes, the 1965 war brought home to U.S. officials serving in the region that the arms supply policy had led to regional military confrontation, not the result intended by the policy. The 1967 arms policy, which provided for a cash supply of non-lethal weapons on a relatively even-handed basis to both Pakistan and India, commanded substantial consensus in the Islamabad and Delhi embassies. Despite the 1970 "one time exception" to the general embargo on lethal weapons, and despite increased concern to respond favorably to Prime Minister Bhutto's request for arms, the consensual possibilities on arms policy remain viable.

Present trends in the region also conspire to make arms aid a more promising subject for regional coordination than it appears at first sight. To some extent since the 1965 war, and certainly since 1971, the notion that India is the dominant power in the area has been increasingly shared by all embassies in the region, although there are differences concerning the interpretation of that position. This relationship is generally accepted by the Pakistan government, although it emphasizes that in its view Indian "dominance" makes India that much more dangerous and Pakistan that much more insecure. But the sharp competition that existed when "balance" between India and Pakistan was sought by both the government of Pakistan and the U.S. ambassadors to Pakistan no longer exists. In so far as the government of India preferred a Bhutto government to foreseeable alternatives, and insofar as the Bhutto government's viability depended on success in its effort to get arms from the U.S., the government of India muted its opposition to limited arms supplies to Pakistan. Such a perspective could enable the Islamabad and Delhi embassies to see the issue through similar lenses.

With respect to Diego Garcia also, the sharp differences that characterized both the embassies and the clients on various arms issues a decade ago is no longer visible. The Dacca government shares New Delhi's opposition to Diego Garcia, but lacks Delhi's sense of the facility's saliency to regional security. The Pakistan government, although not opposed to U.S. policies as articulated by the U.S. Navy, would like to avoid the issue. On the one hand, the government of Pakistan finds it useful to oppose India and to side with the U.S. and the People's Republic of China. On the other hand, supporting Diego Garcia as a full fledged "base", because it puts the GOP on the side of American "militarism", "imperialism", or "capitalism" alienates many third world nations from Pakistan or puts Pakistan in explicit opposition to their policies and concerns. Not least among them is Iran, which has its own ambitions (and capabilities) in the Indian Ocean area.

While the two embassies do not view the issue in the same light, their differences are not so sharp as they were when the

USG military and intelligence interests in South Asia meant arming Pakistan and locating facilities there.

The preceding remarks suggest that the conventional view shared by officials in the region and in Washington, that regional coordination of military policy including arms is impossible, is, if not mistaken, at least less correct than is supposed. To what extent regional coordination on military matters appears impossible because habit linked to bilateral modes of thought blocks a regional perspective, and to what extent it appears impossible because of fundamental differences in the outlook and assumptions of the principle regional actors is a question that remains for the future.

Embassy personnel in the South Asia regions see a number of problems attending regional coordination. They are apprehensive about the exacerbation of conflict among embassies where the problem is distributing limited resources among countries. More fundamental if less articulated is the fear of abandoning a known and rewarding orientation, that of representing a host country's views and interests, for an unknown and potentially costly orientation, that of representing a "regional" perspective. What if an ambassador or other official agreed to consider an issue from the perspective of "the other" country? The cost in Pakistan, for example, and thus the cost to the official and the embassy might be quite high. Critical Pakistani counterplayers might fear or suspect that "their agent" would help "the other side". To the extent that these attitudes depend upon the conflictual history of the two main actors on the subcontinent, India and Pakistan, these apprehensions may deserve less weight at a time when the level of tension appears to be abating. But to the extent that they are rooted in the relationship between foreign and host country counterplayers, they remain an impediment to regional perspectives and policy formulation.

Embassy spokesmen are also apprehensive, as was previously suggested, about a strategy of regional coordination because they do not believe they command the necessary expertise. Regional perspectives, policies or coordination, if they are to exist, are a job for Washington, not for bilaterally defined organizations and roles.

The assets of regional organization include the appearance,

on a common agenda, of policy perspectives arising from country missions. At best, their confrontation might produce some consensus; at least it would promote clarification of costs and benefits, and the increased understanding comparison brings. How important is arms aid to Pakistan to the internal politics of India and Pakistan ? How important to the structure of their respective foreign alliances ? What are the comparative political implications of food short falls in Pakistan, Bangladesh, and India ? How should these implications affect policy if at all ? Ambassadors can now formulate recommendations without substantial information and concern about the cost of their recommendation in the adjoining country, a condition which may create incompletely grounded recommendations and an incompletely argued case. Even where such confrontations do not produce consensus, they will produce a better understanding of trade-offs.

Strengthening regional coordination requires organizational means that can articulate and represent regional problems and priorities, i.e. organizations and procedures that can define a regional policy arena and regional interests. The purposes of regional coordination could be served by the periodic convening at rotating centres in the region, of regional conferences, organized on a functional basis such as economic development, including aid; military policy, including arms; culture and science. Such conferences would include not only the relevant functional officers, who do not always (for example in the case of AID or USIS) command the required standing in their embassies, but also officers who, because of their rank, can speak authoritatively with other embassies. They should further include relevant actors from Washington, from desk officer and country director to deputy assistant secretary and assistant secretary. Conferences should be mandated to convene at times of regional crises; to generate and share information; and to recommend policies that bear on medium and long term regional needs and problems. There are precedents for such assemblies in the regional meetings of U.S. chiefs of mission with the assistant secretary and of late, in the peripatetic activity of the secretary of state. But this proposal aims for a broader institutionalization of intra-regional and regional-Washington exchange.

2. Coordination Across the Sovereignty Barrier

State sovereignty expressed in terms of national jurisdictions and boundaries limits, in principle, the scope and degree of coordination in international relations. Coordination across the sovereignty barrier involves some form of influence or participation by one state in the affairs of another. Under asymmetrical conditions of dependence or coercion, such participation is likely to be seen as intervention. The limits on participation are set by legal and prudential considerations, legal in that states are called upon by law to recognize each others' sovereign autonomy, prudential in that the dependency or coercion associated with intervention generates political costs.

Legal prohibitions and political costs have not, however, eliminated the practice of intervention by means such as military force, covert operations or economic relationships. Here we are concerned with the more benign and "voluntary" forms of intervention that can accompany the dependency inherent in asymmetrical economic and political relationships. What special sensibilities or obligations does coordination across the sovereignty barrier entail?

Several cases reported in this study speak to this question. They emphasize an appreciation of the political and ideological environments in which counterplayers dwell. Bjorkman's study of President Johnson's short tether policy in supplying food to India in 1966-67 provides an example of flawed coordination, in which insensitivity to political consequences on the other side of the sovereignty barrier generated unnecessarily high political costs. President Johnson's grasp of the internal politics of his own nation was not parallel by an understanding of the constraints that affect leaders of other countries. The policy was pursued when Mrs. Gandhi had only recently succeeded to office and when her parliamentary support was increasingly precarious. Accepting foreign aid was problematic and politically dangerous. President Johnson's implicit conditions for food aid, muting criticism of U.S. policy in Southeast Asia and publicizing India's dependence, did not make Mrs. Gandhi's efforts to establish her authority easier. These acts contributed to discrediting an economic policy that, at that time and subsequently, could have been mutually advantageous to America and India.

Sensitive coordination is especially important for economic programs that require political and administrative support in the host country and at home. They oblige foreign policy managers to respond to two environments simultaneously. The cooperative rural electrification program discussed by Susan Hadden required operating agencies to face in two directions at once. On the U.S. side of the sovereignty barrier, AID benefited from some very persuasive lobbyists, including John Lewis, AID Director in India, who appealed to the belief of senators and congressmen on the critical agricultural committees that cooperative rural electrification was an American invention suitable for export. On the Indian side, they found ways to adapt the program to satisfy Indian official notions of how cooperative rural electrification should be organized and administered. This kind of political bridging of the sovereignty barrier is essential if bilateral assistance programs are to be mutually fruitful.

Decentralization is a key to successful coordinations across the sovereignty barrier of development and cultural programs. Decentralization does not come naturally to embassies; a few senior officials are expected to deal with their counterparts at the host capital. Counterparts often expect embassies to deal only with them, and tend to suspect relations with organizationally inferior levels. But a more flexible and segmented structure is necessary, especially for economic and people-to-people programs. Charles Lenth shows that the Peace Corps was initially handicapped by an excessively centralized and federally insensitive liaison mechanism located in the Indian Planning Commission, and by its failure to recognize the requirements of states whose characteristics and needs differed markedly. In time, the Peace Corps in India improved its liaison relationship by shifting it to the Finance Ministry's Department of Economic Affairs, and improved its operations in the states by dealing directly with state governments in the context of central supervision. Such direct lines pre-supposed mutual confidence—especially confidence from the Indian end—that cannot always be achieved. The examples adduced in the Hadden paper reveal similar successful uses of decentralized arrangements (with state electricity authorities).

The comparative record in India and Pakistan of U.S.

military personnel and missions provides important illustrations of the variations and possibilities in cross sovereignty barrier coordination, and the conditions of decentralization. The friendly relations between the U.S. and Pakistan before and during its military regimes arose in part out of the positive experience that U.S. military officers in World War II had with future Pakistan military personnel. American generals were among General Ayub Khan's earliest lobby in the U.S. supporting his requests for arms. Relations between U.S. and Pakistani military personnel were personal, direct, and based on their common military identities. They remained close up to 1971. In India, by comparison, where Prime Minister Nehru maintained civilian control over the military establishment, relations with foreign military missions were handled through intermediary civilian officials. A common community of military functionaries was discouraged. Even after the Sino-Indian war in 1962, when American military assistance reached its peak and U.S. military attaches and mission members came to know Indian military personnel, the GOI continued to interpose a civilian screen.

The contrast suggests that cross sovereignty barrier coordination has political consequences as well as conditions; bringing together functional experts on both sides can enhance communication and create a community of interests. If that community of interests is perceived as threatening by the host country, as was direct collaboration among military officers by the government of India, such coordination may he resisted. Where it is regarded as benign, as was the case with rural electrification and other AID programs in India, or military collaboration in Pakistan, it can enhance communication and relations in ways that promote commonly intended goals.

The possibility that cross sovereignty barrier coordination can be criticized as undesirable sets limits on its use. Because direct channels to and collaborative arrangements with internal program agencies can become fair game for domestic politicians in the host country, they are peculiarly vulnerable. Thus if U.S. government officials in Bangladesh try to insist on better control of food (and other) smuggling into the Calcutta region and on an increase in food production as conditions for food aid, they may open the way to political costs that outweigh the hoped for economic benefits. Susan Hadden reports in the case of rural electrification, that Indian officials were eager to have AID impose higher rates for electricity on Indian states unwilling on their own responsibility to do so. By shifting the responsibility to the U.S., raising rates might have become politically easier for the central and state governments. AID resisted the invitation (except in the most limited sense) in part because it believed the political consequences should be borne by the local governments.

U.S. officials also need to recognize that various local constituencies may respond differently to American programs, and calculate the consequences of local actions accordingly. Pleading political neutrality is no alternative for shrewd political judgment once cross sovereignty barrier relations are established. If Indian central government officials had succeeded in convincing AID to help them raise electricity rates, state governments, which were opposed, would have criticized and opposed the U.S. effort. A judgment concerning these responses had to be made. Similarly, when the Advanced Research Projects Agency, part of the Defense Department, financed research by American scholars on India's Himalayan borders, the project had the tacit support of high officials in New Delhi. This could not, however, protect the American scholars from the parliamentary criticism that followed the exposure of DOD sponsorship and support, exposure which spurred punitive measures against foreign cultural and educational institutions. Contradictory responses must be anticipated and weighed.

Cross sovereignty barrier coordination is less problematic for international or multilateral agencies than it is for U.S. sponsored bilateral programs. International agencies are less susceptible to charges that they are vehicles for imposing external national political interests. But they are far from immune, as the World Bank found in 1966 when, involved in the economic arrangements associated with the devaluation of the Indian Rupee, it was accused of being the agent of disadvantageous U.S. intervention in the Indian economy. Generally, however, the supra-national standing and impartial expertise of multilateral institutions such as the World Bank and IDA, helped them to coordinate across the sovereignty barrier in ways and to a degree not normally available to national actors.

3. South Asia-Washington Coordination

Coordination between the South Asia embassies and Washington bureaus typically involves preliminary informal communication. The "official and informal" (not part of official records) letter is particularly significant, as are memos to the secretary which explore policy positions in a tentative way. They represent a step beyond the "official and informal" letter. Communication by inference, when embassy officials deduce or infer the department or USG position from statements by the national security advisor or the secretary of state, is especially important. Such forms of informal communication precede, for the most part, cable traffic that establishes "facts," takes positions and makes recommendations. Once a situation starts hardening, the telephone becomes particularly important because oral communication can "restore" the fluidity of preliminary informal exchanges. Embassy calls to Washington require special skills though, since it must be assumed that they may be subject to unfriendly monitoring and because talk is now in the context of interests, stakes, "effectiveness," etc. Such informal means are particularly important for effective intervention, manipulations or control of the decision making process. Knowing, by phone or otherwise, on whose desk a piece of paper may be sitting, who is chairing a key committee or when a decision is to be made or a meeting held, can make all the difference in the choice of strategy and means and ultimately for success and failure.

Travel back and forth between the field and Washington is not a significant form of communication and coordination yet it may be the most promising underutilized means available. It allows the field officer to confront directly the bureaucratic stakes and congressional interests vital to policy making. It allows Washington officials to experience the policy environment in which embassy officials dwell. A single act of peripatetic diplomacy, not uncharacteristic for the ambassadors accredited to India, who frequently are recruited from domestic politics, illustrates the importance of exchanging venues.

The PL-480 rupee settlement, achieved in 1973, reverses the usual center periphery image of relations between Washington and the field. Ambassador Moynihan, like Chester Bowles and John Kenneth Galbraith before him came to Washington where he successfully converted an infinite into a finite problem by disposing at a discount India's accumulated debt of three billion dollars in rupees. He deliberately selected the problem for special emphasis because of its promise for improving Indo-U.S. relations and became increasingly aware that success or failure here would make or break his embassy. Officials who worked with the ambassador in preparing the coalition of thirty U.S. rupee spending agencies to support the settlement before Congress, thought its successful conclusion depended heavily on the ambassador's political skills, strategy and connections, a view with which he concurs. Ambassador Moynihan was able to call upon Secretary Schultz's cooperation at Treasury; persuaded Secretary Butz at USDA to lend his support; mobilized the support of presidential assistant Kissinger and in turn gained President Nixon's consent at San Clemente. Having spoken to the president last, he made sure that he kept and used that strategic and psychological advantage. But above all, he participated in the Washington arena.

Ambassador Moynihan mobilized the appropriate congressional support for the settlement by enlisting the aid of his friend, former speaker John McCormack, and talking personally with forty senators and congressmen. His inadvertent failure to approach Senator Harry Byrd almost proved fatal to his purpose because, as a result of Byrd's initiative, the Senate on September 28, 1973, voted to prevent the administration from settling the three billion dollar debt at two-thirds discount without Congressional approval. Good State Department liaison and support from the highest levels of the administration led, eventually, to the defeat of the rider and a happy ending to a complex and perilous maneuver.

Ambassador Moynihan believes that the settlement could not have been made through the institutional apparatus of the Department of State. His leadership to the finale was, no doubt, central. But many elements of the agreement, including the concept of a substantial discount, were prepared through normal bureaucratic channels. He added two elements:

(1) orchestrating legislative support for the measure by carefully attending to Congressional opinion; (2) assuring that the field and Washington pushed in the same direction by personally shuttling back and forth between locales. The personal influence he exercised was no doubt special; but the devices he used are amenable to more general application.

The PL-480 settlement suggests the utility of more frequent Washington-Field movement, particularly opportunities for representatives from the field to inform and influence elected and appointed officials in Washington. The regional conference proposed in section VI-E (Recommendations) would also facilitate such exchanges.

4. The Embassy and the Country Team

While one encounters in the field and in Washington the conception of a "country team," it is not clear to what extent it corresponds to reality. John F. Kennedy's memo of May 29, 1961, designed to re-instate the ambassador as its head has been, at best, imperfectly realized. A considerable portion of the mission's bureaucracy responds to two captains, and the ambassador is likely to be the less significant in the contest between him and, for example, Agriculture, Defense, CIA and AID officials subject to dual lines of command. It should not be surprising if they are sometimes more attentive to their agency's drum than to the ambassador's.

Three examples suggest the nature of these relationships. At Dacca, where food aid was of critical concern in the summer of 1974, the USDA policy statement reporting Secretary Butz' calculatedly pessimistic estimates (after the Russian wheat deal) about the U.S.'s capacity to give aid, came directly to the Agricultural attache. He in turn turned them over to USIA officials who put them out through press releases to local newspapers. Neither the Agriculture nor the USIA officials cleared them with embassy political or economic officers, despite their considerable significance as a statement of U.S. policy.

In Delhi, at the same time, Ambassador Moynihan, who was taking a more skeptical view than the Defense Department of the Diego Garcia facility, on the whole managed embassy responses on this issue, and on India's nuclear explosion, without substantial input, let alone help, from local DOD representatives.

In Islamabad, the AID director, who recognized that economic policy was not to the fore in embassy planning, was nevertheless disconcerted by the omission of economic concerns from an important planning document drafted by the political officers. It was more by accident than design that the document came his way in time to permit some consideration of economic policy.

In all three locations there was agreement that some of those who sit in country team meetings, such as the DOD representative, the public affairs officer or the AID director, do not always have the same access to information as members of the country team at or near the top of the foreign service hierarchy. This, *inter alia*, limits their participation. The result is to narrow the range of issues, the dimensions of policy and available modes of action. And those who are not informed do not, in turn, always inform. But the mix varies, depending on the extent to which the mission of an agency conforms to current embassy and ambassadorial policy. In Islamabad, the defense attaches have easy access to the ambassador, are heard, and participate, in effect, in political reporting, while the AID director remains autonomous and isolated. In Delhi, in recent years, with minimal action in either sphere, little is seen or heard from DOD or AID. The facts were different in the Bowles embassy, when the AID director and the ambassador collaborated closely.

The effectiveness of coordination in South Asia is also related to the size of the embassy. Small embassies such as those in Colombo and Dacca are sufficiently intimate to avoid the complexity that accompanies higher levels of differentiation. In Dacca, where the embassy circle is rather intimate but formal, officials regard the post as well coordinated. The size of the country team in Islamabad and Delhi precludes intimacy. Country team meetings, too large for serious discussions of policy or of the prior identification of problems that need attention, have become largely informational. The ambassador may tell the team about his latest trip to Washington or something of his recent talks with the prime minister or other high officials, and top officials may tell other top officials and a few slightly more junior ones what is going on, what is on their minds or what they think needs doing.

Coordination is also related to host country conditions. These can encourage decentralization or centralization of data gathering and political reporting. In Pakistan, Prime Minister Bhutto like President Yahya Khan before him chose to talk at length and individually with the U.S. ambassador, a practice that affects the pattern and style of embassy work and coordination. Ambassador Byroade played a lone hand, talking frequently and at length with the prime minister, preparing his reports for Washington and occasionally sharing some of his thoughts with subordinates. In India, prime ministers have remained more distant, sometimes very distant, from U.S. ambassadors. To know is to infer or deduce from facts and clues rather than to be told. Under such circumstances, political officers, not the host country prime minister, brief the ambassador.

It is not self-evident that organizational solutions short of organizational integration that eliminates most non-State personnel from embassy staffs can solidify the country team. Favorable ecological circumstances—small embassies—cannot be duplicated in all locations. Personalistic solutions are more likely. Ambassadors who are aware that career patterns, organizational location, and service ideology place FSOs in more advantageous positions than agency and service representatives can correct the balance, up to a point, by deliberate effort. By extending the distribution of critical cable information and inviting responses and by insisting on and practicing consultation, he can generate more participation and broaden his information and option base. Given the multiple channels and multiple loyalties of embassy organization, coordination under present conditions depends ultimately on the ambassador's energy, skill and personal authority.

VI. Recommendations

A. Context

Our recommendations assume the restoration of responsibility for the conduct of foreign policy to a smaller and revitalized Department of State whose secretary is the president's senior foreign policy advisor. The principal means to this end is the institutionalization of deliberative coordination in the context of governmental pluralism. We have discussed in Sections I and II of this report the background, evidence and reasons for a State Department centered strategy and the meaning and benefits of deliberative coordination. Worth reiterating here is the importance of deploying professional knowledge in ways that enhance its authority and influence over policy formulation and management.

Our recommendations do not require but certainly would benefit from a variety of organizational and procedural changes.[57] Reducing substantially the size and complexity of the Department of State by eliminating functions and redundancy is one such change. The elimination of nine of its sixteen bureaus, headed by assistant secretaries (or equivalents) is a possibility that has figured in previous organizational reform proposals, notably the Hoover Task Force Report of 1949,[58] and is worth pursuing. The unprecedented boldness of Congress' recent reorganization suggests that institutional inertia can be overcome, even in the face of substantial vested interests.

We have not argued in detail the case for such changes, but we recite them briefly here to suggest the context in which our main recommendations would thrive.

Elimination of nine bureaus would leave the geographic bureaus (now five) with approximately 1000 personnel as the department's central component. A sixth bureau for multilateral affairs could absorb the functions and some of the personnel of the present Economic (EB), Oceans on International Environmental and Scientific Affairs (SCI), and International Organization (IO) bureaus. Non-redundant activities of the six remaining bureaus can be assigned to the regional and multilateral bureaus, to the secretary's office or (as we recommend below) to autonomous or multilateral agencies outside the department. The disappearance of the affected bureaus,

57. For a more detailed version of the assumptions, evidence, argument and prescriptions discussed below see John F. Campbell, *The Foreign Affairs Fudge Factory* (New York, 1971), particularly Chapter 9.
58. Harvey H. Bundy and James Grafton Rogers, *The Organization of the Government for the Conduct of Foreign Policy*, Task Force Report on Foreign Affairs (Appendix H). 1975.

Congressional Relations (H), Public Affairs (PA), Educational
and Cultural Affairs (CU), Intelligence and Research (INR),
Politico-Military Affairs (PM), and the Office of Legal Adviser
(L), would eliminate superfluous and confusing mediation, often
bypassed in any case, by enabling the secretary's staff and the
geographic bureaus to deal directly with Congress, DOD and
CIA as well as with information and law (cultural exchange will
be dealt with below) through small press and legal staffs in the
secretary's office.[59] Finally, we envisage the day when State
will be given responsibility and commensurate authority for
(1) preparing a single, government-wide foreign affairs budget
and (2) for all governmental personnel sent abroad on foreign
missions.[60]

The excess staffing at the secretary's level (the seventh
floor) also merits attention. The chain of command over the
assistant secretaries should be reduced to two, the secretary
and his deputy, the under secretary. A deputy under secretary
for foreign economic policy should act as the chief economic
advisor to the secretary and handle the department's relations
with Treasury, Commerce and other economic agencies. A
second deputy under secretary for national security police
should monitor for the secretary the department's relations with
DOD, CIA and the military services, including maintaining
representatives on their staffs. A small secretariat able to
monitor and arrange the flow of business within and outside
the department and to give independent advice on day to day

59. The visa work of the Bureau of Security and Consular Affairs (SCA)
can be transferred to the Immigration and Naturalization Service
(INS) in the Justice Department, already responsible for the entrance
of aliens and its passport responsibilities further automated. An
assistant secretary for administration, responsible to the secretary
and the six other assistant secretaries, can reduce substantially the
50 per cent of State employees now allocated to support and house-
keeping jobs.

60. A deputy under secretary for budget, replacing the deputy under
secretary for management would prepare, with the agreement and
cooperation of other interested agencies and, after transferring it to
State, the help of OMB's international division, an integrated foreign
affairs budget for the executive branch. The regional assistant
secretaries should review expenditure plans and ambassadors should
justify and control expenditure in their countries.

matters and a small policy planning staff, independent of but not divorced from operations and able to provide on its own initiative as well as on request independent studies and advice, should complete the staffing of the secretary's office.

Of equal importance if the Department of State and its secretary are to be the president's principal advisors and instruments in the conduct of foreign policy is the restoration of the National Security Council to something that more closely approximates Congress' legislative intent in creating it. The NSC has become a highly bureaucratized, cumbersome White House foreign office. Overweighted with representatives of military and intelligence agencies at the policy, committee and staff levels, it has shifted the concerns and objectives of foreign policy from diplomatic means and a political conception of the national interest to military means and a crisis laden conception of national security. The NSC conducts foreign policy in the context of hierarchy and imperative coordination, its staffs and committees shielded from accountability to Congress and public opinion by secrecy and executive privilege, its decisions, despite interdepartmental committees and review groups, often taken in isolation from the professional knowledge of career officials.

We envisage a small (about 20) flexible staff (divorced from policy management and operations) prepared to give and evaluate advice, to extend the president's reach by asking questions and providing information, to insure that those who should be are heard, and to check on implementation. It would put the president's views and policies into draft form and communicate them to those for whom they are intended. Its principal officers would be an assistant for foreign and defense policy and a deputy assistant for foreign economic policy. The present elaborate structure of permanent committees, which make work and waste time, isolate the president from meaningful advice, and inhibit his capacity to direct and control, would be dismantled. The NSC itself would confine its attention and energies to topics and advice for which it was originally intended, the defense budget and military strategy, i.e., a national security, not a foreign policy, agenda. A president able and willing to foster and use a lean, coherent and revitalized State Department is likely to be a president who wants a small, personal White House staff and an NSC that confines itself to narrowly defined military and intelligence agendas.

B. Assistant Secretary Policy Planning Council

Our first recommendation is the creation of an Assistant Secretary Policy Planning Council mandated to identify national interest and formulate and manage policies in ways that take account of regional perspectives. The Council would consist of the State Department geographic assistant secretaries. It would be supported by the Secretariats (S) and by planning teams located in the bureaus. Deputy assistant secretaries would assume larger operating responsibilities so that assistant secretaries can devote the time and attention to their Council responsibilities.

The Council's proceedings would be rooted in deliberative coordination in a collegial context. It would be in a position to manage the dimensions of complexity specified in Part IV of this report in terms of levels, time, function and region. Staffed by professionals close to operations, it would be in a position to use normal diplomacy over a wide range of problems including many that count as crises under current arrangements.

Several advantages attend such a device : (a) It avoids the irrelevance and busy work that have come to characterize the National Security Council's committee and review system by relating planning to operations. Instead of adding yet another layer to those the president now struggles to control, it counters the tendency for staffs to duplicate line operations by vesting policy planning and management in line officials. (b) The Council's recommendations would capture a view-point different from the Policy Planning Staff whose orientation would remain to the Secretary's responsibility to advise the president about strategic diplomacy at the global level. The Council would attend to those contextual evaluations and judgements based on detailed country and regional knowledge that presidential advisors and staffs miss or ignore. (c) The Council would institutionalize and make more visible professional knowledge and experience; (d) the Council would create a collegial context of deliberation in which officials at equivalent organizational levels can freely exchange views, represent interests, and bargain.

The Council would meet regularly on an agenda of leading regional and interregional problems, including crises. The proposed deputy under secretaries for foreign economic policy and for national security policy would, ordinarily, sit with the Council to insure liaison and coordination with the departments and agencies that fall within their responsibilities. Participants would share a regional perspective on the one hand but speak from divergent regional contexts on the other. Deliberation would involve providing reasons and justifications that made sense across regions as well as in regions.

It is widely believed that operations and planning do not go well together, that planning, if it is not to be subsumed by operations, has to take place outside their framework. We are not sure whether to count this belief as an argument against giving the assistant secretaries responsibilities for policy planning and management or as a criticism of the assistant secretary role as it is now defined. If a substantial portion of the assistant secretary's operational responsibilities were given to the deputy assistant secretaries, the assistant secretary's potential as a policy planner would be enhanced.

Another objection to such a scheme is that FSO's are not suited to policy planning ; neither their training nor experience prepares them for it. The operational and bilateral modes of thought and action to which they are accustomed are difficult to transcend. Difficult but not impossible. In-service mid-career training, particularly at universities, can help the right kind of officer to work effectively in the policy planning medium. Equally important would be lateral appointments from outside. In any case we do not concede as self-evident that FSO's are constitutionally incapable of moving from "operations" to planning ; it is a matter for empirical investigation whether assistant secretaries do not think like planners because their roles do not encourage them to do so or because their training and experience preclude their doing so. If getting to be an assistant secretary depended in part on showing talent in this direction it would be surprising if thinkers as well as doers did not surface on the way to the top.

C. A Southern Asia Bureau

The proposal to create an Assistant Secretary Policy Planning Council raises the question of how effectively South Asia would be represented in such a group. Are NEA and its assistant secretary the appropriate organizational form and leadership for managing the South Asia policy arena ? Would an organizational arrangement other than NEA be more effective and appropriate ? Our response to these questions is that NEA should be separated into Near East and South Asia components and that South Asia be joined to South East Asia, now part of the East Asia Bureau. It is often argued that such a division would hurt South Asia by depriving it of the influence that a large and prestigious bureau provides, particularly one whose assistant secretary, even if sometimes ill-informed about or indifferent to the region, often has the caliber and standing to command a hearing laterally and upward.

Divergent career lines already separate Near East from South Asia personnel. Near East normally received the lion's share of attention in NEA ; it holds six country directorates compared to two for South Asia, a ratio of 3 to 1 although the population ratio is the inverse. The assistant secretary typically is more informed about and engaged with the Middle East. Given the oil crisis and the continuing Israel-Arab confrontation, this skewing of attention and interest will increase. By the standard of the Latin American and African bureaus which deal with regions of comparable or lesser consequence in population, military and economic terms. South Asia easily meets the test of bureau standing.

It may be that South Asia should be joined to a region other than the Near East, i.e that NEA is not the right combination. For example, on the analogy of the European Bureau, South Asia might be joined to East Asia in a mammoth Asia Bureau. But the imbalance of such a bureau would not avoid the difficulties for South Asia that already exist in NEA and would compound them with those that trouble the European Bureau. such as the proliferation of functional units that parallel those in the department and a vast array of country directorates ; including one dealing with a super-power.

Another plausible option is to join South and South East Asia in a Southern Asian bureau. The transformation of China from a hostile to a friendly power, the dissolution of America's strategic commitment in South East Asia and the fact that South East Asia's economic, political and cultural characteristics are more similar to South than East Asia, all point in this direction. A southern Asia bureau that combines scale, relatively uniform circumstances, a common geopolitical context and a good balance in country directorates makes more sense than present arrangements (NEA and EA) or than a separate South Asia Bureau. On balance, then, we recommend that South Asia be separated from NEA, South East from EA, and the two joined in a new Bureau of Southern Asian Affairs (SA).

D. Insulating Selected Programs in Multilateral and Autonomous Agencies

We have argued in Part IV-B that one of the most difficult problems associated with the time dimension of complexity is the relationship of long run and short run interests and objectives. We noted that there is pronounced propensity to sacrifice long run goals to the requirements of leverage and the political need for immediate gains. An organizational solution to this dilemma is the use of agencies that are insulated from the vicissitudes of short run political circumstances and the struggle for power in domestic and international politics.

Insulation will not survive short run political pressures if it is not grounded in good reasons that can be publicly stated and defended ; if those reasons are not appreciated and defended by the president and Congress ; and if they do not command public understanding and support. Among the policies and programs discussed in this report we believe that those directed to economic growth and redistribution and people-to-people diplomacy have the kind of governmental and public support required for such a defense.

In the light of these considerations we recommend that (1) economic aid in the form of loans and credits be concentrated in multilateral agencies such as IDA and regional development banks, (2) that cultural and educational programs now located in the State Department's Bureau of Educational and Cultural Affairs. HEW's Office of Education and in other agencies be transferred to a new autonomous agency, the

Foundation for Education and Culture, described and justified in V C U, "Insulation in Practice : Cultural and Informational Agencies," and (3) that a people-to-people program such as the Peace Corps that relies on volunteers and operates at the grass roots level be located in on autonomous agency similar to the Foundation for Education and Culture.

E. The Regional Conference

We propose the creation of a Regional Conference designed to promote regional coordination in the field and in Washington. Regional conferences lasting two or three days would be convened quarterly at rotating centers in the region and in Washington. Conferences would be organized around topics of common interest to the region such as food and agriculture, economic development, military policy, oceanic problems, nuclear proliferation, population, trade, education and culture, and science and technology. They would be attended by approximately forty persons who would, in a concluding plenary session, review the reports of topically grouped workshops in an attempt to formulate common understandings and recommendations. Such sessions and the documents they produce could do what policy papers drawn up by NSC interdepartmental groups now attempt to do.

The objectives of the Regional Council are like those of chiefs of missions conferences but go beyond them by stressing exposure to the political environment and presenting problems of the region and by aiming to deliberate in ways that promote coordination and policy guidance. The first objective, exposure to the political environment of the host countries, can be aided by inviting as guests to plenary or workshop sessions elected or appointed officials, scholars, and leaders of thought and opinion of the host country (which includes from time to time the USA).

USG participants would include not only officials whose work and qualifications relate to the topic of the conference but also ambassadors or DCMs, assistant and deputy assistant secretaries and, on occasion, the secretary, under secretary or deputy under secretaries. (We take note of Secretary Kissinger's penchant for peripatetic diplomacy and, in the Regional Conference, propose to institutionalize it.)

The Conference is also designed to promote field-Washington coordination. The operational routines, policy agendas and, most important, environmental contexts of the center and the periphery generate markedly different perspectives. Neither believes that the other is sufficiently alive to its setting, constraints and problems. The Conference exploits an underutilized resource for the conduct of foreign policy, modern means of rapid travel, to remedy these difficulties by creating new lines of discourse within the region and between it and Washington.

Conferences in Washington will expose field officials to the relevancies of bureaucratic, congressional and national politics; to policy agendas as Washington sees them; and to political sentiment on the Hill. Such experiences will refresh their appreciation of the relatively modest domestic standing of matters that seem critical in Dacca or Islamabad.

The Regional Conference would be staffed by a small regional secretariat headed by a Regional Coordinator at the rank of Deputy Assistant Secretary. The secretariat would generate and gather information relevant to the topic and agenda of particular sessions, facilitate communication, and plan and coordinate conference agendas. Every effort should be made to prevent the regional secretariat from becoming a place where routine tasks are performed. The regional secretariat is meant to provide horizontal coordination among embassies. Its staff should know the region, have served there, and have a good command of programs, including those on the margins of the State Department and outside it.

We began this report by observing that prescriptions for administrative reform have a cyclical quality. Those that originated in the New Deal era to strengthen presidential management and leadership of the executive branch prospered and grew during and after World War II in response to America's role as a world power. In the 1960s the need for presidential power became the dominant theme of the literature on domestic and foreign policy and in the early 1970s the principal problematic of presidential practice.

We propose in this report counter-cyclical measures designed to correct the excesses of presidential power in the conduct of foreign policy. They include proposals to counter imperative with deliberative coordination; the NSC system with a strengthened and re-organized State Department, including an Assistant Secretary Policy Planning Council and Regional Conferences; hierarchical norms and relationships with collegial ones; the general knowledge of policy intellectuals with the professional knowledge of career officials; and a global dominant view of world politics with one that gives global, regional and bilateral relations their due.

If implemented, these prescriptions will in time no doubt lead to other excesses, but in the historical context of the 1970s we find them appropriate remedies for the era's presenting problems.

ONE

CASE STUDIES :
I. DIPLOMATIC-STRATEGIC

A. South Asia and U.S. Military Policy

Stephen P. Cohen

I. Introduction

Between 1965 and 1974 two Administrations had to fashion a coherent strategic and military policy towards South Asia in the face of extraordinary complexity. This complexity is most evident in two areas of choice : the proper integration of American regional military interests with her global strategy, and the wise use of military means in the service of this integrative process.

There is no doubt that the U.S. has pursued "global" or grand strategic objectives in the world since 1945. At this level critical variables have included Soviet, Chinese, European and (now) Japanese capabilities and intentions. What has been in doubt is the relevance of this global pattern of interaction to American involvement in regional sub-systems such as South Asia. At one extreme, should South Asia be treated on its own terms, free from superpower competition ? At the other, should American policy in the region be guided exclusively by global and superpower considerations ?[1] A striking characteristic of American policy towards South Asia has been the oscillation between these two views : one purpose of this paper will be to

---

1. For a discussion of this problem see Wayne Wilcox, Leo E. Rose, and Gavin Boyd, eds., *Asia and the International System* (Cambridge: Winthrop Publishers, 1972, v), and more recently, William P. Bundy, "International Security Today", *Foreign Affairs* 53, 1 (October, 1974). 24-44.

describe this oscillation and identify the important organizational and issue-related causes for it.

A second area of complexity confronting U.S. military and strategic policy is the extraordinary militarization of relations in South Asia.[2] Military tension between India and Pakistan—erupting in open warfare twice since 1964—has become a regrettably permanent feature : this has in turn provided the opportunity for major external powers to provide hardware and weapons to both sides. For the U.S. this presents a number of difficult problems : how effective are weapons as instruments of American policy ? Who is to implement an arms program, and who is to evaluate it ? Can arms transfers enhance bilateral relations in what is almost a zero-sum environment, should they serve America's *regional* interests, or can (and should) they serve extra-regional global American interests ? Thus, what confronts American policy-makers is both complexity of *situation* as well as complexity of *choice*.

One issue has dominated American military policy in South Asia : the transfer of weapons.[3] The bulk of this paper will examine the determination of arms transfer policy in the 1965-74 period with special attention to two decision points. These are the reformation of weapons policy in 1966-67, and the "one-time" exception to that policy of 1970. The two decisions illustrate radically different judgements of both the strategic importance of South Asia and the use of weapons as an instrument; the decisions were also concluded via two different organizational patterns. To provide a broader base of comparison we will also examine another decision with military implications : the proposed expansion of the facility on Diego Garcia. This episode provides additional confirming evidence about the way in which America's South Asian

2. Stephen P. Cohen, "Security Issues in South Asia," *Asian Survey*, XV (3), March, 1975.

3. By transfers I include a wide variety of programs : direct grants, loans, and sales of equipment (the latter for hard or soft currency and by deferred or immediate payment). In addition, military assistance may also take the form of cash subsidies to the recipient state. Quite often, as in the case of both India and Pakistan, a military relationship will encompass a mix of several programs. Additionally, it may also involve direct cash subsidies in local currencies.

military policy has been made in recent years and helps provide some additional basis for evaluation of that policy.

II. No Arms for the Poor : State Gains Control

By many standards, the 1965 Indo-Pakistan war was a success. From the military point of view it was, according to participants on both sides, "a bloody good show", with just enough casualties to toughen the troops but not so many that eyebrows were raised.[4] For the political leadership in each country the war served a purpose : for the Pakistanis it was vital in their attempt to keep the Kashmir issue alive and before world opinion, for Lal Bahadur Shastri, it was a successful baptism under fire. True, much of the moderate East Bengali leadership was incensed at the lack of preparedness in East Pakistan —but at the time this was a grievance which was merely noted, although it was to surface again in 1971.

Yes, the war was useful, and not only for the South Asians. China was able to demonstrate her continuing and firm support of Pakistan through a bit of saber rattling in the Himalayas (and they were to repeat the effort in 1971); the Soviet Union demonstrated that it had established itself on the Sub-continent by hosting a reasonably successful summit conference at Tashkent. And what of the United States ? An ally, Pakistan, and a sister democracy, India, had fought a war which was widely viewed as subsidized by American taxpayers. The U.S. played little or no role in ending that war, and had received no thanks from either side; what was there to rejoice about ?

Very simply, the war came at the right moment for the U.S. in the way that some calamities are welcomed by debtors and bigamists. For this was precisely the position of the U.S. vis-a-vis India and Pakistan. It had undertaken substantial arms programs in both countries, and attempted to manipulate their relationship for the presumed benefit of all three parties, with dismal results. Promises had been made to both sides which could not be kept without antagonizing one state or the

4. For three contrasting views see Russell Brines, *The Indo-Pakistani Conflict* (New York : Praeger, 1968), Lt. Gen. B.M. Kaul (Indian Army), *Confrontation With Pakistan* (Delhi : Vikas Publications, 1971), and Brig. Gulzar Ahmed (Pakistan Army), *Pakistan Meets Indian Challenge* (Rawalpindi : Al Mukhtar Publ., n.d.).

other : the 1965 war enabled the U.S. to get out of these commitments with some shred of dignity and then actually proceed to construct a reasonably intelligent arms policy.

Before describing this effort, note should be made of the way in which the U.S. painted itself into a corner in South Asia, and the enormous military impact it had come to have upon a region which by no stretch of the imagination was strategically vital.

The U.S. had been engaged in the transfer of weapons and war material to South Asia since the mid-1950's. Indeed, transfers occurred earlier, if one takes into consideration the weapons and military infrastructure left in the region as a consequence of World War II. The military importance of weapons transfers from the U.S.A. was historically crucial. Pakistan would not have become a serious military power without U.S. equipment. Virtually her entire Army and Air Force were equipped with relatively modern U.S. weapons, most notably M-47 and M-48 Patton Tanks (once the main battle tank of NATO), F-86 Sabre aircraft, and F-104 supersonic fighters (also frontline NATO equipment), and B-57 light attack jet bombers. In addition, engineering, communications, and transportation equipment was lavishly supplied. These transfers led directly to Indian purchases (largely from the U.S.A., Britain, but later from France and the Soviet Union) of equivalent weapons and very heavy Indian investment in a domestic arms industry.

Until 1962, U.S. weapons were largely a Pakistani asset and an Indian problem. However, after the conflict with the Chinese, they were given and sold to India for the explicit purpose of defense against further Chinese incursions.[5] To this end, the U.S. provided equipment for six so-called mountain divisions, road-building and engineering equipment, and the beginning of a modern air defense system orientated towards the Himalayas.[6] In addition, parts of several ammunition and

5. See K. Subrahmanyam, "Military and Foreign Policy", *Foreign Affairs Reports* (New Delhi), XVII, 11 (Nov., 1968), p. 118, for an Indian analysis.

6. This system, "Star Sapphire," has just been completed. Earlier, the U.S. had sold at concessional rates significant numbers of World War II Sherman Tanks (800) and medium C-119 transports (55).

arms factories were shipped to India, although not all of these were completed before the 1965 war. Negotiations for modern supersonic aircraft fell through, as did talks about refurbishing the aging Indian Navy. According to the terms of the assistance, this equipment was to be used only against the Chinese. A huge U.S. military mission was installed in New Delhi to inspect the disposition of American aid.[7]

This U.S. Military Supply Mission to India (USMSMI) housed in a rented maharajah's palace, operated under direct orders from the Department of Defense. But it was not the first such mission in South Asia : a gigantic Military Assistance Advisory Group had been in Pakistan for years, directing the flow of American weapons and training in that country.

Both of these missions were classic expressions of then-prevalent assumptions concerning the utility of direct military-to-military ties in furthering U.S. policy. As Selig Harrison and others have noted, the Pakistan aid program was based on the belief that even before Ayub's coup the military was a dominant power in that country and that U.S. military personnel were perfectly capable of dealing with them.[8] At that time State was thought to be unable to handle such large military assistance programs so it seemed perfectly natural to let the military do it. They did, with characteristic zeal. Ties between U.S. officials and Pakistani generals date from the early 1950's, and remain a factor in bilateral relations.[9] State Department officials even today note with a mixture of sarcasm and awe the power of Pakistanis—especially the right "martial" types—to influence visiting American dignitaries.[10]

7. Most of this equipment has stayed in the Himalayas, but some can be used against Pakistan as well as China (the radar net, mountain divisions in Kashmir). There are some indications that the Indian military has spread around equipment intended for the mountain divisions to other units.

8. Selig Harrison, *India, Pakistan and the United States* (Washington : The New Republic, 1959).

9. Stephen P. Cohen, *Arms and Politics in Bangladesh, India, and Pakistan* (Buffalo : SUNY, Council on International Studies, 1973).

10. Typically a senior American officer has been met in Rawalpindi by a higher ranking Pakistani officer, or, in the past, by Ayub or Yahya, and in New Delhi by a middle-ranking civilian Defense Ministry bureaucrat.

The officers attached to USMSMI had no such ego-building experience. The Indian Government had long been wary of close relationships between their own generals and foreign military personnel : they were quite aware of developments in Pakistan. While their fears of a foreign-inspired coup among their own military may have been exaggerated, they were deeply felt, and Indian civilians in the Ministry of External Affairs and the Defense Ministry were scrupulous in restricting contacts between their own and the U.S. military.

Thus, when the 1965 war finally came the American military found themselves to be the subject of exaggerated expectations in Pakistan and exaggerated suspicions in India. Pakistan expected more help than it could get; India, needing less, was angry when even that was not forthcoming.

Even to the U.S. military the war seemed to undercut much of the rationale for the military aid programs in both India and Pakistan. True, there were still "interests" in both countries, especially Pakistan, in the sense that a number of American generals tended to view substantial U.S. programs and installations as interests in themselves—deriving interest from program. But even in Pakistan this "interest" had deteriorated, and the spy-bases and radar installations located in Peshawar and Gilgit had lost much of their value. Besides, as a number of U.S. officers had observed, India demonstrated substantial improvement over her inept performance against China three years earlier. A number of younger U.S. Army and Air Force officers (the two services most concerned with South Asia at that time) argued for an arms policy which at the very least would not antagonize this growing power.

If Pakistan had lost much of her military lobby by 1965 she had begun to lose support among State Department professionals even earlier. The rapid move of India towards the West after the 1962 India-China war raised the strong possibility that she could become a de facto ally of the U.S., and a strong, powerful, democratic one at that. This position was argued by both Galbraith and Bowles, sometimes to excess, but was shared by foreign service professionals who had seen duty in both countries.[11] While there was some sense of

11. For a view of the U.S. policy process in the period after the 1962 Indo-China conflict see Shivaji Ganguly, "U.S. Military Assistance

competition between the embassies in Rawalpindi and Delhi before 1965, the war had done much to crystallize opinion and bring them together.

Their shared analysis of both military and strategic possibilities in South Asia remains almost intact today, and is worth presenting in summary form :[12]

(a) Militarily, Pakistan could no longer hope to obtain any kind of strategic superiority on the Subcontinent even with a major external arms supplier. This judgement was confirmed by the outcome of the 1971 war and was based largely upon a significantly better Indian performance in 1965 than 1962. Although the war of 1965 was something of a stalemate, and almost degenerated into a war of attrition, it was precisely that kind of war which India was best able to mount against the numerically smaller Pakistani forces. No amount of bluff and bravado about the martial races of Pakistan could conceal the fact that Indians fought well also. Pakistan, in short, was clearly not—and could never become—the dominant or even major military power on the Sub-continent.

(b) America had few if any *direct* or bilateral military interests in South Asia itself. While the area remained of political importance for a number of reasons (see below) these did not necessarily have military implications. It seemed unlikly that the Soviet threat to the Subcontinent would take military form, the Chinese struggle with India seemed to have cooled down considerably. The Chinese even failed to intervene during the 1965 war, when such intervention would have had a great impact. And, as noted above, the spy bases and other installations in Pakistan were no longer vital to U.S. strategic planning, having been largely replaced by satellites.

(c) the U.S. did retain some bilateral non-military

in India 1962-63 : A Study in Decision-Making", *India Quarterly* (July-Sep., 1972), 1—11.

12. I have drawn these from various conversations, official statements, and actions.

interests in the region. The general goals of economic development, humanitarian relief, encouragement of democratic regimes, favorable bilateral ralations and the reduction of Sub-continental tensions were (and still are) shared by foreign service professionals dealing with the region. Strategically, they viewed the region as important in the Cold War, but not as important as in the 1950's but this importance was based on non-military grounds.

(d) As between India and Pakistan, few in Rawalpindi, New Delhi or Washington would be willing to argue for an either/or choice. India was important because of its size, democratic political system, and economic difficulties; Pakistan was itself regarded as a substantial nation, but in addition had been a loyal American ally for a number of years. Politically, India had excellent ties with the non-aligned world, Pakistan with a number of Arab states and other American allies. Of greater concern were the ties of the two states with the two great Communist powers : India with the Soviet Union, Pakistan with China.

While there are of course individual exceptions, it must be stressed that even in 1970 there was remarkable agreement on the above analysis among civilian FSOs dealing with South Asia. This shared perception of local conditions and American interests made it possible for a major step in American military involvement in South Asia to be taken.

Shortly after fighting broke out between India and Pakistan in 1965 the USG announced an embargo on military shipments to both India and Pakistan. By the time the war had terminated plans were underway in Washington to study the entire U.S. arms program for the region. The embargo had had an uneven impact, because Pakistan had been almost totally dependent upon the U.S. for her weapons, while India's military had British, French, and indigenous equipment.[13] In

13. For a careful study of India's attempts to achieve self-sufficiency in crucial major weapons systems see Wayne A. Wilcox, "The Indian Defense Industry : Technology and Resources", in Frank B. Horton III, et al. (eds.) *Comparative Defense Policy* (Baltimore : Johns Hopkins University Press, 1974), pp. 479—481.

fact, the USG never did give or sell frontline combat weapons (tanks and aircraft) to the Indian armed services which had viewed America as the best possible source of weapons. When the then Defense Minister (Y.B. Chavan) went to the Soviet Union in 1964 to examine Soviet weapons he was accompanied by a group of reluctant Indian officers; ultimately it became clear that American weapons were not to be forthcoming, and the Indian military settled for what they could get.

While the Pakistanis had held discussions with the Chinese for some time concerning arms assistance, the 1965 war made this an urgent priority. The Chinese rapidly became Pakistan's major arms supplier, and today just under half of her combat aircraft and well over half of her medium tanks are of Chinese origin.[14]

These developments were of some concern to the MAAG mission in Rawalpindi and they kept pressure on DOD to support the lifting of the embargo to Pakistan. But DOD itself was having second thoughts on arms programs in general, and Pakistan in particular. By coincidence, a major DOD study of military assistance had been completed in 1965 and concluded that most current programs were in great need of reform.[15]

An initial break in the embargo occurred in early 1966 as a consequence of urgent pleas from both the U.S. and Pakistani military in Rawalpindi. India and Pakistan could purchase for cash or credit and on a case-by-case basis, "non-lethal" end items. Additionally, they could purchase spare parts for non-lethal material on a cash basis only. Crucially, India and Pakistan were to be treated *identically*, a reflection of the rough equality of U.S. interests in both states. Further, a unique

14. This is according to recent International Institute for Strategic Studies figures, which are accurate. In terms of American equipment, this amounted to over 80 per cent of Pakistan's weapons at the peak of the aid program, but is now around 35-40 per cent, and declining. During the 1971 War "friends" of the Pentagon were anxious to prove that weapons used by the Pakistan Army in East Bengal were of predominately Chinese origin. Several articles making this point were inserted in the *Congressional Record* of Nov. 16, 1971, by Cong. John Schmitz (Rep., Calif.).

15. For a discussion see Roger E. Sack, "United States Military Aid to the Ayub Khan Regime", a companion paper being presented to the Commission. The organization of the Government for the conduct of Foreign Policy.

distinction had been introduced into the arms assistance program : "lethal" vs. "non-lethal" equipment. The former were presumably weapons that fired, the latter included un-armed transport (air and ground), communications equipment, and logistics and engineering supplies.[16] This relaxation of the embargo was no boon for Pakistan. In fact, like the total embargo, it favored India, which had been making large purchases of U.S. "non-lethal" equipment for several years. But the new policy had another effect : it stimulated the Indian and Pakistani search for new sources of weapons.

Meanwhile, the State Department's India and Pakistan desks had undertaken a careful search for an arms policy which would maximize what they perceived to be American interests in the region. A virtual embargo might have been continued had India and Pakistan not been so successful in obtaining outside sources of weapons from the two Communist powers, France, and Great Britain. Additionally, Pakistan was still putting heavy pressure on the USG and tried to exploit what they perceived as a sympathetic Lyndon Johnson. According to several sources however, Johnson declined to intervene in the decision-making process on the side of the Pakistanis and the final policy determination was formulated within the regional bureau of the State Department.

This policy, announced on September 23, 1967, remains in effect to day. It consisted of the 1966 modification of the 1965 embargo, plus the following points :

(a) All equipment assistance on a grant basis would be terminated (with the minor exception of the provision of road-building equipment for India to use in constructing the East-West Highway in Nepal),

(b) Withdrawal of the substantial U.S. Military Supply Mission and MAAG groups in India and Pakistan, respectively,

Resumption of grant aid training programs on a limited scale,

16. For the official policy statements plus supporting data see : 93rd Congress, House Committee on Foreign Affairs, Subcommittee on the Near East and South Asia, *Hearings* (United States Interests in and Policies Toward South Asia), March, 1973, and *Report*, May, 1973.

(c) "Willingness to consider on a case-by-case basis the cash sale of spare parts for previously supplied lethal equipment".[17]

The criteria for the case-by-case consideration of spare parts were to be the recipient's critical need, "contribution to reduction of military expenditures or arms limitations and contribution to reasonable military stability" within the Subcontinent.[18] Thus, the U.S. did not declare its intention to withdraw *entirely* from its earlier efforts to seek some balanced relationship between India and Pakistan, but it did state that such efforts would be quite restricted. The U.S. would not rebuild or expand Pakistani force levels; at the very most it would guarantee that they would remain at approximately 1965 levels. A number of DOD, MAAG, and attache studies had already determined that these levels were adequate for Pakistan's internal security and for her defense against India. The U.S. had tried to remove itself from a position of major arms supplier in South Asia, while still maintaining some limited military-to-military contact and holding some leverage over Pakistan (via decisions on spare parts) and therefore (indirectly) over India as well.

The reaction to this policy statement was stunned anger in Pakistan and wary relief in India. On balance, the policy favored India, to the degree that the U.S. would no longer be Pakistan's major arms supplier. U.S.-Pakistani relations hit an all-time low in the years following the 1966-67 policy decisions, as Pakistan felt vulnerable and betrayed. She even accepted some Soviet military equipment, a development which sent tremors of concern through the Indian government. Ironically, the Soviet justification for arms to Pakistan was the same as that invoked by the Americans: it was needed to provide a token balance to Chinese arms aid. The Soviets now argued in New Delhi that their supplies to Pakistan made that state dependent upon her—the identical argument used before 1965 by the USG in both New Delhi and Rawalpindi. The Soviets, in brief, had assumed much of the same responsibility for balancing Indian-Pakistani relations that the U.S. had carried for a number of years. And the USG, deeply embedded in the

17. *Hearings, op. cit.,* p. 86.
18. *Ibid.*

Vietnam struggle, was perfectly willing to let the Soviets assume that responsibility.

Maintaining the 1967 arms restrictions has been a difficult task, complicated by continual pressure from Pakistan and its supporters and the occasional difficulty of knowing exactly what U.S. policy *is*. Such a policy is not self-enforcing; it depends upon knowledgeable individuals defending it from encroachment, nibbling tactics and sheer ignorance. At present, the critical officials are the desk officers and Country Directors for India and Pakistan, plus the Deputy Assistant Secretary of Defense (ISA) that deals with South Asian matters. He, in turn, is assisted by two military officers of colonel rank (who may, however, be drawn from any of the three services), who deal, respectively, with South Asia and the Indian Ocean region. There is close continuing relationship between these two officers and the desk level FSOs in the State Department : they form the key relationship in the application of the 1967 and related policy decisions. Others may be brought in for special reasons, but *policy* implementation lies in the hands of these half-dozen individuals.

My observations of this process in recent years indicates some weaknesses. Desk officers usually come to their positions with considerable area expertise, but military experience ranging from very little to advanced training at a war college. They must cope with a variety of complicated military-related issues : when is a weapon "offensive" or "defensive"; what is a spare part and what is a complete weapons system (a 105 mm. shell would be the former, a hand grenade the latter); what are India and Pakistan's "real" military needs, as opposed to their announced needs; what civilian and commercial equipment has military application; what is a "lethal" vs. a "non-lethal" item of military equipment.

The first determination of such issues is made by these civilian officials, and they are on occasion unable to muster the necessary expertise. Their counterparts in ISA *will* have technical expertise, but may or may not have area knowledge. When ISA did have officers with both kinds of skills the task of coordination and implementation of policy was enormously simplified, and lower-level officials were quite effective in their presentation and defense of existing policy. Thus, during the

entire Bangladesh crisis, the 1966-67 policy *was never broken*
by the U.S. although a self-imposed embargo was accidentally
violated, and illegal third-country transfers of weapons may
have been winked at. All of these violations were initiated
at the highest levels of the U.S. government, and working
level officials were deliberately deceived on more than one
occasion.

In retrospect the 1966-67 policy decision to remove the
USG from the South Asian strategic balance of power was a
remarkable achievement brought about because of several
unusual circumstances. The bilateral military programs in
both India and Pakistan were proving to be personally and
politically unsatisfactory to those involved in them; they meant
that the USG was fueling both sides of an arms race; external
Communist threats to the region seemed to have declined;
American resources and war material were urgently needed
elsewhere; the bureaucratic and public lobbies favoring arms
supplies to India or Pakistan were sobered by the 1965 war.
Finally, a President preoccupied by the Vietnam conflict was
unwilling to intervene on behalf of one or the other country,
and permitted the State Department to make a final determination of U.S. policy. But, as one participant in the process at
that time noted, "policy" is a slippery concept : it can serve
indefinitely as a guide to future action, or it can be swept away
tomorrow. America had a "policy", but even it was to be made
subject to "exceptions".

III. Let There Be One, Two, Many Exceptions

When Richard Nixon acceded to the Presidency in 1968 he
was determined to make a mark in foreign policy above and
beyond the immediate requirement of terminating American
involvement in the Vietnam war. With Henry Kissinger as
mentor and executor he fashioned a global foreign policy for
the United States and presented it to the world during his
1969 trip around the world. Unlike the crude anti-communism
of earlier administrations or the *ad hocism* of Johnson, the
Nixon Doctrine envisioned a world made up of several
important power-centers, and predicated U.S. foreign policy
upon successful dealing with these centers. The "battleground"
of the Cold War, the so-called Third World, was clearly

relegated to a subservient position in this scheme of affairs, important only as individual countries had a special relationship with one of the major power centers.

Pakistan was one such country. It had stubbornly pursued close ties with China despite American and Soviet objections.[19] It is quite probable, therefore, that when Nixon visited Pakistan in 1969, he initiated discussions about future U.S.-Chinese relations. At the same time he listened with considerable sympathy to President Yahya Khan's request for a change in the 1966-67 arms assistance policy. For reasons which we may never know, Nixon is reliably reported to have said to those in his party that the U.S. should "do something for Pakistan".[20] This could have been a *quid pro quo* for Pakistan's role in making the China trip possible, it could have grown out of Nixon's long-standing interest in Pakistan itself, or both motives may have played a part.

The command to "do something for Pakistan" came back to the State Department through NSC and State Department channels. Do what for Pakistan? The India and Pakistan desks were to have their first taste of the new, Kissinger-ized system of decision-making.

As a group, the two dozen or so senior officials in Delhi, Rawalpindi, and Washington were not inclined to do anything for Pakistan.[21] They understood that Pakistan needed weapons, that the Pakistanis had continued their pressure to have the 1966-67 policy altered, but by and large they were pleased with the state of affairs in South Asia. No major war appeared likely in the foreseeable future and relations with India were reasonably good. In their view the demand to "do something" probably stemmed from the President's personal interest in the fate of the generals in Pakistan; they were hardly inclined to

19. See Shivaji Ganguly, *Pakistan-China Relations, A Study in Interaction* (Urbana : Center for Asian Studies, 1971).

20. This is one version reported (and presumably believed by) a number of officials in State; they speak of offhand and casual presidential commitments, and the one-time exception seemed to be this at one time. In retrospect the commitment may not have been so casually entered into.

21. A few exceptions, especially the various U.S. ambassadors to Pakistan, have consistently argued over the years for increased military assistance to Pakistan.

sympathize, and none were aware of the secret plans being made for the China trips of Kissinger and Nixon.

The initial reaction of State was to temporize. Presumably, the decision to assist Pakistan was a whim, and could be dragged out. Thus, papers circulated from the regional desks to NSC and back for numerous modifications and adjustments, coordination with the Pentagon being handled by the staff of the Assistant Secretary of Defense for International Security Affairs. A number of study papers were prepared with various choices laid out for NSC and presidential action. To the dismay of the now perplexed desk officers and country directors in State, several of these were sent back with the demand that more "real" choices be presented. At least one desk officer noted at the time that he was not really sure whether *anyone* at NSC was reading the papers from State, or whether he might not be performing make-work tasks. State was in no hurry to rush to a decision but then the NSC staff seemed to be demanding something from State, but not specifying what that something should be. However, since State officials were unaware of the new importance of the Pakistan-China link, they were unable to formulate a policy to accommodate this development. They were serving as technical advisors, blindly offering up suggestions without a clear understanding of the reasons for making an exception to the 1966-67 policy. Some thought that it was Pakistan's relationship with Iran and the Middle East which had triggered presidential concern, but offered this explanation to a visitor with only half-hearted enthusiasm.

State pondered the demand to "do something" for a number of months. Then, in mid-1970, after a meeting with CENTO ambassadors, President Nixon was approached by the Pakistani Ambassador, who reminded him of the 1969 pledge. Furious at the news that "something" had not yet been done, Nixon turned to an aide and demanded immediate action. The bureaucracy was jolted, and a package deal was finally put together.

This was announced in October, 1970 as a "one-time exception" to the 1966-67 policy. Pakistan was to be offered the right to purchase—for cash and hard currency—a number of M-113 armored personnel carriers (303) as an alternative to their request for M-48 tanks. Additionally, the U.S. would enter into negotiations for the purchase of a limited number of combat aircraft—but not the "hot" F-104's so desired by the Pakistan Air Force. And that was all : no really new "offensive" weapons was provided (as the APCs were defined as "defensive") and the aircraft were to be replacements for interceptors Pakistan had lost by attrition and accident (but not combat). The entire one-time exception was publicly justified as a "symbolic offset to Pakistan's growing dependence on Chinese arms". In retrospect this seems an almost comical assertion in view of the fact that Pakistan was by then serving as an intermediary with the Chinese. With the benefit of hindsight the one-time exception emerges as a symbolic reassurance *to* the Chinese that the U.S. would assist a mutual friend. One can only speculate whether the Chinese actively lobbied for the one-time exception as an indication that in areas where their interests were parallel, the U.S. and China could work together, and that the U.S. was willing to share the Chinese' burden in maintaining the Pakistani military.

If such cooperation later was a Chinese or Pakistani expectation the actual content of the one-time exception must have been a disappointment, more symbol than substance. The weapons to be provided were not particularly crucial for Pakistan nor were the terms very good. Pakistan had hoped and tried for weapons through the "third country route", obtaining U.S.-origin equipment from Iran, Saudi Arabia, Turkey, or West Germany.[22] However, Congress had passed restrictive legislation concerning "third-country" transfers and was watching the situation very closely. The White House

---

22. When India or Pakistan wanted to buy U.S.-origin weapons from third countries (Great Britain, West Germany, Iran, Turkey) they had to obtain American permission for the transfer under present agreements. This meant that both South Asian states plus one or more NATO or CENTO allies were simultaneously lobbying the U.S. Government, creating a very complicated and delicate political problem. There have been transfers from the U.K. to India and from West Germany to Pakistan via Iran; some of the latter raised legal and political difficulties. For extensive documentation and testimony see, U.S. Congress, Joint Economic Committee (Subcommittee on Economy in Government), *Hearings* on Economic Issues in Military Assistance, January-February, 1971.

staff had suggested using third-country transfers as the vehicle for providing weapons under the "one-time exception", but it was pointed out by the Country Directors of India and Pakistan that this would require a determination that the U.S. would be willing to provide those weapons to Pakistan *directly*. Neither State nor the White House staff seemed to be eager to claim that U.S. policy now included the provision of "offensive" weapons. Even the President did not demand this. He was interested only in some visible, public show of sympathy for Pakistan and "symbolic" support was indeed enough.

Ironically, Pakistan will never receive the aircraft that were being negotiated under the one-time exception agreement, and only recently received shipment of the APC's. When fighting broke out in East Pakistan in 1971 a new embargo was imposed on shipments of weapons and war material to both India and Pakistan; despite some leakage of largely Pakistan-owned equipment, the embargo was effective. The APC's, which had been partially paid for, were manufactured right through the Bangladesh crisis and waited for shipment until 1973 when delivery was resumed. Even as the last shipment was arriving in Karachi, though, Pakistan undertook a new campaign to have the U.S. make what could well become "the second one-time exception".

In recent years many Washington officials have looked back upon the "one-time exception" with a sense of frustration and concern. Insisting that it really was "exceptional", a "deviation" or an "aberration" because of the extreme degree of Presidential initiative, they nonetheless feared a repetition of the episode. It made the working-level officer quite sensitive to South Asia's marginal place in the Nixon-Kissinger world order, and such officials became adept at justifying or explaining bilateral policy issues in terms of broader strategic and political consequences. One senses that they did this more out of duty than conviction.

IV. Diego Garcia and the Politics of Persistence

Diego Garcia, a small island located 1000 miles to the southwest of the Indian Subcontinent in the Indian Ocean, has been the object of American naval planning for over thirty years.[23] This interest was intensified in the mid-1960's when the U.S. Navy launched a full-scale effort to obtain Diego as a transit base for ships proceeding to or from Southeast Asia. A project manager was appointed, studies were made, and the "facility" became an annual object of negotiation between the Navy and civilian managers in the Department of Defense. As Earl Ravenal has testified, the staff of ISA/DOD took up the challenge and pointed out that refueling could be done more efficiently and cheaply in the Persian Gulf, that developing a U.S. facility would anger littoral states without yielding any particular benefit and that even a small facility might be the prelude for a larger and unnecessary establishment.[24] Thus, until very recently, successive Navy project managers for Diego Garcia have had limited success. A small breakthrough occurred in the late 1960's when Diego was leased from the British and used as an electronics communications facility.

All of the public evidence available (and much of the private evidence) indicates a single-minded and intensive Navy interest in Diego, with annual requests for a major facility and the grudging but hopeful acceptance of funds for a minor one. In the scheme of things, until 1973, the Navy was the only agency which wanted to expand Diego Garcia, and they were successfully neutralized by civilian DOD officials in ISA working in collaboration with regional and functional bureaus (Political Military Affairs) of the State Department. Interest outside of these bureaucratic groups, and among the littoral states, was relatively insignificant.

The Middle East war of 1973 changed the entire political, strategic, and bureaucratic context. The Navy claimed that its ship movements in and around the Indian Ocean area (including the Gulf) were artificially constrained because of lack of support facilities (similar complaints had been registered in

23. For an alleged chronology of Navy interest, see : U.S. Congress, Committee on Foreign Affairs, Subcommittee on the Near East and South Asia, *Hearings* (Proposed Expansion of U.S. Military Facilities in the Indian Ocean), Feb-March, 1974, p. 156. The Navy claims initial interest in the 1960's, but studies underway indicate a much earlier concern with an Indian Ocean facility.

24. *Ibid.* p. 86.

1971 during the sailing of the *Enterprise* into the Bay of Bengal).[25] The Navy was concerned about distances, cost, and the larger Soviet naval presence in the Indian Ocean region, which required a bigger balancing force. Suddenly, the notion of an expanded Diego Garcia facility seemed to make considerably more sense to a number of DOD and State Department officials at all levels, although there was still no unanimity about either the role or mission of such a facility.

However, even before these issues could be fully discussed within the bureaucracy, the decision was made to go ahead with the expansion of Diego Garcia and raise it to the level of a significant support facility (although something less than an Okinawan or Guam-type base). It is widely believed in official Washington that the surprise decision was made "over breakfast" between Secretaries Henry Kissinger and James Schlesinger.[26] A supplementary appropriation bill was rushed to Congress, all out staffing was begun within the bureaucracy, and littoral states were hastily consulted and/or notified. In brief, Diego was to be expanded, and *then* the expansion would be properly justified in and out of the U.S. government.

The sudden unexpected expansion of Diego Garcia caused as much difficulty for the Administration as the idea of expansion itself. The announcement came during a period of great suspicion over executive secretiveness and stealth, and generated enormous opposition within Congress, the press, and to a lesser extent, the bureaucracy.

Gradually, a full-fledged political battle began to shape up. Some ambassadors to littoral states expressed their strong private dismay at the way in which the Diego Garcia expansion program was being handled; Congress took testimony from a number of well-informed critics of Diego, and even the C.I.A. seemed to be contradicting Administration and Navy estimates

25. See the testimony of Admiral Zumwalt, *op. cit.*, pp. 129 ff.
26. There are various apocryphal stories circulating among the reasonably well-informed. One version has Diego Garcia 'traded" by Kissinger for DOD support on the SALT talks; another has it that the Secretary of State thought the island was so unimportant that he "gave" it to the Navy. Both interpretations are possible and not incompatible. If true, the most important aspect of these perceptions is that the decision to expand did come from the very top of the bureaucracy and was only then staffed out in the State Department.

of the degree of threat from the Soviet Union in the Indian
Ocean.[27] A number of supporters of an expanded Diego
Garcia facility, within and out of the Government, expressed
public and private reservations over the Navy's actual intentions, fearing a bloated, vulnerable, and costly base which in
turn would be used to justify additional aircraft carriers,
possiblytrapping an undue portion of the American fleet on the
wrong side of the Suez Canal.

At the time of writing funds for the expansion of Diego
Garcia remain bottled up in Congress, despite direct and
public Presidential support for what has now become a "base".
It is clear that an initial attempt to rush expansion only led to
greater Congressional and public skepticism, which in turn has
finally brought about a public and bureaucratic debate over
the strategic utility of Diego Garcia.

V. Conclusions

A comparison of the three decisions we have described in
this report leads to several conclusions about foreign policy
decision-making.

The locus of decision was different in each case. In 1967 it
was at the working level of the State Department, the one-time
exception was essentially a Presidential command, and the
Diego Garcia expansion decision was taken at the Secretarial
level. Thus, one came from the "bottom up" and two from the
"top down". The latter two decisions were staffed-out only
after the basic decision was made.

Other patterns emerge : the two arms assistance decisions
were characterized by very heavy foreign governmental input,
and strong representational roles on the part of the U.S.
ambassadors to India and especially Pakistan. Diego Garcia
has had very little foreign input, except in the negative sense

---

27. The testimony of the Director of the C.I.A. lent some support to
those who were opposed to Diego Garcia. William Colby noted
three times in that testimony that it was the C.I.A.'s judgment that
an increase in the U.S. presence in the Indian Ocean region would
lead to an increase in the Soviet force levels. However, he did also
state that should the U.S. do nothing, Soviet force levels would
gradually increase anyway. His testimony before the Subcommittee
on Military Construction (Senate) is reprinted in the *Congressional
Record* of August 1, 1974.

that several littoral countries oppose an enhanced American presence in the Indian Ocean. Littoral sentiment has been heavily discounted by most participants in the decision-making process, unlike the two arms assistance decisions, when it was one of the main factors.

Another difference between the decisions has been the role of the Pentagon. As we have argued above, the U.S. military had begun to lose interest in South Asia by 1965 because of local and global developments. While simple program interest and inertia led them to urge a continuation of *some* military relationship with India and Pakistan, no single service or branch was willing to mount a defense within the U.S. bureaucracy on behalf of MAAG or USMSMI programs. However, Diego Garcia had been a pet project of the Navy for a number of years and it had assiduously built up support among the other two services as well as its traditional supporters in Congress and among the public.

Finally, the public and Congress have played quite different roles in the three decisions. Again, the major contrast is between Diego and the two arms assistance decisions. Diego has become a minor cause celebre, and was even the subject of a question at President Ford's first press conference ; hardly any politician or journalist has taken a substantial interest in arms assistance to South Asia (except during the Bangladesh crisis). For Diego, the Navy mobilized its entire Congressional and public-relations lobby ; arms assistance was simply not a matter of much public interest in the U.S. in either 1967 or 1970. At the very most a few scholars expressed their concern publicly but with no perceptible impact. Also, a few arms manufacturers lobbied the Pentagon and the State Department to have various restrictions relaxed or eliminated. But these companies are probably more interested in selling equipment and weapons to India (the larger market) than Pakistan, and have had no substantial impact on policy-making.

As we have indicated, *evaluation* of the three decisions in this case study presents certain problems and is strongly affected by one's stance or perspective. From the viewpoint of American relations with South Asia as a *region* the original 1967 arms assistance cut-off made considerable sense and the subsequent

one-time exception of 1970 was calamitous. It further strained
relations with India without substantially aiding Pakistan and
kept alive the hope in both countries that the U.S. might once
again enter into a permanent and arms assistance relationship
on the Subcontinent.

But from a so-called "global" perspective a different calculation was made by Kissinger and Nixon. Did not the enormous gain of better U.S.-Chinese relations (including the effect
of this on U.S.-Soviet relations) outweigh the temporary and
relatively trivial setback to U.S.-Indian relations? When one
adds the gains the U.S. obtained in Pakistan itself, the impact
of this on Iran and the Middle East, *and* the success of the
China trip, it would seem to outweigh the losses suffered in
U.S.-Indian relations. Is not India, in the global scheme of
things, a marginal factor anyway? Put in these terms the one-
time exception was a sound decision as was U.S. policy in
Bangladesh.

However, this *ex post facto* rationalization is no more
complete than a purely regional perspective. Had a broader
circle of participants been involved in the actual policy decisions
during the 1970-71 period it is quite probable that a way could
have been found to minimize the harmful impact on U.S.-
Indian relations and still bring off the China visit. The fundamental *organizational* implication of our study of U.S. strategic
and military policy in South Asia pertains to the form and
quality of coordination of that policy with other, allegedly
more important areas. Are bilateral ties ("good" relations
with India and Pakistan) to be consistently sacrificed to extra-
regional considerations? If not, who is to determine when
relations with South Asian policy must suffer, when an extra-
regional interest must give way, or whether regional and
global policies can be integrated and coordinated? One solution would be to insist upon more interregional transfers of
personnel and periodic consultation between relevant Country
Directors (most urgently, the India, China, and Soviet CD's).
But this is obviously not enough. Additionally, the Assistant
Secretaries might consult more frequently with each other on
issues which cut across their geographic boundaries. The
Bureau of Political Military Affairs and the Munitions Control
Board cannot bring about such coordination in military and

arms assistance matters because they lack day-to-day contact
with the regions. Ultimately, however, even this is not enough
in a situation where policy is made at the very top of the
hierarchy, as in the one-time exception and Diego Garcia cases.
The failures in these decisions were not of organizational
structure but of leadership, and of a leadership which felt
comfortable with an organizational structure which could be
manipulated to permit the intermittent shutting off of
influence and participation of some concerned actors.

On the other hand, if one takes the view that U.S.-South
Asian relations should be permanently subordinated to some
global vision then the present structure *is* perfectly adequate.
It provides for extraordinary regional expertise without
regional influence within the State Department. South Asia
claims only half of an Assistant Secretary's responsibilities
(and probably the lesser half). American interests in South
Asia receive attention at higher levels, but relatively little
advocacy. Yet one must ask whether the present organization
reflects a realistic judgment of the region's importance. It does
if one gives overwhelming weight to security and strategic concerns and is prepared to perpetually subordinate humanitarian,
developmental, and certain libertarian and ideological interests.
A kind of Seeley's Law appears to operate in these matters at
least in recent years : the U.S. will eagerly trade off "soft"
long-term interests, for which there is a small and weak
Washington constituency, for "hard" and short-term military
and global gains which may have a tremendous political and
domestic payoff. The tragedy does not lie in the fact that
government seeks such visible tangible gains, but that it does
so little to reconcile them with other, longer run interests.

Our case study shows that such a reconciliation is possible.
The 1967 revision of arms assistance policy was the result of
a confluence of favorable forces, and any organizational
reform should be directed towards creating such a situation.
In that case relatively little attention was paid to global
military or strategic considerations: U.S.-regional relationships
had high priority. It was what I have elsewhere termed a strategy of bilateral or balanced relations, in which South Asia
would not be treated as a dependent variable vis-a-vis the rest

of the world.[28] That decision did not please the states of the Subcontinent, but it did establish the basis for a realistic relationship between the U.S., India, and Pakistan by removing a terrible impediment to normal economic, political, and cultural ties. Had regional factors been given at least as great a weight in policy as global factors in formulating American policy in South Asia from 1969 onward, it is not likely that the U.S. would again be the object of military presure from both Pakistan and India—the former pleading for another dose of weapons, the latter threatening to develop nuclear arms. It may well turn out that the gains of 1970-71 will be paid for during the rest of the decade.

28. Stephen P. Cohen, "U.S. Policy in South Asia", unpublished memorandum, Center for Asian Studies, University of Illinois at Urbana, June 15, 1972. See also William Bundy, *op. cit.* and William Barnds, *India, Pakistan, and the Great Powers* (New York : Praeger. 1972).

CASE STUDIES :
I. DIPLOMATIC-STRATEGIC

B. After The "Tilt" : The Making Of [U.S. Foreign Policy Towards Pakistan, 1972-1974[1]]

Gerald A. Heeger

> The essence of ultimate decision remains impenetrable to the observer—often, indeed, to the decider himself.
>
> —*John F. Kennedy*

Within the past few years there has been a spate of books about government decision-making in general and about that process in the creation of foreign policy in particular.[2] As one scholar has characterized the principal paradigm of these studies : "The decisions and actions of governments are intra-national political resultants : *resultants* in the sense that what happens is not chosen as a solution to a problem but rather results from compromise, conflict, and confusion of officials with diverse interests and unequal influence; *political* in the sense that the activity from which decisions and actions emerge

1. Data for this study were collected, in part, through interviews conducted at the Department of State, June-September, 1974.
2. See, for example, Roger Hilsman, "The Foreign Policy Consensus", *Journal of Conflict Resolution*, (December, 1959), 361-382; Richard C. Snyder, H.W. Bruck, and Burton Sapin, *Foreign Policy Decision-Making* (Glencoe, III. : Free Press of Glencoe, 1962); Karl Deutsch "Problem Solving : The Behavioral Approach", in Arthur S. Hoffman, ed., *International Communication and the New Diplomacy* (Bloomington : Indiana University Press; 1968); Glenn D. Paige, *The Korean Decision* (New York : The Free Press, 1968); Graham T. Allison, *The Essence of Decision* (Boston : Little, Brown and Co., 1971).

is best characterized as bargaining along regularized channels among individualized members of government".[3]

This "governmental politics" paradigm has proved to be an extremely useful means of comprehending foreign policy-making, and it will be utilized, to some degree, in this study as well. Yet the paradigm has its costs. Studies utilizing it often succumb to a kind of intellectual "tunnel vision". Viewed as resultants, as the end-points of a process, government decisions assume an autonomy from one another that does not exist in reality. Often ignored is the role which one decision—in terms of the way in which that decision was made as well as its content—can play in shaping the policy-making environment in which future decisions are to be made.

This is no small point. Placed in the context of foreign policy decision-making, it raises a multitude of questions concerning the relationship between the top-most and the lower levels of the foreign affairs bureaucracy. To what degree, for example, do policy outcomes influence the selection of information subsequently provided to decision-makers by middle level bureaucrats ? Is it true that bureaucracy is characterized solely by its inertia, its lack of response to innovative direction; or, rather, are particular bureaus and offices able to recast their interests and perceptions in terms of new goals and directives from the top ? If such "coherence" can be achieved, can it go too far, yielding a policy process which is increasingly blind to policy options ?

This study is about such problems. Concentrating on a period in American-Pakistani relations which follows a major crisis and an active Presidential involvement in the making of policy towards Pakistan, it examines the relationship between earlier Presidential decisions and subsequent policy made by middle level State Department bureaucrats. More specifically, it suggests that the enigmatic basis of Presidential decisions and the isolation of regional bureau personnel from "global" policy making have functioned to restructure perceptions of South Asia and Pakistan on the part of the "working level" State Department officials primarily concerned with those areas. Such a "restructuring" may give the President and his advisors greater control over the foreign policy-making process. It may

3. Allison, *op. cit.*, p. 162.

also, however, limit information made available to high-level decision-makers and serve to mute the clear policy choices essential to the creation of a rational foreign policy.

Shaping the Policy-Making Environment : The President, the State Department and South Asia, 1969-1971

The President

It would be less than useful to attempt a detailed assessment of the presidential role—both potential and actual—in the formulation of American foreign policy in South Asia. Such a study demands volumes, not paragraphs. On the whole, however, it is possible to say that presidential involvement in the making of South Asia policy has been intermittent and crisis-oriented. This has traditionally posed problems for the regional bureaucracy concerned with South Asia: for, Presidents have tended to intervene into the policy-making process with seemingly little regard for coordinating their "crisis" policies with previously existing short and long-term goals.

In spite of Richard Nixon's well-known concern for rationalizing both the foreign policy machinery and the presidential role in that machinery, it does not appear—at least insofar as South Asia is concerned—that his presidency varied from this pattern of intermittent involvement. In 1970, for example, it was largely at the President's instigation that a "one time exception" sale of "lethal" military equipment was made to Pakistan. Although the sale was officially justified as an attempt to counter Pakistan's growing dependence on China for military supplies, it had apparently been pressed for by the President with little regard for its possible "fit" into ongoing South Asia policy. As it was, the maneuver proved too limited to accomplish its official goal but sufficient to disrupt the effort (since 1966-1967) to wean Pakistan gradually away from the United States so as to strengthen U.S. ties with India.

Events surrounding the emergence of Bangladesh provide, of course, the most graphic examples of the nature and impact of intermittent Presidential involvement in South Asia. It was largely because of the President's intervention that the United States initially assumed its "non-condemnatory" policy vis-a-vis Pakistan's crackdown on Bengali dissidents, that a more antagonistic policy towards India was articulated, and, when war between India and Pakistan came, that a "tilt in favor of Pakistan" was attempted. Again, ongoing policies were radically affected.

More important—at least insofar as the policy-making process is concerned—was the extremely episodic and secretive nature of Presidential involvement. It gave no indication to the foreign affairs bureaucracy of the exact interests of the President. This posed serious problems for the bureaucracy. It is one thing to make policy when the President's positions are known, i.e., as Morton Halperin has noted :

. . . Obviously, the deeper the President involves himself in operations, the more influence he will have over what is being done. In part, this is simply because he is able to do more of it himself, but also the President, by devoting a substantial amount of time to an issue, makes it clear to his subordinates that it is something that he cares a great deal about. Officials recognize that to fight the President on such an issue is likely to cost them dearly in terms of their relation to the President.[4]

It is quite something else when the "degree of presidential involvement" is less than clear. During the crisis, President Nixon was explicit about Pakistan's being "something that he cares a great deal about". Yet, the reasons for that concern and, therefore, an assessment as to whether those reasons were salient in a radically altered South Asia remained elusive—at least at the lower levels of the bureaucracy. As one official commented : "The problem was not the fact that policy was made in response to a crisis. South Asia policy is generally a crisis-to-crisis thing. The problem was that these particular policies did not really provide any direction for the period following the war".

The Nixon Foreign Policy System and the Bureau for Near Eastern and South Asian Affairs
Throughout the 1971 crisis in South Asia, the regional

---

4. Morton Halperin, *Bureaucratic Politics and Foreign Policy* (Washington, D.C. : The Brookings Institution, 1974), p. 289.

bureau within the State Department closest to the crisis, the Bureau for Near Eastern and South Asian Affairs, appears to have played a less than consequential role in the actual policy-making process. That role was less the result of the crisis itself than of the whole structure of the foreign policy process in existence at that time. As I. M. Destler has suggested in his study of Presidential-State Department relations, the initial Nixon foreign policy system (and the one largely intact when the South Asia crisis occurred) was one of leaving the State Department and building above it.[5] The National Security Council and, more particularly, the National Security Council staff and its chief, Henry Kissinger, comprised the focal point of the policy-making system. As was the case with policy analysis in general, regional affairs were brought into the policy process not through the standard department and bureau lines, but rather through a variety of NSC-centered committees. Destler summarized the system thusly :

> To support the NSC and strengthen central management of foreign policy issues, a network of general inter-agency committees was established. The Johnson Administration's IRG's were re-named IG's (Interdepartmental Groups,) with . . . State's Assistant Secretaries remaining as Chairmen . . . these State-chaired groups reported . . . to the Kissinger-chaired NSC Review Group . . . resolving one serious problem in the Johnson system—its lack of any strong link to the Presidency. Another change was that the main role of the regional groups was not operational coordination, as it was intended to be under Johnson, but overseeing the preparation of NSC policy papers. These were then examined by the Review Group . . . After appropriate revision, the most important papers were presented to the President and the National Security Council.[6]

As Alexander George has noted, the Nixon-Kissinger-NSC-focused system had the advantage of involving more

5. I.M. Destler, *Presidents, Bureaucrats, and Foreign Policy* (Princeton : Princeton University Press, 1972), p. 132.
6. *Ibid.*, pp. 121-122.

personnel at the working-levels of the bureaucracy more systematically in preparatory stages of the policy-making process than was the case in earlier administrations.[7] A number of South Asia bureau personnel, for example, participated in the creation of the National Security Study Memoranda on South Asia. On the other hand, as George has also noted, the NSC-focused system also served to weaken the bureaus and bureau heads in their roles as policy advocates and advisors.[8] Instead of bureaus functioning to support the involvement of their senior staff members and heads in the final stages of the policy-making process, near or at the locus of decision-making, the input of bureau expertise was primarily restricted to the earliest stages of that process. From there it was distilled into a limited number of policy options by the NSC committees chaired by Dr. Kissinger and, through him, presented to the President. The Assistant Secretaries, for example, appear to have had only limited participation in the policy process. Their principal access was to the Secretary of State and not to the White House; and even where they did function within the NSC-system, their role was limited. The Interdepartmental Groups which they headed functioned to coordinate the NSSMs assigned to them but as little else. Such committees could not serve as platforms for the Assistant Secretaries on critical policy issues simply because the "action", the focus of decision-making, lay elsewhere, in the proliferation of committees chaired by Kissinger himself.[9]

The 1971 South Asia crisis brought these discontinuities in the policy process to the fore. With no systematic access to critical decision levels on a "crisis" basis, the personnel of the Bureau of Near Eastern and South Asian Affairs was pervaded by a strong sense of isolation from the policies that were being produced. To varying degrees, all of the FSO's working in the

7. Alexander L. George, "The Case of Multiple Advocacy in Making Foreign Policy", *American Political Science Review* LXVI, 3 (1972), p. 754.

8. *Ibid.*

9. These committees included the Under Secretary-level Washington Special Action Group (WSAG), established to oversee crisis management, and the Defense Program Review Committee as well as more specialized groups such as the "Forty Committee" which supervised covert intelligence operations.

South Asia section of the bureau were critical of the reluctance of the United States to pressure the Pakistani government against further action against the Bengali dissidence.

This situation worsened as the "tilt" became more formal. When an "official" rationale for the policy was given—that India had launched its attack despite the fact that the United States was on the verge of success in bringing about negotiations —it was almost immediately rejected throughout the Bureau. March to December, 1971, to quote one respondent, was "an orgy of second-guessing in the Bureau as those of us here at the time sought some rationale for the South Asia policy. I have never had the feeling of isolation from the logic of a policy as bad as then". This isolation was to continue to be a major characteristic of the South Asia policy-making process.

The Making of United States Policy Towards Pakistan, 1972-1974

If nothing else, the events of 1971 made obvious the limits of actual American interests in South Asia. The loss of a war by an ally and the animosity between the United States and India were irritants; yet, they were irritants which seemed to have no long-term consequences for the United States. Accordingly, the absence of any immediate American interests of any significance served as a kind of base line for American policy, giving the United States considerable freedom to formulate its policy towards the countries of South Asia on the basis of its conception of a desirable international order.

Yet, policy is seldom generated on the basis of such "cosmic" considerations. There are real, more mundane issues which demand a response on the part of policy-makers, and the linkages between such mundane problems and "cosmic", "globalist" considerations are seldom clear. Nor do "globalist" considerations always easily point to a single best policy.

It is in terms of these problems that, after 1971, difficulties arose in the American foreign policy-making process regarding South Asia in general and Pakistan in particular. On the one hand, a consensus rather quickly emerged among policy-makers as to the role of South Asian countries in the international order and as to specific policies vis-a-vis those countries. On the other hand, the continuing isolation of the regional bureau from the goals of the larger foreign policy structure sought by the President resulted in ambiguity as to the extent of the linkage between American policy towards Pakistan and American policy elsewhere, particularly towards China. Thus the policy-making process became an extremely limited one in terms of the kinds of options it could consider.

The end of the Indo-Pakistani war presented the United States with sharply defined limits in terms of further aid to Pakistan. In the first place, the decisiveness of Pakistan's defeat was visible to all. If President Nixon had any aspirations to continue the "tilt"—and there is no evidence of this—India's overwhelming victory foreclosed that option. There was no realistic way that the ratio of power on the subcontinent could be returned to its pre-1971 status. President Nixon, himself, rather quickly acknowledged India's regional dominance :

> We are prepared for a serious dialogue with India on the future of our relations . . . . our political as well as our economic relationship will be the subject of our dialogue. If India has an interest in maintaining balanced relationships with all major powers, we are prepared to respond constructively. Of interest to us also will be the posture that South Asia's most powerful country now adopts towards its neighbors on the subcontinent.[10]

Secondly, Congress' vociferous reaction to the "tilt", set alongside its growing unwillingness to countenance military assistance programs which seemed only to feed local wars, served as a continuing restraint on the options available to policy-makers. A GAO report in February, 1972, confirming the shipment of $4 million in military equipment to Pakistan after March 25, 1971, the alleged cut-off date for such shipments, and the Administration's admission that Jordan had transferred American-supplied jet aircraft to Pakistan during the war (a violation of the Foreign Assistance Act) renewed Congressional resistance to any possible resumption of military supplies to Pakistan.

10. Richard M. Nixon, *United States Foreign Policy for the 1970's : A Report to the Congress*, 1972 (Washington, D.C. : Government Printing Office, 1972).

What emerged in the context of these constraints was a rather broadly shared view of South Asia within the regional bureau, not unlike that which had been characteristic of the bureau in the late 1960's, i.e., that: (1) Pakistan could no longer aspire to superiority or even to parity vis-a-vis India in terms of military capability; (2) South Asia was an area of low priority for the United States except to the degree that affairs within the subcontinent were seen to impinge upon American relations with other regions and, especially, with other great powers; (3) Pakistan could remain a concern for the United States not only because it was an ally but also because its further fragmentation could jeopardize stability on the subcontinent and, more importantly, elsewhere in Asia and in the Middle East.[11] Policy was formulated on the basis of this consensus, "catalyzed", so to speak, by Bureau personnel but often "cued" in terms of timing by the highest levels of the foreign affairs bureaucracy and the President.

Economic assistance to Pakistan is illustrative of this process. The war's end found substantial agreement within the Bureau that economic assistance programs throughout the subcontinent should be restarted as quickly as possible. Insofar as Pakistan was concerned, it was felt that an early start of economic aid would emphasize to Pakistan, as one State Department official commented, "that economic and food assistance was where the American emphasis was and should be". Proposals to this effect were quickly cleared with the senior levels of the Department and, apparently, with Kissinger. Despite this consensus, however, the resumption of aid to Pakistan—or to any other South Asian country—seems to have awaited Presidential "cue". Aid to Pakistan was rather quickly resumed, following a statement by the President that Pakistan had returned to normal and that, as a result, aid to Pakistan was no longer subject to congressional restriction. Presidential reluctance to "cue" similar policies, it might be added, appears

11. These were not formal policy guidelines but, rather, were common "themes" which have tended to recur in assessments made by State Department officials in their discussions of South Asia. Stephen Cohen, in another study prepared for the "organization of complexity" project, also discusses these "themes". See his "South Asia and United States Military Policy".

to have been primarily responsible for the initial American hesitation to extend a systematic economic assistance program to Bangladesh and to renew suspended economic assistance programs to India. (The latter were not restored until March, 1973.)

White House "cues" were not always so clear, however. This was especially the case with the issue of renewed military assistance to Pakistan. As was the case with the economic assistance issue, a consensus as to the desired direction of American policy seems to have been easily obtained within the Bureau itself. The United States, it was generally agreed, had no real role to play in an arms race in South Asia, especially as an arms supplier to Pakistan. Several things, however, seemed to deter officials within the Bureau from pressing for a decision on the issue. First, it was generally recognized that any decision—for or against further arms sales to Pakistan—would require a release of that equipment already owned by Pakistan but not transported there because of a total embargo placed into effect at the outbreak of the 1971 war. Such a transfer, especially in the light of the GAO revelations about previous arms shipments to Pakistan, threatened to seriously inflame Congressional tempers. Second, the position of President Nixon and Dr. Kissinger was still ambiguous. Pakistan remained a formal ally, and the President had publicly expressed his continuing close friendship with that country. Technically, the Presidential pronouncement of a "return to normal conditions" in Pakistan cleared the way for renewed military as well as economic assistance. Yet, the White House had made no effort to move the State Department in that direction. In general, it evinced little or no visible concern to re-evaluate American arms policy in the subcontinent. No systematic NSC study to that effect, for example, was undertaken. In this context, despite a general consensus on the appropriate policy, the issue was simply postponed by the bureau.

However, the question of renewed military sales to Pakistan continued, in a less than critical way, to plague the State Department throughout 1972. It hampered not only American efforts to get Pakistan to focus on its economic needs, but also the Department's efforts to re-establish sound ties with the Indians. So long as the potential of renewed arms assistance to Pakistan existed Indo-American relations remained troubled. There were more mundane problems as well. Logistical problems caused by the need to store and maintain the embargoed Pakistani-owned equipment, for example, were becoming irritants. In any case, by early 1973, it appears that there was general agreement at all levels that a decision on an arms policy for South Asia could not be indefinitely postponed, that some decision had to be made. The means by which White House acceptance of this proposition was communicated to the Bureau remains obscure. That such communication did occur is apparent; according to officials interviewed, there was little doubt as to the White House view by this time.

A set of proposals was formulated within the Bureau and rather quickly translated into policy. The decision provided that : (1) shipment of Pakistan would be allowed for $1.1 million in military equipment previously ordered but barred from shipment by the total embargo imposed in 1971; (2) the "total" embargo of 1971 would be relaxed while reaffirming the 1967 policy decision to limit military sales to non-lethal items and spare parts for equipment previously supplied; (3) delivery to Pakistan would be permitted for the 300 armored personnel carriers contracted for during a "one-time exception" sale in October, 1970.[12] Coupled with this decision were announcements that $87 million in economic aid previously suspended was being restored to India, and that India would be allowed to complete the purchase of $19 million in communications equipment for an air defense system.

It was in terms of "global" foreign policy—of South Asia's linkage to the major themes of American foreign policy—that the isolation between the regional bureau and the White House (and Dr. Kissinger) was most acute. I.M. Destler has commented that :

The Nixon NSC system had been partially designed and totally explained as a means of enhancing the quality and

12. From the testimony of James Noyes, Deputy Assistant Secretary of Defense for Near Eastern, African, and South Asian Affairs, House Foreign Relations Committee, Subcommittee on Near East and South Asia, "United States Interests In and Policies Toward South Asia", (Washington, D.C. : Government Printing Office, 1973), p. 88.

responsiveness of the bureaucracy's contribution to foreign-policy decision-making. But it became increasingly, in practice, a vehicle for excluding or diverting the bureaucracy while Nixon and Kissinger did the "real" business on their own. The primary targets of attention were China, Russia, and Vietnam. Kissinger handled the most critical negotiations personally, even secretively, keeping the rest of the U.S. bureaucracy in the dark. His one client was the President.... [13]

The problem for the regional bureaucracy at that time was to assess correctly to what degree, if any, South Asia related to the "primary targets of attention". The relative isolation of the bureau from systematic discussion on these issues made such an assessment, at best, extremely difficult. The lack of concrete data on this subject makes any discussion necessarily intuitive. Yet, if interviews within the bureau are any indication, it would seem that the isolation of the regional bureau from the rationale of the White House's actions during the 1971 South Asia crisis resulted—especially in 1972 and early 1973—in a tendency among the regional bureaucracy to over-stress the role of China in South Asia, particularly as a factor in U.S. policy towards Pakistan. Rather than focusing on Pakistani interests and activities in South Asia and suggesting appropriate policy responses, these functionaries appear, to an increasing degree, to have focused on their interpretation of Chinese interests as the crucial variable in determining American policy towards Pakistan. Chinese interests were (and to a considerable extent are) assumed to have been explicitly defined to the White House; and policy options considered within the Bureau tended to reflect that assumption. Bewilderment as to the rationale for American actions in South Asia during 1971 was replaced by a widespread conviction that those actions were part of a general White House effort to enhance American relations with the People's Republic of China.

Presidential "cues" as to the linkage between American South Asia policy and its China policy were certainly visible.

13. I.M. Destler, "The Nixon System: a further look", *Foreign Service Journal*, February, 1974, p. 10.

In his discussion of the South Asia crisis in the 1972 foreign policy report to the Congress, President Nixon gave particular emphasis to the impact that the events in South Asia might have for China and, indirectly, for Chinese-American rapprochement :

> . . . it was our view that the war in South Asia was bound to have serious implications for the evolution of the policy of the People's Republic of China. That country's attitude toward the global system was certain to be profoundly influenced by its assessment of the principles by which this system was governed—whether force and threat ruled or whether restraint was the international standard.[14]

The communique issued at the end of President Nixon's visit to China also figured here. Although the communique revealed significant differences in the degree of support expressed for Pakistan by the United States and China, it also revealed significant congruence of American and Chinese interests in the subcontinent. Yet none of these "cues" offered any guidance as to specific policies or positions which might be desired by the White House. This lack of consultation perpetuated the "second guessing" which became so characteristic of the regional bureaus during the 1971 crisis.

The effect that this stress on China's role in South Asia had on actual policy decisions is difficult to judge—largely because it seems to have influenced the selection of information by policy-makers rather than policy choices directly. That is to say, the emphasis placed on China's role in Pakistan appears to have further reduced the salience of local and regional issues which cannot be linked to China or one of the other great powers. Information on local and regional issues, while circulated at all levels, appears to have been given relatively little weight. Complaints were made not only that the present system was too centralized, that too many issues required clearance at the senior-most decision-making levels, but also that their assessments of local and regional problems, which they believed had relevance for American policy, did not always get a proper review. Isolation and the possible misconceptions

14. Nixon, *op. cit.*

spawned in that isolation served to limit the information brought into the policy-making process.

Organization and Policy : An Assessment

It would not be new or startling to state that, under Henry Kissinger, presidential-level involvement in and control of foreign policy formation and implementation substantially increased. Operating within a policy framework which allowed a high degree of discretionary presidential action, the President and Henry Kissinger were able to impose a significant degree of coherence on American foreign policy. This was particularly true of American foreign policy actions directed at the great powers, which comprised the principal focus of the Nixon-Kissinger foreign policy structure. Here the "Nixon-Kissinger diplomacy at the top" was able to alter significantly the direction of American foreign policy and to secure major bilateral agreements.

The Nixon-Kissinger system has, however, demonstrated some limitations. One particular limitation has been its relatively closed character, its inability to integrate the foreign affairs bureaucracy into the policy-making process. This, in itself, would not be a criticism if the Nixon-Kissinger system had not needed such a bureaucracy. This was not the case, however, for the range of problems which could be dealt with within the framework of personal diplomacy was, in fact, very narrow. Although this was true even for American relations with the major world powers, where the breadth and complexity of relations required extensive staff support, it was particularly true of American relations with countries and areas which were viewed as having relatively low priority in the American foreign policy structure. The emphasis placed by the White House on the great powers meant that the bureaucracy, more specifically the regional bureaucracy, would have to be the focus of policy-making for these countries.

Yet, the peculiar kind of centralization in the Nixon-Kissinger policy-making system frustrated this very possibility. The NSC-focused foreign policy system organized by Nixon and Kissinger, as was noted earlier, yielded a policy structure in which assessments by the particular offices and bureaus most concerned with a problem were screened through the NSC system. The particular offices and bureaus were not linked directly to any "arena" whereby their data and assessments could be presented undistilled to the President. As Alexander George has noted :

> ... While providing orderly procedures for widespread participation of foreign policy specialists in the departments and agencies in the "search" and "evaluation" phases, the present NSC system restricts the process of "choice", and not merely the final decision to the President. Those few advisors who participate in the final discussions before he makes his choice of policy all largely depend on the same body of distilled analysis of options that has emerged from the centralized, "advocate-free" search and evaluation system.[15]

Thus what emerged was not so much an orderly presentation of options, as President Nixon was seeking when he organized the system, but an ignorance of options. The President and his Adviser for National Security Affairs seem to have been isolated from the input of the regional bureaus in the State Department, at least insofar as South Asia was concerned. While the expertise of individual bureau personnel was sought in the formulation of the NSSMs, neither their individual points of view nor the bureau's point of view were really considered during the 1971 crisis.

Such isolation had consequences not only for the top levels of decision-making but for the middle levels as well. Isolation of the latter from anything but the most preparatory stages of the decision-making process made it difficult for bureau personnel to comprehend the basis for the policy choices made. Decisions assumed the character of "lightning bolts" from above, mysterious in substance and inexplicable in cause. Several things seem to have happened in this context insofar as the making of South Asia policy was concerned. First, the regional bureau, unable to assess the White House's perspective on South Asia, was extremely reluctant to assume the initiative for making specific policies. There was a regional bureau view of American policy in South Asia. This was not, however,

15. George, *op. cit.*, p. 755.

translated into policy unless Presidential "cues" were clearly given. In the absence of such cues, given the focus of the Nixon-Kissinger system on other areas and issues, there was really no "South Asia" or "Pakistan" policy. Second, the absence of an apparent rationale for the 1971 decisions at the top stimulated a search for one in the middle level of the bureaucracy. The rationale which "working level" officials ultimately assumed to be the basis of policy and which they, in turn, adopted as the premise of their policy assessments may have been wholly erroneous. The continuing isolation of those officials from the final stages of the decision-making process would only perpetuate the possibility of error.

The secretiveness with which foreign policy was conducted during this period had much to do with this problem of isolation on the part of the regional bureaucracy. Henry Kissinger has been quoted as saying, "No foreign policy—no matter how ingenious—has any chance of success if it is born in the minds of a few and carried in the hearts of none". Despite this admirable sentiment, secrecy has been a much discussed characteristic of the Nixon administration and its foreign policy—not only secrecy between the Government and the people but also secrecy within the Government itself.

In their recent study of Kissinger, Marvin and Bernard Kalb repeatedly relate how Dr. Kissinger has misjudged or misevaluated other Governments' positions despite the fact that more realistic assessments were available to him elsewhere in the bureaucracy.[16] Secrecy had a no less grave effect on the rest of the bureaucracy, intensifying, in particular, the isolation of the "working level" officials. Insofar as Pakistan policy was concerned, the secretiveness surrounding the decisions during the 1971 crisis and the restructuring of the United States' policy toward China served only to accentuate the gap between the geographic bureau and the President and his chief foreign policy advisor. The continuing secrecy of China policy placed it outside of the standard "clearance" procedure whereby Desk Officers consult with their counterparts in other bureaus and departments on issues of mutual concern. Lacking this, the

16. Marvin Kalb and Bernard Kalb, *Kissinger* (Boston : Little, Brown and Co., 1974).

actual "weight" of a particular variable, e.g., China's interest in South Asia, could be wholly misperceived.

Set against the background of a Nixon-Kissinger "world-view" which minimized the role of "third world" states such as those in South Asia and which tended to consider those countries only in terms of their linkages to major powers, organization and secrecy telescoped to inhibit the ability of those middle-level bureaucrats responsible for assessing changing local and regional circumstances and their possible impact on U.S. interests from doing just that.[17] The premises of the Nixon-Kissinger "world-view" were challenged less and less by the people best equipped to make such challenges—the regional bureaucracy. What ensued as a result was less policy than self-fulfilling prophecy.

Correcting the problems discussed here requires both organizational and intellectual changes. So far as the first is concerned, the issue is not so much one of a "White House-focused" system as opposed to a "strengthened State Department" as it appears to be one of developing ways in which options not be so finely distilled before they reach the apex of the decision-making process. Ironically, President Nixon himself expressed this point most succinctly in his first "U.S. Foreign Policy for the 1970's" address :

> The new NSC system is designed to make certain that clear policy choices reach the top, so that various positions can be fully debated in the meeting of the Council. Differences of view are identified and defended, rather than muted or buried. I refuse to be confronted by a bureaucratic consensus that leaves me no options but acceptance or rejection

17. On the Nixon Doctrine, which was first discussed by President Nixon during his Guam press conference on November 3, 1969, see Richard M. Nixon, *U.S. Foreign Policy for the 1970's : A Report to the Congress*, 1971 (Washington : Government Printing Office, 1971); and President Nixon's Kansas city speech on July 6, 1971, *Department of State Bulletin* (July 26, 1971). The best systematic critique of the Doctrine and its practical implications can be found in Robert E. Osgood, et al., *Retreat From Empire* ? (Baltimore : The Johns Hopkins Press, 1972).

and that gives me no way of knowing what alternatives exist.[18]

Alexander George has suggested that "the executive would be in a position to make better decisions if multiple centers of analysis and stronger staffs were available to senior departmental officials who serve as advisers to the President in the final stages of foreign policy decisions".[19] It would seem that this recommendation is a useful one. Regional bureaus must be strengthened and, more importantly, the individuals who head them must be participants in the decisive stages of policy process.

Intellectual changes are more difficult to obtain. The tendency of the "big-power" balance of power to occupy almost completely the focus of American foreign policy demands considerable re-evaluation. In the absence of such a re-evaluation, an organizational framework which constantly makes senior policy-makers aware of inputs ignored by their general intellectual paradigm is all the more necessary.

18. Richard M. Nixon, *United States Foreign Policy for the 1970's : A Report to the Congress*, 1970 (Washington, D.C. : Government Printing Office, 1970).
19. George, *op. cit.*, p. 754.

CASE STUDIES :
I. DIPLOMATIC-STRATEGIC

C. The Breakup of Pakistan

Philip Oldenburg

Introduction
Chronology

The crisis of the breakup of Pakistan can be divided, in terms of U.S. participation, into roughly four major phases. The first began with the Pakistan army crackdown in the East Wing of Pakistan on the night of March 25/26, 1971.[1] This followed a three week period of civil disobedience and the exercise of *de facto* governmental power by the Awami League led by Sheikh Mujibur Rahman. The Awami League had won an overwhelming victory in the December 1970 election for the Constituent Assembly, the climax of a movement toward greater autonomy for East Pakistan which began in 1954 or perhaps even earlier. The drive for autonomy was fueled by the economic, political and bureaucratic discrimination against East Bengal by the West Pakistan-dominated central government, exacerbated by the West Pakistani belief (held particularly by the Punjabi-dominated military) that Bengalis were culturally and racially inferior.

The crackdown, in which Sheikh Mujib was captured and thousands of Bengalis were killed—students, Hindus, and

1. All dates with no year given are from 1971. The most readily available detailed chronology for the 1971 crisis can be found under the heading "Pakistan" in the *New York Times Index 1971*; *A Book of Record*, pp. 1287-1310. (Cited hereafter as : NY Times Index.)

members of the police and army, particularly—precipitated a full-scale civil war, a declaration of independence by the Awami League leaders who had fled to India, and, in the view of most observers within the State Department and without, the inevitable breakup of Pakistan. As Tajuddin Ahmad, Prime Minister of the Awami League government-in-exile, put it in April, "Pakistan is now dead and buried under a mountain of corpses".[2]

The second phase of the crisis began with the announcement of Henry Kissinger's visit to Peking (July 15) and the signing of the Indo-Soviet friendship treaty (August 9). This phase featured the build-up of guerrilla forces (the Mukti Bahini) inside East Bengal, and the increase of direct and indirect Indian support, against the backdrop of a refugee population in India of nearly ten million by November. It ended with the outbreak of full-scale war between India and Pakistan on December 3rd.

The third phase was the war, in which India, with the help of the Mukti Bahini, quickly defeated the Pakistan army in the East, and while fighting a holding action on the ground on the western front, used air and naval power to damage Pakistan's military capability. The final phase began with the transfer of power to Sheikh Mujib on January 12, 1972 and ended with U.S. recognition of Bangladesh, on April 4, 1972.

Decision-Making and Rationales

Virtually all the decisions made by the U.S. in this crisis originated in the White House. By and large, explicit rationales for those decisions were *not* communicated to State Department officials, still less to the Congress and the public. Since the end of the crisis, some rationales have been presented, most

2. Marta Nicholas and Philip Oldenburg, compilers; Ward Morehouse, general editor, *Bangladesh : the birth of a nation; a handbook of background information and documentary sources* (Madras : M. Seshachalam, 1972), p. 82. (Cited hereafter as : Bangladesh handbook. This contains the "Anderson Papers" reprinted (in pp. 112-34) from the *New York Times* of January 6 and 15, 1972; the Kissinger background briefing of December 7, 1971, reprinted (in pp. 134-42) from the *Congressional Record—Senate*, December 9, 1971; Mrs. Gandhi's letter to President Nixon, reprinted (in pp. 143-45) from the *New York Times* of December 17, 1971; and other documents.)

notably by President Nixon in his "State of the World ' message to Congress of February 9, 1972, but what interviewees* agreed were the *real* reasons for U.S. policy have never been publicly stated. I will discuss some of those decisions in detail below, mentioning others only briefly because of lack of information and space. Having presented what I believe the rationales of each of these decisions were, I will move to a detailed discussion divided into two parts : the facts of the case, and the implications. The study will conclude with a brief sketch of the implications of these decision cases taken together.

Those decisions I will discuss in detail are :

(1) the decision *not* to comment on the initial "bloodbath" in East Bengal, and, later, the decision not to criticize Pakistan as the killing continued;

(2) the decision to cut off most arms aid to Pakistan, while continuing to supply some;

(3) the decision to provide humanitarian relief to refugees in India and to the people who stayed in East Bengal;

(4) the decision to pursue a political solution of the crisis with the Pakistanis, the Indians, and the exiled Bengali leadership;

(5) the decision first to attempt to prevent the outbreak of war between India and Pakistan and then to end it once it had begun.

The rationale for the first decision was that the civil war was an internal affair of Pakistan; but the reason for not letting concern for violations of human rights override that principle was the "historical coincidence" that Pakistan was the intermediary in the arrangement of the opening to China. These

* Much of the material in this study is drawn from interviews with government officials and private individuals, conducted in the summer of 1974. The line of argument presented is entirely my own, however, and when it is necessary to identify the source of a statement as an interview, an asterisk in parentheses is placed in the text, thus : (*).

delicate negotiations, which were initiated in 1969[3] and had reached the stage of the exchange of notes via Pakistan by early 1971, became very serious on March 15th, and a specific invitation (in a sealed envelope) for either Kissinger or Rogers to visit China was conveyed by the Pakistan Ambassador some time before April 6th.[4] Presumably the secrecy of the negotiations, and thus the opening itself,[5] would have been jeopardized by an "unfriendly" gesture to Pakistan at the very moment a breakthrough was achieved.

The reason for not criticizing Pakistan over the violent repression in East Bengal is tied to the generally favorable position vis-a-vis Pakistan that the U.S. adopted. As stated publicly, the pro-Pakistan "tilt" was meant to retain "leverage" with President Yahya Khan. It is likely that the desire to remain the friend of China's friend contributed to the decision, as did the factor of President Nixon's personal rapport with President Yahya, and his positive feeling toward Pakistan. (This factor has been emphasized by too many to be discounted, despite Kissinger's remark that "I do not think we do ourselves any justice if we ascribe policies to the personal pique of individuals".)[6]

The rationale for cutting off arms aid was simple : the Pakistan army was making use of them in a situation contrary to the agreement under which the U.S. supplied them. The

3. G.W. Choudhury, *The Last Days of United Pakistan* (Bloomington : Indiana University Press, 1974), p. 68. Choudhury was a senior advisor to President Yahya at the time, "one of the very few whom [Yahya] took into his confidence about his top secret mission [to Peking]". (Ibid., p. 70.)

4. See Marvin Kalb and Bernard Kalb, *Kissinger* (Boston : Little, Brown, 1974), pp. 237-38. Unfortunately, they do not give a date, but simply set the time as cherry blossom season in Washington.

5. On President Nixon's and Kissinger's belief that secrecy was required, see I.M. Destler, "The Nixon System, a further look" *Foreign Service Journal*, February 1974. See also Secretary Rogers' reply to a question at the Sigma Delta Chi convention, *Department of State Bulletin*, Vol. LXV, No. 1693 (December 6, 1971), pp. 652-53.

6. Made in his background briefing of December 7th. As reprinted in Bangladesh handbook, p. 139. The remark refers to Nixon's alleged hostility to Mrs. Gandhi; in the earlier part of his reply, Kissinger denies that either he or President Nixon had a preference for Pakistan or for Pakistani leaders.

reason for continuing a comparatively small flow of spare parts, etc. was symbolic, and was tied to the general pro-Pakistan U.S. stance. The decision to provide humanitarian relief needed no justification, but the proportions of aid given to India compared to aid earmarked for East Bengal underlined the White House position that humanitarian aid was to be the "centerpiece" of the U.S. political-diplomatic effort.

The "political solution" was juxtaposed to a military solution : if the U.S. and others did not succeed in getting a political settlement of the civil war, India in one way or the other would see that Pakistan was broken up. The rationale was that the U.S. did not wish to see the breakup of Pakistan occur, especially with outside intervention, because that would "destabilize" the region. The need to preserve Pakistan's "integrity" was even greater in view of her alliance to the U.S. and friendship with China.

The decision to exercise U.S. influence first to prevent the outbreak of war between India and Pakistan and then to end it was of course justified on the ground that war is not a way to solve international disputes (a rationale which, it should be noted, the U.N. General Assembly agreed with by a vote of 104 to 11, with 10 abstentions). A deeper rationale for the U.S. was that since India would win decisively, the "destabilization" of the subcontinent would occur. Also, the defeat of a U.S. ally would place the U.S. in a weak position vis-a-vis the USSR in upcoming summit talks. This latter reason bulks very large during the war. And underlying the "tilt" which was made explicit during the war—i.e. the war should stop because Pakistan was losing it—is the personal factor of President Nixon's attitude. In Kissinger's words at the Washington Special Action Group (hereafter WSAG; the minutes constitute the bulk of the "Anderson Papers") meeting, ". . . the President is not inclined to let the Paks be defeated".[7]

Let me discuss briefly decisions on economic aid to Pakistan and on the recognition of Bangladesh. The focal points for Congressional action during the crisis were the Gallagher and Church/Saxbe amendments to the Foreign Aid bill which would have cut off economic aid to Pakistan until the civil war

7. "Anderson Papers" as reprinted in Ibid., p. 125. All statements about WSAG deliberations hereafter are from this source.

ended. The administration not only opposed those amendments, it also dissented from the Aid-Pakistan consortium recommendation to suspend aid to Pakistan (made in the wake of the leaked World Bank report which noted that the repression in East Bengal was so severe that economic aid could not be utilized there). Again, the rationale for this policy was to preserve leverage with the Pakistanis.[8]

Finally there was a decision to delay the recognition of Bangladesh—the U.S. recognized Bangladesh on April 4, 1972, fully two months after most of the nations of Europe had extended recognition and nearly a month after Indian troops had left Bangladesh. No plausible rationale was ever given to the State Department (*), still less the Congress,[9] but it was clearly tied to the China opening—President Nixon postponed considering it until after his trip to China (in late February 1972). Certainly, too, there was a desire to defer to Pakistan, even as the Muslim nations of the Middle East and Africa were doing.

Violent Repression; and the Register of Dissent
The Facts
After the crackdown on March 25/26 a decision was made to downplay the seriousness of the action and to avoid admitting to the facts of the "blood-bath". In the initial phase of the civil war, there was, as Senator Kennedy said on the Senate floor on April 1, 1971, "indiscriminate killing, the execution of political leaders and students, and thousands of civilians suffering and dying every hour of the day".[10] It soon became clear from press reports that Hindus were being singled out

8. See the study for the Commission by Joan Hochman, printed in Appendix H.
9. *Recognition of Bangladesh,* Hearings before the Committee on Foreign Relations, U.S. Senate, March 6 and 7, 1972; testimony of Christopher van Hollen, Deputy Assistant Secretary for Near East and South Asia, pp. 6-25, passim.
10. As reprinted in *Relief Problems in East Pakistan and India, Part I,* hearings before the subcommittee to investigate problems connected with refugees and escapees of the Committee on the Judiciary, U.S. Senate (hereafter : Kennedy subcommittee), June 28, 1971, p. 87.

for killing,[11] and by June the London *Sunday Times* could use
the title "Genocide" for its introduction to one of the best
accounts of Pakistan army activities.[12] Senator Kennedy, in a
news conference in New Delhi in August, called the Pakistan
military action "genocide",[13] but that word was absent from
debate by public figures both before and after August.[14]

The administration was even less willing to come to terms
with the possibility that "genocide" was occurring in the

11. Many reports, from the onset of the crisis, mention this; see, for
example, some of those reprinted in *Ibid*, pp. 95 ff. : Peggy Durdin,
"The Political Tidal Wave That Struck East Pakistan" (reprinted
from the *New York Times Magazine* of May 2, 1971), *Ibid*.,
pp. 95-105; Mort Rosenblum, "Army, Rebels Fight Over Ruined
Pakistan" (reprinted from the *Baltimore Sun*, May [?] 1971), *Ibid*.,
pp. 110-11; *et al.*

12. As reprinted in *Ibid*., pp. 118-20; the article introduced is by
Anthony Mascarenhas, "Why the Refugees Fled", *Ibid*, pp. 120-32.

13. New York Times Index, p. 1296, col. 1 (original article : *New York
Times*, August 16, 1971, p. 6.).

14. The International Genocide Convention (not ratified then by the
U.S.), defines genocide as "acts committed with intent to destroy, in
whole or in part, a national, ethnical, racial, or religious group . . ."
Quoted in Michael Bowen, Guy Freeman, Kay Miller (Roger Morris,
Project Director), *Passing By; The United States and Genocide in
Burundi, 1972* (Washington : The Carnegie Endowment for Interna-
tional Peace, 1973), p. 18. In addition to eyewitness testimony (see
note 11, above), the fact that after May virtually all the refugees were
Hindus supports the view that actions by the Pakistan army in East
Bengal constituted genocide by this definition. However, the
language used in public even by critics of U.S. policy did not include
the word "genocide"; for instance, in Senator Kennedy's report
Crisis in South Asia, we get only an indirect usage : "Our national
leadership has yet to express one word that would suggest we do not
approve of the genocidal consequences of the Pakistan Government's policy of repression and violence". (*Crisis In South Asia*, a
report by Senator Edward M. Kennedy to the Kennedy subcommittee, November 1, 1971, p. 55.) Nor is there any evidence that a
"demand" was made by any member of Congress, or by any FSO, to
condemn Pakistan for committing "genocide". There was some
indirect evidence in the interviews I had that policy positions which
would have had the U.S. strongly condemn the killing—and place the
blame on the Pakistan Government—were put forward within the
State Department; the issue was raised, even if the word "genocide"
was not used.

later phase of the civil war than they had been willing to condemn the initial violence of March. The first indication of this stance was Washington's resistance to the Dacca Consul-General's decision to have Americans evacuated from Dacca in the first week of April (*), at a time when Pakistan was claiming that the situation had already returned to normal. According to Senator Kennedy, "instead of calling it an 'evacuation' . . . the State Department reached into its bag of euphemisms and termed the exodus of Americans a normal 'thinning out' ".[15]

The U.S. issued a statement deploring the violence at the end of the first week of April, but one view is that that actually represented a decision *not* to pressure Pakistan because it was made so late, nearly two weeks after the crackdown. U.S. officials were reluctant to make public mention of the widespread killing or of the facts on actions which could be labelled "genocide". Archer Blood, Consul-General in Dacca until early June, testified before Senator Kennedy's subcommittee on refugees on June 26th. Part of his testimony is worth quoting at length :

SENATOR FONG : When the insurgents were put down, were there actions taken by the East Pakistan Army which forced the people to leave ?

MR. BLOOD : I don't see any direct relationship between the level of insurgency and the flow of refugees.

SENATOR FONG : Then why would the refugees leave ?

MR. BLOOD : . . . And, subsequently, many Hindus have left because of the way they were treated.

SENATOR FONG : Did many of them leave because they say conditions were imposed on the Hindus that they thought they couldn't live with ?

MR. BLOOD : I assume so, yes.

SENATOR FONG : What would those conditions be, sir ?

MR. BLOOD : I wouldn't want to go into every detail, because we have reported this in the classified messages—. . . . I would prefer not to answer in open session . . .[16]

The official position was that the refugee outflow was due

15. *Crisis in South Asia*, p. 56.
16. Relief Problems in East Pakistan and India, Part I, Kennedy subcommittee hearings, June 28, 1971, p. 46.

to continued fighting and the poor economic situation. U.S. efforts were thus aimed at stopping the "fighting" (between the Pakistan army and the Mukti Bahini guerrillas) not at stopping the killing of Hindus and the destruction of their property. Official policy plus the constraints of "cliency" make it most unlikely that "genocide" ever figured in any private communication with the Pakistan government.[17]

While the Dacca consulate was urging condemnation of the violence, seconded by the New Delhi embassy, the Islamabad embassy discounted the reports from Dacca on the grounds that the consulate officials, being limited in their movements, could only be getting "partial" reports (*). The fact that the Islamabad embassy seemed to give greater credence to its Pakistan government sources than to its own officers in the field, despite close personal ties between the Deputy Chief of Mission and the Consul-General, must have hurt the morale of officers in Dacca. On the other hand, the Islamabad embassy protested on July 15 to the State Department that field reports on predictions of possible famine in East Bengal were being denied in public statements in Washington.[18]

All interviewees agreed that the "tilt" policy position of the U.S. did not affect the reporting of facts to Washington. Even after it had surfaced, during the war, Consul-General Spivack cabled details[19] of his and U.N. Assistant Secretary General Paul Marc Henry's inspection of damage and bomb-rack fragments which indicated Pakistani responsibility for the bombing of the Dacca orphanage (which was blamed on India with much publicity). The Islamabad embassy sent in a report to Washington in which the Defense Representative to Pakistan and the Defense Attache questioned Spivack's conclusion.[20]

The discounting of reports because of their tone and the presumed "cliency" bias of the drafters extended to the

---

17. Roger Morris, "Clientism in the Foreign Service" *Foreign Service Journal*, February 1974. Ambassador Farland, while perfectly correct in his relationship with the Government of Pakistan and his superiors in Washington, did "represent" the point of view of Pakistan to Washington (*).

18. See *Crisis in South Asia*, p. 57, for excerpts from the cable.

19. Jack Anderson, with George Clifford, *The Anderson Papers*, (New York : Random House, 1973), pp. 242-45.

20. *Ibid.*

reporting of facts as well as to the presentation of estimates and advice on policy. (Ironically, the presumed cliency of Dacca begat cliency in Islamabad.) But the professionalism of the Foreign Service dictated that the reporting of facts known to be unpalatable not stop.

Implications

The maintenance of contact with the Pakistanis, both in the context of the opening to China and with a view toward exerting "leverage" in the future (once the situation in the East had become clear), was clearly a matter of great importance. One non-U.S. source, who discussed the findings of the leaked World Bank report of July with Yahya Khan, says the Pakistan President could not credit its finding that official violence had and was occurring in East Pakistan. The result of a U.S. decision to raise the question of "genocide" might thus have resulted in cutting off communication with the Pakistanis (and especially with Yahya Khan) rather than in changing Pakistan's policies.

Most sources agreed that almost everyone at the State Department recognized what was going on in East Bengal and would have liked to see if not a U.S. condemnation at least a dissociation of the U.S. from the Pakistan regime. The facts reached the policy-makers in the White House, although there is some difference of opinion on how forceful and articulate the presentation of State Department views were; according to one official, lower levels of State felt it could have been much better, but according to Marvin and Bernard Kalb, Assistant Secretary of State Sisco "battled" with Kissinger in WSAG meetings in December.[21]

Those within the system were apparently satisfied with the channels of dissent open to them. "Official informal" letters were seen by my sources as having considerable importance in making an impact on policy decisions in most cases (in part because they are considered leak-proof, and the leaks of dissent positions seemed to distress the dissenters as much as anyone), but, it was implied, not in this crisis, because policy was being made beyond the reach of the "official informal".

21. Kalb and Kalb, pp. 258-59.

No one who dissented from U.S. policy in this crisis resigned. It would not be necessary or desirable for an FSO to threaten to resign whenever he objected strongly to a decision. But if the forceful presentation of policy alternatives is considered desirable, it might be worthwhile to make it easier for the FSO to leave the Service, by training him during his career so that he could enter a different career (e.g. university teaching, international business), or by bringing in people from outside the Service into middle-level slots.

Finally, the existence of career sub-cultures, FSOs with academic interests, for example, can provide sub-communities of knowledgeable professionals who can informally sustain the dissenter in responsible dissent. There is some evidence that the South Asia specialists—encompassing both India and Pakistan "wallahs"—constituted such a sub-community in 1971.

The Arms Aid Cut-Off Decision; and the Use of Public Statements

The Facts

A decision was made to cut-off the supply of arms to Pakistan. In a letter to Senator Kennedy dated April 20, 1971, David Abshire, Assistant Secretary for Congressional Relations, wrote, "we have been informed by the Department of Defense that [no non-lethal military end items (of) spare parts and ammunition have] been provided to the Pakistan government or its agents since the outbreak of fighting in East Pakistan on March 25-26, and nothing is presently scheduled for such delivery".[22] But "delivery" here meant that items contracted for and licensed for export before March 25 were considered "delivered" even though they had not left U.S. shores. This continued movement of arms to Pakistan was revealed in a *New York Times* article— presumably as the result of a leak—while the Indian Foreign Minister was returning from Washington to Delhi with what he thought were assurances that Pakistan was not receiving U.S. arms. These events contributed to Indian distrust of the U.S. (which became crucial in U.S. attempts to prevent a war; see below).

A General Accounting Office report released on February

22. *Relief Problems in East Pakistan and India, Part I*, Kennedy sub-committee hearings, June 28, 1971, p. 82.

4, 1972[23] revealed that not only had $3.8 million worth of
Munitions List articles been exported under valid licenses, but
also "Department of Defense agencies, despite departmental
directives issued in April, continued to release from their stocks
spare parts for lethal end-items" and "the U.S. Air Force delivered to Pakistan about $563,000 worth of spare parts between
March 25 and mid-July 1971 on a priority basis using the
Military Airlift Command. Some of these spare parts were
needed to place inoperable aircraft, such as F-104's, into oper-
able condition."[24] It was discovered in late August that until
the practice was stopped by informal order on July 2nd and
formally on August 12th, "military departments" entered into
foreign military sales contracts of about $10.6 million with
Pakistan . . ., "[25] though no licenses were issued for these contracted items. On November 8th the State Department revoked all outstanding licenses (for goods worth about $3.6
million) and the flow of arms to Pakistan ended.

There were several factors at work here. On one level
there was something of a bureaucratic "snafu" (*) in the
instances of continued spare parts supply. This might of
course be interpreted as a deliberate effort on the part of
Defense agencies to continue supplying a country they considered to be a good ally. The "business as usual" signing of new
contracts was justified as proper because U.S. military supply
policy was "under review". If the continued supply under valid
licenses had been a "snafu" in which State Department and
Defense Department signals had gotten crossed, then presumably shipments would have ceased when it was revealed in late
June. But the licenses were not revoked until November—and
Kissinger wondered aloud in the WSAG meetings whether
that step had been wise—making it clear that the supply of
a limited amount of arms to Pakistan had been U.S. policy.
Christopher van Hollen, Deputy Assistant Secretary for NEA,
in testimony before Senator Kennedy's sub-committee on
October 4, made U.S. policy explicit :

23. *Relief Problems in Bangladesh*, Kennedy subcommittee hearings,
    February 2, 1972, Appendix III, pp. 85-92.
24. *Ibid*, p. 90.
25. *Ibid*. Note that none of these shipments were illegal, nor did they
    violate overall U.S. policy on arms to Pakistan.

SENATOR FONG : The administration did not feel it should revoke the licenses that had been issued?

MR. VAN HOLLEN: That is correct. The judgement was made that this would be a political sanction, and that it would not be in keeping with our efforts to maintain a political relationship with the Government of Pakistan, looking toward the achievement of certain foreign policy objectives of the United States.[26]

That is, these arms shipments were continued as part of U.S. attempts to maintain "leverage" on Pakistan.

During the December war, Jordan and possibly other countries offered to transfer U.S. supplied weapons to Pakistan. The question was discussed in two of the WSAG meetings whose minutes were leaked. State Department and Defense Department officials pointed out that it would be illegal for the U.S. to permit third country transfers, since the U.S. itself was barred from supplying arms to Pakistan. Kissinger, however, asked that King Hussein be kept in a "holding pattern", noting that the President "may want to honor" requests from Pakistan for military aid of this kind.[27] It was later reported that "military sources" disclosed that Libya and Jordan had indeed provided aircraft to Pakistan.[28]

Humanitarian Assistance; and the Role of Congress
The Facts

One interviewee told me that in August the President described the relief effort—which would be carried on no matter what, for humanitarian reasons—as the centerpiece of the U.S. political effort vis-a-vis Pakistan. This view of U.S. policy was however not conveyed downward even to middle-level State Department officers. The decisions was to provide aid both to the refugees in India and to those in the East (especially in the cyclone-affected areas) who did not leave. The threat of famine would be met and India's burden would be shared. Congress,

26. *Relief Problems in East Pakistan and India, Part III,* Kennedy sub-committee hearings, October 4, 1971, p. 376. Christopher van Hollen's testimony.
27. "Anderson Papers" as reprinted in Bangladesh handbook, pp. 132 and 125.
28. *New York Times,* March 29, 1972, p. 1.

on the other hand, wanted to give more aid for refugee relief than the administration requested, and less to the people in East Pakistan, on the grounds that with a crippled transport system and the acknowledged diversion of some relief supplies and transport vehicles to the Pakistan army, there was no guarantee that such aid would reach those for whom it was intended.[29]

The amount of U.S. assistance was consistently overstated by U.S. spokesmen, including the President, even after the crisis was over. A GAO report of June 29, 1972 listed authorized contributions for victims in India as $94.5 million, and pointed out that of the $276.7 million authorized for victims in Pakistan (and this included "old" money intended specifically for pre-March cyclone damage relief and normal bilateral food aid), $ *201.2 million (73 per cent) was not implemented.* The repeated U.S. assertion that the U.S. was contributing "more than the rest of the world combined"—a formulation the Delhi embassy finally gave up protesting(*) —appears to have been a self-serving public relations effort. The World Bank's estimate of the cost of refugee relief to India was $700 million by March 1972 (India claimed in the U.N. debate in December that she was spending $3 million a day); the U.S. thus would contribute about 15 per cent of the total and the "rest of the world" about the same or more,[30] leaving India with nearly 70 per cent of the cost of refugee relief.

29. The position that the bulk of U.S. relief should go to East Pakistan was congruent with administration policy after August to portray the refugee outflow as the result of the threatened famine. But before August, the official view that all was "normal" in East Pakistan as the Government of Pakistan contended led the administration to resist Congressional efforts - especially those of Senator Kennedy— to get recognition of the danger of famine. Aid to the refugees in India, I surmise, was to ease India's burden so that she would not have that excuse to go to war to stop the drain on her economy. Interviewees, however, discounted these explanations for the "humanitarian aid was centerpiece" view.

30. As of October 19, 1971, the U.S. had contributed 42 per cent of the "world's" total to refugee relief in India (and 71% of the total for East Pakistan relief). *Ibid.* p. 40. Senator Kennedy, pointing out India's burden, concludes "we realize how little the outside world is really doing, and how paltry the American contribution is comparatively". (*Ibid.*, p. 41.)

There was, moreover, a coordination of public utterance in this instance. Another GAO report (of April 20, 1972, but requested in July 1971 by Senator Kenneddy) stated in the introduction :

> Our review efforts were impeded by Department of State and AID officials. They withheld and summarized records prior to our access and thereby limited information needed for a complete and thorough report. In connection with the GAO review, U.S. Embassy officials in Islamabad were instructed not to make available messages reporting on sensitive discussions with the GOP [Government of Pakistan], Government of India, or U.N. agencies, or certain sensitive documents relating to development of U.S. policy.

Implications

The U.S. relief effort provided a major focus for Congressional attention to the 1971 crisis. While the GAO, an arm of the Congress, was having difficulty in conducting its investigation, Senator Kennedy was able to get copies of confidential cables from Pakistan. Congressional sources I spoke with seemed satisfied with the institutional arrangements in the foreign policy field, arguing that the lack of Congressional activity during the crisis (the Foreign Relations Committee never held a public hearing, for example) reflected not the lack of power or expertise but the lack of Congressional interest in foreign policy and especially vis-a-vis South Asia.

The Congressional concern with humanitarian issues reflected the U.S. public perception of the problem—a record amount of money was contributed to refugee relief from private sources—but Congress had little impact in the face of a U.S. policy which sought first to downplay the refugee issue, then to shift the focus of concern from refugees and from "genocide" to East Pakistanis suffering because of civil strife (cause unspecified), and finally, to overstate the amount of U.S. assistance.

The Political Solution; and the "Checklist" Danger
The Facts
President Nixon in his "State of the World" message of February 9, 1972 called "the problem of political settlement

between East and West Pakistan" "the basic issue of the crisis".[31] In May, in letters to President Yahya and Prime Minister Gandhi, President Nixon referred to the necessity of a "political accommodation";[32] by summer, this was communicated to "all parties" as being a political solution "on the basis of some form of autonomy for East Pakistan".[33]

During August, September and October, eight contacts with the "Bangladesh people" in Calcutta were made, according to Kissinger.[34] And, according to President Nixon, "by early November, President Yahya told us he was prepared to begin negotiations with any representatives of this group not charged with high crimes in Pakistan, or with Awami League leaders still in East Pakistan".[35] One interviewee felt that the contacts were a "sterile exercise" and another felt that they were not serious, since follow-up cross-checks were discouraged by Washington. The difficulty here was perhaps differing perceptions of what the contacts meant.

These contacts were to lead to negotiations between Pakistan "and Bangladesh representatives approved by Mujibur", according to Kissinger.[36] The negotiations never began, nor was the U.S. ever involved "on substance".[37] The next step was to establish contact with Mujib to get his approval of Awami League negotiations, and Kissinger claimed that the U.S. "had the approval of the Government of Pakistan to establish contact with Mujibur through his defense lawyer", and that India had been so informed.[38] Prime Minister Gandhi, however, wrote to President Nixon on December 15th that "there was not even a whisper that anyone from the outside

---

31. *U.S. Foreign Policy for the 1970's: The Emerging Structure of Peace*, A report by President Richard Nixon to the Congress, February (9) 1972, (hereafter: State of the World message) p. 159.
32. *Ibid.*, pp. 159-60.
33. *Ibid.*, p. 162.
34. Kissinger backgrounder, as reprinted in Bangladesh hand-book, p. 136.
35. State of the World message, p. 162.
36. Kissinger backgrounder, as reprinted in Bangladesh hand-book, p. 140.
37. *Ibid.*, p. 141. These points only emerged from close questioning of Kissinger at the backgrounder of December 7th.
38. *Ibid.*, p. 140.

world had tried to have contact with Mujibur Rahman".[39] And Ambassador Keating, reacting to the news of Kissinger's backgrounder, pointed out that a move to contact Mujib had been rebuffed on December 2nd, and the initiative had been suggested on November 29th[40] (*one week after the war had begun, by President Nixon's account*).[41]

The negotiations, President Nixon admits, were to be with those not charged with "high crimes",—i.e., the entire top leadership of the Awami League. Given the gap between "contacts" (the latest in October) and the attempted contact with Mujib (end of November), plus the conditions set by Yahya in "early November", one can understand the belief that it was all a "sterile exercise".

There is also some doubt in another area, the proposal for a timetable for East Pakistan's autonomy. The U.S. claim was that "in mid-November, we informed India that we were preparing to promote discussion of an explicit timetable for East Pakistani autonomy".[42] Kissinger told the press, "we told the Indian Ambassador . . . that we were prepared to discuss with them . . . a precise timetable for the establishment of political autonomy in East Bengal".[43] Ambassador Keating, relying on

39. Kissinger backgrounder, as reprinted in Bangladesh hand-book p. 144.
40. *Ibid.*, p. 134.
41. The Pakistan point of view was that the war broke out with India's large scale incursion in support of Mukti Bahini operation on November 21st. President Nixon's phrase was "when war erupted toward the end of November" (State of the World message, p. 164). This view is supported by Wayne Wilcox (*The Emergence of Bangladesh*, Foreign Affairs Study 7, American Enterprise Institute for Public Policy Research, Washington, 1973), p. 51, but a *New York Times* report of November 24th (NY Times Index, p. 1301, col. 3) says that "U.S. officials . . . dispute Pakistani charge that India has launched fullscale invasion", and an important Pakistani General (Farman Ali), as reported on November 26th (*Ibid.*, p. 1302, col. 1), said that "field reports indicate conditions on East Pakistan border [were] returning to normal tenseness". India, of course, held that the war began with the Pakistani air attacks on 8 Indian airfields on December 3rd; most observers agree.
42. State of the World message, p. 162.
43. Kissinger backgrounder as reprinted in Bangladesh hand-book, p. 137.

the news report, pointed out that he had not been informed of
this "critical fact" that "Washington and *Islamabad* were prepared" to discuss the timetable (emphasis added).[44] But it seems
clear from another remark by Kissinger that the U.S. was seeking a timetable from India;[45] he also said "[India] knew that
we believed that political autonomy was the logical outcome
of a negotiation . . ."[46] Prime Minister Gandhi indeed wrote
that "the United States recognized that . . . unquestionably
in the long run Pakistan must acquiesce in the direction of
greater autonomy for East Pakistan . . ."[47] There is no indication, however, that *any* timetable for political autonomy (which
went beyond the scheduled restoration of civilian government
in East Pakistan) was presented *to Pakistan*, or that the U.S.
had publicly favored autonomy in a form acceptable to the
Awami League.

Many officials, both in Delhi and Islamabad, believed by
April that Pakistan would break up, and this assessment was
supported by the intelligence community (*). Those in
Islamabad felt that direct Indian intervention would be inevitable while those in the Delhi embassy felt that the guerrillas
would succeed on their own (*). An interim solution of autonomy leading to independence was not ruled out as unacceptable to the Bengalis (and to India, who did not recognize an
independent Bangladesh until December 6, despite considerable
internal political pressure). Whether such a facade would have
been acceptable to Pakistan is questionable. The Pakistan
government's qualified amnesty, its willingness to accept a limited U.N. role, and the return of East Pakistan to "civilian
rule" under a man totally unacceptable to the Bengalis—all
pointed to as significant steps by President Nixon—were dismissed by the Awami League. The proposal to station U.N.
observers on the border was called a "non-starter" by the Delhi

---

44. "Anderson Papers" as reprinted in *Ibid.*, p. 133.
45. Kissinger backgrounder as reprinted in *Ibid.*, p. 138. "We were
    urging movement at the greatest speed that the Pakistan political
    process could stand. We felt that one way to resolve this would be
    for the Indians to give us a timetable of what they would consider a
    reasonable timetable . . ."
46. *Ibid.*, p. 139.
47. Mrs. Gandhi's letter to President Nixon, as reprinted in *Ibid.*, p. 144

embassy (*). Ambassador Keating dismissed the amnesty
proposal in only slightly less direct terms.[48]

Implications

Ambassador Keating concluded his December 8th cable by
implying that he realized he might not have been informed of
some of the specific developments mentioned in the story of
Kissinger's backgrounder. Several interviewees agreed that no
"political solution" was pressed on Pakistan until very late,
and none could say what that solution was. If indeed it was
formulated as a package by the White House, it was certainly
not presented as such to the State Department. The proper
presentation of alternative policy proposals was frustrated in
this instance by the lack of policy guidance. State Department
officials seemed to have had no idea that the White House felt
it was pressing a coherent strategy toward getting a political
solution, and was forced to react to proposals piecemeal.

There is a danger inherent in compiling a "policy checklist"
and then ticking off items as they are accomplished (or partially
accomplished), because one has the illusion that the policy,
overall, is then "working". The U.S. managed to get Yahya to
agree to a series of steps—maybe the civilian government was
not acceptable to the Awami League, but at least it was a *civilian* government; maybe Mujib would not get a public trial and
would not be permitted to participate in negotiations, but at
least he was *alive*; maybe the amnesty was less than complete,
but at least Yahya had accepted the idea in principle; etc.—
and the President and Mr. Kissinger apparently felt that progress was being made. And so they were angry (if not furious)
with India for not giving Pakistan time to come to accept a
political solution in such terms. But it was obvious to many
officials at State that these steps came far, far too late to provide the basis for a solution; that satisfying a number of items
on the checklist did not constitute a viable policy or strategy
of action.

The review process in charting policy progress must be
constant : whether an objective has been achieved "too late" is
the kind of judgment that demands considerable reliance on
the area experts (centered on the Country Director), who have

48. "Anderson Papers" as reprinted in *Ibid.*, p. 133.

a feel for the political parameters of a situation. High-level decision-makers, especially in the White House, have neither the time nor the expertise to develop such judgment adequately. In this instance, apparently, the White House relied on its own judgment, and wound up pressing for a solution which the Bengalis would have accepted before March 25th but which would not do in the fall of 1971. The White House belief that the U.S. could play the role of honest broker seemed to fly in the face of Indian distrust of U.S. motives and allegiance; area experts in the State Department who did keep the situation under review were not so sanguine. To the extent that the White House belief that a political solution was aborted by Indian actions influenced U.S. policy during the December war and after, this instance points to the failure of a White House centered system.

Prevention of War ; and Policy-Making Crisis by Crisis
The Facts
The danger of India going to war against Pakistan was clear from the first phase of the crisis. On May 28, President Nixon wrote to both President Yahya and Prime Minister Gandhi urging "restraint" and warning of the danger of war,[49] In the second phase of the crisis (August-November), it seemed to be only a matter of time before war broke out. U.S. policy was to urge restraint on India and Pakistan, as part of a diplomatic effort which included humanitarian relief and the effort to broker a political solution. Specific suggestions focused on a disengagement of Indian and Pakistani troops from East Pakistan borders, and the U.S. supported a Pakistani proposal that U.N. observers be posted on the border. India rejected these moves on the grounds that the threat of war arose from the situation in East Bengal, not border confrontations.

When the war broke out on December 3rd, President Nixon apparently felt that India had not given the U.S. time to achieve a solution to the crisis, and that India was thus the "aggressor". As the war developed, officials from the U.S. ambassador to the U.N. on down followed instructions to "tilt" in favor of Pakistan. The minutes of the WSAG meetings reveal that from the outset no one believed that India

49. State of the World message, pp. 159-60.

would halt until she had achieved an independent Bangladesh, resolutions in the U.N. calling for a cease fire notwithstanding. The focus of attention in WSAG was the halting of the war against West Pakistan. President Nixon reported in February that "during the week of December 6, we received convincing evidence that India was seriously contemplating the seizure of Pakistan-held portions of Kashmir and the destruction of Pakistan's military forces in the West. We could not ignore this evidence. Nor could we ignore the fact that when we repeatedly asked India and its supporters for clear assurances to the contrary we did not receive them".[50] He continued, "if we had not taken a stand against the war, it would have been prolonged and the likelihood of an attack in the West greatly increased . . . The war had to be brought to a halt".[51]

The means to this end that President Nixon mentioned was the United Nations, but it is not implausible that the U.S. did threaten to cancel the upcoming U.S.-USSR summit unless the Russians put pressure on India to stop. The sending of the *Enterprise* task force into the Bay of Bengal, after the war in the East was won, has been interpreted as a signal to the USSR and to Pakistan that the U.S. would not let an ally "go under".[52]

An important aspect of this case is the seeming gap in communication between India and the U.S. The U.S. urged "restraint" on India; India would say "yes, but only when the Pakistan army in East Bengal shows 'restraint' ". More directly, after Mrs. Gandhi's trip to Washington in early November, during which she repeatedly said that India was nearing the end of her tether, she said that reports "that she and President Nixon found no common ground in their talks are entirely correct".[53] The U.S. standing vis-a-vis India, and the influence it could hope to exercise was of course seriously

50. State of the World Message, p. 165.
51. *Ibid.*, p. 166
52. Reports of the *Enterprise* task force movements first appeared on December 13th (when it went through the Straits of Malacca), when the Indian army was within artillery range of Dacca. The most detailed account of the task force deployment is in Anderson, *op. cit.*, pp. 259-69 (the chapter is titled "The Brink of World War").
53. N.Y. Times Index, p. 1301 (news story of November 16).

undercut by the clear U.S. commitment to an undivided Pakistan and its unwillingness to condemn Pakistani excesses.

Another instance of communications breakdown: President Nixon claimed that no assurances denying the report of Indian intentions to seize Pakistan-held Kashmir had been received. The CIA report which I infer had touched this off held that Mrs. Gandhi intended to "straighten out the southern border of Azad [Pakistan held] Kashmir", and to "eliminate Pakistan's armor and air force capabilities".[54] In the WSAG meeting of December 8, however, Assistant Secretary Sisco reported that India's "Foreign Minister Singh told Ambassador Keating that India has no intention of taking any Pak territory".[55] And in a public statement in New York on December 12th, Singh said India had no wish to "destroy Pakistan".[56] But, as Sisco also pointed out, "Kashmir is really disputed territory".[57] On balance, he doubted that India had any intention of breaking up West Pakistan.

President Nixon apparently wanted more ironclad assurances; the State Department spokesman reported on December 15th that "India has not replied to U.S. request for assurances it will not attack West Pakistan after defeating Pakistan in the East."[58] (General Niazi, the commander of the Pakistan army in the East, had asked the U.S. to convey his request for a cease fire on the morning of December 14th, Washington time). It is difficult to understand why Washington expected India *not* to attack while Pakistan continued to wage war in the West. Even before the outbreak of the war, on December 2nd, Mrs. Gandhi said: "If any country thinks that by calling us aggressors it can pressure us to forget our national interests, then that country is living in its own paradise and is welcome to it".[59] In the event, President Yahya only agreed to the Indian cease-fire offer under pressure (*). Yahya's broadcast to

54. "Anderson Papers" as reprinted in Bangladesh handbook, p. 128.
55. *Ibid.*, p 130.
56. NY Times Index, p. 1306, col. 2.
57. "Anderson Papers" as reprinted in Bangladesh handbook, p. 130.
58. NY Times Index, p. 1307, col. 1.
59. Quoted in Robert Shaplen, "The Birth of Bangladesh—II", *The New Yorker*, February 19, 1972; as reprinted in *Relief Problems in Bangladesh*, Kennedy subcommittee hearings, February 2, 1972, p. 117.

the nation, delivered four hours before the cease-fire was announced, in which he spoke of a fight to victory, suggests that the cease-fire was indeed hard to accept. Here, as in much of the crisis, the U.S. misunderstood both the Indian position and, probably, the intensity of Pakistani feeling.

Implications

Communication and contact between the countries involved was not impeded by cliency—the unwillingness to carry unpleasant messages to the government concerned, e.g., as it had been in the 1965 war, when Ambassador Bowles was said to have shown such reluctance—nor by any other organizational constraint. There may well have been failures in communication at even the most rudimentary level : misunderstanding Pakistani English usage, for example (*). More important is the apparent belief that conveying a message means that the recipient has digested its meaning. This dichotomy is neatly illustrated by the words of an American official in Islamabad, speaking around November 20 : "we've been in it up to our necks—making suggestions. talking privately with Yahya and others night and day—but this is a closed society. They don't pay any attention—there's no flexibility left. We no longer have any reason to expect the Pakistanis to behave".[60] One suspects that India and Pakistan had similar difficulties in conveying *their* position to American officials.

There are two facets of the communication problem which relate to the U.S. effort to prevent a war. (1) The problem of ambiguity in statements and intentions, and the possibilities of "weathervaning" in analysis which this opens up, and (2) the variant definitions of the size and time dimensions of the "crisis" itself.

President Nixon and Henry Kissinger were apparently unsatisfied with Indian assurances because of the ambiguity inherent in any interpretation of a domestic political situation —they overestimated the importance of Indian "hawks" like Defense Minister Jagjivan Ram, in this instance—and in the less than sweeping nature of the assurances received (which

60. Quoted in Robert Shaplen, "The Birth of Bangladesh—II", *The New Yorker*, February 19, 1972; as reprinted in *Relief Problems in Bangladesh*, Kennedy subcommittee hearings, February 2, 1972, p. 114.

were, to be sure, perfectly understandable from the Indian standpoint). Ambiguity can be used as a tool, however : Kissinger emphasized in the WSAG meeting of December 8th that "we cannot afford to ease India's state of mind" presumably about U.S. intentions to come to Pakistan's assistance.[61] Ambassador Keating had made it clear to Indian officials that third country transfers of weapons required U.S. approval and was told by Under Secretary of State John Irwin, on Kissinger's orders, "in view of intelligence reports spelling out military objectives in West Pakistan, we do not want in any way to ease Government of India's concerns regarding help Pakistan might receive from outside sources".[62] Again, there is no reason to believe that India or Pakistan would not pursue *their* foreign policy vis-a-vis the U.S. by using the same technique.

Although as noted above interviewees agreed that the reporting of facts to the highest levels was not restricted, I was told that there was "weathervaning" in analysis : the preferences of the top levels were fed back to them. The ambiguity which is inherent in the communications between nations—and to a degree within one nation's foreign service—opens the way to anticipatory compliance in reporting and analysis that does not compromise professional responsibilities.

The second facet of the communication problem here has to do with the dimensions of the crisis and ideas of crisis management. The U.S. treated the threat of war and its outbreak as a separable crisis amenable to what one interviewee called the "standard crisis manual" which says "first, urge restraint; second, get the fighting stopped; third, get the parties talking". India's position was that the crisis of a threat of Indo-Pakistan war could not be and should not be separated from the overall crisis which began on March 25th.

U.S. policy toward South Asia was very much a crisis by crisis affair. From the U.S. point of view "the crisis" did not mean the totality of events in 1971 (as it did for India and Pakistan), but rather a series of interrelated crises, like the war. Officials were taking up new posts in the summer of 1971, as is usual, and though the overall crisis was relatively subdued—no headlines, just one constant stream of refugees—they did not

61. "Anderson Papers" as reprinted in Bangladesh handbook, p. 132.
62. Anderson, *op. cit.*, p. 228.

go into the details of previous "crises". Nor were the ex-incumbents sought out when new "crises" or decisions were encountered. Familiarity with the current file coupled with overall expertise was believed to be sufficient.

In 1971 decisions were made at the White House. During the "smaller" crises—the initial crackdown, the first realization of the magnitude of the refugee flow, the December war, etc.—raw intelligence reports and reports of facts direct from the field reached the highest policy-making level and probably were read. During the less active phases, analytic reports warning of the danger of continued armed violence against Hindus by Muslims reached that level (*), but there is little reason to believe that it made an impact. By the time of the crisis of the war Indian motives might well have been difficult to discern or appreciate. A problem in an area like South Asia which is a low priority in U.S. national interest terms has to be more serious than in other areas before it reaches a "crisis" level, and the failure to appreciate the dimension of the crisis from the point of view of the other parties is exacerbated by the tendency to shift not only decision making *but also analysis* to levels in which expertise is severely limited. It is hardly surprising that the U.S. failed to head off war on the Indian subcontinent in 1971.

Conclusions

From the point of view of the White House, I suspect, U.S. policy in South Asia in 1971 was a qualified success. The key goal of the opening to China was not jeopardized by events on the South Asian subcontinent. The progress toward detente with the USSR was not harmed, and valuable lessons were learned on how effective ties with the Soviet Union could be. Relations with Pakistan remained firm, with all that meant for U.S. flexibility in the Middle East (recall that Middle Eastern nations, by and large, gave Pakistan considerable support during 1971). Relations with India were none too good to begin with; a further deterioration could be borne with equanimity, with the added thought, perhaps, of letting the Russians enjoy that headache for a while. Bangladesh and Sheikh Mujib —with whom the U.S. had had close ties—might well want U.S. friendship and aid to counterbalance India and the USSR.

On the other hand, of course, Pakistan had been reduced in power, though India's military development since 1965 precluded a position of parity for Pakistan in any case. A nation state, an ally, had been dismembered by its neighbor, but Pakistan was, in the view of some observers, doomed from its birth, and in the view of others, better off without the drain East Pakistan was becoming. Vigorous U.S. opposition to the war had been concurred in by almost all the nations of the world, and especially third world nations. The U.S. was vilified in moral terms both at home and abroad, but in the context of the war in Vietnam (which was to be ended, after all, with the help of new relations with China and U.S.–USSR detente), that was hardly unusual. Moral outrage evaporates while national interests remain; even India would come around eventually.

But couldn't U.S. policy have been better? (In both senses of the word : couldn't the opening to China have been achieved *without* the costs incurred in South Asia, and *with* the U.S. supporting a democracy instead of yet another military regime, condemning officially sanctioned violence against the civilian population and making every effort to get it stopped?) And would a different organizational structure have made any difference ?

There were, on the whole, no problems in the flow of information upward, nor in the carrying out of instructions from the White House. There is no indication that President Nixon or Kissinger felt any lack in the information they received or in the responsiveness of officials in Washington or in the field (with the exception of Kissinger's famous remark in the WSAG meeting that he was "getting Hell from the President every half hour" because State Department officials were not "tilting" sufficiently toward Pakistan).[63]

There were, however, severe restrictions in the flow of information downward. Rationales for policy never reached lower levels of State. Similarly, the upward flow of analysis and advice was impeded because it had to be considered irrelevant. Until July 15, when the China opening was announced, the State Department was working in the dark— receiving no guidance on what the reasons for U.S. policy were

63. "Anderson Papers" as reprinted in Bangladesh handbook, p. 115.

and sending up analysis and policy advice which had to be ignored, since it could not confront the real rationale. Even after July 15, rationales for U.S. policy which took account of the China opening were not spelled out, and so meaningful alternatives could not be presented.

The secrecy of the rationale for U.S. policy meant that there was no one other than President Nixon and Kissinger who could make decisions, even on minor matters. They were the only ones able to monitor effectively the implementation of the decision, and they alone could assess its impact in terms of the goals they had set. But they also did not have the time (or the expertise) to perform those tasks well—the delay in the recognition of Bangladesh is a case in point.

Alternatives to policy were not presented effectively to decision-makers in the White House, as might be expected under the circumstances. Those sending up proposals were unaware of the "global strategy" which determined U.S. decisions. Moreover, their proposals would inevitably be framed in terms of U.S. policy toward the region or to one country or the other, and would be discounted accordingly. Ultimately, the serious consideration of bilateral and regional dimensions of policy while global objectives are pursued— sorely needed as the U.S. dealt with South Asia in 1971— depends most on having a President or Secretary of State willing and able to work with knowledgeable professionals and with organizational arrangements that effectively represent them.

CASE STUDIES :
I. DIPLOMATIC-STRATEGIC

D. The U.S. Response to the JVP Insurgency in Sri Lanka, 1971

Barnett R. Rubin

Introduction

This is a case study of the U.S. government's response to a military political emergency of moderate importance. Although it took place at a time when the Nixon-Kissinger National Security Council (NSC) system dominated American foreign policy, the emergency was mainly handled within the State Department, where the regional bureau staff had the action. Recourse was had to the Political Military Affairs (PM) and Intelligence and Research (INR) Bureaus in State, as well as to the Office for International Security Affairs (ISA) of the Defense Department, and to the Senior Review Group (SRG) of the NSC in the White House. The President personally made one major policy decision, which was communicated to State at an SRG meeting. Nevertheless, no agency opposed the action leadership of the Bureau for Near East and South Asia Affairs (NEA) in the State Department. Most of the coordination took place within that bureau, at the level of the country director. The policy proved a successful one, and this case gives an idea of the conditions under which a State Department, regional bureau centered foreign policy process can work, and what its limitations might be.

U.S.-Sri Lanka Relations until the Attack on the U.S. Embassy

Towards noon on March 6, 1971, the Deputy Chief of the U.S. Mission in Colombo, who was charge d'affaires during the home leave of Ambassador Robert Strausz-Hupe, was chairing a meeting of his staff on the second floor of the American Embassy in a room which overlooked the embassy compound's front yard and the wall along the Galle Road. To the rear, but not visible from this room, lay first the railroad tracks of the southwest coastal line and then the Arabian Sea, at this season placid, brilliant, and warm. Ceylon, as the Republic of Sri Lanka was known prior to January 25, 1972, bears a superficial resemblance to paradise, and although the Sri Lanka cabinet was proposing a new law to deal with a threat of violent insurrection reported by the Criminal Investigation Department (CID), the men in Mr. Petersen's office had little reason to suspect an impending break in their routines.

Elsewhere, some of their governmental colleagues were backing, or even sponsoring, an incursion into Laos by the South Vietnamese military. There were protests heard from sources in the U.S. and around the world, including, of course, numerous members of the government of Sri Lanka. These protests underlined some of the delicate diplomatic problems these men had been dealing with for the past year.

Prime Minister Mrs. Sirimavo Bandaranaike's United Front (UF) of her own radical nationalist Sri Lanka Freedom Party (SLFP), the Trotskyist Lanka-Sama Samaja Party (LSSP), and the Communist Party (Moscow Wing) had swept 116 out of 150 seats in the parliamentary elections of May, 1970. The UF then proceeded to implement the radical activist foreign policy for which it had campaigned. Many UF members harbored a suspicion that the U.S. had played a role in their electoral defeat in 1965, and might now try to sabotage or overthrow their government. Over the next few months they followed a policy of uniting with friends to oppose enemies. They expelled Western organizations such as the Peace Corps, and the Asia Foundation (a private U.S. organization). They suspended diplomatic relations with Israel and established them with North Vietnam, the Provisional Revolutionary Government of South Vietnam, East Germany, and North Korea. They invited a large group of Chinese technicians and construction workers to build an international conference hall in memory of S.W.R.D. Bandaranaike, Mrs. Bandaranaike's husband, the founder of the SLFP, who was assassinated by a communalist Buddhist monk in 1959. Her government opposed much of U.S. policy in Asia, particularly in Indochina and the Indian Ocean.

It was the Sri Lanka government's stand on the Indian Ocean which most concerned the U.S. During her first term as prime minister (1960-1965), its policy was that no naval vessel could dock in Sri Lanka without declaring that it carried no nuclear weapons. The U.S. responded that it never made such declarations, but would take the feelings of the littoral countries into account. This assurance sufficed for the more pro-Western government of Dudley Senanayake's United National Party (UNP) from 1965 to 1970, but when Mrs. Bandaranaike returned to power her government reactivated the note on non-nuclear declarations. U.S. Navy ship visits came to a halt.

The government of Sri Lanka was suspicious of the continued Anglo-American naval presence in the Indian Ocean, particularly of the plans to build a naval communications facility on the island of Diego Garcia, one thousand miles south of Sri Lanka. Mrs. Bandaranaike criticized these plans at the Commonwealth Heads of Government Conference held in Singapore in January, 1971, where she also started a campaign to have the Indian Ocean declared a nuclear-free "Zone of Peace".

Nevertheless, during the few months before March, 1971, there were signs that U.S.-Sri Lanka relations might be improving. During the UF's most radical foreign policy period, immediately after its election, the U.S. did not overreact. The embassy sent notes of regret over UF actions like the recognition of the Indochinese revolutionary governments, but it did not recommend any sanctions. Soon the UF government realized that they were not going to get as much aid from the socialist countries as they had hoped. The U.S. diplomatic mission, led by Ambassador Strausz-Hupe, was trying to reassure the UF that the U.S. would not interfere in Sri Lanka's politics and had no desire to overthrow the government.

Besides the gradually developing improvement in U.S.-Sri Lanka relations, there were several other reasons for the men in Mr. Petersen's office to feel reasonably secure. Plentiful and powerful as they were, the radicals in Sri Lanka had no tradition of organized political violence. The conventions of parliamentary democracy had been more or less observed through five changes of government and seven national elections in the last twenty-five years. Politics aside, the people seemed friendly and easy going. The Sinhalese majority had been Buddhist since the time of Ashoka, and its leaders proclaimed non-violence an essential part of the national culture.

So it was with shock, surprise, and a feeling of growing uncertainty that the diplomats in Mr. Petersen's office heard the shouts of a mob and the crash of broken glass and saw Molotov cocktails explode beneath their windows. Three minutes later the commando raid from the Galle Road was over. The hundred and fifty or so participants had coalesced, accomplished their limited goal, and scattered into the city and along the sea front with discipline and precision. They left behind a fatally stabbed Ceylonese policeman, the remains of six or seven home-made bombs, an equal number of prisoners in the hands of the police, the burnt shells of a few embassy cars, and a pile of leaflets denouncing U.S. aggression in Laos, signed by the "Mao Youth Front".

The DCM picked up the phone and called the Director General of the Sri Lanka Foreign Office to inform him, protest, and ask for protection and compensation. Other members of the staff drafted a flash cable to Washington which arrived on the desks of the desk officers in the India-Nepal-Ceylon (INC) country directorate, the State Department Bureau of Intelligence and Research (INR), the Office for International Security Affairs of the Defense Department (ISA), and the national Security Council at the White House on top of the morning traffic on March 6.

The JVP and the "Mao Youth Front"
Over the next few days the minds of the speculative in Colombo were exercised by the puzzle of the "Mao Youth Front". The name had never cropped up before. Some of the country's youth had organized New Left (or "ultra-left") groups, which were commonly referred to collectively as the "Che Guevara movement". The largest and best organized of these groups called itself the Janata Vimukti Peramuna (JVP) which means People's Liberation Front.

The JVP dated back to 1966, when its best known leader, Rohan Wijeweera, resigned from the Communist Party (Peking) and began to organize among students and other youths. Wijeweera was educated at Moscow's Lumumba University, and probably received some training in North Korea, but the Russians apparently found him too radical and cancelled his scholarship while he was home.

Wijeweera and his colleagues called into question the legitimacy of the Ceylonese Marxist tradition as practiced by the Old Left parties. The JVP held that the old left parties (primarily the LSSP and the CP-Moscow and sometimes the CP-Peking as well) had capitulated to bourgeois nationalism and revisionism by allying themselves with the SLFP and choosing the "parliamentary path to power". But the JVP was by no means ideologically orthodox or consistent. It was both indigenous and eclectic. The Indian political scientist K.N. Ramachandran has described its ideology as, 'molded out of diverse elements, such as a general Marxist-Leninist outlook, a Maoist itch for revolutionary practice, the Guevarist obsession with instant revolution, Sinhalese ethnocentrism, and the frustrations smoldering in the subconscious of the unemployed youth".[1]

The JVP was thus not unlike other youth organizations growing up during the 1960's all over the world, such as the Naxalites in India or certain factions of SDS in the U.S. The difference was the wide range of its appeal. As was amply demonstrated by the events of April, 1971, the JVP caught the imagination and enlisted the support of thousands, mostly unemployed or underemployed youths and students, who had been educated in traditional style Sinhalese medium schools. The most important reasons for their allegiance were frustration over the lack of opportunity for the rapidly growing youthful population, the absence of visible economic progress, and their feeling of alienation from the closed and privileged ruling elite, almost all of whom, regardless of political allegiance, lived in a few well to do neighborhoods in Colombo, com-

1. K.N. Ramachandran, "China's South Asia Policy", *Journal of Institute for Defense Studies and Analysis* (JIDSA), IV : 1 July, 1971, p. 54.

municated, with each other in English, and married only among themselves.

The JVP made its debut in the society of Ceylonese politics during the elections of 1970. It supported what it considered progressive candidates of the UF while emphasizing that its support was based on agreement with the more radical aspects of the UF's program, such as the nationalization of foreign owned banks and plantations. The UF viewed the JVP as primarily directed against the UNP, and some of its members considered the JVP's paramilitary preparations a possible aid. When the UNP government arrested Wijeweera on the grounds that the JVP was plotting to attack polling booths, the JVP mounted a poster campaign for his release with astonishing rapidity and coordination. After their victory the UF government released Wijeweera, whose followers launched a short lived campaign of thuggery against UNP supporters.

Starting in August, 1970, the JVP held large public rallies all over the country to explain their program to the public. They began to form ties with like minded groups among the urban workers and even the plantation workers of recent Indian origin, whom they had originally wanted to expel from the country as agents of "Indian expansionism".[2]

Meanwhile, in domestic as well as in foreign affairs, the UF was coming up against unforeseen contradictions. To nationalize the foreign banks, whose short term credits were enabling the government to buy rice, or the foreign (mostly British) owned tea plantations, would have meant a loss of precious foreign exchange. The UF did not abandon its goals, but it moved more slowly and cautiously than its campaign rhetoric had led many of its supporters to expect.[3]

To the JVP, this caution looked like the expected sellout. They continued their preparations, political and military, for revolution. The UF, which had dismissed the "reactionary" police officials responsible for intelligence on the JVP, remained largely ignorant of these developments. This ignorance was

2. Jayasumura Obeysekara, "Revolutionary Movements in Ceylon", in Kathleen Gough and Hari P. Sharma ed., *Imperialism and Revolution in South Asia*, p. 389.

3. Urmila Phadnis, "Insurgency in Ceylonese Politics: Problems and Prospects", JIDSA, III: 4, April, 1971, p. 591.

compounded by the failure of the UF to appreciate the depth of the criticism made by the JVP. Its members persisted in believing that any leftist movement in the country would be directed only against the UNP and imperialism. Even when, in early 1971, the CID made disturbing reports of preparation for insurrection, the reaction of the UF, especially of the more radical members, was that "reactionaries", domestic and/or foreign, had to be behind it if it was directed against them. These reports nevertheless were disturbing enough that on March 1, 1971, Mrs. Bandaranaike's cabinet approved a proposal by Minister of Justice Felix Bandaranaike to offer a bill entitled, "An Act for the Prevention of Violent Insurrection".

By this time the JVP was suffering from internal dissension. Mahinda Dharmasekera (popularly known as "Castro"), one of the JVP's cofounders, argued for immediate attack on imperialist targets as part of a long range revolutionary strategy, rather than the policy of careful preparation for a successful revolution in 24 hours, the strategy followed by the main body of the JVP under Wijeweera. He and a group of followers split off from the JVP and prepared to go on the attack. And so they did, on March 6, 1971, under the pseudonym of the "Mao Youth Front".

Government Crackdown and Insurgency

After the attack the embassy staff had to re-define the tasks at hand. They organized increased security measures (such as taking unusual routes to and from the embassy) to avoid kidnappings or attacks. To their Ceylonese counterparts they argued that the attack was directed not primarily against the Americans, but rather against the government of Sri Lanka.

Mrs. Bandaranaike quickly deplored "this high handed attack against the diplomatic mission of a friendly country" and condemned "the miscreants responsible for these criminal acts".[4] After a seven hour cabinet meeting the government decided on a dual strategy : a military crackdown to destroy the JVP and other groups stockpiling arms, and a political offensive to deprive the JVP of mass support by picturing it as the tool of reactionary forces who opposed the march toward socialism.

The government called out the armed forces, who began

4. *Ceylon Daily News*, March 7, 1971.

arresting suspects. They uncovered surprisingly large caches of homemade bombs, stolen guns, blue uniforms and revolutionary literature (including North Korean literature). A bomb factory was discovered on March 15 when it exploded, killing five young men. (This explosion, which took place in the constituency of former UNP Prime Minister Dudley Senanayake, was widely publicized by the government.) Mrs. Bandaranaike then declared a state of emergency. To the subdued bemusement of the UNP, Rohan Wijeweera was re-arrested, and another poster campaign was mounted for his release. On March 20 an explosion in a university hall at Peradeniya led the army and police to a huge cache of dynamite, gelignite, gasoline, detonators and hand bombs. The next day Mrs. Bandaranaike invoked additional emergency powers providing for the death penalty for certain offenses. By the end of March almost 400 people had been arrested.

Government ministers held meetings all around the country denouncing the JVP as the tool of reactionary forces. Some government ministers believed, or at least charged, that the CIA had organized the attack on the American Embassy in order to weaken the government. All evidence, including these men's subsequent behavior, indicates these charges were false. The American diplomats, especially those such as the labor attache who were regularly in touch with the leftists, tried to convince them that they were equally ignorant and equally endangered.

The embassy also kept up a steady stream of reporting to Washington, which was mostly based on conversations with counterparts in the Sri Lanka government and other embassies, such as the Canadians and especially the British, who were particularly well connected with Ceylonese military officials. The U.S. defense attache, a navy commander, had special responsibilities for gathering information on the military situation. Despite the hopes of some Ceylonese, who called the Americans for information, believing that the CIA knew everything, the U.S. seems to have had no reliable sources of intelligence on the JVP.

The remaining JVP leaders faced an unhappy problem. Their forces were poorly armed, and they were losing men and supplies daily. Their organization in the cities was still extremely weak. They had relatively strong forces in many Sinhalese villages, but none on the plantations. They decided that rather than allow their organization to be dismantled by the government without a fight, they would counter-attack with all the forces at their disposal. The first strike was to be aimed at the undermanned rural police stations, which might provide additional arms. There was also an ill-conceived plan to paralyze the central government by kidnapping or killing the prime minister and other government figures in Colombo.

Shortly before the attacks were scheduled to go off, a bhikku who had been involved in the plan to seize government ministers confessed to the police, leading to the destruction of the JVP's Colombo group. Before the rest of the armed forces and police could be notified, on the night of April 5-6, the insurgents struck, with devastating effect. No one knows how many there were. Estimates give a hard core of 3000 to 5000 with supporters somewhere between 20,000 and 100,000; at one point, the Sri Lanka government estimated 80,000.[5] The government forces of about 7000 army regulars, 1900 navy, 1500 air force, and 12,500 police, were outnumbered.[6] Their equipment, which had never before been used in combat, was meager and aged. Mrs. Bandaranaike appealed for military aid, which eventually came from India, Pakistan, the U.S., Britain, the U.S.S.R., Yugoslavia, and Egypt.

On April 17, the North Korean embassy was ordered closed and all staff and their families ordered to leave the country immediately. The Sri Lanka government never announced what the North Koreans had been doing, but it is possible to piece together an account. The North Koreans had organized North Korea-Ceylon Friendship Societies all over the island. These societies distributed large quantities of revolutionary literature, much of which had been found in insurgent hideouts. A few of the insurgent leaders had received some training in North Korea. The North Koreans may also have brought large amounts of foreign currency into the country which they changed on the black market and distributed to the JVP, but evidence for this is equivocal. There is no evidence of any arms aid to the JVP.

5. *New York Times*, April 10, 1971; April 11, 1971.
6. Phadnis, *op. cit.*, p. 610.

With the help of their new military equipment, the government forces moved from the defensive to a position of strength by the end of April. Mrs. Bandaranaike called upon the insurgents to surrender over May 1-4, and almost 4000 did. The government forces then went on the offensive. By the end of June, almost 14,000 alleged insurgents were in detention camps, and most of the rest had lain down their arms and gone home.[7] No one knows how many were killed. The government claims that 60 of the government forces and 1200 insurgents died. Other sources gave fatality estimates as high as 6000, including civilian deaths. A widely accepted compromise figure is about 3000 insurgent and civilian deaths.[8]

Sri Lanka and the International System
During the insurgency, India lent Sri Lanka six helicopters with crews, sent five frigates to seal off the island's coast from any outside intervention, sent 150 troops to guard the airport used for delivery of aid, and provided arms, ammunition, and full kit and equipment for 5000 combat troops.[9] Great Britain ferried supplies of arms and ammunition from Singapore, provided seventeen scout cars, and delivered six Bell helicopters that the U.S. had sold for transfer to Sri Lanka. Pakistan lent two helicopters with crews and provided hand grenades and communications equipment. The USSR provided five MIG-17 jet fighters and a MIG-15 trainer along with sixty Russian maintenance and training personnel, who were asked to leave Sri Lanka in June. The UAR and Yugoslavia provided small amounts of arms and ammunition.[10]

7. The "insurgents" in the camps included many who had been only marginally involved with the JVP, but who surrendered out of fear of reprisals or at their parents' urging.
8. S. Arasaratnam, "The Ceylon Insurrection of April, 1971 : Some Causes and Consequences", *Pacific Affairs*, 43 : 3, Fall, 1973, p. 363.
9. It was widely believed in Sri Lanka that India's reaction indicated the existence of contingency plans for intervention in Sri Lanka and a readiness to implement them. Indian government sources claim that the Indian aid in fact was delayed by the lack of any such contingency plans and, only timely improvisation provided what aid was forthcoming.
10. IDSA, *India in World Strategic Environment, Annual Review*, 1970-71 : 7, p. 379.

The U.S. sold and delivered 8000 pounds of spare parts for four Bell helicopters the UNP government had bought in 1968. Washington approved the sale of six surplus helicopters to the British for transfer to Sri Lanka. And on June 7, 1971, President Nixon formally determined that the national security of the U.S. and the cause of world peace would be strengthened by a $3 million grant of military assistance to the government of Sri Lanka.

Clearly, the greatest resource which the government of Sri Lanka had at its command was its legitimacy within the international system. The linkages of Sri Lanka to the international system formed the context within which U.S government officials evaluated and acted upon the requests for aid which they received. It would be well to review these linkages before describing their activities.

It is a truism that Sri Lanka is of interest to global powers because of its "strategic location". It is also a euphemistic way of saying that Sri Lanka contains no natural, economic, or human resources which are of intrinsic interest to the U.S. or any powerful nation.[11] Nor do American companies have substantial holdings in Sri Lanka.[12] As a result of this lack of direct, bilateral linkages, the U.S. government maintains a consistently low level of involvement in Sri Lanka. This is difficult to keep in mind in a paper devoted largely to U.S.-Sri Lanka relations, but it has important practical implications for the nature of U.S. policy and the way that policy is formulated and carried out.

Within the South Asia region, Sri Lanka is of interest to India and, less so, to Pakistan. The tribulations of the Tamil minority in Sri Lanka have often been echoed in the Lok Sabha by the DMK. More important, Sri Lanka functioned as

11. Partial exceptions are China, which receives a good part of the island's rubber production in return for rice (but is not dependent on Sri Lanka for rubber) and Great Britain, some of whose tea companies have holdings there.

12. The American and British oil companies' holdings were nationalized by Mrs. Bandaranaike's first government in 1962. The U.S. felt the compensation offered was inadequate, and cut off aid under the Hickenlooper amendment. Relations were poor until the UNP government settled the matter on terms acceptable to the U.S. in 1965.

a base for expansion in India by colonial powers—Portuguese, Dutch, and British—and Indian defense planners include the island within the Indian defense perimeter. The growth of Sri Lanka-Chinese friendship has caused them some discomfort.[13] Prior to the completion of its disintegration in December, 1971, Pakistan relied on Sri Lanka as a stopping off point for transportation and communication between its two halves in the event of hostilities with India. Sri Lanka played that role in 1965 and again in 1971. Stability in Sri Lanka was thus linked to stability on the subcontinent.

What interest the global powers have in Sri Lanka is mainly based on its geographic position and its influence among other nonaligned countries. Sri Lanka lies at the center of the Northern Indian Ocean, along the sea route from the Persian Gulf to Southeast Asia and Japan, or midway between the two great Soviet naval bases of Vladivostok and Sevastopol. The naval base at Trincomalee was a link in the chain of British bases from Suez to Singapore until S.W.R.D. Bandaranaike asked the British to leave in 1956. Since then no foreign power has been granted any base in Sri Lanka, and despite occasional alarmist rumors that the Chinese or Soviet navies have been given Trincomalee, no foreign power is like to get one in the near future.

The late 1960's saw a change in the naval power configuration in the Indian Ocean. The Labour Government in Britain began a policy of disengaging from the East of Suez. The base in Aden was evacuated, and the base in Singapore was turned over to local sovereignty. The U.S. and Britain announced a plan under which active naval bases would be replaced by a chain of staging posts for long range aircraft, naval fuelling, and communications. This policy led to the decisions to establish the British Indian Ocean Territory (BIOT) and the Anglo-American "facility" on Diego Garcia.[14]

13. One example among many : J.I.S. Kalra, "Growing Navy Needs Greater Punch", *Illustrated Weekly of India*, June 23, 1974, p. 23 : "China has made it quite clear that the Indian Ocean comes under its sphere of influence. And if Pakistan, Ceylon, and some East African countries provide the Chinese with base facilities, the menace would assume astounding proportions".

14. IDSA, *India in World Strategic Environment, Annual Review*, 1969-70, pp. 252-3.

In March, 1968, the Soviet Navy put in its first major appearance in the Indian Ocean, making calls around South Asia, the Arabian Sea, the Persian Gulf, and East Africa. The U.S. and Britain began to be concerned over Soviet "expansion", especially in the light of the increase of Soviet influence in the Middle East. After the reopening of the Suez Canal, the Soviets seemed likely to link up their Mediterranean fleet, based at Sevastopol, with their Pacific fleet, based at Vladivostok. Sri Lanka, as noted, is right in the middle. The U.S. navy task force in Bahrein was decrepit and superannuated. The navy inaugurated a policy (since spring, 1971) of detaching part of the Seventh Fleet in the Pacific to make calls around the Indian Ocean from time to time. Stops at Colombo for bunkering and shore leave facilitate these trips.

China's policy makers also became concerned over the Soviet expansion, which they christened "The gunboat policy of the new czars".[15] China is competing with the Soviets for influence in most of the Indian Ocean littoral areas, such as Southeast Asia, the Middle East, East Africa, and, of course, South Asia. China's navy has also embarked on a program of intensive ship building and expansion. The Chinese, perhaps because of their concern with Soviet activity, have been relatively quiet about U.S. activity in the area.

U.S. Interest in Sri Lanka at the Time of the Insurgency
No one in the U.S. government expects to get a military base in Sri Lanka. The U.S. government wants Sri Lanka to permit occasional visits by ships of the U.S. Navy, to refuse to give base facilities to any power, and not to oppose U.S. naval activity too vehemently in international forums, where Sri Lanka is influential, especially in matters pertaining to the sea or to non-alignment, out of proportion to its size.

Because of the low level of involvement in Sri Lanka, there are few bureaucratic struggles over policy toward that country within the U.S. government. The one service with a particular bureaucratic interest in Sri Lanka is the Navy, and there have been some relatively minor disagreements between the Navy and State. Generally, State wants the Navy to be restrained in order not to place the government of Sri Lanka

15. IDSA, *India in World Strategic Environment*, *Annual Review*, 1969-70, p. 267.

in an awkward position, while the Navy feels State over-estimates the amount of restraint needed. But the activation of the facility on Diego Garcia, an island conveniently devoid of population, politics, and governments, would render these arguments moot. The Navy also realizes that in any situation of actual international conflict it would be unable to use Sri Lanka—a Seventh Fleet destroyer escort called there in October, 1971, but the *Enterprise* did not call in Sri Lanka during the Indo-Pak war. Ship visits serve mainly political rather than military purposes.

When the requests for aid against the insurgents were received, all U.S. government participants agreed that a JVP victory would have been contrary to the interests of the U.S. Although the JVP was an indigenous organization with little or no foreign support, a JVP government would presumably have been anti-American and favorable to China or Russia (or both : no one was quite sure), as well as disruptive to stability in Sri Lanka and the region, which the U.S., as a *status quo* power, attempted to maintain. The decision makers saw Sri Lanka as an increasingly friendly non-aligned country of some strategic importance, whose government was under attack by forces likely to align themselves against the U.S., and which had requested aid in order to strengthen itself.

The aid was also likely to reassure the UF government regarding U.S. intentions and make it politically easier for Mrs. Bandaranaike to improve relations with the U.S. Although this was not raised explicitly in discussions in Washington, it was generally understood that "improved relations" would manifest themselves in U.S. ship visits and a more tolerant attitude toward U.S. activity in the Indian Ocean and the region. In the context of competition in the Indian Ocean there was some discussion of the need to offset the Russian aid (although in itself there was nothing objectionable in their aid). But the Russians did not really enter the picture with military aid until after the major U.S. decisions had been made.

Given the desire to improve relations, the fact that the Sri Lanka government would probably win regardless of what the U.S. did, and what was then called the "Nixon Doctrine", that the U.S. should not take on primary responsibility for defense of the whole world but should share the burden with other interested countries, NEA, in consultation with ISA, initially determined that U.S. interest would be served best by staying in the background. The policy was to encourage those countries with a more direct interest, such as India and Britain, to give aid. Later, in response to a request from Mrs. Bandaranaike, the President decided to enter into a direct non-lethal military supply relationship with the Ceylonese government. This decision was consistent with the increasing warmth of U.S.-Sri Lanka relations.

Whatever different perceptions of U.S. interest there were, were differences of emphasis, and complemented rather than contradicted each other. Policy disagreements were only on matters of detail, and they reflected personal opinions rather than bureaucratic view points.

Request for Aid I : Helicopter Spare Parts
On the night of April 7, the defense attache, who was stranded in his home in Colombo by the curfew, received a visit from the Commander of the Sri Lanka Air Force and the Permanent Secretary of the Ministry of Defense. The Deputy Chief of Mission, who had a pass enabling him to go out in the curfew, was also asked to come. (Ambassador Strausz-Hupe returned from leave either the next day or the day after.) The Ceylonese informed the Americans that the situation was serious and that they badly needed spare parts for their American helicopters. The defense attache noted that U.S. military planes were not allowed to land in Sri Lanka. He was assured there would be no problem. The Americans then pointed out that they lacked reliable intelligence on the insurgency, and could not very well ask Washington for aid without full information. The Ceylonese assured them that they would be briefed fully and regularly. The Americans were driven to the American Embassy in a Sri Lanka Air Force jeep. They sent off a cable relaying the request.

The cable arrived in a State Department bureau, NEA, which was already overloaded with work. Since March 25, when Yahya Khan ordered the crackdown in East Pakistan, the staff of the Pakistan-Afghanistan (PAF) country directorate had been working around the clock in the seventh floor Emergency Control Center. The Deputy Assistant Secretary for South Asia, Christopher Van Hollen was similarly preoccupied with Pakistan. Assistant Secretary Sisco's time was taken up not only by the crisis in Pakistan, but also by the up coming Middle East peace initiative (the so-called "Rogers Peace Plan"). The INC Country Director (CD), David Schneider had to monitor India's reaction to the Pakistan crisis, but, since the outbreak of the insurgency, he had devoted most of his time to the situation in Sri Lanka. Together with Andrew Kay, the Ceylon desk officer, and Peter Burleigh, the Nepal desk officer who had also served in Sri Lanka, he set up an *ad hoc* operations center in the country director's office, which was manned around the clock. The desk officers prepared daily situation reports (SITREPs), which were ready for distribution by 8 A.M. The CD briefed his superiors on the basis of these SITREPs. He also discussed the situation with them daily at meetings on Pakistan that were being held in Secretary Rogers' office. Present at the meetings, besides Rogers, Sisco, Van Hollen, and Schneider, were Special Deputy Assistant for press affairs Robert McCloskey and PAF CD William F. Spengler.

The problem posed by the request for helicopter spare parts was more practical than political. There was no real question of how to respond, nor were there any legal difficulties in the way of direct supplying of spare parts for equipment bought under a Foreign Military Sales Credit agreement. The State Department Bureau of Political Military Affairs raised no objection, nor did ISA. The Secretary of State gave his approval, and Dr. Kissinger indicated White House agreement. Despite the non-controversial nature of the decision, approval by the White House was required by the law governning military assistance.

The main problem then became finding the spare parts, getting an airplane to the proper place, and getting the parts flown to Sri Lanka. This process involved close collaboration of the NEA staff with their counterparts in ISA. After a few days of chaotic phone calling, during which the formal division of labor was overlooked in the interests of efficiency, the spare parts, which had been found at the Bell factory in Texas, were loaded on a USAF C-141 transport plane and flown off to Sri Lanka. The defense attache was given a lift to the Bandara-

naike International Airport in a Ceylon Air Force helicopter
in order to meet the incoming delivery on April 13. He was, he
says, favorably impressed by the speedy delivery. So, too, were
the Ceylonese.

Request for Aid II : Helicopters

The Sri Lanka government requested additional aid from
many countries. They especially asked for helicopters, which
they had found useful for observation and for breaking up
concentrations of insurgents during the day, enabling the army
to get some rest. Apparently, on or about April 10, the
embassy received a request for helicopters on an emergency
basis from the Commander of the Ceylon Air Force.

This request presented the NEA bureau with several
problems. The Ceylonese were asking the U.S. for direct
supply of new equipment to fight the insurgents, yet several
cabinet ministers had accused the U.S. of organizing the
insurgency. Furthermore, it was assumed that India and
Britain, Sri Lanka's Commonwealth partners, who traditionally
had a more direct interest in Sri Lanka's security, would bear
most of the aid burden. The bureau thus recommended that
the U.S. stay in the background and coordinate its actions
with governments that were more directly interested. There
was also a legal problem : the U.S. had no continuing military
assistance program in Sri Lanka, and any direct aid would
have required either an Act of Congress or a formal presidential determination. Either of these procedures would be
relatively slow. They further recommended, in agreement with
ISA, in line with the U.S. desire for a low level of involvement
and the policy, followed since 1966, of providing only "non-
lethal" military aid to South Asia, that any helicopters provided by the U.S. be unarmed.

The U.S. embassy in New Delhi contacted the Indians, to
seek their assessment of the situation and find out what they
intended to do. The U.S. embassy in London contacted the
British government. The State Department also worked with
the British embassy in Washington. The British supplied arms
and ammunition from Singapore, but they said they were
unable to supply helicopters. ISA meanwhile had dug up

six surplus helicopters of the type the Ceylonese were already using, which were stored at the Air Force base in Port Lewis, Washington. The bureau recommended that these helicopters be sold to the British for transfer to Sri Lanka, in order to stress the Commonwealth ties and evade the slow legal procedures required for direct U.S. aid. This recommendation was cleared with the PM and European Affairs Bureaus and by the Secretary of State.

Under Sec. 506 (a) of the Foreign Assistance Act, such a transfer of military aid by the recipient to a third country required the "consent of the President". This consent was obtained through the SRG. On April 13 there was an SRG meeting on Pakistan. At that time such meetings were held about once a week. As the Pakistan crisis deepened later in the year these meetings became the controversial WSAG meetings. At the end of the meeting on April 13, the insurgency in Sri Lanka was discussed. The SRG approved the proposal to send helicopters to Sri Lanka through the British. After the meeting, Gen. Haig called Gen. Purlsley (Secretary Laird's military aide) and instructed him to have the helicopters flown from Port Lewis to an RAF base in England. On April 16 the RAF landed the helicopters at Bandaranaike International Airport.

Request for Aid III : A Shopping List
Some time between April 14-18, the defense attache was asked to come to Sri Lanka Army Headquarters. He met the Commanders of the Army and Air Force, who told him that now that the insurgency was coming under control, they were starting to plan for the future. They did not want to be caught in such an unprepared state again. They requested a whole "shopping list" of items to be delivered on a long term rather than an emergency basis. The list was intended to fill in the major deficiencies in the equipment exposed by the insurgency, which were in the areas of communication, observation, and transportation. They asked for more helicopters, fixed wing transport planes, field radios, road building equipment, and certain lethal items such as machine guns, rifles, and ammunition. The defense attache returned to the embassy and talked the request over with the DCM and the Ambassador. They sent off a

cable describing the request and endorsing it, [with appropriate qualifications].

This request required a different kind of policy decision in Washington, one having to do not with the reaction to the crisis but with shaping U.S.-Sri Lanka relations for the next few years. The Ceylonese were asking the U.S. to enter into a direct long term military supply relationship. Before NEA had formulated a recommendation, the president made a decision on his own initiative. On April 19, at another SRG meeting mainly concerned with Pakistan, Dr. Kissinger said that the president wanted to be helpful, and directed Sisco to have his bureau put together a package in response to the request. The avowed purpose of the aid was to improve U.S.-Sri Lanka relations, to reassure the UF government about the U.S.'s intentions toward it, and to continue to build upon the mutual interest that had been growing.

NEA had to find legal authority for the aid, decide the terms under which it would be given, fix a budget, and determine the content of the package. These four things were all done at once, and not necessarily in any logical order, in collaboration with the PM bureau, ISA, the embassy in Colombo, and the government of Sri Lanka. I have not been able to reconstruct the process in full detail, but I can outline the role played by each group.

The subsidiary policy issue of what the general "thrust" of the aid should be was settled jointly by NEA and ISA. Both agreed not only to continue the policy of giving "non-lethal" equipment, which ruled out guns and ammunition, but further, to give equipment which, as far as possible, would serve dual purposes, military and developmental, or "civic action" equipment as described in section 505 (a) of the Foreign Assistance Act. The purpose of the aid was to improve relations, not to build a sophisticated military machine. This decision was also consistent with the main body of the request made by the Ceylonese.

There was no question that the aid had to be in the form of a grant, given Sri Lanka's economic situation, which the insurgency had seriously aggravated. The legal authority for grant aid coincidentally solved the budgetary question. A military aid specialist in either State's PM bureau or in Defense informed NEA that if the president made a formal determination under section 503 of the Foreign Assistance Act that military aid to Sri Lanka would "strengthen the security of the United States and promote world peace", he could then authorize a grant of military assistance under section 614(a). Under the rules of eligibility in section 506(b), the grant could not exceed $3 million in any fiscal year unless the President determined, among other things, that the recipient would use the arms to strengthen "the defensive strength of the free world". Such a determination, besides its innately dubitable qualities, might have created political difficulties with Congress or with the non-aligned Ceylonese. NEA had been estimating the needs of the Ceylonese at about $2 million, but they decided to go for the legal limit.

The budget figure was sent to the embassy in Colombo and conveyed to the Ceylonese military by the American defense attache. The military commanders, in consultation with Permanent Secretary of Defense Ratnavale and Mrs. Bandaranaike, as well as with the U.S. defense attache, prepared a more detailed list for transmittal to Washington, in view of the "dual purpose" policy and the budgetary requirements.

NEA sent the list to ISA for pricing. It turned out to overrun the budget, and had to be sent back to Sri Lanka, where, presumably, the different military services tried to make sure that the reductions were equally shared. Eventually, the CD received an agreed upon list which he incorporated into the memorandum he drafted for the president. This memorandum, after being approved by NEA, the PM bureau, and the Secretary of State, was signed by President Nixon on June 7, 1971.

Procurement and delivery were the responsibility of the Department of Defense, under the supervision of ISA. The first installment was delivered on January 25, 1972, by the Seventh Fleet supply ship *Mobile*. The decision to deliver the aid by a navy ship rather than by merchant marine or by air was made mainly on the basis of economy and convenience, though the Navy was naturally happy to have an opportunity for friendly contact with Sri Lanka. Some NEA officials at first questioned the political wisdom of this decision. They thought it might seem like a sneaky way of getting a ship visit. But they did

not press the point. In fact, the delivery made a fine ceremony
—Mrs. Bandaranaike turned out to meet the ship and had
lunch on board as the ambasador's guest. The last delivery,
which the ISA desk officer personally accompanied, was made
by air in early 1973.

Better Relations with Sri Lanka

The timely and tactful aid given by the U.S. played a role
in consolidating the tentative steps that had been taken toward
an improvement in relations. The destruction wrought by the
insurgency intensified the need for aid. The U.S. and China
became the biggest donors.[16] The rapprochement between the
U.S. and China made it easier for the Ceylonese to befriend
both countries, while the Soviet Union and India became
objects of suspicion in influential circles.

There was plenty of speculation in Sri Lanka about what
big power, if any, was behind the activities of the North
Koreans. A number of incidents cast suspicion on the Soviets.
There were reports from Mexico of the arrest of a guerrilla
group whose leaders had been trained at Moscow's Lumumba
University and in North Korea. When the North Koreans left
Sri Lanka, staff of the Soviet embassy saw them off at the airport. The Soviet embassy also took over responsibility for
North Korean interests in Sri Lanka. Furthermore, after
delivering their aid, which was useless for fighting the insurgents, arrived late, and was accompanied by an oversized
military mission, the Soviets may even have made a clumsy
attempt to secure a permanent presence in Sri Lanka, which the
Ceylonese naturally rejected.

Later events in 1971 consolidated these suspicions. The
Indo-Soviet pact was widely regarded in Sri Lanka as a betra-
yal of non-alignment by a neighbor the Ceylonese have viewed
as expansionist for at least two thousand years. They were
concerned by the influx of sophisticated Soviet military equipment into India and by the actions of the Soviet Union and

16. In a letter to Mrs. Bandaranaike, Chou-En-Lai denounced the insur-
    gents as ultra-leftists infiltrated by foreign spies. I have not discussed
    China's attitude to the insurgency because they did not give military
    aid. There is no indication that the activities of the Chinese affected
    the U.S. government's activities.

India in the December war, which destroyed the South Asian "balance of power" which Sri Lanka, as well as the U.S. and China, had favored. By early 1972 many Ceylonese defense strategists concluded that Soviet expansion in the Indian Ocean area was the primary external threat to Sri Lanka.[17] Not surprisingly, this conclusion affected the way they viewed U.S. activity in the region. Around the time of the Indo-Soviet treaty, partly in response to the efforts of the U.S. ambassador and defense attache, the government of Sri Lanka agreed in principle to consider requests for U.S. navy ship visits as a sign of a more even handed foreign policy. The first visit under the new policy took place on October 11, 1971, about a week before Mrs. Bandaranaike's visit to the U.S. to present the Indian Ocean Peace Zone proposal to the U.N. and meet with President Nixon. Like so many world leaders, Mrs. Bandaranaike hit it off with President Nixon, who viewed her as quiet and practical.

In March, 1972, she welcomed Admiral John S. McCain, Commander of the Pacific Fleet on a three day "orientation visit" to Sri Lanka. The "chop line" dividing the Pacific from the Mediterranean Fleet had been moved westward in January, bringing Sri Lanka (and Diego Garcia) within the Pacific Fleet's official range. Admiral McCain was visiting littoral countries wherever possible to work out plans for future relations. The government of Sri Lanka let him know that in the absence of fulfilment of the plan for an Indian Ocean Peace Zone, Sri Lanka would not single out U.S. naval activity in the Indian Ocean as a target for criticism.

Evaluation of Information

The information available to the decision makers was imperfect in certain ways. In particular, no one knew how many members or weapons the JVP had, how it was organized,

17. For a pseudonymous account of this process, seemingly written by an insider, see Pertinax, "Ceylon's Non-Alignment after the Indo-Pak War : Can SWRD's Dynamic Neutralism Flourish Today ?" *Tribune*, 17 : 29, May 20, 1972. U.S. officials maintained an attitude of agnosticism toward charges of Soviet involvement in the insurgency. Whether or not they actually believed the Soviets were involved, they didn't consider this question to be of great importance.

what international contacts it had, or what, exactly, it intended to do. A little while before the attack on the embassy, the CIA seems to have believed that an insurgency was likely, but this view affected policy about as much as an article in a journal of political science. This view was apparently not based on definite inside information, but on an intelligent reading of the situation. What evidence there is indicates that the CIA did not infiltrate or develop sources within the JVP.

The main, one might almost say the exclusive, source of information during the crisis was foreign service reporting both directly, in cables, and indirectly, as analyzed by State's Intelligence and Research Bureau. (INR was most useful for coordinating information on the activity of other aid donors, since it received cables from all U.S. missions.) The foreign service reporting formed the basis for the daily situation reports composed by the desk officer and used by the country director to brief higher officials.

Although the U.S. mission in Colombo was well aware of JVP's existence, the staff never went out of their way to find people who could tell them about it. Given the suspicions of the U.S. current in the UF and the ambassador's overriding goal of allaying these suspicions and improving relations, the mission made it a policy to restrict travel and unofficial contacts. It seemed better to remain ignorant of some things than to do anything which might have been misconstrued as subversive. For the month or two before the attack on the embassy, this general policy was reinforced by security considerations, as information on the JVP's preparations trickled out.

Hence the U.S. government had no specific warning of the attack on the embassy or the insurgency, had no idea how strong or extensive an insurgency the JVP was capable of mounting, and remained unsure of the extent of the insurgency for some time after its outbreak. Nevertheless, it was about as well informed as any other government, including Mrs. Bandaranaike's. Once the crisis was on, the mission's development of a good working relationship with government and military officials in Colombo provided Washington with reliable information from Ceylonese official sources. Although many questions, such as the number of insurgents and the extent of foreign involvement, were never completely answered, the

decision makers had enough information to decide the issues
confronting them. The lack of information was partly the
result of a political calculation, the justice of which was proved
in the event.

Evaluation of Field Organization

The embassy played a somewhat limited role during the
crisis. Most of the staff's time was taken up with gathering
information. The defense attache, the ambassador, the deputy
chief of mission, and the first secretary also received and
evaluated the aid requests before sending them on to Washington. But this evaluation never included the full range of policy
considerations that were introduced to the discussions in
Washington. During the insurgency, embassy reporting focused
mainly on the insurgency itself and issues directly involving the
U.S. For them the question was, how can we respond to this
crisis in such a way as to improve relations ? They did not
simply become advocates of "their" government's requests.
Although they endorsed the requests, they did so after noting
possible reasons for reserve, such as UF ministerial accusations
of CIA involvement with the JVP. But details of policy, such
as the decisions to supply only non-lethal equipment and to send
the helicopters through the British, originated in Washington.
Officials who participated in the Washington meetings on the
crisis repeatedly mentioned that they considered the U.S.'s
reaction to the insurgency in the light of the "Nixon Doctrine".
Those in the embassy were aware of wider policy considerations, but did not take the time to think through the full
implications of those considerations, such as the "Nixon
Doctrine", for U.S. policy.

At the times other than crisis, the embassy had more initiative in shaping U.S.-Sri Lanka relations. Both before and after
the insurgency the trend toward improvement of relations was
assisted considerably by the personal efforts of Ambassador
Strausz-Hupe, a Viennese born professor of international
relations from the University of Pennsylvania. President
Nixon originally nominated Strausz-Hupe to be ambassador to
Morocco, but the Senate Foreign Relations Committee found
his views too right wing and blocked his confirmation until he
was renominated for the presumably less important post of

ambassador to Sri Lanka. His political philosophy did not seem to hamper his relations with Mrs. Bandaranaike and her cabinet, with whom he got on "swimmingly", nor did he have any conflicts with the professionals working under him in the mission. The excellent personal relations between the ambassador and the prime minister created an atmosphere which facilitated the work of other members of the mission and contributed to the entente.

The ambassador also worked to obtain permission from the Government of Sri Lanka for the renewal of ship visits. The defense attache, a Navy officer, participated actively in this effort. The decision to provide military aid increased both the frequency and the intimacy of his contact with Ceylonese officials concerned with defense, both in the military and civil services. He took advantage of these contacts to argue that renewed ship visits would bring benefits of many kinds to Sri Lanka, including the financial benefits of foreign exchange. After some discussion the officials agreed, and, in due time, the government of Sri Lanka approved the proposal.

The defense attache was distinct in belonging to a service (the Navy) which had a well defined specific area of a concern in Sri Lanka. Because of the Navy's "primary interest" (among the military services) in Sri Lanka, Navy officers are routinely assigned the defense post in Colombo. The attache's duties include not only contact with the Sri Lanka government, but liaison with sea captains, the updating of harbor maps, and other duties concerning maritime matters. There is no evidence that this particular interest (or any disagreements between the navy and State in Washington) led to conflicts in the Colombo Embassy.

Evaluation of Decision Making in Washington
The NEA bureau had the action in Washington. The country director in particular did almost all of the drafting of policy documents and hence most of the coordination of information and policy inputs from different sources. Much of the evaluation of alternatives and options went on in the daily meetings in Secretary Rogers' office, rather than in NSC papers prepared for the president. The NSC and its subgroup, the SRG, were accessible to the State Department officials working on the case,

and provided quick clearances and quick communications of the President's decision. ISA and the military services were content to act as support for State; they provided information on "nuts and bolts" questions without pushing for greater authority or special military interests. In this case policy making was centered around the country director, who worked closely with those immediately above and below him, coordinated matters with horizontal counterparts in other agencies, and had easy access to the Secretary of State and the White House whenever necessary. The treatment of this case thus differed considerably from that of other foreign policy questions at the same time. The policy making process resembled the organizational model that inspired the institution of the country director in the first place, but was never fully realized.

These characteristics of the organizational environment were mainly determined by the simultaneous crisis in Pakistan and the lack of strong bureaucratic or national interest in Sri Lanka. The crisis in Pakistan prevented the action from going above the country director's level and provided him with greater access to higher officials. The Deputy Assistant Secretary and the Assistant Secretary were too preoccupied with Pakistan to take much responsibility for Sri Lanka. The same is true of counterparts in other agencies such as (ISA or NSC) who worked on South Asia. The Pakistan crisis was also the reason for the daily meetings with Secretary Rogers and the weekly meetings of the SRG, where all South Asia officials from country director up were present. The country director did not normally have such frequent access to high officials, especially on matters pertaining to Sri Lanka.[18]

The lack of strong interest removed another possible source of challenges to the CD's authority. The Defense Department had no reason to demand more of the action, which might have led to the formation of an interdepartmental working group or

18. One official suggested an analogy with the Sino-Indian war, which occurred during the Cuban missile crisis. The analogy applies in so far as the action officers had a great deal of initiative because superior officers were preoccupied. It does not apply in that the Cuban missile crisis sealed off access to higher levels by the South Asia line men rather than opened it. In the spring of 1971, there was a crisis in both the country directorates under the South Asia DAS.

pushed the level of policy formation up to the White House. Nor did the NSC regard the insurgency as a vital national security matter which needed to be centered in the White House.

Unlike the Embassy staff, the officials who worked on this case in Washington viewed the issue in the context of broad foreign policy considerations. They tried to apply the "Nixon Doctrine" and considered Sri Lanka's position in the international political system. Whatever differences (if any) might have existed in the initial approaches of the country director, deputy assistant secretary, assistant secretary, and secretary of state, they seem to have reached a consensus during their daily meetings. It seems apparent in this case that constant contact with high level officials and increased responsibility for policy lead working level line officers to see issues in a broader perspective. "Clientelism" may not be built into the regional and subregional roles *per se*, but into the organizational structure which isolates the line officers from decision making and planning.

It is possible only to speculate about the view from the Oval Office. It is possible that Nixon and Kissinger saw improved relations with Sri Lanka as a way of enlarging common interests with China. This consideration might have been behind the President's quick positive response to Mrs. Bandaranaike's request for direct aid, while NEA was still unsure what to recommend. But even if other participants were ignorant of some motivations behind the President's decision, the decision appeared reasonable in the light of what they did know.

Last, one should not forget that small crises create small problems. Suppose the insurgents had managed to capture parts of Colombo or the airport. It might have appeared that only direct foreign military intervention could have defeated the JVP. India might well have moved to take such action, which would have threatened to place an Indian military presence along what was then Pakistan's only route of transportation between its East and West wings. Such a development would have summoned the attention of partisans of India and Pakistan to the crisis in Sri Lanka. At that point the problem would have required a coordinator with more clout than the

CD, and the conflicts that surfaced later in the year might have come to the fore then. Although the country director centered process functioned well in this case, it was as much because of the weakness of the insurgency, a factor out of the U.S. government's control, as because of the virtues of the process.

Recommendation
Since this is a case of success in planning and implementation, recommendations take the form not of correcting flaws in the policy process, but of drawing positive lessons. The major respect in which this case differed from other cases was in the high involvement of the regional bureau line officers in the policy making process. Such involvement both brings regional expertise to bear on problems where it is needed and forces the experts to apply their expertise within a larger policy context.

This suggests not only that the State Department be given a greater role relative to the NSC in foreign policy planning, but that within State itself policy planning should more deeply involve the line officers. Those with responsibility for setting policy would have to change their pattern of consultation. At present, the regional staffs provide informational inputs early in the policy process, but later policy evaluation is done elsewhere. Under the system proposed here, the regional bureau officials would be involved in discussion and drafting of policy papers at every step of the process. Such an arrangement could operate within the present system of formal organization, but it would require a commitment from the highest levels to change the informal processes through which policy is formulated.

ANNEX:

BIBLIOGRAPHY

Anand, J.P., "British Military Presence East of Suez", *Journal of the Institute for Defense Studies and Analysis* (JIDSA), IV : 2, Oct., 1971.

Arasaratnam, S., "The Ceylon Insurrection of April, 1971: Some Causes and Consequences", *Pacific Affairs* 43 : 3, Fall, 1973.

Bharati, Agehananda, "Revolution in Sri Lanka", *Quest*, Jan.-Feb., 1973.

Bhargava, G.S., "Civil Violence and External Involvement : The Indian Sub-Continent", *JIDSA*, IV:2, Oct., 1971.

Dubey, Swaroop Rani, "Sri Lanka: A Survey of Events: 1970-72", *South Asian Studies* VIII:1, Jan., 1973.

IDSA, *India in World Strategic Environment, Annual Review*, 1969-70,Delhi, 1970. 1970-71, V. I, II, Delhi, 1971.

Iqbal, Mehrunissa, "The Insurgency in Ceylon and its Repercussion", *Pakistan Horizon*, XXV : 2, Second Quarter, 1972.

Muni, Anuradha, "Sri Lanka's China Policy : Major Trends", *South Asia Studies*, VIII:I, Jan., 1973.

Obeyesekera, Jayasumuna, "Revolutionary Movements in Ceylon", in Kathleen Gough and Hari R. Sharma, ed., *Imperialism and Revolution in South Asia*, Monthly Review Press, N.Y., N.Y., 1973.

Pertinax, "Ceylon's Non-Alignment after the Indo-Pak War : Can SWRD's Dynamic Neutralism Flourish Today ?" *Tribune*, 17 : 29, May 30, 1972.

Phadnis, Urmila, "Insurgency in Ceylonese Politics: Problems and Prospects", *JISDA*, III:4, April, 1971.

——, "Trends in Ceylon Politics", *India Quarterly*, XXVII:2, April-June, 1971.

——, "The U.F. Government in Ceylon : Challenges and Responses", *The World Today*, June, 1971.

——, With S.D. Muni, "Emergence in Bangladesh: Response of Ceylon and Nepal", *South Asian Studies*, VII:2, July, 1972.

——, "Infrastructural Linkages in Sri Lanka-India Relations", *Economic and Political Weekly*, August, 1972 (Special edition).

——, "Sri Lanka Today", *Current History*, 63:375, Nov., 1972.

Politicus, "The April Revolt in Ceylon", *Asian Survey*, XII:3 March, 1972.

Prasad, D.M., "Ceylon's Foreign Policy under the Bandaranaikes 1956-1965 : A Study in the Emergence and Role of Non-Alignment," *The Indian Journal of Political Science*, July-Sept,. 1972.

Ramachandran, K.M., "China's South Asia Policy", *JIDSA*, IV:1, July, 1971.

"U.S. Strategy Beyond Vietnam : Exclusive Interview with Defense Secretary Melvin R. Laird", *U.S. News and World Report*, LXX:20, May 17, 1971.

Warnapala, W.A. Wiswa, "Sri Lanka in 1972: Tension and Change", *Asian Survey*. XIII:2, Feb., 1973.

Wilson, A. Jeyaratnam, "Ceylon : a New Government Takes Office", *Asian Survey*, XI:2, Feb., 1971.

——, "Ceylon : A Time of Troubles", *Asian Survey*, XII:2, Feb., 1971.

Newspapers:
Ceylon Daily News
New York Times

CASE STUDIES :
II. ECONOMIC POLICY

A. Public Law 480 and the Policies of Self-Help and Short-Tether : Indo-American Relations, 1965-68

James Warner Bjorkman

American agricultural abundance offers a great opportunity for the United States to promote the interests of peace in a significant way.

John Fitzgerald Kennedy, 1958

Food is power and the basis of a happier world.

George S. McGovern, 1962

Food, and the ability to produce it, and the means of teaching others to produce it, are the most powerful weapons that America possesses.

Orville L. Freeman, 1966

We know that a grain of wheat is a potent weapon in the arsenal of freedom.

Lyndon Baines Johnson, 1968

I. Introduction

The politics of food and agricultural aid have become an increasingly large component of American foreign policy. Unlike traditional foreign policy concerns like diplomacy, espionage, and war, food policy deals with a very prosaic subject. But it is a vital subject on which the strength of nations both morally and physically, depends. Since *Famine 1975!* (Paddock and Paddock, 1967) and *The Limits to Growth* (Meadows *et al.*, 1972), the imperatives of agricultural production and distribution systems have become increasingly apparent to policy-makers both here and abroad.

The Achilles heel of writings on contemporary problems is the seeming impossibility of political prediction, and evaluations of a particular decision's consequences are likewise unlikely. Although retrospectives often seem passe, a historical case example permits judicious estimates of such causes and consequences. No single study can discuss all the issues involved in the political economy of foodaid, but an example focussed on Public Law 480 can illuminate the operation of US food policies toward the Republic of India. The time-period selected for detailed examination lies in the mid-sixties and coincides with the troubled presidency of Lyndon Baines Johnson. The period was selected because it spans the revision of ground-rules for American food policy and because it illustrates the vulnerability of a seemingly well-insulated program to presidential manipulation. It also marked a reorientation of India's strategy for economic development, even as Indo-American relations cooled.

Two broad decisions within the PL-480 ambit have been selected for special consideration. These are the requirement that India demonstrate sincere efforts at 'self-help' before foodaid would be granted, and LBJ's 'short-tether' on food shipments during the latter half of the 1965-67 drought. The self-help provisions include a discussion of their origin, the negotiating of their terms, and the monitoring of their implementation. And the short-tether policy includes its source, its coordination with other nations, and its political effects.

After the background of PL-480, its shifting complex of players, and its mechanisms for coordination and surveillance have been discussed, a narrative history will be presented of PL-480 programs in Indo-American relations and how they affected bureaucratic politics in the respective countries. This history indicates how an incremental policy affected by many players was abruptly placed under close presidential supervision, and describes some effects of this changed situation on the US policy-making system. The essay ends with brief observations and recommendations about coordinating American foreign policies.

II. Background of a Well-Insulated Program

The Agricultural Trade Development and Assistance Act of 1954 authorized the "sale" of American farm surpluses to other countries on concessional terms. These terms included payments in foreign currency, reduced rates of interest, and grace-periods before repayments began. Proceeds from these commodity sales were deposited in special local currency accounts. Other than a small percentage transferred to the United States Government (USG) for use by its in-country agencies, the counterpart funds in these accounts belong to the recipient country.[1] The USG cannot spend this balance because "in essence, with the exception of the portion set aside for US uses, counterpart is a conditional grant—the condition being agreement by the United States on the final uses of the funds" (Galdi, 1974 : 5).

The 1954 Act had several goals which can be rank-ordered. First, it sought to protect and sustain standing patterns of American agricultural commerce or, in other words, to ensure the profitable disposal of American farm produce; second, to expand old markets and develop new ones for US agricultural goods; and third, to help other countries to grow to the point of economic self-sufficiency. No specific assistance, however, would be allowed that jeopardized America's international or domestic commercial interests.

Furthermore, PL-480—as this Act of the 83rd Congress came to be called—included non-agricultural aims. It authorized the purchase of goods and services on behalf of other countries, the promotion of trade, and the financing of international educational exchange. Like the successive Mutual Security Acts of the 1950s, PL-480 also sought to purchase materials for the US strategic stockpile, pay US obligations overseas, and provide military equipment, materials, or facilities. Over time, amendments and extensions added other aims to Section 104.[2]

The act is administered through the Commodity Credit Corporation (CCC) under a remarkably flexible financial arrangement. US domestic agricultural policy is committed to a price-support program and, therefore, to a type of national

1. Through 1971 when PL-480 shipments to India were interrupted, 87 per cent of PL-480 receipts had been earmarked for use in India (63 per cent for loans, 18 per cent for grants, and six per cent for the so-called 'Cooley loans' to American business ventures) and the remaining 13 per cent had been allocated for use by USG agencies (Veit, no date : 4).
2. See Annex A.

subsidy for agriculture. In order to respond to market forces, CCC was designed to operate independently of the Congress since market fluctuations made it impractical to put line-items for specific commodities in the annual budget. Thus, in 1949, Congress reluctantly agreed to allot CCC a blanket authorization against which annual appropriations are requested. Other than the comparable example of the Tennessee Valley Authority, CCC's authority is unique in American government.

In order to finance commodity "sales" abroad, the funding arrangements for PL-480 provide an annual ceiling between $1.5 and $3 billion with which to pay the CCC for its surplus commodities. Since CCC goods cost cash dollars, congressional appropriations are required to pay for the commodities purchased. Appropriations, of course, entail taxation to pay for government expenditures, which put a strain on the normal domestic US budget. In turn, the US Treasury accepts foreign currencies as payment for the PL-480 goods overseas, although after 1971 most sales were shifted into freely convertible currencies.

In addition to the annual appropriations for PL-480, there are "reflows" which come back from overseas agreements. These reflows now total about $200 million per year and can be carried over to subsequent years. As a consequence of these cumulative reflows, the CCC budget for PL-480 can always facilitate the export of US agricultural commodities. Furthermore, CCC is empowered to purchase commodities on credit, using its reflows and annual appropriations as security collateral. In 1975 Title I had about $10.8 billion on tap for underwriting concessional sales while Title II, which authorizes the outright donation of surplus commodity stocks through voluntary agencies, had about $1.4 billion.

These funding arrangements through CCC have always provided the PL-480 program with considerable fiscal autonomy. It is not subject to quick congressional leverage since the purse-strings cannot be drawn shut very easily—a situation which is perhaps the *sine qua non* of a well-insulated program. Until the Soviet wheat deal of 1972,[3] the Commodity Credit

---

3. Although CCC is formally within the jurisdiction of USDA, the negotiations for the ultimate signing ceremony of the Soviet-American wheat deal occurred in the US Department of Commerce.

Corporation had operated prudently and responsibly within the increasingly restrictive constraints of the American executive budget. Since that deal, the problem confronting PL-480 operations has not been one of funds to cover exports but the availability of the commodities themselves.

III. The Range of Players : Organizational Actors and their Interests*

Like all programs attesting to the high art of the politically possible, PL-480 met a number of needs simultaneously. As a staff member of the Senate Committee on Agriculture and Forestry put it, "PL-480 was an act which has been all things to all people". The attached chart depicts some of the organizational players involved in the PL-480 program during the mid-'60s. Most importantly, it provided a vehicle to dispose of the unwieldy American farm surpluses generated by price-supports so that, while *American farmers* received cash for their produce, the *United States Department of Agriculture* (USDA) saved the costs of commodity storage. As the annual carry-overs of surplus commodities diminished, the payoffs from PL-480 became less economical and more political.

American shipping interests, including both the heavily subsidized *merchant marine fleet* and the *maritime unions*, received welcome business since at least half of all PL-480 goods had to be transported on American bottoms. In 1964, a representative year before the massive shipments to India, "the total value of freight payments for the movement of PL-480 cargoes amounted to almost $222 million, including more than $81 million in rate premiums which represented the difference between world market rates and the rate required by US-flat ships" (N. Johnson, 1965 : 1). Cargo-preference requirements originated in the Merchant Marine Act of 1936 but were reinforced in its 1965 amendments after the Joint Economic

---

However, recent presidential interventions in CCC operations and their consequences for domestic inflation and American investments in Siberia are beyond the scope of this case-study.

* See also the schematic representation : Chart I.

Committee had sharply criticized the Agency for International Development (AID) and other USG agencies for shipping such a small percentage of US-financed goods on American vessels. Furthermore, while shipping charges are paid by recipient countries, the USG financed the "differential" between world-rates and American-rates of shipping. Until 1969[4] USDA financed this "differential" for PL-480 shipments from its own dollar budget.

Initially the *US Department of State* had opposed PL-480 because of its presumed repercussions on international trade and because it was assigned to "those cowboys" at USDA.[5] When PL-480 did pass Congress, the State Department then proceeded to ignore it during the 1950s. By the time Foggy Bottom awoke to the considerable political leverage afforded by PL-480 shipments, USDA would not relinquish its control. Over time, State/AID came to value PL-480 because the provision of food supplies was a very direct, immediate gesture of goodwill and was also a disguised source of development capital. For the humanitarian interests which persist in the American character, the PL-480 program offered tangible evidence of our native generosity. And even the cold-warriors couldn't take full offense at PL-480 because, although India maintained neutrality in the "Dullesian" anti-communist crusades, it was an operational democratic state with "a democratic political accountability almost as real and exacting as

4. In contrast to previous presidencies, the Ford Administration's strategy for making the US merchant marine more competitive entails subsidies for ship-construction and for flying the American flag rather than the imposition of cargo-preference requirements. While the American shipping fleet and the maritime unions are both well-entrenched interests in US politics, GOP administrations tend to favor the former and Democratic administrations the latter.

5. One experienced interviewee observed that during the Marshall Plan, to the disgust of domestic American agriculture, the State Department persistently slighted US exports in favor of European-grown agricultural produce. Thus when PL-480 was drafted in 1954, it was specifically designed for USDA's interests. The bill's basic intent was to move surplus commodities but not to interfere with commercial trade.

ublic Law 480 Policy : A Simplified Chart

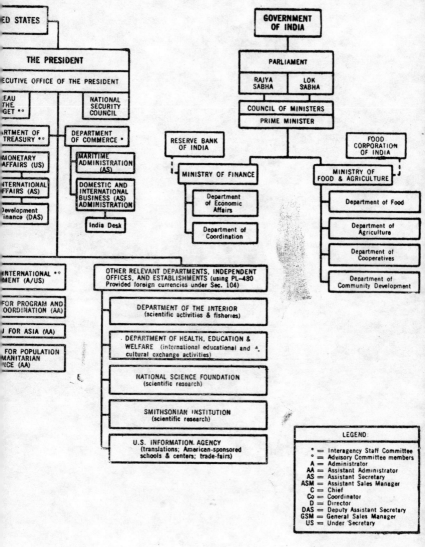

ED STATES

THE PRESIDENT

ECUTIVE OFFICE OF THE PRESIDENT

REAU
THE
GET **

NATIONAL
SECURITY
COUNCIL

ARTMENT OF
TREASURY **

DEPARTMENT
OF COMMERCE *

MONETARY
FFAIRS (US)

MARITIME
ADMINISTRATION
(AS)

NTERNATIONAL
FFAIRS (AS)

DOMESTIC AND
INTERNATIONAL
BUSINESS (AS)
ADMINISTRATION

Development
inance (DAS)

India Desk

NTERNATIONAL **
MENT (A/US)

FOR PROGRAM AND
OORDINATION (AA)

FOR ASIA (AA)

FOR POPULATION
MANITARIAN
NCE (AA)

OTHER RELEVANT DEPARTMENTS, INDEPENDENT
OFFICES, AND ESTABLISHMENTS (using PL–480
Provided foreign currencies under Sec. 104)

DEPARTMENT OF THE INTERIOR
(scientific activities & fisheries)

DEPARTMENT OF HEALTH, EDUCATION &
WELFARE (international educational and
cultural exchange activities)

NATIONAL SCIENCE FOUNDATION
(scientific research)

SMITHSONIAN INSTITUTION
(scientific research)

U.S. INFORMATION AGENCY
(translations; American-sponsored
schools & centers; trade-fairs)

**GOVERNMENT
OF INDIA**

PARLIAMENT

RAJYA
SABHA

LOK
SABHA

COUNCIL OF MINISTERS

PRIME MINISTER

RESERVE BANK
OF INDIA

FOOD
CORPORATION
OF INDIA

MINISTRY OF FINANCE

MINISTRY OF
FOOD & AGRICULTURE

Department
of Economic
Affairs

Department of
Coordination

Department of Food

Department of
Agriculture

Department of
Cooperatives

Department of
Community Development

LEGEND
* = Interagency Staff Committee
° = Advisory Committee members
A = Administrator
AA = Assistant Administrator
AS = Assistant Secretary
ASM = Assistant Sales Manager
C = Chief
Co = Coordinator
D = Director
DAS = Deputy Assistant Secretary
GSM = General Sales Manager
US = Under Secretary

(Facing Page 206)

Chart I : Some Organizational Players in

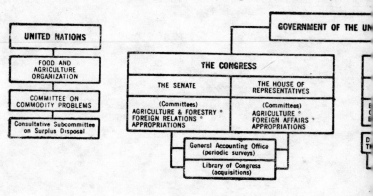

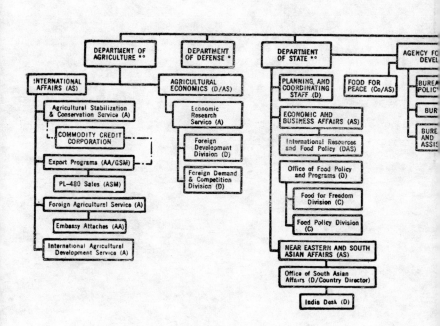

UNITED NATIONS

FOOD AND AGRICULTURE ORGANIZATION

COMMITTEE ON COMMODITY PROBLEMS

Consultative Subcommittee on Surplus Disposal

GOVERNMENT OF THE UN

THE CONGRESS

THE SENATE	THE HOUSE OF REPRESENTATIVES
(Committees) AGRICULTURE & FORESTRY ° FOREIGN RELATIONS ° APPROPRIATIONS	(Committees) AGRICULTURE ° FOREIGN AFFAIRS ° APPROPRIATIONS

General Accounting Office (periodic surveys)

Library of Congress (acquisitions)

DEPARTMENT OF AGRICULTURE °°

INTERNATIONAL AFFAIRS (AS)

Agricultural Stabilization & Conservation Service (A)

COMMODITY CREDIT CORPORATION

Export Programs (AA/GSM)

PL–480 Sales (ASM)

Foreign Agricultural Service (A)

Embassy Attaches (AA)

International Agricultural Development Service (A)

DEPARTMENT OF DEFENSE °

AGRICULTURAL ECONOMICS (D/AS)

Economic Research Service (A)

Foreign Development Division (D)

Foreign Demand & Competition Division (D)

DEPARTMENT OF STATE °°

PLANNING AND COORDINATING STAFF (D)

FOOD FOR PEACE (Co/AS)

ECONOMIC AND BUSINESS AFFAIRS (AS)

International Resources and Food Policy (DAS)

Office of Food Policy and Programs (D)

Food for Freedom Division (C)

Food Policy Division (C)

NEAR EASTERN AND SOUTH ASIAN AFFAIRS (AS)

Office of South Asian Affairs (D/Country Director)

India Desk (D)

AGENCY FO DEVEL

BUREA POLIC

BUR

BURE AND ASSIS

that of the United States government itself" (Lewis, 1964 :
273).

The *US Department of the Treasury* at first did not object to
PL-480 because the American balance of payments in the 1950s
was healthy and in fact through PL-480 the US Government
reduced its storage costs for surplus commodities. Although
agricultural exports account for up to a quarter of total US
exports, for many years long-term credit sales in soft-currencies
were permissible. As the balance of payments turned unfavorable, the Treasury sought cash rather than credit sales and
emphasized sales in convertible currencies. Nonetheless,
because PL-480 funds existed for American use, US
Embassy and AID Mission operations in excess currency countries like India have had virtually no balance of payments cost to
the United States.

In the *United States Congress*, three sets of committees are
relevant : agriculture, foreign affairs, and appropriations. Within the jurisdictional division of power on the Hill, PL-480 falls
under the House and Senate *agriculture committees*. The *foreign
affairs committees* have an obvious interest in trying to handle
this major component of foreign economic aid since in some
years PL-480 aid totaled nearly one-third of all non-military
assistance. The third set of Congressional committees are those
dealing with appropriations, since the surplus commodities
must still be paid for and then reallocated as foreign aid. In
simple terms, the *appropriations committees* are interested in
keeping government expenditures, and therefore taxes, down.
Give-away programs (other than porkbarrel projects) have
never been popular with these committees, even when the proceeds go to the powerful agricultural barons.

Finally, the *Government of India* (GOI) had a considerable
stake in the PL-480 program. The GOI received the food
supplies necessary to maintain political stability while it
devoted its slim resources to industrial investments (the Nehru-
Mahalanobis strategy of development). And in fact, by
allowing India to concentrate on industrialization, PL-480
indirectly helped US firms to sell India capital goods. Furthermore, at a time of general inflation, Nehru in particular
repeatedly pointed with pride to the cheap-food policy of his

government.[6] While price indices of all other commodities kept
rising, the prices of wheat and other foodgrains were held in
check through 1963 by PL-480 imports (Bhatnagar, 1969 :
250-259). As under the old CCC strategy in the US, economic
analyses indicated that the price of wheat in India varied
more with government wheat-stocks than with domestic production, so ample PL-480 imports were desirable. Fortunately,
payments for the American-provided grainstocks could be
deferred to the distant future through 'credit sales' while
reaping immediate benefits. Of course, like all governments,
the GOI was not monolithic. Its *Finance Ministry* worried
about the inflation caused by additional rupee-revenue flowing
through the economy, while the *Ministry of Food and
Agriculture* sought the contradictory policies of cheap food for
the consumers and better prices for the producers.

Thus, in the period examined, a pattern of interests
emerged among those playing an active role in PL-480
decisions. These interests involved three sets of basic issues :
economic, budgetary-finance, and political, which were of
varying concern to the many participants as PL-480 policy
evolved over time.

Economic issues concerned the transfer of real resources
from the US into the Indian economy, the actual terms of
individual agreements, the US balance of payments, and
transfers within the US to the agricultural sector. Until about
1964, AID wanted to free up indigenous resources and precious
foreign exchange for India's industrial undertakings and the
large-scale projects necessary to build up an infra-structure for

6. The success of the GOI's cheap-food policy until 1963 and the
   dilemmas thereafter are indicated by the index numbers of December
   wholesale prices for Indian food articles :

1952=100.0	1964=166.0	1969=227.3
1960=117.0	1965=173.2	1970=235.6
1961=117.8	1966=204.1	1971=241.1
1962=122.8	1967=239.3	1972=287.9
1963=136.1	1968=227.3	

SOURCE : *Agricultural Situation in India*, Department of Economics and
Statistics, Ministry of Food and Agriculture, Government of India
(various years).

future development. The GOI wanted the same as well as an adequate supply of grain to keep food prices down.

USDA had originally wanted to dispose of its surplus commodities and secondarily to develop or expand markets. Later, when reserve stocks of commodities grew scarce and claims could only be made on America's long-range agricultural production capacity, USDA wanted assurance that accidental over-runs in production could be absorbed by CCC. In the latter post-1964 period, USDA also sought to stimulate agricultural development in India in order to wean India from its increasing dependency on US grain reserves and to strengthen India's ability to purchase US products commercially. In both periods, USDA sought to ensure price stability and economic well-being for its primary domestic constituency, the American farmers.

Meanwhile, the Department of the Treasury became increasingly concerned about the adverse balance of payments and regarded PL-480 "sales" as a drain on America's potential hard-currency assets. The same issue (but for obviously different reasons) agitated other producer nations which earn a substantial portion of their foreign exchange from agricultural exports. Through the United Nations' Food and Agriculture Organization (FAO), such countries as Australia, Argentina, Canada, the Netherlands, and Denmark (plus, recently, other members of the European Economic Community) kept track of American PL-480 negotiations and shipments so that the usual marketing patterns in world agricultural trade were not disrupted.

Budgetary-finance issues dealt with taxation and the internal contours of the American budget. The Bureau of the Budget (BoB) and the Congress knew that PL-480 costs real dollars, which have to be appropriated in order to pay for agricultural commodities. Since 1964 when the CCC appropriation peaked at $1.6 billion, about one billion dollars have annually been allocated to the CCC for financing Titles I and II of PL-480. Appropriations for this budget item entail taxation to pay for government expenditures, curtail other domestic programs, and place a drain on the US Treasury.

In addition to the natural Treasury and BoB interests in fiscal responsibility, the Appropriations Committees are concerned. As Galdi (1974 : 8-9) reports, "the fact that the local currencies obtained are not dollars and not convertible is frequently misunderstood, especially when it comes time to spend them". The original relevance of the 1966 Mondale-Poage amendment[7] was that the US Executive could use PL-480 funds for certain purposes without undergoing the appropriations process.

The GOI was also concerned about the domestic fiscal effects of PL-480 agreements, since the rupees they generated were permitted to have an inflationary effect on the Indian economy. Such inflation was caused not only by expenditures of blocked rupees through loans and grants but also by the multiplicative effects of an increased money supply in the central budget. The US goods supplied under each PL-480 Agreement were, in turn, sold by the Food Corporation of India and the proceeds, after committing about ten percent to USG use, were added to the annual GOI budget.[8]

Political issues comprise the more traditional concerns of US foreign policy, although there was a growing concern for the US balance of payments during the latter half of the decade. The State Department and the President usually wanted *quid pro quos* of support for (or, at minimum, neutrality towards) American diplomatic positions, both bilaterally and through international organizations. Treasury and BoB had greater interest in improving American leverage over international commerce in order to correct the shortfalls in the US balance of payments. Meanwhile, PL-480 Agreements automatically meant involvement in and interference with a recipient country's internal affairs. As the conditions of each Agreement became more explicit and more oriented toward self-help, PL-480 became a lever to redirect and restructure the Indian domestic economy. This leverage was of critical interest to AID and to USDA for their development projects and strategy. It was also of increasing concern to the Government of India, which regarded such conditions as an infringement on its national sovereignty. At the same time, within the GOI were

7. See Section 104(k) of Annex A.
8. The Khusro Report (1968) also correctly predicted that inflation would worsen when the PL-480 shipments ceased and the buffer stocks in the Food Corporation of India declined.

competing factions who were respectively weakened or strengthened by US decisions about PL-480 and the resources it provided.

IV. Mechanisms for Coordination and Surveillance : The Agreement Process

Including the Executive Office of the President and five major Cabinet Departments as well as various committees, of the US Congress, PL-480 had ramifications throughout much of American government. The oldest of the formal coordinating devices for PL-480 is the Interagency Staff Committee (ISC) which has operated since 1954. Chaired by USDA, the ISC has representatives from State/AID (two masquerading as one), Treasury, Commerce, Defense, and the Bureau of the Budget (now Office of Management and Budget). Other departments and agencies which are concerned with specific phases of Title I programs and with uses of foreign currencies but which are not voting members of the ISC include the Office of Emergency Planning, the US Information Agency, the National Science Foundation, the Department of the Interior (for fisheries) the Library of Congress, the Smithsonian Institution, and the Department of Health, Education, and Welfare.

The ISC is a working-level committee whose members, all career bureaucrats, proceed only through consensual decision-making. If problems cannot be resolved in ISC deliberations, decisions are deferred until representatives can consult with their parent agencies. Or the decisions may be taken by other agency personnel on a bilateral basis at an appropriately high level, reaching up to and including the Department Secretaries themselves. In recent years, as commodities have become more scarce, higher-level decision-making has become more common; and in 1973 a more permanent committee was convened under the chairmanship of OMB's Associate Director. During the mid-1960s, however, although BoB became more important as the Planning, Program, and Budgeting System (PPBS) was increasingly adopted by the federal government, only the ISC provided working-level coordination of PL-480 on a sustained basis.

The extension of PL-480 (PL88—638) in 1964 established a joint executive-congressional advisory committee to review

Title I currency uses and to consult about loans, sales agreements, and convertibility terms. The House in particular wanted more systematic knowledge about PL-480 operations. In 1966 PL89-808, which completely restructured PL-480, expanded the joint committee to include the Secretaries of State and Treasury, as well as four additional congressional members from the agricultural committees. These latter four were dropped again in 1968. Chaired by its congressional members on a rotational basis, the Joint Committee has met but twice since 1966. Many interviewees mentioned that the Joint Committee's large size and high-status personnel made its meetings exceedingly difficult to arrange.

Congressional supervision of PL-480 programs, particularly toward India, is poor. The Congress is not a unified actor in PL-480 affairs and is characterized by jurisdictional disputes. Its Committees spend as much time squabbling among themselves as overseeing the Executive Branch. Also Congress is understaffed and over-crowded with only a spasmodic interest in and knowledge about the PL-480 program. To expect the Congress to monitor the PL-480 program is probably like asking blind men to describe an elephant. Futhermore, knowledge of and sympathy for India is rare on Capitol Hill. Most Congressmen, Senators, and staff regard Indians as poor, inept and arrogant. Their concern for the region is minimal and declining in an era of accelerated non-interventionism.

The relative importance of these coordinating devices varies at different phases of the process for contracting a PL-480 Agreement, a process which has changed over the years toward increasingly formalized procedures. At first contacts were informal and could start during a luncheon engagement between USG and GOI officials. Later the USG began to ask the GOI to provide a formal request and a justification, and then would try to supply its needs. Finally by the late' 60s, PL-480 was drawn into the planning-programming-budgeting process. The program's procedures became particularly rigid under LBJ who required pre-clearance for any agreement with ten selected countries receiving the bulk of US economic aid.

During the mid-'60s, the standardized procedures for contracting a PL-480 agreement with India were as follows. (1) India would approach the US Embassy in Delhi with a request for food aid, along with a justification. Informal consultations among Embassy personnel and GOI bureaucrats generated the contours of most requests. Often the Embassy took the initial initiative.

(2) The Embassy would transmit the request back to Washington for submission to the Interagency Staff Committee. In addition, the Embassy staff collected relevant information about the country's needs and prospects, to accompany the request. There seem to have been as many channels for transmitting information as there were attaches and administrators in Delhi although all were formally responsible to the Ambassador. That is, despite most information being transmitted through the State Department's cables, Treasury, AID, and USDA could and did receive information independently of one another.

(3) The broad outlines of the potential agreement were generated by the ISC. Decision-making in that body was consensual and, if disagreements occurred, the problem was passed to superior levels of government. After 1966 and coincident with ISC's initial discussions about each individual agreement, the State Department through its Food for Freedom Division in the Economic Bureau alerted other producer-nations about the pending negotiations and potential "sale". Usual Marketing Requirements were calculated on the past five years' average and advice was solicited.

(4) When the ISC had agreed on the outlines of an agreement and no objections had been received or acknowledged from the big three producers (Canada, Australia, and Argentina —with the EEC being added in later years), the US Embassy in Delhi was authorized to commence negotiations with GOI representatives. The ISC document served as the basic negotiating instrument. At this time, the Consultative Sub-committee on Surplus Disposal of the Food and Agriculture Organization's Committee on Commodity Problems was notified in order to alert the rare country that might not already have been consulted.

(5) Negotiations took place in Delhi with varying numbers of participants. The larger the individual Agreement proposed or the more comprehensive its terms, the higher the ranks of the players involved. The American Ambassador and the AID

Mission Director might well consult with members of the Indian Council of Ministers. In exceptional cases, special delegations from Washington would join the negotiations. The negotiation of self-help provisions in particular required, or at any rate inspired, participation by USDA experts.

Within the GOI, foreign aid negotiations were highly coordinated. The Ministry of Finance served as focal point and all other ministries, including the Food and Agriculture Ministry deferred to its lead. The Delhi venue for negotiating PL-480 terms made the US Embassy a critical link in the government-to-government relations that characterized PL-480 programs.[9] In the American Embassy, the Minister for Political and Economic Affairs headed the American negotiating team, under ambassadorial guidance. He relied heavily on a staff team comprised of AID, USDA, and Treasury representatives. The Agricultural Attache in particular was a major participant, although as an agent of USDA, he often was motivated more by the interests of American commercial agriculture than by general foreign policy considerations.

(6) When the terms of an Agreement had been mutually devised, the Agreement required formal approval by both governments. Signing ceremonies were often regarded as major diplomatic events so their sites alternated between national capitals.

V. PL-480 in the Mid-Sixties : Self-Help and the Politics of an Era

The Washington Scene

Prior to becoming Secretary of Agriculture, Orville Freeman had expressed an interest in the agricultural economies of less-developed countries (LDCs). Freeman believed that American agriculture could make considerable contributions to the rest of the world and one of his conditions for taking up JFK's offer was a chance to stress this developmental theme. The pragmatic basis of his reasoning was later borne out by USDA studies which demonstrated that to the extent a

9. Almost 100 per cent (and never less than 93 per cent) of all American agricultural exports to India occurred through official governmental channels; the private grain trade was virtually nil.

country absorbs PL-480 aid and grows economically, that country comes to purchase more and more US goods. Trade relations are built up, and what begins as concessional sales later shifts into straight agricultural commerce. Taiwan, Spain, Japan, Israel, and Korea are all cited as examples of a successful market development policy. It therefore made good business sense to American agriculture to see that LDCs develop to the point where they could pay for American goods with cash.

Furthermore, it was clear to USDA economists, if not to many in AID, that most LDCs were neglecting agriculture in favor of industrialization. Certainly such a skewed development strategy characterized India during the Nehru era. Whether Freeman sought to improve India's agricultural base enough to permit future commercial sales or just wanted to end the assumption that the US was obligated to supply India's food needs on a concessional basis, he bid for control over agricultural development in the LDCs. The problem was that responsibility for economic development aid had previously been almost completely within the Agency for International Development or its predecessors.

Freeman entered the bureaucratic battle with several advantages. First, he already had an instrument in the PL-480 program which was a direct avenue into the LDCs. Concessional sales, originally stimulated to dispose of unwanted American surpluses, had been underway since the mid 1950s. Second, by virtue of PL 83-690, the Agriculture Attaches in US embassies, while nominally subject to the Ambassador as head of the country-team, were actually USDA personnel rather than in the Foreign Service. Third, USDA had a powerful domestic constituency which the State Department did not. And fourth, the Secretary had a good friend in the White House both before and after 23 November 1963.

Perhaps because of his Vietnam burden, LBJ became the even better friend. The quarrels between LBJ and Fulbright over foreign policy were not secret and were increasingly evident in the annual foreign aid bills, over which the Foreign Relations Committee had jurisdiction. Agricultural aid, however, was a large and enlarging portion of total economic aid and PL-480 was the major source of food-aid. Since PL-480 was under the jurisdiction of the agricultural committees and since the deployment of PL-480 commodities was decided by the ISC chaired by USDA, Fulbright's influence over foreign policy could be diminished if the agricultural component of foreign aid were shifted elsewhere. Freeman was a trusted lieutenant, with an acceptable ideological position, who aspired for control over US policy toward agriculture in LDCs. And in addition, Freeman shared LBJ's conviction—at least vis-a-vis India—that only a strong dose of self-help would ensure the type of national commitment necessary to remove LDCs from excessive dependence on US grain-bins. [0]

The origin of the 'self-help' concept in agriculture is somewhat disputed, but the drive toward its implementation is generally conceded to have come from USDA. State/AID did not need to be converted about self-help's value, but there was a question of its priority among other goals. During the early 1960s, for example, it was often erroneously assumed that capital investments achieve a higher payoff in industry than in agriculture (Singh, 1963, quoted by Lindblom, 1964b: 8). Therefore, Freeman argued that only agricultural experts could really specify a less developed country's agricultural needs. The State Department was too concerned with diplomacy and AID with industrial projects to pay sufficient attention to the agricultural basis of an LDC's economy.

At the same time, the importance of self-help in agriculture was being promoted in India by various non-governmental agents as well as by technocrats within the Ministry of Food and Agriculture (if not in the Planning Commission).

10. As a basic foreign policy aim, all countries seek to keep others mildly dependent in order to influence their behavior. But there are always questions about the appropriate mix of independence and dependence, as well as questions of what lever works best when trying to deflect or halt another country's unwanted policies. Food supplies are, unfortunately, a crude and ugly weapon to use among nations. Human malnutrition and starvation are conditions guaranteed to soften all but the hardest hearts, for the strong humanitarian streak in the American character, however ungraciously acknowledged or delivered, tempers its more materialistic and realpolitik aims. Allowing people to go hungry when food supplies are available is not a 'clean' instrument of foreign policy, either in world or domestic public opinion.

Public and private research organizations such as the Indian Council of Agricultural Research, the Ford Foundation, and the Rockefeller Foundation repeatedly stressed the value of developing India's agricultural sector and had offered practical schemes to improve production. Leading nationalist economists such as V.K.R.V. Rao, M.L. Dantawala, K.N. Raj, V.M. Dandekar, and Gyan Chand also supported a strategy of "self-reliance" in agriculture.[11] Furthermore, agricultural technocrats such as M.S. Swaminathan, B.P. Pal, M.S. Randhawa, and especially N. Sivaraman, who staffed the GOI's Department of Agriculture, argued forcefully for greater emphasis on agricultural development. Until the 1965 confrontations with Pakistan and the subsequent cut-off of US aid painfully demonstrated India's vulnerability, however, the Planning Commission continued to favor investments in the industrial sector.

The campaign for "self-help" proceeded slowly and by a circuitous route. In 1961, when the International Cooperation Administration was reconstituted into the Agency for International Development, the Food for Peace program was not assigned to the new agency. Agricultural pressures were marshalled to keep PL-480's Title I "sales" in USDA while promotional responsibilities for its Title II grants and donations through voluntary agencies were assigned to a newly created post in the Executive Office of the President. The Office of Food for Peace was mainly a publicity vehicle as well as a safe haven for George McGovern, the defeated Congressman from South Dakota, until the 1962 Senate race.

In 1964 and again in 1965, PL-480 was marginally amended to extend the USDA Secretary's powers over counterpart funds. And in early 1966, a complex inter-agency agreement was signed which exchanged USDA and AID personnel and strengthened the former's role in planning, implementing, and evaluating technical assistance in agriculture overseas. But despite these marginal successes, Freeman's original aspiration seemed stymied in the bureaucratic jungle of jurisdictional dickering.

11. See, for example, Chand, 1965; Rao, 1965; Raj, 1966; Dandekar, 1967; as well as the entire collection of articles from *Yojana*, 1965, entitled "The Meaning of Self-Reliance".

In fact, through an administrative maneuver, USDA almost lost its international food-aid program in 1965. The problem of PL-480 in foreign policy had been, and is, that no single agency is administratively responsible for it. The ISC coordinates among many interested parties, but it cannot take authoritative decisions. This peculiar "headless" administrative arrangement was devised by one of Eisenhower's Executive Orders which is still operational. In 1965, some members of the ISC thought they had agreed on a new Executive Order which would assign responsibility for PL-480 to the newly created "War on Hunger" office within AID. That draft order went to LBJ for his signature but on Freeman's (rumored) advice, the President decided not to sign it. Rather LBJ decided to coordinate the program himself and required that all PL-480 Agreements with the ten major recipient countries be cleared by him personally.

Presumably LBJ did not want to augment the powers of State/AID, to which he had already transferred the White House's Office of Food for Peace established by JFK.[12] In contrast to his predecessor, LBJ did not really like State Department types or even foreign policy. He felt ill-at-ease on international affairs (especially toward Europe) and much preferred domestic policies and their intuitively understandable protective interests. Furthermore, in LBJ's particular conception of politics, there were international and domestic payoffs in wielding PL-480, which he did not want to relinquish. Thus the foundation for the "short-tether" policy had been laid considerably before it was applied.

In February 1966 LBJ sent Congress a special message to pass his Food-for-Freedom program and thereby drastically restructure PL-480.[13] Since US grain stocks had peaked in 1960,

12. This White House office, which had been renamed Food for Freedom in line with LBJ's manipulation of verbal symbols, should not be confused with the operational office of Food for Peace, which was transferred to the 'War on Hunger'. That FFF office is, apparently, the predecessor of the division now found in the State Department's Economic and Business Bureau, which is responsible for furnishing a delegate to the FAO's Consultative Subcommittee on Surplus Disposal.

13. The nomenclature expressed a symbolic squabble between Congress and the Executive. PL-480 had come to be known as 'Food for Peace'

economic reasons to dispose of surplus commodities were no longer pressing. Through a combination of acreage controls, large PL-480 shipments, and expanding commercial exports, grain stocks had been almost halved (Schnittker, 1966) and the annual storage costs had been substantially reduced. Indeed, a number of Congressmen claimed the well-being of the US was threatened because grain reserves were so low. Their fear, while premature in 1966, has become more valid today.

Interviewees note that USDA drafted the bill revising PL-480 in order to get a major share of the action. In large measure, USDA was successful although its success must be qualified. PL-480/808 retained its conventional statement of intent "to increase the consumption of United States agricultural commodities in foreign countries, to improve the foreign relations of the United States, and for other purposes". But a new preamble to the Act read:

> "The Congress hereby declares it to be the policy of the United States to expand international trade; to develop and expand export markets for US agricultural commodities; to use the abundant agricultural productivity of the United States to combat hunger and malnutrition, and to encourage economic development in the developing countries, with particular emphasis on assistance to those countries that are determined to improve their own agricultural production; and to promote in other ways the foreign policy of the United States." (7 U.S.C. 1691)

In order to promote these developmental goals, a new Title IV specifically enhanced USDA's role in international affairs without, however, assigning it exclusive responsibility. In his special message on the Food-for-Freedom program, LBJ had emphasized that "the Departments of State and Agriculture

---

but LBJ wanted 'freedom' to be the hallmark of his foreign policy. For a time there was a tug-of-war between FFP and FFF—both complicated by the 'War on Hunger'—but FFP ultimately won the day. Congress does have greater staying power than a President, and also the earlier phrase had taken firm root in the media. FFF still exists in one anachronistically titled office in the State Department, where bets are occasionally taken about its prospective longevity.

Figure 1—North America's Emergence as The World's Bread Basket. Numbers in bars represent millions of metric tons

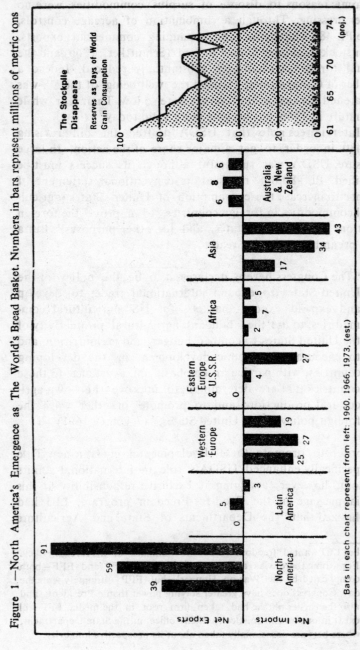

Bars in each chart represent from left: 1960, 1966, 1973. (est.)

Source: Brown and Eckholm, 1974a; 6—E. As based on U.S. Dept. of Agricultural data.

and the Agency for International Development will work together even more closely than they have in the past in the planning and implementation of coordinated programs". He sought to reassign functions among government departments and thereby shift the balance of bureaucratic power.

But suspicious even of loyal lieutenants, President Johnson kept ultimate control over PL-480 in his own office. The revised Act substantially strengthened the President through a new section[14] which empowered him to terminate any PL-480 agreement with a country judged to be in adequately performing its stipulated self-help program. After spelling out some anticipated self-help measures, the section specified that "each agreement entered into under this title shall describe the program which the recipient country is undertaking to improve its production, storage, and distribution of agricultural commodities; and shall provide for termination of such agreement whenever the President finds that such program is not being adequately developed". Thus, while USDA became explicitly associated with economic development efforts in the LDCs, the President's own powers were also considerably augmented.

Nonetheless, Freeman had achieved a qualified success in expanding his department's role in international agricultural development. With White House support, USDA had stolen a march on State/AID and, indirectly, on Fulbright. The following year, 1967, the foreign affairs committees tried to assert jurisdiction over PL-480 by placing agricultural and food aid in the annual foreign aid bill but, as one senior staffer of the House Foreign Affairs Committee put it, their attempt was a "total nonstarter". The powerful agricultural committees had approved of USDA's enhanced role[15] and the result of this jurisdictional dispute was a foregone conclusion. By the mid-1960s, problems began to appear in the US balance of payments and a messy war in Southeast Asia was well underway which went unsupported by those nations rebuilt two decades before by American capital and know-how. Americans had become disillusioned with foreign aid and with the ingratitude of other peoples so that, unlike the staunch political support on

14. Annex B provides the full text of Section 109.
15. Pithy evidence from a 1966 Senate hearing on the "Food for Freedom Program and Commodity Reserves" is provided in Annex C.

which the agricultural committees could depend, the foreign
affairs constituency was weaker than ever.[16]

In short, while USDA's success did not amount to total
control over foreign agricultural development policy, the
revised bill did strengthen Freeman's authority over the
quantity of PL-480 commodities available for any country and
did establish some new USDA programs in the international
field.[17] And perhaps USDA's greatest accomplishments lay in
reorienting AID's development strategy and in sharing the
planning and execution of the revised strategy's agricultural
component. Under Eisenhower, USDA was not connected in
the affairs of the International Cooperation Administration.
Ezra Taft Benson, the previous Secretary of Agriculture,
regarded PL-480 as just a messy method for disposing of
agricultural surpluses and was not interested in development
per se. Neither, to a great extent, were the State Departments
of Dulles and Herter.

Even after 1961 and Freeman's avowed interest in international development issues, AID did not draw upon USDA's
resources. One reason lay in reciprocal jurisdictional jeal-
ousies, for the Food for Peace Program had been kept outside
the new agency. Another was that AID concentrated primarily
on a strategy of industrial development. When David Bell
became Administrator, AID's relationship with USDA improved but he still tried to duplicate expertise already available in
USDA. Senator Humphrey of Minnesota then introduced an
amendment to an annual AID bill which, while emphasizing
that AID was the "operating agency" for international agricultural development efforts, arranged for 'cooperative agreements' between USDA and AID. In 1964, in order to fulfil
these cooperative arrangements under which AID financed a
series of teams contracted from USDA, Freeman established
the International Agriculture Development Service.

16. It has also been suggested that Senator Fulbright, being equally
    interested in relieving the rice-glut of that year which plagued his
    Arkansan constituents, did not press the fight for jurisdictional
    reassignment very hard.
17. See, respectively, Sections 401 and 406 of Annex D. Ironically, the
    annual funds authorized for Section 406 programs were *not* appro-
    priated by Congress during Freeman's final two years in office.

This contractual arrangement, while an improvement over the vacuum of the past, was still unsatisfactory to Freeman. As he testified in 1966 on behalf of revising PL-480 (*Hearings*, 1966 : 47-48) :

> The Secretary of Agriculture will need to take into account the foreign policy aspects of food aid and the degree of success of self-help efforts in recipient countries before he can make final determination about commodity programs.

*   *   *   *

> The new Food for Freedom program contemplates closer coordination of food aid with other assistance programs directed toward food and agriculture in recipient countries.

*   *   *   *

> The Department of Agriculture and the AID have for several years been developing closer working relationships with each other in the food aid part of US assistance programs. But the kind of unified efforts to which the President referred means that Agriculture will also be called upon to participate in the planning of agricultural assistance activities and in reviewing the progress made in agricultural development.
>
> This means that we are called upon to develop closer interagency operating relationships that will involve the Department of Agriculture in a shared concern for not only the food component of assistance programs but also that part of economic assistance that relates to self-help in the agriculture related sectors of developing nations.
>
> This planning is primarily the responsibility of the AID . . . [but] Mr. Bell has indicated his hope that the USDA will be increasingly helpful in this area. We have just signed a new interagency agreement under which AID seeks to—'enlist as fully and effectively as possible on a partnership basis the pertinent resources of the Department in planning, executing, and evaluating those portions of the foreign assistance program in which it has special competence'.

Members of the Senate Committee then interrupted to cross-examine Freeman on these cooperative arrangements :

> SENATOR YOUNG. May I ask a question at this point, Mr. Chairman ?
> THE CHAIRMAN. Yes, sir.
> SENATOR YOUNG. To what agency would the costs of this program be charged, the cost of assisting other countries to produce more ?
> SECRETARY FREEMAN. To the AID Agency in the State Department.
> SENATOR YOUNG. But not to Agriculture ?
> SECRETARY FREEMAN. Not to Agriculture.
> THE CHAIRMAN. Why was it necessary to enter this agreement that you speak of ? I thought there was always full cooperation among the agencies in respect to Agriculture and AID. Weren't you consulted in the past by the AID Agency as to food production abroad ?
> SECRETARY FREEMAN. Some.
> THE CHAIRMAN. Not too much ?
> SECRETARY FREEMAN. No.

The Congress did oblige by enhancing both USDA's control over food-aid and its role in international agricultural development policy. But USDA's influence over the latter was due more to its resident expertise than its formal responsibility.

Once associated with foreign agricultural policy, USDA began to relax its battle on behalf of "self-help". True, self-help provisions were written into every subsequent PL-480 Agreement[18] whose fulfilment was purportedly the basis for allowing further concessional sales. But the criteria of "self-help" actions were not explicit and, when objectified, were not closely monitored. Some typical criteria were (1) proportion of national budget allocated to agriculture; (2) emphasis on provision of chemical fertilizers, either through foreign imports or domestic production (which opened an avenue to foreign investment); and (3) extension of power generation and electrification, provided the rate-structure was modified to remove

18. Annex E. presents a representative example of a PL-480 Agreement with 'self-help' provisions contracted between the United States and India.

subsidies and make the user pay appropriate costs. AID devised "check-lists" against which to measure a country's performance but such monitoring was unimpressive. Instead of holding countries to their targets, US decision-makers were satisfied with a country's "best efforts".

By the end of LBJ's Administration, "self-help" had been considerably de-emphasized. The State Department had always contended that self-help requirements could never really be enforced without some sharp political repercussions, and USDA soon agreed. In the field the US Embassy and the AID Mission were responsible for assessing the progress toward self-help and the recipient country had to submit reports on its performance twice each year. USDA assigned responsibility for evaluating the information compiled to the International Agriculture Development Service, which was abolished in 1969. Since then, as a further demotion, evaluations of "self-help" efforts have been conducted by the Foreign Development Division of the Economic Research Service. The USDA's Assistant Secretary for International affairs and Commodity Programs once again emphasized commercial trade almost exclusively.

The problems with "self-help" and the coordination it presumed were evident in all phases of PL-480 in India. Officials of the New Delhi Embassy from that period suggest that the ISC's formal instructions for each PL-480 Agreement contained one item of essential information and a lot of "boiler-plate". The essential item was the amount of specific commodities to be authorized under the Agreement and the balance included the conditions sought as *quid pro quos*. The latter "boiler-plate" were not too meaningful a set of requirements, a conclusion supported by a ranking member of the AID policy planning team in Washington at that time. Few new commitments to agricultural development were ever extracted from the GOI since the terms in the Agreements were usually projects already about to get underway.

The AID planner further observed that "the idea of self-help provisions is a reasonable one, and the recipient countries agreed. But the teeth in those agreements were often quite weak. India, for example, had 'food zones' which obstructed the movements of its own commodities from surplus to shortfall areas. Overall efficiency would suggest that these zones be abolished, and one indicator that self-help was really underway would have been to require the elimination of these zones by a fixed date. But such blatant interference was impossible because it raised questions of national sovereignty". As the AID official quipped, "you can't have a report card for a country". And so "self-help" increasingly became mere window-dressing rather than an enforceable criterion for action.[19]

Even granting that self-help may have been a temporary touchstone for US foreign agricultural policy after 1966, it was poorly coordinated and suffered the drawbacks of any dyarchy. Responsibility for it resided in AID, but the necessary expertise lay in USDA. Progress reports by recipient countries and the American field personnel were evaluated by a relatively low office in USDA and by AID's Washington bureaus, but in reality these evaluations rarely surfaced. The results of these investigations were seldom brought before the ISC during its deliberations on subsequent PL-480 Agreements. And since USDA remained primarily interested in maintaining and developing its hard-currency foreign markets (a position much appreciated by the Treasury and by BoB), the "self-help" provisions were more an excuse to diminish shipments of food-aid and end Indian dependency on US supplies. As one wag put it, "there is never enough self-help !" And then, of course, there were the extra-regional policy considerations to the east.

An Indian Chronology
Before discussing LBJ's "short-tether" policy on PL-480 shipments, some developments in India should be reviewed which are relevant to self-help and the struggle between USDA and State/AID. American foreign policy-making does not occur in

19. Much more contributory to meaningful American help for Indian agricultural development were the monthly "world problem-solving luncheons" regularly held in Delhi by representatives of USDA (the Agriculture Attaches and an Economic Research Service man), AID, the Rockefeller Foundation, the Ford Foundation, Peace Corps, and CLUSA (the Cooperative League of the USA). Informal consultations, it is commonly agreed, produced more coordinated leverage on Indian agriculture than all the public PL-480 pronouncements and requirements.

a vacuum, and changes in India affected the fates of bureau-cratic players in Washington. Furthermore, there is some evidence that through PL-480 the USG tried to influence the Indian Cabinet's composition and general policies.

Under Nehru and his economic advisor, P.C. Mahalanobis, the Government of India had pursued a heavy-industries strategy of economic development. PL-480 shipments were welcomed as a cushion in years of agricultural shortfalls and, as a perfectly rational reason not to invest scarce resources in rural development schemes. They also helped to ensure that urban food prices remained low. During a 1961 world-trip, a member of Freeman's staff asked a ranking Indian official about India's grain reserves and received the ingenuous reply : "Oh, they're in Kansas".

As Ministers of Food and Agriculture, neither S.K. Patil[20] nor his successor, Swaran Singh, were particularly interested in agriculture *per se*, a fact that attests to the low salience of agricultural policy in the Nehruvian years. Shortly before Nehru's death in May, 1964, Freeman again visited Delhi and found Swaran Singh noncommittal about "self-help" pro-posals. Freeman did, however, leave behind a standing offer to provide whatever help he could to solve India's food problems, should the GOI so desire. And the Bowles Embassy continued to press for a shake-up of Indian thinking on agri-cultural policy.

After Nehru's death, a period of collective and confused political leadership occurred. Then in July 1964 Prime Minister Shastri had a mild heart attack and the collective leadership decided that Nehru's practice of reserving the External Affairs Ministry along with a number of other portfolios for the

20. In Washington, D.C. on 4 May 1960, Patil and Eisenhower had signed a PL-480 Agreement for 17 million tons of food-grain, the largest Agreement ever signed. At a time when US farm surpluses were still accumulating, the deal made economic sense to USDA. It also established a well-insulated crutch for India that justified the remark about Kansan reserves and also allowed Patil to neglect the agricultural sector for the next four years. Patil, it should be noted, was political boss of Bombay, the great metropolis of western India, and had greater interests in industry and commerce than in the rural sector. Patil was concerned, however, about ensuring cheap food-stuffs for the urban consumer.

Prime Minister, was too great a task for the ailing Lal Bahadur. Swaran Singh, who had gained minor diplomatic experience in 1963 as Nehru's surrogate in a series of discussions[21] with the Pakistani Foreign Minister, then Zulfikar Ali Bhutto, became Minister of External Affairs. And in the same cabinet reshuffle, Chidambaram Subramaniam became Food Minister. The latter's appointment was yet another example of the low salience of domestic agricultural policy in India, since Subramaniam was a relatively junior member of the Cabinet. At the same time Subramaniam, who had previously served as Minister of Steel and Heavy Industries, was recognized as an accomplished administrator and technocrat.

Subramaniam soon expressed interest in Freeman's offers, which had been supplemented and supported by Bowles and the AID Mission. Most American participants from the period credit the turn-around on agricultural policy in India to him. Like Freeman, Subramaniam was not an agriculturalist but he was an experienced politician who knew how to get things done. Subramaniam began to push for the modernization of agriculture through the application of new high-yielding seeds, the expansion of fertilizer production, farm mechanization, and the spread of irrigation facilities and electricity. Since its First Five-Year Plan and the Community Development program, India had sought to expand its agricultural production but only at a modest rate of about five-to-ten per cent. Agricultural accomplishments measured up to these goals, but Subramaniam sought to double and triple crop-yields with the new techniques.

The path to increased agricultural production was not, however, easy. The year of 1965 proved to be one of turbulence and trouble for India. In January, language riots occurred in Madras over the mandatory shift to Hindi as the national language. Subramaniam submitted his resignation over this issue, but Shastri refused to accept it. From April through June, India confronted Pakistan in the Rann of Kutch incident, while the Chinese increased tensions on the northern border.

21. President Kennedy, in hopes of resolving the Kashmir dispute, had persuaded the two belligerents to conduct these meetings. The Sino-Indian conflict of 1962 had placed a new dimension on this old problem.

Then the main monsoon failed and by late July, the country's food situation began to deteriorate. Furthermore, on September 1st, Pakistan attacked the Chamb sector of Kashmir and by the 6th Ayub Khan broadcast : "We are at war with India". Two days later the US suspended all military and economic aid to both belligerents. A cease-fire was arranged in less than a month and Shastri and Ayub agreed to January discussions under Soviet auspices in Tashkent.

Given these dilemmas, the Indian Cabinet belatedly re-emphasized its agriculture-first strategy of development. Subramaniam was authorized to accept standing offers of American technical aid and to reach an understanding with Freeman in order to ensure adequate supplies of grain. The unfolding effects of the drought were most pronounced in the Hindi-heartland of northern India, which had always been the sheet-anchor of the Congress Party. Concessional rates would allow the GOI to provide cheap food to the masses in the Indo-Gangetic plain, so US food shipments were a guarantee of political stability in India and indirectly underwrote its Congress government.

On 25 November 1965, Subramaniam and Freeman met in Rome to hammer out an agricultural package for India. Both agreed on the importance of self-help, and Subramaniam made it clear that American pressures for self-help would help him in the Indian Parliament as well as supply needed leverage on his own Cabinet colleagues. He returned to India armed with a package of promises and penalties. The situation also allowed Freeman, back in Washington, to emphasize the importance of USDA in stimulating agricultural development. "Self-help" helped to advance the careers of two political bureaucrats in their respective countries and became as well as code-word for re-orienting the GOI's development strategy. On 7 December 1965 the GOI announced its new farm program, and LBJ immediately ordered a speed-up in the shipping of 1.5 million tons of wheat to India to meet the food crisis. Thereafter, says LBJ in *The Vantage Point* (1971 : 226), he gave Freeman the ball to carry. Within seven months, he retrieved it on a re-bound.

In January 1966 Shastri signed the Tashkent Declaration and then died of a heart attack. Eight days later Indira Gandhi became Prime Minister as India's food shortage worsened. She immediately appealed to other countries for assistance, and the American Embassy in Delhi supported her request with extensive documentation on the disaster confronting India. In February Vice-President Humphrey travelled to New Delhi to announce new loans totalling $150 million for purchasing essential raw materials for industry and also for fertilizer imports. And LBJ revived his invitation to the Indian Prime Minister for a state visit.

In March Indira Gandhi came to Washington for formal discussions, just as India and the USSR signed an agreement in Delhi about building the Bokaro steel plant. After their meeting, LBJ sent Congress a special message about emergency food aid for India, and also lobbied actively and personally among the Senators and Representatives. Johnson's rhetoric was passionate and inspiring :

> India is a good and deserving friend. Let it never be said that "bread should be so dear and flesh and blood so cheap" that we turned in indifference from her bitter need.

The Congress obliged almost immediately with a unanimous joint resolution, and favorable exchanges between the USG and the GOI became fairly common.

In the following three months, in response to the World Bank's Bell Report and as articulately promoted by Indian civil servants and politicians like L.K. Jha, I.G. Patel, S. Bhoothalingam, and Ashok Mehta, the GOI's policy of limited economic liberalization was underway. The GOI changed its foodzone policy (slightly); liberalized its import requirement; delicensed a number of industries; signed a pact with the American International Oil Company for a Madras fertilizer plant; and on 5 June announced the devaluation of the rupee by over one-third.

The United States, in turn, agreed to send India 3.5 million more tons of foodgrains under PL-480; committed another $50 million to expanding Indian power generation plants; and loaned the GOI $33 million for the Beas Dam Project. In July, even as evidence accumulated that for a second straight year the monsoon played fickle with India, the US signed another $150 million loan for industrial and agricultural production, while the Government of India accepted in principle the recommendations of the Swaminathan Committee on industrial development procedures, and de-licensed still more industries.

Operation Short-Tether

Then a critical event occurred which derailed the entire train of events. On a July 1966 state visit to Moscow, Prime Minister Gandhi signed a communique which criticized the "imperialists in South East Asia". The communique was allegedly written by a very young Indian Foreign Service officer and was signed, unread.

Indian comments on Vietnam may have been a necessary trade-off between sovereignty (in foreign policy) and dependency (in agricultural aid) and therefore a type of symbolic horse-trading for domestic consumption. The relationship should have been intuitively obvious to a consummate politician, but President Johnson did not always appreciate the democratic imperatives of other countries. LBJ was infuriated and descriptions of his reaction range from the violent to the obscene. He was particularly angry since Shastri's last message to him from Tashkent had praised LBJ's "determined effort . . . to bring about a peace in Vietnam". Despite the grim drought ironically coupled with floods, LBJ strictly applied the short-tether policy on grain shipments to India from August onwards.

The justification for short-tether had been laid earlier, and mildly practiced. On 30 June 1965 the four-year PL-480 agreements signed under JFK with both India and Pakistan terminated. During July and August, negotiations were underway to provide another agreement, but for one month's duration only. LBJ's stated aim was to keep recipients on a short leash in order to force their attentions toward domestic agriculture. His instructions to the bureaucracy, in the recollections of one AID official, were : "don't be easy on them; let them get cracking and show they seriously mean business in boosting food-production". Furthermore, during the 1965 Executive Order issue, LBJ had drawn the many strings of PL-480 into his own hands and assumed direct control for some ten major recipient countries. By March 1966, when testifying on the proposed revision of the act, Freeman also argued

against multi-year agreements and advocated a shortened—
although not arbitrarily tight—tether on PL-480 agreements :

> The new Food for Freedom program can truly be an
> instrument under which the millions of lives that are now
> threatened by famine under present trends can be saved.
> But this will result only if it proves effective in changing
> those trends by stimulating, encouraging, and if necessary,
> insisting on effective self-help measures. This may mean
> agreements for no longer than 1 year, with provisions for
> periodic reviews of progress made toward self-reliance.

In November 1966, LBJ obtained congressional action on
his Food-for-Freedom message and signed PL-89-808 into law.
Then Freeman, with a formally acknowledged role in foreign
economic affairs, sent several USDA experts to estimate India's
harvest. In November LBJ also told Freeman and others than
he had decided to end the "giveaway" days and would not
move on PL-480 without congressional agreement.

Furthermore, in contrast to his earlier instructions to the
bureaucracy, LBJ's public explanation for short-tether was to
force other countries to share the burden of food-aid for India.
He wanted Canada, Australia, and other major wheat producers to supply some of the grain needed. Thus, when in March
1967 he did send another message to Congress on behalf of
Indian food-aid, he sent Freeman and Eugene Rostow to testify
that the US wanted a 50-50 principle of sharing the burden
with other countries. In December 1966 LBJ persuaded
Congress to send a fact-finding delegation to India, and that
team subsequently recommended 1.8 million tons of PL-480
grain for the February-April shipments. LBJ, however, refused
to send more than half that amount as America's share.

The international response was not overwhelming. India's
estimated food needs for 1967 were ten million tons of imports,
towards which the US had already committed 3.6 million tons
of PL-480 grain. In mid-December Canada announced a grant
of about 200,000 tons of wheat to India and, after extensive
diplomatic pressure, Australia announced a grant of 150,000
tons. The US was startled and angered to learn, however, that
the Indian High Commission in Canberra and the Australian

Wheat Board had also concluded a hard-currency sale of another 150,000 tons. The Soviet Union contributed 200,000 tons of emergency food aid, too.

But LBJ wanted more action on the 5.7 million tons deficit which India still needed. He asked the World Bank president, George Woods to organize as many nations as possible into a food-aid consortium for India, and Woods agreed. LBJ also sent Eugene Rostow, Under Secretary of State for Political Affairs, around the world to generate support for India's food needs. Pledges worth about $200 million were grudgingly obtained, although many countries bluntly felt that "twenty people are being saved today so that forty can starve tomorrow".

India in 1967 was like a ship adrift. The Government of India continued to delicense additional industries but its policy of economic liberalism was flagging. Indira Gandhi had been strongly criticized by many older leaders for devaluing the rupee, especially since exports did not rise as anticipated. Bhagwati and Desai (1970: 487-490) describe numerous reasons why the experiments with economic liberalism did not work, but by early 1967 the GOI began to sign economic cooperation pacts and trade protocols with Soviet-bloc nations. The strategy of administrative markets revived in Indian economic planning.

Despite India's food needs, Indo-American relations grew increasingly distant. During the Six-day War in West Asia, India strongly criticized Israel and took over US-UAR relations after they were severed. Greetings were also sent to Ho Chi Minh in Hanoi on his 77th birthday and in November Indira Gandhi attended the 50th anniversary celebrations of the Russian Revolution in Moscow. LBJ grudgingly authorized repeated PL-480 shipments but only after holding every one up long enough to indicate his displeasure. During 1967, agreements totalling over six million tons were authorized, along with several loans for fertilizer imports. But LBJ was clearly unhappy with India as well as increasingly absorbed by his Vietnam policies.

LBJ's short-tether policy, which others have dubbed "the great hold-up" or "the tight-rope tether", illustrates the pernicious effects of excessive coordination. It also illuminates how a program, well-insulated from Congressional supervision and control, can be wielded as a weapon of executive policy. The bureaucratic politics paradigm of behavior is adequate up to a point, and has revealed reasons and methods by which self-help provisions got written into law. But the paradigm loses applicability as soon as the highest elected official takes a direct interest in whatever the subject is at hand.

The views, moods, and actions of a President of the United States are subject to a different calculus than that applied to other players. With reference to the subcontinent of South Asia, LBJ, like many of his former peers in Congress, disliked Indians and admired Pakistanis. LBJ's associates often comment how he anthropomorphized politics for, rather than seeing nations of people, the President saw countries in terms of discrete personalities. Based on his assessment of selected leaders, LBJ regarded Indians as weak and indecisive. And although he had vowed to "help that girl" after his first meeting with Indira Gandhi, he reportedly had also concluded that she was a "typical woman in politics" who tended toward the opaque if not the vacuous.[22] His lack of confidence in the Prime Minister's ability or that of her colleagues, presaged Myrdal's classification of India among the "soft states" of the world, but LBJ's view had considerably more impact.

LBJ's personal dislike for Indians would not have explained his behavior, however, because as his domestic policies demonstrate, he had great compassion for the poor and the unfortunate. But LBJ was infuriated at Indian pronouncements on Vietnam and American policies there. In retrospect, Mrs. Gandhi could have been much more vocal in leading Asian opposition to the war, and her remarks sound more like products for domestic consumption than like leverage on the international scene. But LBJ was excessively preoccupied with

22. In contrast to this characterization by a White House insider, Bhatia (1974: 193) comments that "the President told Ambassador to India Chester Bowles that he had been 'particularly impressed by the political astuteness she displayed' during those parleys." And according to other hearsay, LBJ likened Indira to a "cross between Barbara Ward and Lady Bird", which surely indicated high praise. But these interpretations seem less consonant with his subsequent behavior, especially when the following year LBJ and the Congress gave exaggerated attention to Indira's domestic rival, Morarji Desai, on his official visit to Washington, D.C.

and sensitive about his policies toward Southeast Asia. And while by now this explanation has a hackneyed flavor, it still seems accurate.

The self-help policy, which was objectively sensible and necessary for balanced economic development, became tainted as an American strategy foisted upon India. The technological package of hybrid seeds, chemical fertilizers, electrified irrigation and easy credit required sustained application over the long-term rather than on a month-to-month basis. LBJ's tether was clearly tied more to political events than to economic performance. Consequently, like the whole strategy of economic liberalization of which it was a part, the self-help policy was discredited in India as a device for systematic national humiliation. In the long run, LBJ's short-tether policy and his lack of respect for the Indian leadership were political mistakes.

Short-tether did have a salutary effect on American government, however, for it managed to unite USDA, the State Department, AID, and the Congress in favor of an uninterrupted flow of foodstuffs to India. Many interviewees commented that previously warring interests learned to cooperate against Johnson in order to release the food shipments for India, a unity which LBJ interpreted as proof that his subordinates were all soft-headed.

More seriously, the short-tether policy reduced LBJ's own credibility as a competent guardian of American interests. Tying everything to his Vietnam policy was damaging enough in itself, but the President also discredited pro-American forces within the Indian establishment. Two cases illustrate the ill-effects of trying to coordinate policy at the White House level, when its occupant has more pressing concerns elsewhere.

The most blatant example dealt with Subramaniam, a very competent Minister skilled in combining political insights and administrative ability. Subramaniam had become clearly identified with technological attitudes and pro-American affiliations, but he was also a man getting things done. Although under considerable pressure within India, Subramaniam maintained his progressive policies toward India's agricultural problems. Then one day in May 1966, LBJ unceremoniously and imperiously summoned Freeman and Subramaniam to his Texan ranch—Subramaniam all the way from India. Right up to the presidential press conference, nobody, including Freeman, knew the President's intentions. His decision, announced with great pride, was to approve a new PL-480 Agreement. This decision, in itself, was fine but the circumstances of its announcement made Subramaniam look like an American puppet and weakened him further at home. His 1967 electoral defeat was probably due more to linguistic quarrels than his American connections, but Subramaniam's power within the Cabinet had eroded considerably.

The second case dealt with those Indian bureaucrats who consistently advocated economic liberalism, a policy regularly promoted by the US government. Their prescriptive recommendations failed for many reasons—some would say they were never really tried—but the decision to devalue was predicated upon an expectation that sufficiently large doses of economic capital would be forthcoming to provide the big push. The World Bank's Bell Report of 1965 had lead the GOI to assume that massive foreign aid commitments from the Aid-Consortium would follow upon changes in the rupee's exchange rate, relaxation of administrative market controls, and re-emphasis on the agricultural sector. The successive droughts in themselves were probably sufficient to prevent success, but along with the short-tether food policy came a mere trickle of foreign aid. Part of the problem surely lay in India's inadequate absorptive capacities for the Consortium's first instalment of $ 900 million, but perhaps the US also cannot afford extensive involvement in more than one Asian country at a time, if that. The choice actually made between a peripheral state of Southeast Asia and a major state of South Asia bore decidedly recurrent ill-consequences.

VI. Concluding Observations and Comments

As representative American policies toward agricultural and food aid, self-help and short-tether suggest the merit of moderation in all things. Neither succeeded fully, although both had identifiable effects at home as well as in India. On reflection perhaps self-help, and certainly short-tether, violated the first rule of diplomacy, namely that nations should never threaten actions which they are not prepared to back up.

The rationale for both policies' objectives had been fairly well thought out. LDCs, with development strategies skewed toward industrialization, had to rebalance their industrial projects with agricultural investments. Self-help was a code-word for such reorientation. And in terms of yearly evaluations of performance, short-tether was a reasonable condition for external assistance. Application of a shorter-tether in periods of crisis in order to encourage other countries to share the burden of food-aid is somewhat less reasonable or realistic.

The adoption of self-help as a US policy was a slow process, but the trend was based on extensive and accurate information about agricultural development. The options of indiscriminately continuing US food-aid policies and of ending food-aid altogether had been considered and properly rejected. The latter was inhumane and the former would lead to excessive dependency and future disaster. Consequently, in the phase of policy-formulation, self-help seems to have been thought through, while short-tether was not. The former calculated the range of relevant issues, consulted most appropriate participants, and was assigned to middle-level government agencies capable of executing the policy. The latter, in all cases, was the reverse. It sought very short-term payoffs, was basically a presidential whim, and was decided at the rarefied pinnacle of the governmental hierarchy.

Parenthetically, the analyses above indicate that Lyndon Baines Johnson was the prime actor in PL-480 during the mid-sixties. By asserting presidential control over a semi-insulated program, LBJ required his personal clearance for all shipments of food to major recipients. And as Chester Bowles' memoirs also indicate, LBJ's erratic and capricious behavior in some-times withholding, sometimes releasing shipments authorized under PL-480, complicated most of the natural dilemmas. His method of control disrupted normal program operations because officials in both countries were unable to deal with each other on the basis of minimally confident expectations. Evidently Johnson's preoccupation with Vietnam led him to withhold economic aid elsewhere as the war absorbed increasing amounts of America's wealth. At the same time, the Congress whittled down its appropriations for development loans, many of which were understood to be destined for India. The general conclusion emerges that India's trial of a liberal economic policy failed in large part because the anticipated, if not explicitly promised, support was forthcoming neither from the US nor from the World Bank as a whole.

By its implementation phase, because self-help took so long to adopt, most participants understood its intent. The series of reports and consultative committees envisaged suggested that those responsible for self-help activities would be thoroughly supervised, but operational difficulties and jurisdictional rivalries made such monitoring inadequate. US-AID, for example, often appreciated self-help as an idea but not for the leverage it gave USDA over agricultural development. On the other hand, despite some prior intimations, the application of the short-tether was abrupt and surprised many of those affected. Short-tether was, however, extensively monitored in the sense that the President alone was responsible for the decision and its implementation. Ironically, the resources of presidential authority and interest devoted to short-tether were commensurate to the task set forth, while the resources devoted to self-help were not.

Assessments of the outcomes of the two policies and the participating organizations were provided *inter alia* above. But in brief summation, self-help did have an impact on re-orienting Indian agricultural strategy, although other pressures, both internal and international, lead to the GOI's 1965 decision as well. In the long run, the well-intended US pressures and requirements for a public Indian profession of faith in a pro-agriculture development strategy had considerable political costs. Even when advice is correct, nations like people don't like to accept it and implicitly admit past errors.*

Furthermore, some issues require more insulation than others. Like population programs and environmental issues, food problems necessarily involve higher costs if and when they are sacrificed to short-run political goals. These social issues need longer gestation periods and time perspectives, attainable only by a degree of insulation from direct control by Presidents

---

* Editor's Note : In retrospect, India's relative inattention to agricultural investment up to 1966-67 co-incided with non-availability of new agricultural technology. Investment began after new technology made substantial returns possible.

and their political appointees. But since much visible foreign policy deals with political problems and crises of a short-run nature, programs with longer-term objectives are at a disadvantage. Too much insulation, of course, may entail neglect and ultimate asphyxiation because every viable program requires a real constituency. The question is, what domestic costs and benefits are associated with any particular program or policy. Rather than prescribing a series of autonomous but centralized programs, insulation may best be achieved through a loosely articulated process of decision-making with multiple access-points and considerable slippage.

The principle bureaucratic players involved in self-help were USDA, AID, and the State Department, in descending order of interest and commitment. Other actors and agencies participated much more minimally, although USDA drew considerably on the system of land-grant universities and their institutes of agriculture. The principle players were not, however, well-coordinated; and the relations between overseas and Washington-based units in each agency were not strong. Congress had an overall interest in whatever impact self-help would have on American agricultural exports for hard-currency and thereby on the US balance of payments. Congressional interest, however, declined in proportion to the diminishing stock of surplus commodities.

Short-tether also had an impact : it discredited the sensible US policies toward Indian agricultural development and toward the general Indian economy. Its postulated aim of encouraging other nations to share in the burden of providing food-aid was not achieved either, but it did serve to diminish the moral standing of the United States overseas. The short-tether participants can be summed up in a simple dichotomy : LBJ versus the rest. Even loyal lieutenants like Freeman and Rusk ended up opposing an increasingly crotchety President in order to release the badly needed foodgrains. The American people, Congress, and bureaucracy came to regard LBJ's short-tether as an ill-disguised halter systematically choking Indo-American relations. While the US may be ambivalent toward South Asia, its actions since 1950 of offering India over $4 billion in economic aid and supplying over $4 billion of foodgrains against soft-currency payments, suggest some understanding of India's importance in a stable, friendly South Asia.

In conclusion, the case-study above suggests considerable merit in an incremental and somewhat disjointed system for administering US food and agricultural policies. There are times when rapid and coordinated actions are needed, but past events have indicated the ability of the current distribution of offices and reponsibilities to cope with such crises. During the drought years, the ISC had worked well-enough in obtaining the necessary food supplies and expediting their shipment. Despite presidential harassment, the ISC and supplementary task-forces had resolved the formidable technical problems in one of history's largest relief programs. Consequently, the best approach to self-help would probably have been to pass the word among participating departments that the Congress and the President wanted agricultural development promoted at all possible opportunities because, given the subtleties of international relations and of persuasive pressurizing, a decentralized system is more appropriate than a sharply articulated hierarchy.

In any case, when an issue is important enough to merit unflagging attention by the occupant of the White House, constitutional provisions are still sufficient to allow the Chief Executive maximal participation. In crisis conditions, the most that bureaucrats can do is present necessary information and choices, argue the alternatives and consequences cogently, and then abide by the legitimate policy-makers' decisions—or else publicly resign with a reasoned explanation of why the policy-makers are wrong. At times executive leadership is necessary; at times reforms are required to strengthen the bureaucracy and thereby brake determined but short-sighted leaders. But theories of democratic government require active, involved political leadership even though it occasionally rejects the best professional advice from knowledgeable specialists. Short of a platonic state, there is no solution to this creative tension. And notwithstanding any of the above, in food and agricultural aid as well as in other policies of economic development, American foreign policy-makers might well heed Hirschman's long-standing advice (1964: 54) : "We must recognize that there are tasks that simply exceed the capacities of a society, no matter to whom they are being entrusted".

ANNEX A :

USES OF FOREIGN CURRENCIES : SECTION 104
OF PL 83-480 (AS AMENDED)

SEC. 104* Notwithstanding any other provision of law, the President may use or enter into agreements with foreign countries or international organizations to use the foreign currencies, including principal and interest from loan repayments, which accrue in connection with sales for foreign currencies under this title for one or more of the following purposes :

(a) For payment of United States obligations (including obligations entered into pursuant to other legislation);

(b) For carrying out programs of United States Government agencies to—

(1) help develop new markets for United State agricultural commodities on a mutually benefiting basis. From sale proceeds and loan repayments under this title not less than the equivalent of 5 per centum of the total sales made each year under this title shall be set aside in the amounts and kinds of foreign currencies specified by the Secretary of Agriculture and made available in advance for use as provided by this paragraph over such period of years as the Secretary of Agriculture determines will most effectively carry out the purpose of this paragraph : *Provided,* That the Secretary of Agriculture may release such amounts of the foreign currencies so set aside as he determines cannot be effectively used for agricultural market development purposes under this section, except that no release shall be made until the expiration of thirty days.

* Public Law 85-128, 71 Stat: 345, approved 13 August 1957 (7 U.S C. 1704a), provides that "Within sixty days after any agreement is entered into for the use of any foreign currencies, a full report thereon shall be made to the Senate and House of Representatives of the United States and to the Committees on Agriculture and Appropriations thereof".

following the date on which notice of such proposed release is transmitted by the President to the Senate Committee on Agriculture and Forestry and to the House Committee on Agriculture, if transmitted while Congress is in session, or sixty days following the date of transmittal if transmitted while Congress is not in session. Provision shall be made in sale and loan agreements for the convertibility of such amount of the proceeds thereof (not less than 2 per centum) as the Secretary of Agriculture determines to be needed to carry out the purpose of this paragraph in those countries which are or offer reasonable potential of becoming dollar markets for United States agricultural commodities. Such sums shall be converted into the types and kinds of foreign currencies as the Secretary deems necessary to carry out the provisions of this paragraph and such sums shall be deposited to a special Treasury account and shall not be made available or expended except for carrying out the provisions of this paragraph. Notwithstanding any other provision of law, if sufficient foreign currencies for carrying out the purpose of this paragraph in such countries are not otherwise available, the Secretary of Agriculture is authorized and directed to enter into agreements with such countries for the sale of agricultural commodities in such amounts as the Secretary of Agriculture determines to be adequate and for the use of the proceeds to carry out the purpose of this paragraph. In carrying out agricultural market development activities, non-profit agricultural trade organizations shall be utilized to the maximum extent practicable. The purpose of this paragraph shall include such representation of agricultural industries as may be required during the course of discussions on trade programs relating either to individual commodities or groups of commodities;

(2) finance with not less than 2 per centum of the total sales proceeds received each year in each country activities to assist international educational and cultural exchange and to provide for the strengthening of the resources of American schools, colleges, universities, and other public and nonprofit private educational agencies for international studies and research under the programs authorized by Title VI of the National Defense Education Act, the Mutual Educational and Cultural Exchange Act of 1961, the International Education

Act of 1966, the Higher Education Act of 1965, the Elementary and Secondary Education Act of 1965, the National Foundation on the Arts and the Humanities Act of 1965, and the Public Broadcasting Act of 1967;

(3) collect, collate, translate, abstract, and disseminate scientific and technological information and conduct research and support scientific activities overseas including programs and projects of scientific cooperation between the United States and other countries such as coordinated research against diseases common to all of mankind or unique to individual regions of the globe, and promote and support programs of medical and scientific research, cultural and educational development, family planning, health, nutrition, and sanitation;

(4) acquire by purchase, lease, rental, or otherwise, sites and buildings and grounds abroad, for United States Government use including offices, residence quarters, community and other facilities, and construct, repair, alter, and furnish such buildings and facilities;

(5) finance under the direction of the Librarian of Congress, in consultation with the National Science Foundation and other interested agencies, (A) programs outside the United States for the analysis and evaluation of foreign books, periodicals, and other materials to determine whether they would provide information of technical or scientific significance in the United States and whether such books, periodicals, and other materials are of cultural or educational significance, (B) the registry, indexing, binding, reproduction, cataloging, abstracting, translating, and dissemination of books, periodicals, and related materials determined to have such significance; and (C) the acquisition of such books, periodicals, and other materials and the deposit thereof in libraries and research centers in the United States specializing in the areas to which they relate;

(c) To procure equipment, materials, facilities and services for the common defense including internal security;**

** Section 505(e) of the Foreign Assistance Act of 1961, as added by the Foreign Assistance Act of 1966, Public Law 89-583, 80 Stat. 803, approved September 19, 1966, and redesignated by the Foreign Assistance Act of 1967, Public Law 90-137, 81 Stat. 459, approved November 14, 1967, provides as follows: "(e) From and after the

(d) For assistance to meet emergency or extraordinary relief requirements other than requirements for food commodities : *Provided*, That not more than a total amount equivalent to $5,000,000 may be made available for this purpose during any fiscal year;

(e) For use to the maximum extent under the procedures established by such agency as the President shall designate for loans to United States business firms (including cooperatives) and branches, subsidiaries, or affiliates of such firms for business development and trade expansion in such countries, including loans for private home construction, and for loans to domestic or foreign firms (including cooperatives) for the establishment of facilities for aiding in the utilization, distribution, or otherwise increasing the consumption of, and markets for, United States agricultural products : *Provided however*, That no such loans shall be made for the manufacture of any products intended to be exported to the United States in competition with products produced in the United States and due consideration shall be given to the continued expansion of markets for United States agricultural commodities or the products thereof. Foreign currencies may be accepted in repayment of such loans;

(f) To promote multilateral trade and agricultural and other economic development, under procedures, established by the President, by loans or by use in any other manner which the President may determine to be in the national interest of the United States, particularly to assist programs of recipient countries designed to promote, increase, or improve food production, processing, distribution, or marketing in food-deficit countries friendly to the United States, for which purpose the President may utilize to the extent practicable the services of nonprofit voluntary agencies registered with and

sixtieth day after the date of enactment of the Foreign Assistance Act of 1966, no assistance shall be provided under this chapter to any country to which sales are made under title I of the Agricultural Trade Development and Assistance Act of 1954 until such country has entered into an agreement to permit the use of foreign currencies accruing to the United States under such title I to procure equipment, materials, facilities, and services, for the common defense including internal security, in accordance with the provisions of section 104(c) of such title I". [22 U.S.C. 2314(e).]

approved by the Advisory Committee on Voluntary Foreign Aid : *Provided*, That no such funds may be utilized to promote religious activities;

(g) For the purchase of goods or services for other friendly countries;

(h) For financing, at the request of such country, programs emphasizing maternal welfare, child health and nutrition, and activities, where participation is voluntary, related to the problems of population growth, under procedures established by the President through any agency of the United States, or through any local agency which he determines is qualified to administer such activities. Not less than 5 per centum of the total sales proceeds received each year shall, if requested by the foreign country, be used for voluntary programs to control population growth;

(i) For paying, to the maximum extent practicable, the costs outside the United States of carrying out the program authorized in section 406 of this Act;

(j) For sale of dollars to United States citizens and non-profit organizations for travel or other purposes of currencies determined to be in excess of the needs of departments and agencies of the United States for such currencies. The United States dollars received from the sale of such foreign currencies shall be deposited to the account of the Commodity Credit Corporation; and

(k) For paying, to the maximum extent practicable, the costs of carrying out programs for the control of rodents, insects, weeds, and other animal or plant pests; *Provided*, That—

(1) Section 1415 of the Supplemental Appropriation Act, 1953,*** shall apply to currencies used for the purposes specified in subsections (a) and (b), and in the case of currencies to be used for the purposes specified in paragraph (2) of sub-

---

*** Section 1415 of the Supplemental Appropriation Act, 1953, provides that "Foreign credits owed to or owned by the United States Treasury will not be available for expenditure by agencies of the United States after June 30, 1953, except as may be provided for annually in appropriation Acts and provisions of the utilization of such credits for purposes authorized by law are hereby authorized to be included in general appropriation Acts". Public Law 547, 82nd Congress, 66 Stat. 662, approved July 15, 1952 (31 U.S.C. 724).

section (b) the Appropriation Act may specifically authorize the use of such currencies and shall not require the appropriation of dollars for the purchase of such currencies,

(2) Section 1415 of the Supplemental Appropriation Act, 1953, shall apply to all foreign currencies used for grants under subsections (f) and (g), to not less than 10 per centum of the foreign currencies which accrue pursuant to agreements entered into on or before December 31, 1964, and to not less than 20 per centum in the aggregate of the foreign currencies which accrue pursuant to agreements entered into thereafter : *Provided, however*, That the President is authorized to waive such applicability of section 1415 in any case where he determines that it would be inappropriate or inconsistent with the purposes of this title,

(3) No agreement or proposal to grant any foreign currencies [except as provided in subsection (c) of this section], or to use (except pursuant to Appropriation Act) any principal or interest from loan repayments under this section shall be entered into or carried out until the expiration of thirty days following the date on which such agreement or proposal is transmitted by the President to the Senate Committee on Agriculture and Forestry and to the House Committee on Agriculture, if transmitted while Congress is in session or sixty days following the date of transmittal if transmitted while Congress is not in session,

(4) Any loan made under the authority of this section shall bear interest at such rate as the President may determine but not less than the cost of funds to the United States Treasury, taking into consideration the current average market yields on outstanding marketable obligations of the United States having maturity comparable to the maturity of such loans, unless the President shall in specific instances after consultation with the advisory committee established under section 407 designate a different rate : *Provided, further*, That paragraphs (2), (3), and (4) of the foregoing proviso shall not apply in the case of any nation where the foreign currencies or credits owned by the United States and available for use by it in such nation are determined by the Secretary of the Treasury to be in excess of the normal requirements of the departments and agencies of the United States for expenditures in such nations for the two

fiscal years following the fiscal year in which such determination is made. The amount of any such excess shall be devoted to the extent practicable and without regard to paragraph (1) of the foregoing proviso, to the acquisition of sites, buildings, and grounds under paragraph (4) of subsection (b) of this section and to assist such nation in undertaking self-help measures to increase its production of agricultural commodities and its facilities for storage and distribution of such commodities. Assistance under the foregoing provision shall be limited to self-help measures additional to those which would be undertaken without such assistance. Upon the determination by the Secretary of the Treasury that such an excess exists with respect to any nation, the President shall advise the Senate Committee on Agriculture and Forestry and the House Committee on Agriculture of such determination; and shall thereafter report to each such Committee as often as may be necessary to keep such Committee advised as to the extent of such excess, the purposes for which it is used or proposed to be used, and the effects of such use. (7 U.S.C. 1704.)

SELF-HELP MEASURES : SECTION 109 OF PL 83-480
(AS AMENDED)

SEC. 109 (a) Before entering into agreements with developing countries for the sale of United States agricultural commodities on whatever terms, the President shall consider the extent to which the recipient country is undertaking wherever practicable self-help measures to increase per capita production and improve the means for storage and distribution of agricultural commodities, including :

(1) devoting land resources to the production of needed food rather than to the production of nonfood crops—especially nonfood crops in world surplus;

(2) development of the agricultural chemical, farm machinery and equipment, transportation and other necessary industries through private enterprise;

(3) training and instructing farmers in agricultural methods and techniques;

(4) constructing adequate storage facilities;

(5) improving marketing and distribution systems;

(6) creating a favorable environment for private enterprise and investment, both domestic and foreign, and utilizing available technical know-how;

(7) establishing and maintaining Government policies to insure adequate incentives to producers;

(8) establishing and expanding institutions for adaptive agricultural research;

(9) allocating for these purposes sufficient national budgetary and foreign exchange resources (including those supplied by bilateral, multilateral and consortium aid programs) and local currency resources (resulting from loans or grants to recipient governments of the proceeds of local currency sales);

(10) carrying out voluntary programs to control population growth.

(b) Notwithstanding any other provisions of this Act, in agreements with nations not engaged in armed conflict against Communist forces or against nations with which the United States has no diplomatic relations, not less than 20 per centum of the foreign currencies set aside for purposes other than those in sections 104 (a), (b), (e), and (j) shall be allocated for the self-help measures set forth in this section.

(c) Each agreement entered into under this title shall describe the program which the recipient country is undertaking to improve its production, storage, and distribution of agricultural commodities; and shall provide for termination of such agreement whenever the President finds that such program is not being adequately developed. (7 U.S.C. 1709.)

TRANSCRIPT ON INTERAGENCY RELATIONSHIPS IN FOREIGN AGRICULTURAL DEVELOPMENT POLICY

Participants : Senator Allen J. Ellender of Louisiana, Chairman of the Committee on Agriculture and Forestry, United States Senate; and the Honorable Orville L. Freeman, Secretary of Agriculture, United States Department of Agriculture.

THE CHAIRMAN. Have you any kind of agreement between the State Department and you ?

SECRETARY FREEMAN. Yes. I have had long discussions with Mr. Bell in connection with this, and he has volunteered and urged, and since he has been in the AID agency he has advocated a stronger working relationship, and it has improved very significantly since he became Administrator of the program.

And one of the ways to make it work more efficiently has been for them to contract with the Department to take on a special project or in some cases possibly in the agricultural development in a country. Then the appropriation goes to AID. They contract with Agriculture. We then carry out to meet the contracted objective. We have been learning how to use this device and it is becoming more and more important.

THE CHAIRMAN. I presume you are not giving up any of your authority. I hope.

SECRETARY FREEMAN. No, sir.

THE CHAIRMAN. Neither to AID nor the State Department ?

SECRETARY FREEMAN. No. Quite the contrary. This means that we will be more intimately involved in both the planning and the evaluation of the results. I might just add, to be sure the record is straight, that the so-called PASA's are merely an effort to formulate more effectively the effort we have tried to try over a long period of time.

THE CHAIRMAN. It is my hope that the Department of Agriculture will remain at the top of the heap instead of at the bottom in handling such a program as you are now proposing.

SECRETARY FREEMAN. I believe the Department has an important contribution to make.

THE CHAIRMAN. We will see that that happens as far as I am concerned.

SOURCE : Hearing on "Food for Freedom Program and Commodity Reserves" on 2 June 1966 (Washington: U.S. Government Printing Office), p. 49.

SELECTED SECTIONS OF TITLE IV OF PL 83-480
(AS AMENDED)

SEC. 401. After consulting with other agencies of the Government affected and within policies laid down by the President for implementing this Act, and after taking into account productive capacity, domestic requirements, farm and consumer price levels, commercial exports, and adequate carryover, the Secretary of Agriculture shall determine the agricultural commodities and quantities thereof available for disposition under this Act, and the commodities and quantities thereof which may be included in the negotiations with each country. No commodity shall be available for disposition under this Act if such disposition would reduce the domestic supply of such commodity below that needed to meet domestic requirements, adequate carryover, and anticipated exports for dollars as determined by the Secretary of Agriculture at the time of exportation of such commodity. (7 U.S.C. 1731.)

SEC. 403. There are hereby authorized to be appropriated such sums as may be necessary to carry out this Act including such amounts as may be required to make payments to the Commodity Credit Corporation, to the extent the Commodity Credit Corporation is not reimbursed under sections 104 (j) and 105, for its actual costs incurred or to be incurred. In presenting his budget, the President shall classify expenditures under this Act as expenditures for international affairs and finance rather than for agriculture and agricultural resources. (7 U.S.C. 1733.)

SEC. 405. The authority and funds provided by this Act shall be utilized in a manner that will assist friendly countries that are determined to help themselves toward a greater degree of self-reliance in providing enough food to meet the needs of their people and in resolving their problems relative to population growth. (7 U.S.C. 1734.)

SEC. 406. (a) In order to further assist friendly developing countries to become self-sufficient in food production, the Secretary of Agriculture is authorized, notwithstanding any other provision of law—

(1) To establish and administer through existing agencies of the Department of Agriculture a program of farmer-to-farmer assistance between the United States and such countries to help farmers in such countries in the practical aspects of increasing food production and distribution and improving the effectiveness of their farming operations;

(2) To enter into contracts or other cooperative agreements with, or make grants to, land-grant colleges and universities and other institutions of higher learning in the United States to recruit persons who by reason of training, education, or practical experience are knowledgeable in the practical arts and sciences of agriculture and home economics, and to train such persons in the practical techniques of transmitting to farmers in such countries improved practices in agriculture, and to participate in carrying out the program in such countries including, where desirable, additional courses for training or re-training in such countries.

(3) To consult and cooperate with private nonprofit farm organizations in the exchange of farm youth and farm leaders with developing countries and in the training of farmers of such developing countries within the United States or abroad;

(4) To conduct research in tropical and subtropical agriculture for the improvement and development of tropical and subtropical food products for dissemination and cultivation in friendly countries;

(5) To coordinate the program authorized in this section with the activities of the Peace Corps, the Agency for International Development, and other agencies of the United States and to assign, upon agreement with such agencies, such persons to work with and under the administration of such agencies: *Provided,* That nothing in this section shall be construed to infringe upon the powers or functions of the Secretary of State;

(6) To establish by such rules and regulations as he deems necessary the conditions for eligibility and retention in and dismissal from the program established in this section, together with the terms, length and nature of service, compensation,

employee status, oaths of office, and security clearances, and such persons shall be entitled to the benefits and subject to the responsibilities applicable to persons serving in the Peace Corps pursuant to the provisions of section 612, volume 75 of the Statutes at Large, as amended; and

(7) (a) To the maximum extent practicable, to pay the costs of such program through the use of foreign currencies accruing from the sale of agricultural commodities under this Act, as provided in section 104 (i).

(b) These are hereby authorized to be appropriated not to exceed $33,000,000 during any fiscal year for the purpose of carrying out the provisions of this section. (7 U.S.C. 1736.)

SEC. 407. There is hereby established an Advisory Committee composed of the Secretary of State, the Secretary of the Treasury, the Secretary of Agriculture, the Director of the Bureau of the Budget,* the Administrator of the Agency for International Development, the chairman and the ranking minority member of both the House Committee on Agriculture and the House Committee on Foreign Affairs, and the chairman and the ranking minority member of both the Senate Committee on Agriculture and Forestry and the Senate Committee on Foreign Relations. The Advisory Committee shall survey the general policies relating to the administration of the Act, including the manner of implementing the self-help provisions, the uses to be made of foreign currencies which accrue in connection with sales for foreign currencies under title I, the amount of currencies to be reserved in sales agreements for loans to private industry under section 104 (e), rates of exchange, interest rates, and the terms under which dollar credit sales are made, and shall advise the President with respect thereto. The Advisory Committee shall meet not less than four times during each calendar year at the call of the Acting Chairman of such Committee who shall preside in the following order: The chairman of the House Committee on Agriculture, the chairman of the Senate Committee on Foreign Relations, the chairman of the Senate Committee on Agriculture and Forestry, and the chairman of the House Committee on Foreign Affairs.** (7 U.S.C. 1736a.)

* Office of Management and Budget.
** Amended by PL90—436, 82 Stat. 451, approved 29 July 1968.

REPRESENTATIVE PL-480 AGREEMENT WITH INDIA, SIGNED 20 FEBRUARY 1967

1. The two governments have consulted on the problems arising out of the gap between food production and food consumption. India has launched strong programs of economic and agricultural development accompanied by appropriate measures of import liberalization, which this agreement is designed to support.

2. The two Governments are agreed that planning for food sufficiency is an integral part of the development process and necessarily the first priority in economic planning. Nevertheless programs to achieve food sufficiency will be self-defeating if they are achieved at the expense of development in other sectors of the economy.

3. The Indian Government, as a part of its overall development program for the fiscal year beginning April 1967, is giving priority to its programs to improve production, storage and distribution of agricultural commodities, particularly food crops. Subject to the overall development of the economy and the availability of adequate amounts of foreign exchange, the following general targets were established for 1967-68 within the framework of the draft outline of the fourth Five Year Plan of the Indian Government.

(a) Fertilizer production—535,000 nutrient tons of nitrogen (N), 250,000 nutrient tons of phosphate (P_2O_5).

(b) Fertilizer imports—850,000 nutrient tons of N, 250,000 nutrient tons of P_2O_5 and 300,000 nutrient tons of potassium (K_2O).

(c) Acreage to be placed under new varieties of seeds:

Rice . . . . 6,000,000 acres
Wheat . . . . 3,500,000 acres
Maize, Bajra, and Jowar . . . . . 5,500,000 acres

(d) Crop protection—125 million acres to be sprayed.

(e) Irrigation—an increase in minor irrigation of 3 million acres, of which 2.4 million will be new command areas, 300,000 acres improvement in existing systems and 300,000 acres provided with supplementary irrigation; and concentration on use of irrigation for intensive production.

(f) Agricultural credit—an increase of over Rs. 1,000 million in agricultural credit—short, medium, and long-term—administered through government agencies, cooperatives and land development banks.

(g) Storage—owned by the Food Department and the Food Corporation of India will increase from 2 million tons capacity to 2.5 million tons. The Central and State Warehousing Corporation will increase their modern storage capacity by 0.35 million ton (to 1.8 million tons) and the States and co-operative societies will increase their facilities on modern construction designs by 0.5 million ton (to 2.5 million tons).

4. Further the following is also recognized:

(a) With respect to pricing, the timely announcement of the food grain price support at levels suffcient to encourage greater production is important so that the cultivator will base his cropping pattern on certain knowledge of the return of his expenditure, and

(b) With respect to distribution, a satisfactory distribution policy is heavily dependent on the availability of stocks under the control of the Central Government, and it is the intention of the Indian Government to increase the end of year grain stocks through implementation of price support and food distribution policies.

(c) With respect to investment, implementation of the targets set forth in paragraph 3 above and of the general agricultural development program calls for a significantly larger investment in agriculture in 1967-68 than in the previous year.

5. The Indian Government has announced its intention of

accelerating domestic production capacity for fertilizer and other industrial inputs for agriculture. The Indian Government has also announced its determination to call on all possible sources of financing for these undertakings, including private investment, and has declared that it recognizes in the context the importance of policies designed to secure a favorable investment climate.

Agreement signed 24 June 1967 (1st Supplementary)

1. As part of its efforts to increase the domestic production of fertilizer needed to achieve its target of food sufficiency and to reduce the demand for foreign exchange, the Government of India is accelerating its efforts to assess and if feasible develop indigenous sources of phosphate rock.

2. The Government of India has also announced its determination to give high priority to the implementation of a massive countrywide family planning program in order to limit the growth of population and ensure a better standard of living for its people.

3. The Government of India has announced that it is undertaking measures to systematically reduce the rate of food grain losses due to pests, particularly insects and rodents.

4. The Government of India anticipates that foodgrain acreage will increase by about 10 million acres by 1970-71 over the total area in 1964-65, while the area under cotton is expected to remain unchanged during the same period. In seeking to increase foodgrain production; the Government of India is developing and implementing a policy of announced incentive prices, improved information and extension programs, and other appropriate means.

SOURCE: *Food for Freedom, New Emphasis on Self-Help*, The Annual Report of the President on Activities Carried Out under Public Law 480, 83rd Congress, as Amended, during the Period January 1 through December 31, 1967; 90th Congress, 2nd Session, House Document No. 296 (Washington, D.C.: U.S. Government Printing Office, 1968), pp. 72-73.

SUGGESTED READINGS

Abel, Martin E., "The 1966 Amendments to Public Law 480." Washington : Economic Research Service, US Department of Agriculture (November, 1966).

Allison, Graham T., *Essence of Decision* : *Explaining the Cuban Missile Crisis.* Boston : Little, Brown and Company, 1971.

Allison, Graham T. and Morton H. Halperin, "Bureaucratic Politics : A Paradigm and Some Policy Implications." Washington : The Brookings Institution, Reprint No. 246, 1972.

Analyst, "Politics of PL-480." A four part discussion in *Mainstream* (an Indian leftist weekly) on 16, 23 and 30 October and 13 November, 1965.

"Trading Freedom for US Wheat : Aid with Chains." *Mainstream*, 25 February, 1967, 9-11.

Barnds, William, *India, Pakistan, and the United States.* New York : Praeger, 1971.

Bhagwati, Jagdish N. and Padma Desai, *India* : *Planning for Industrialization* : *Industrialization and Trade Policies Since 1951.* London : Oxford University Press, 1970.

Bhardhan, Kalpana, "Do Foodgrain Imports Affect Production?" *Economic and Political Weekly*, I, 1966, 541.

Bhatia, Krishan, *The Ordeal of Nationhood* : *A Social Study of India Since Independence, 1947-1970.* New York : Atheneum, 1971.

Indira : *A Biography of Prime Minister Gandhi.* New York : Praeger Publishers, 1974.

Bhatnagar, Satvir K., "An Analysis of Wheat Prices in India, 1954-67, With Particular Reference to PL-480." *Indian Journal of Economics*, X, 1969, 249-265.

Brown, Lester R. and Erik P. Eckholm, "Grim Reaping : This Year the Whole World is Short of Grain." *The New York Times*, 15 September, 1974, 6-E.

By Bread Alone. New York : Praeger Publishers, 1974.

Bowles, Chester, *Promises to Keep* : *My Years in Public Life, 1941-1969.* New York : Harper & Row, Publishers, 1971.

Chand, Gyan, "Food and Self-reliance." *Mainstream*, 4 December, 1965 9-11.

Cochrane, Willard W., "Food and Agricultural Policy for India." Report by the Consultant on Agricultural Planning to the Ford Foundation, New Delhi, 24 April, 1968.

Dandekar, V.M., "Food and Freedom." A two part article in *Mainstream* on 25 March and 1 April, 1967.

Destler, I.M., *Presidents, Bureaucrats, and Foreign Policy*. Princeton : Princeton University Press, 1972.

Eldridge, P.J., *The Politics of Foreign Aid in India*. Delhi : Vikas Publications., 1969.

Galdi, Theodor, "The Availability and Use of Local Currencies in U.S. Foreign Aid Programs." A report prepared for the Committee on Foreign Affairs, 93rd Congress, First Session, by the Foreign Affairs Division of the Congressional Research Service, Library of Congress. Washington : U.S. Government Printing Office, 1974.

Ghosh, Arun, "A Recipient Country Looks at Food Aid—Its Benefits and Problems." Statement by the delegate for India at the ninety-ninth meeting of the Consultative Subcommittee on Surplus Disposal of the Committee on Commodity Problems, Food and Agriculture Organization of the United Nations, 20 February, 1964.

Hirschman, Albert O., *Strategy of Economic Development*. New Haven : Yale University Press, 1964.

Hunter, Robert E. and John E. Reilly, *Development Today : A New Look at US Relations with the Poor Countries*, editors. New York : Praeger Publishers, 1972.

Jacobson, Jerome, "PL-480 Consultation Procedures." A statement by the Deputy Assistant Secretary of State for Economic Affairs, before the Subcommittee on Surplus Disposal of the Committee on Commodity Problems, Food and Agriculture Organization of the United Nations, at its 110th meeting, 9 February, 1965.

Jain, A.P., "For a New Food Policy." *Mainstream*, 25 July, 1964, 9-11.

Johnson, Lyndon Baines "Feeding the Hungry : India's Food Crisis." *The Vantage Point : Perspectives of the Presidency, 1963-1969*. New York : Holt, Rinehart & Winston, 1971, 222-231.

Johnson, Nicholas, Letter of 19 November from the Maritime Administrator to Senator Paul H. Douglas of Illinois, Chairman of the Subcommittee on Federal Procurement and Regulation, of the Joint Economic Committee. The letter is included in a report entitled "The Impact of Government-Generated Cargo on the U.S.-Flag Foreign Trade Fleet for Calendar Year 1964," prepared by the Maritime Administration of the Department of Commerce for the subcommittee, 89th Congress, First Session. Washington : U S. Government Printing Office, 1965.

Kalra. O.P., *Agricultural Policy in India*. Bombay : Popular Prakashan, 1973.

Khusro, A.M. *et al. Report of the Expert Group on the Monetary Impact of PL-480 Transactions*. New Delhi : Department of Economic Affairs, Ministry of Finance, Government of India (December 1968).

Krishnanath, *Impact of Foreign Aid on India's Foreign Policy, Economic and Political Development and Cultural Change.* Hyderabad : Rammanohar Lohia Samata Vidyalaya Nyas, 1971.

Lelyveld, Joseph, "U.S. and India : Some Mutual Irritations over Food." *New York Times,* 11 June, 1967.

"A Case Study in Disillusion : U.S. Aid Effort in India." *New York Times,* 25 June, 1974, 6.

Lewis, John P., *Quiet Crisis in India* : *Economic Development and American Policy,* Anchor Books edition. Garden City, New York : Doubleday and Company, Inc., 1964.

"Continuity and Change in U.S. Economic Aid." *Commerce,* annual number, 1966, 89-90.

Lindblom, C.E., "Has India an Economic Future ?" *Foreign Affairs,* XLIV, 1964, 239-252.

"Five Problems in Foodgrain Production : Memorandum to Ambassador Chester Bowles." New Delhi : U.S. Embassy (April, 1964), mimeographed.

"India's Economic Prospects." *Ventures* : *Magazine of the Yale Graduate School,* VII : 1 (Spring, 1968).

Lukas, Anthony, "India Tastes Politics in Food from U.S." *New York Times,* 12 February, 1967.

Mackey, George, "Consultative Subcommittee on Surplus Disposal : Adaptation to Changing Conditions." Report to the Committee on Commodity Problems of the Food and Agriculture Organization of the United Nations, 31 July, 1974.

Meadows, Dennis *et al., The Limits to Growth* : *A Report of the Club of Rome's Project on the Predicament of Mankind,* New York : Universe Books, 1972.

Mehta, Balraj, "Reverse Gear in Agriculture : Spotlight on Subramaniam Plan." *Mainstream,* 25 December, 1965, 8-9.

Paddock, William and Paul Paddock, *Famine 1975*[!] *America's Decision* : *Who Will Survive ?* Boston : Little, Brown and Company, 1967.

Raj, K.N., "Food, Fertilizer and Foreign Aid." *Mainstream,* 30 April 1966, 10-12.

Rao, V.K.R.V., "Agricultural Production." *Yojana,* 24 October, 1965.

Reserve Bank of India, *Report on Currency and Finance,* issued annually, Bombay : The Examiner Press, 1961-1973.

Schertz, Lyle P., "World Food : Prices and the Poor." *Foreign Affairs,* LII, 1974, 511-537.

Schnittker, John A., ' U.S. Food and Agriculture Act of 1965." Remarks by the Undersecretary of Agriculture at the 119th meeting of the Consultative Subcommittee on Surplus Disposal of the Committee on Commodity Problems, Food and Agriculture Organization of the United Nations, 10 January, 1966.

Sen, A.K., "PL-480 and India." *Now,* 12 November, 1965.

Singh, Har Pal, "Capital and Labour Inputs in Agriculture." *The Economic Weekly,* XV, 1963, 1963-64.

Srivastava, U.K., "PL-480 and the Indian Economy". *Asian Economic Review*, XI (February, 1969).

Sundaram, K., "PL-480 Imports—Efficiency in Purchase and Distribution." *Economic and Political Weekly* II, 1967, 487.

"The Relationship between PL-480 Transactions, Money Supply with the Public, and Prices : An Analysis." *Indian Economic Review*, V : 1 (April, 1970).

USDA Economic Research Service, *Changes in Agriculture in 26 Developing Nations, 1948 to 1963*. Foreign Agricultural Economic Report No. 27, 1965.

Veit, Lawrence, "The Economic and Political Ramifications of Local Currency (Rupee) Finance." Unpublished appendix to chapter six of his forthcoming book from the Council on Foreign Relations, New York.

Yojana, *The Meaning of Self-Reliance*. Delhi : Publications Division, Ministry of Information and Broadcasting, Government of India, 1965.

Hearings Before Congress

"Discriminatory Ocean Freight Rates and the Balance of Payments." Before the Joint Economic Committee on 20-21 June, 9-10 October, and 19-20 November 1963 and on 25-26 March, 88th Congress, first and second sessions, 1964.

"Extension of Public Law 480—Titles I and II." Before the Subcommittee on Foreign Agricultural Operations of the Committee on Agriculture, House of Representatives, 88th Congress; second session, 18-20 and 28 February, 1964.

"Extension of Public Law 480, 83rd Congress." Before the Committee on Agricultural and Forestry, United States Senate, 88th Congress, second session, 12 August, 1964.

"Discriminatory Ocean Freight Rates and the Balance of Payments." A Report of the Joint Economic Committee, Congress of the United States, 6 January, 89th Congress, first session, 1965.

"Discriminatory Ocean Freight Rates and the Balance of Payments." Before the Subcommittee on Federal Procurement and Regulation of the Joint Economic Committee, Congress of the United States, 89th Congress, first session, 7-8 April, 1965.

"Food and Agriculture Act of 1965." Before the Committee on Agriculture and Forestry, United States Senate, 89th Congress, first session, 16-18, 21-25, and 28-29 June and 15, July, 1965.

"Emergency Food Relief for India." Before the Committee on Agriculture and Forestry, United States Senate, 89th Congress, second session, 5 April, 1966.

"Discriminatory Ocean Freight Rates and the Balance of Payments." Before the Subcommittee on Federal Procurement and Regulation of the Joint Economic Committee, Congress of the United States, 89th Congress, second session, 6 and 19 May, 1966.

"Food for Freedom Program and Commodity Reserves." Before the Senate Committee on Agriculture and Forestry, United States Senate, 89th Congress, second session, 2-4, 7-8, and 15 June, 1966.

"Extension of Public Law 480, 83rd Congress." Before the Committee on Agriculture and Forestry, United States Senate, 90th Congress, second session, 13-15 March, 1968.

"Cargo Preference Provision of the Export Expansion and Regulation Act." Before the Committee on Banking and Currency, United States Senate, 91st Congress, first session, 10 July, 1969.

Annual *Reports on Public Law 480* by the President to the Congress of the United States, 1966-1972.

CASE STUDIES :
II. ECONOMIC POLICY

B. Assessment of a Bilateral Economic Policy :
A.I.D.'s Program in Support of the Rural
Electrification Corporation

Susan G. Hadden

Introduction

This case study deals with two routine decisions to provide
economic aid to India in the field of rural electrification. The
programs that resulted were very successful, because they were
both timely and well-implemented. They were closely related
to the Indian development effort and therefore received the
closest cooperation of the various Indian officials who were
involved. Despite a few snags during the formulation period,
these decisions reflect a well-coordinated policy effort.

The reasons for the success of these programs would be
valuable to trace and, if possible, duplicate. The important
issues highlighted by the progress of these two decisions are: (1)
The overall question of coordination—within AID, which was
the implementing agency, between AID and other U.S. agencies
and departments, and between the U.S. groups and Indian
government officials. (2) The degree of awareness of the political
context within which aid is being given and the potential
effects of that context on the results of the aid program. Such
awareness of political context is especially critical in all
programs that operate across the boundaries of what the
Rudolph's general report calls the sovereignty barrier; that is,
within the political and bureaucratic arena of recipient
countries. This in turn raises the issue of the nature and extent
of the controls imposed by the donor implicitly with each grant
or loan of money and the political implications of those

controls. (3) Closely related to the previous two, the role of contractors and technicians in formulating, implementing, and evaluating economic aid. This issue is of increasing importance given the fact that contractors are proposed to be increasingly emphasized as a vehicle for delivering economic aid, given the decreasing size of the core of AID staffs. These three major issues will provide the foci for the discussion following a brief chronological outline of the two decisions.

The Rural Electrification Programs

The two drought years in India, 1964-65 and 1965-66, reinforced by the American aid cut-off during the 1965 Indo-Pakistan war, turned the interest of Indian planners and policy-makers towards investing in agricultural production. Attention focused on a package of inputs including fertilizer, pesticides, and improved seeds, all of which work only in the presence of an assured supply of water. The surest source of water in many places is underground water, and the cheapest and most efficient way to lift it is with electrically powered pumps on tubewells. Thus interest in rural electrification entered a new and more productive phase when its applicability to food production was understood.

The two rural electrification programs under discussion here were specifically designed for promoting agricultural uses of electricity. Because the high costs of rural electrification discouraged most State Electricity Boards from investing in it, a program of pilot rural electric cooperatives was designed with AID help. The program had two purposes; first, to determine whether rural electrification costs could be lowered by use of cooperatives rather than government distribution systems, and second, to increase demand for electricity by demonstrating that it was both a cheap and an efficient means of irrigation. AID's main consultant and contractor for this project was the NRECA, the National Rural Electric Cooperative Association, an American agricultural and rural private association. Its role is discussed in detail below.

When the pilot coops were ready to start their construction programs in order to deliver electricity to their members, they had no source of funds. State Electricity Boards were also running into difficulties in raising money for rural electrification projects. This lead to the second project : a Rural Electrification Corporation (REC) which was an autonomous body at the federal (central) level of the Indian government and which could serve as a lending agency both to the coops and to the state boards for rural electrification projects that met certain criteria. AID provided 70 per cent of the funds for the REC and the Government of India (GOI) 30 per cent. These terms were consistent with a condition for participation imposed upon all such grants by Chairman Poague of the Agriculture Committee of the House of Representatives in order to ensure that receiving countries were committed to the programs. The total grant given over a period of five years was Rs. 1051 million ($140 million).

Chronology :

1962, AID begins to fund NRECA International Division.

1965, March Clyde Ellis and Thomas Venables of NRECA visit India, touring rural electrification installations with the India representative of Cooperative League of the U.S.A.

1966, Contract given by AID to NRECA for exploratory study for a rural electrification project.

1966, Fall Four NRECA specialists tour six states surveying sites and holding discussions with state and central officials. Returning, they recommend funding of 5 pilot rural electrification cooperatives and enactment of a rural electrification law similar to that of the U.S.

1967, Draft of the Project Proposal after negotiations with GOI. GOI agrees to set up a central coordinating committee to assure proper involvement and interest of relevant ministries and state officials.

1968, Jan-June. Phases 2-3 (Organization and Engineering) of Five Pilot Coop project implemented by 5 NRECA specialists.

June GOI declares coops to be economically feasible and worthy of incorporation and funding. All-India Rural Credit Review Committee (Venkatappiah Committee) issues report containing chapters on impact of rural electrification on agricultural development.

Aug. Conversation between Venkatappiah and J. Lewis, AID Mission Director in India, in which REC is proposed.

Aug-Dec. AID and Indian Planning Commission, Ministry of Irrigation and Power, and Ministry of Agriculture hold talks on rural electrification.

Dec. Talks made formal—project near approval. AID receives informal Bureau of Budget approval and sets Congressional wheels in motion.

1968 Dec. 20 AID Washington staff meet to discuss whether to announce project under Johnson's administration or Nixon's.

Dec. 29 Three AID and three GOI officials meet, preparing the way for Cabinet-level clearance of REC by GOI.

1969 Jan. 6 India Desk of AID (Washington) chairs meeting to discuss size and feasibility of project and its acceptability to Congress.

Jan. Copies of Project Proposal to incoming U.S. Cabinet. Word received that Indian Cabinet has scaled down project from Rs. 2.5 billion to Rs. 1.5 billion because of inflationary impact. AID informs Delhi of Bureau of Budget clearance of REC.

Feb. Lewis informs GOI that Congressional machinery is moving.

Feb. 13 GOI told to go ahead with its final budget preparations without waiting for final REC approval in U.S. which will be delayed but to keep budget flexible as REC approval likely.

March 3 P.L. 480 Congressional-Executive Advisory Committee meets to discuss REC under chairmanship of Representative Poague of House Agriculture Committee. Poague suggests that the grant be made contingent upon its continued use for rural electrification. Poague also queries giving a grant when U.S. rural electrification program is on a loan basis.

March 4 Lewis tells GOI about Poague condition that money must be used in perpetuity for rural electrification or will be subject to repayment with interest. Indians cannot accept this, suggest alternate arrangements.

March GOI agrees to accept limitation on use of funds for a period of five years.

April Bureau of the Budget declines to deliver the entire sum for REC at once but will make it available in three instalments contingent upon progress.

May Poague is persuaded to drop demand for loan by evidence that U.S. rural electrification program originated with a grant of similar size to that proposed for India.

1969 May Discussion of who owns interest on REC funds which are not immediately disbursed. Resolved in favor of India.

June Agreement to fund REC signed by Lewis and GOI officials.

July REC incorporated in India.

Sept. Five NRECA specialists arrive to help with phase 4 (Construction) of the 5 Pilot Coops.

1971 March BOB requests written justification that REC deserves more money. AID rejects request by saying *it* is the agency to make that judgement. Second instalment released earlier than target date.

July NRECA unable to replace 2 of 5 specialists whose tours are ending; 3 men thus cover 5 widely-separated coops.

1973 June 30 As part of phasing out of all AID projects, GOI requests terminating of both REC and pilot coop projects.

1974 Feb. As part of Rupee Settlement, further funds are guaranteed to the REC.

Organization and Coordination

One prerequisite for the success of programs such as the rural electrification projects just described is coordination among the agencies responsible for formulating and implementing them. Since different problems arose at different points in the history of the project, it will be convenient to discuss organization in terms of two periods, formulation and implementation.

Formulation

One major problem of coordination in the formulation period arises outside the U.S. institutional framework, and requires the synchronization of actors on both sides of the sovereignty line. It appears that India is reluctant to make a formal request for aid without a strong probability that the project will be approved. At the same time, AID is constrained from taking some important steps for obtaining funds and drawing up a formal proposal until it receives a request from India. Pakistan is reported to be considerably bolder in sending proposals for AID's consideration, which speeds up the aid process. In the present case, informal talks were held between AID and the GOI and between AID and BoB, but these were not binding. For example, BoB declined to release all the money for the REC at one time and imposed the three-instalment system very late in the negotiations.

As the accompanying chart shows, AID is organized into a series of functional and area bureaus. Most functional bureaus have some area specialists and each area bureau has some experts in agriculture, capital development, program planning and other fields. Since the policy in AID is to fund projects requested by host governments, the area bureaus have the larger role in policy formulation. Since, as the chronology suggests, negotiations with the government constitute a major part of formulation, the use of area specialists is advantageous. The other bureaus provide support and control. For example, at a January, 1969 meeting in Washington to discuss the REC proposal, AID's India Desk Officer chaired a meeting consisting of representatives from the Asia Bureau's Technical, Engineering, and Development Planning staffs, as well as representatives from the Department of Agriculture and the Bureau of the Budget. No one from AID's specialized Bureau for Technical Assistance or from its Bureau for Program and Policy Coordination was even present. However, coordination between the control bureaus and the area bureau appears to be good, while the Technical Bureau is not usually called in until after the formulation stage.

Another indicator that formulation is largely a country responsibility is that a large part of it is done by the AID Mission in India. Again this follows from the draft Project Proposal's being formulated by representatives of the recipient country. The rural electrification projects had the enthusiastic backing of the AID Mission Director, who indeed had his staff working on rural electrification proposals as soon as the GOI appeared interested in the subject. A small AID staff worked consistently and closely with the relevant Indian officials, some of whose superiors were friends of the Mission Director. The working out of the Project Proposal was speeded by the existence of a small group of concerned staff from both countries, linked by commitment to the program and personal ties. Since a Project Proposal reflects a fairly late stage of negotiations, very little was changed by Washington in the one received from India. One major change in the proposal was of course related to Representative Poague's request that a condition be imposed strictly limiting the use of the grant to rural electrification programs.

Two other groups of actors were very important in the formulation of the project, the OMB and Congress. OMB, which superseded the Bureau of the Budget, derives its power with respect to program formulation and implementation from its authority to approve the actual release of funds, and it has often interpreted that authority generously. In the rural electrification project BOB's slowness in processing the grant prevented its coordination with the formulation of the Indian budget. Also, a great deal of effort was required to obtain release of funds already approved. When the GOI was ready to use the second instalment of REC funds before the target date, OMB sought proof from AID that would allow OMB to judge whether the project was going forward as required.

AID told OMB that it was AID's function to determine whether the conditions were being fulfilled, and this was reluctantly accepted by OMB after AID provided some supporting documentation. As in other intances, it is difficult to halt ongoing projects.

AID's coordination with Congress seems to be very good. Since the two bodies often have conflicting aims and responsibilities with respect to foreign policy, coordination with Congress really means maintaining good ties with staffs and Congressmen and providing them with sound documentation about projects. AID's long-time director, John Hannah, had personal ties with many Congressmen which lent force to the informative memoranda prepared by AID staff.

The REC grant provides a good example of AID's ability to provide Congress with information that makes projects more acceptable and more compatible with the Congressmen's goals. At the meeting of the PL-480 Congressional-Executive Advisory Committee, Representative Poague imposed two conditions on the grant: (1) that the U.S. should give no more than 70 per cent of the needed funds, the other 30 per cent to be provided by India to ensure its good faith (a similar condition is placed on many grants), and (2) that the funds be restricted to use in rural electrification projects forever or else be subject to repayment with interest. This condition was not acceptable to the Indian Government, and through AID's diplomacy on both sides it was subsequently modified to restrict the use of funds to rural electrification for five years. At the same time, Representative Poague and Senator Ellender asked how they could justify to their constituents that India's rural electrification program was being financed by a grant when the American program is based on loan funds. From January to May a large part of AID's internal communications about the REC project were concerned with the early history of the U.S. rural electrification program. At last an AID officer remembered that the program had begun with a *grant* from Congress of almost exactly the same $ 140 million that was being allotted to the Indian grant. Thus Congressional objections were overcome by careful AID staff work.

Implementation

My discussion here will be very brief, as the major part of it falls under the head "Technical Assistance" below. A few comments are in order, however.

The cooperative program was implemented almost entirely by the NRECA personnel, who were given a great deal of freedom in what they did. Indeed, they were praised warmly by an independent GOI Commission report for their ability to overcome obstacles at the state level. AID's contract supervisors in Delhi were not entirely satisfied with the NRECA's performance, especially when it was unable to provide a full complement of personnel in 1971. One NRECA specialist was not encouraged to extend his tour of duty. The contract supervisors were also the project supervisors for the REC program. They exercised almost complete personal discretion, rarely checking with superiors in AID either in Delhi or Washington.

There were some interesting differences in style between the two men who served as REC project supervisors in Delhi. The first was a credit specialist whose previous government experience had been with the U.S. Department of Agriculture and the Farmers Home Administration. He was competent but not knowledgeable about India. He therefore tended to act (or be made to act ?) through his superior in the Economics Section of AID in India who was more familiar with local conditions. He did not communicate directly with Washington. The second man was a long-time resident of India and an agricultural economist; he was very independent in working with the GOI and the REC. He communicated often with his Washington counterpart in the Technical Support Office of AID's Asia Bureau, who was also a close personal friends At the time assignments of supervisory staff were made, the Public Administration section of Asia/Tech had a relatively light work load. Consequently, REC's formal Washington supervisor was located in this division of Asia/Tech rather than in its Agricultural Section. However, all actual supervision was exercised by the friend in the Agriculture Section, which facilitated inter-project coordination and speeded requests for equipment. For example, this officer and the Delhi supervisor agreed to use the Agricultural Production Teams who were working on related projects in India to talk with the cooperatives should they happen to be nearby. Under the formal arrangement, this would probably not have occurred.

Once it was formulated, the REC project was almost self-sustaining, probably due in part to the AID supervisor's competence, and in part to the nature of the project itself. The coop project had more difficulties, but apart from the serious problems of NRECA not providing enough staff, it too does not seem to have suffered from lack of coordination in implementation.

U.S. Controls and the Awareness of Political Effects

Two of the World Bank's criteria for economic aid are that the project should fall in a productive sector and that the investment should generate further investment by private persons. In 1965-69 when the two rural electrification projects were initiated, the agricultural sector in India fulfilled both these criteria, which partially accounts for their success. The programs' formulators were fully aware of this, for in their presentations to Congress they stressed the role of rural electrification in increasing agricultural production and in helping the farmer to help himself.

However, economic projects also have political implications. One important part of assessing an organization's ability to formulate good economic projects is analyzing its ability to foresee and control for the political constraints within which its programs will be working as well as the political impacts of those programs.

AID personnel generally seemed quite aware of the political contexts within which they had to work, but attitudes of many (especially the technicians—see below) were that they didn't care—"politics is for the Indians to worry about". Others were worried about the fact that too careful monitoring of the political implications of their policies would look like meddling in India's internal affairs; this is a legitimate problem which is also discussed below.

A good example of the whole set of problems surrounding the political implications of economic aid programs is found in the REC decision. Electricity is a concurrent power, according to India's constitution; that is, it is a power exercised jointly by the federal government and the states. The State Electricity Boards set electricity rates and decide the details of all but interstate projects. Because they are constrained to operate on a no profit, no loss basis, they tended to ignore rural electrification projects which almost always lose money. Indeed, to induce them to undertake such projects, the GOI had had to provide them with funds. In an effort to increase the rural load, all the states had decided to offer at a subsidized rate that electricity which would be used for irrigation. This further lowered the profitability of rural electrification projects. One major concern of AID was that the REC should fund the most profitable rural electrification projects first, and that it should try to increase the number of such projects by getting the states to raise electricity rates.

It is clear from the discussions that were held with the GOI that many Indian bureaucrats in the Ministry of Irrigation and Power and in the Planning Commission also wanted the rates raised. Thus they were not at all reluctant to accept as a condition of the grant that Boards should be requested to raise rates in areas receiving electricity through REC loans. In fact, the GOI wanted to gain control over the total financial procedures of the State Boards by imposing fiscal constraints on them. It requested AID to make this control a condition of the REC grant. AID refused. It did not have the personnel to both oversee rates and to pursue REC's other objectives. In the absence of sufficient personnel, the program's wider objectives would be affected and it would be open to criticism. Similarly, the REC's wish to enforce higher electricity rates on *all* rural electrification programs in borrower states was rejected because neither AID nor the REC could enforce such a condition, and both agencies would be criticized for interfering in the states' affairs.

These examples do suggest some awareness of India's political reality. Why then did AID agree to impose even the limited condition that the rates should be raised on REC-financed projects when it was clear that the states would be extremely reluctant to do this—and indeed have not done so ? There are two major answers to this question. First, AID is of necessity very responsive to Indian bureaucrats in formulating programs. Implementation is dependent on their goodwill, as is acceptance of further programs, both of which are sought by the agency as part of its own growth and effectiveness. Second, AID officials are unanimous that even if a condition such as this one is not fulfilled, the mere fact that it exists is helpful in paving the way for implementation of the objective sometime. Thus, while reluctant to impose conditions so severe that they would be criticized both for imposing them and for failing to implement them, AID officials *were* interested in calling attention to what they believed would be the best way of carrying out a program.

Never was it specifically mentioned that the states were unlikely to accept the rate raises, but several officials said they vaguely knew that this would happen. No one, however, had consulted the embassy political officers either on this or on any other matter except a joint annual review of the Indian budget. Such lack of consultation on the political implications of economic policy seems to characterize agricultural development issues generally though commercial project officers found embassy people helpful. While AID personnel briefed the embassy on projects in hand, and the ambassador himself was involved in trying to obtain release of the later instalments and persuading congress to accept the REC, generally coordination of political implications of aid was weak.

One reason for lack of coordination was that AID personnel were confident of their own understanding of the Indian political situation. From Lewis on down, there was an extraordinary amount of expertise on India, with a strong appreciation of politics and an interest in Indian culture. The second REC project supervisor shared these qualities, and his sensitivity to Indian political requirements was one of the most important reasons for the success of the REC. But while these particular conditions led to an intelligent review and management of the political implications of aid, one cannot count on the fortuitous selection of politically knowledgeable AID personnel.

Money, especially phased loans or grants, is a powerful tool for controlling behavior. That is of course why the Bureau of the Budget insisted that the REC grant be phased and that further disbursements be conditioned upon proper use of earlier monies. Indian bureaucrats are well aware of this tool and use it themselves in controlling the behavior of the states' electricity rates. However, the exercise of such controls is a touchy matter in international affairs. Indian bureaucrats wanted the U.S. to put strict conditions upon the grant so that they could force the states to adopt the desired behavior without accepting the blame for having imposed the conditions. The U.S. declined to do so.

Bureaucrats in the receiving nation are thus important if unacknowledged actors in aid programs. In this case the GOI wanted the states to adhere to the condition of raising the rates but could not force them to. In other cases, however, it would no doubt be easy enough for the U.S. to be manipulated by the recipient governments into attaining goals other than those the U.S. was trying to achieve. The U.S. government would then be open to criticism both at home and in the recipient nation. While no serious problems appeared in the REC case, they can and have occurred in other instances. Channels for considering political implications of economic aid must, therefore, be established and routinized. Politically sensitive advice must be formally incorporated in aid decisions; embassy political staffs are presumably the most likely agents of such advice. They should explicitly share an obligation for which they will in any case share responsibility if trouble should arise.

The Agents of Technical Assistance

The final issue of importance that is raised by the rural electrification decisions concerns the agents of technical assistance. It is closely related to the issues of political awareness and of coordination raised above. Technicians and contractors are often not aware of political conditions, and contractors are often difficult to coordinate and control during the period of existing contracts. This problem has three aspects : contracts, technicians vs. generalists, and the new administrative procedure for economic assistance.

(1) Contractors

One of the outstanding features of this project is surely the strong reliance on the NRECA for details of the cooperative program. Indeed, much of AID's assistance is delivered through contracts with various people and organizations. This is inevitable given the range of programs undertaken by AID and its limited staff. The NRECA contract is in many respects typical of other AID contracts and it raises many interesting problems in the administration of foreign aid.

The NRECA is a powerful, nationwide, private association originally established to promote rural electric cooperatives in the United States. Its power in U.S. politics stems from the 1940's when America's own rural electrification movement was in its infancy. The establishment of coops in all but two of the 48 states meant that few Congressmen could afford to oppose the coop movement and its regulatory agency, the REA (Rural Electrification Administration).

As so often happens, the public REA and the private NRECA developed such cordial relations that the REA might be considered a "captive" agency. Exchanges of personnel between the two and continuous consultations assure that the organization and program goals of the REA are substantially those of the NRECA. These goals include a very strong commitment to the cooperative form of organization with all of its self-help ethos and populist ideological commitments. Indeed, the NRECA is one of the most important members of the Cooperative League of the U.S.A. In addition, the two groups have a virtual monopoly on managerial and technical expertise in the rural electrification field. Thus AID had to look to the NRECA for technical help on its rural electrification projects, but in doing so it also purchased committed cooperators with strong Congressional influence.

Because of its importance to many under-developed countries, AID was interested in rural electrification from the start. In 1962 it began providing a small grant to NRECA to staff an International Office which would be able to provide AID with expertise in organizing rural electrification projects. Funding of such private groups had several advantages for AID. One is that expertise is always available. More important, it is emphasized by members of both NRECA and the Cooperative League of the U.S.A., which also helped formulate the pilot coop project, that the use of non-governmental agencies to develop and implement foreign aid projects removes some of the appearance of meddling and makes the projects more acceptable to many governments. Finally, such private groups do have Congressional influence which they may use to further foreign aid because of its direct benefits to their institutional maintenance and prestige.

On the other hand, AID may get locked into contracts with

the same agencies over and over again, as it has with NRECA and with the Land Grant Colleges. This is especially likely to happen if AID is funding the agency. Furthermore, this close relationship compounds a problem inherent in many of the service contracts : no sanctions for non-fulfilment of contract. Since the quality of services is difficult to measure, it would be hard to justify the imposition of sanctions. But without competition for contracts the absence of sanctions may lead to complacency, as when the NRECA was unable to provide a consultant for each coop and three men had to direct five widely separated projects, to the detriment of all. Finally, as suggested, purchase of services from a group such as NRECA involved purchase of its cooperative ideology as well. In the Indian project NRECA was firm about the necessity for the program to be cooperative. Pressure from AID (which is, after all, partially funding it) was required before it would consent to advise non-cooperative rural electrification programs.

Because they have their own ends to pursue, the services of such ideologically committed private groups may be purchased more cheaply than those of individual citizens. This creates problems, as noted, but it also indicates the need for further mobilization of private groups. First, by competition with each other, these groups may upgrade the quality of services being delivered. Second, they will help educate Congress in the requirements of foreign aid. Third, private groups will bring to their members broader understanding of other peoples and nations, as NRECA has already done by telling about its overseas programs.

(2) Technicians Vs. Generalists

This issue is as old as administration, but it is still important. AID's contractors as well as the people from AID's Technical Assistance Bureau feel rather strongly that because it is scientific, the expertise they offer is universally applicable. They prefer short terms of duty because they feel they can analyze a problem and suggest the best or the second-best solution very quickly. Needless to say, their solutions often are not feasible because of costs or politics, and their unwillingness to "get involved" is resented by AID country specialists and by nationals alike. The preliminary report by the NRECA team in which it hoped to transfer U.S. organization for rural electrification wholesale to India indicates the sort of naivete that is often found. AID's Technical Assistance Bureau has attempted to develop a core of specialists who have both the requisite knowledge and some experience in trying to apply it in developing countries. But this effort founders on the realization that field men simply cannot keep current enough in their technical areas to be useful. Furthermore, cuts in AID personnel mean that it is increasingly difficult to maintain a staff of country oriented people with the necessary technical expertise.

The rural electrification projects indicate that there is a solution to this problem. A group of country-oriented generalists, including people familiar with agriculture, small industry, etc., should be stationed in each AID country mission. These people would have good relationships with relevant country officials and serve both as program officers and discussants in the informal talks preceding formal program requests. They will have enough professional expertise to gain the confidence of the more specialized technicians called in to advise on specific problems. (Similarly, in Washington, the Technical Assistance Bureau should have at its core a group of technical experts whose secondary competence will be about developing countries.) In order to develop this group of generalist experts, it will be necessary to (1) consistently encourage tours of duty longer than four years (two 2-year terms) in any one country rather than discourage them as at present; and (2) encourage such persons to take paid leaves every four to five years to renew their expertise in their technical fields of specialization. It may be that more and more AID employees will be natives with the proper training, rather than U.S. citizens living long in one country. While this does raise problems of ability to get things done, even natives will find themselves insulated from some accustomed pressures as employees of the U.S. Government.

The problem of the way in which skills of specialists are made available to receiving countries is one of the most important in foreign aid. A know-it-all attitude, or even one that insists that certain technical problems are really the same everywhere, grates on local administrators mired in the complexities of turning theoretical solutions into action. The presence of less specialized but still competent professionals who are attuned to these needs should help mitigate this problem.

(3) *Host Country Direct Recruitment of Technicians*

The old procedure by which technical assistance was given is generally similar to that followed in the rural electrification programs. Since AID is turning more and more to technical assistance and away from large capital development projects, it is of importance to assess the new procedure for rendering technical assistance and to compare it with the old one.

The new procedure essentially consists of giving a large block of money to a country to set up and administer a series of related rural development programs of its own choosing. The choice will be limited by Congressional approval, by AID's assessment of its overall feasibility, and by its relationship to the Congressional guidelines for aid projects (aid the poorest people with programs emphasizing food production, nutrition, health, population control, and education). The country is then responsible for determining whether it requires expert advice, for finding people who fit its requirement, for administering the program and for actually apportioning the monies to the different parts of the project. Following the World Bank's lead, some of the money must be used to hire independent auditing services which will analyze in depth 10 percent of the progress reports originating in the field; AID in turn will spot-check 10 percent of these studies to make sure that the program is in fact directed towards the desired goals.

In some respects this program does not differ markedly from the previous procedure. For example, as early as 1962, John Lewis noted that most AID projects were a result of the host government submitting a list of its own favored development programs from which AID would then choose those it most preferred to fund. Decentralization in administering the program and a spot-check method of assessing its usefulness are also occasionally used. However, the selection by the government itself of advisory personnel is an important new feature which, I believe, is contrary to the best interests both of the U.S. and of the country's development effort. (Of course, even at present, the host government reviews the vitas of all AID-selected potential U.S. advisors and may reject any of them.)

First, it is very difficult for foreign countries to know where to go to select personnel. Negotiating contracts is very difficult without knowledge of current rates; even knowledge of where to place recruiting advertisements may be lacking. On its face the procedure eliminates the difficulty of AID's being locked into relationships with certain groups such as the Land Grant Colleges. In fact it opens governments to serious problems in evaluating personnel and receiving the full services paid for.

Second, where the technicians become employees of foreign governments, they may lose the independence and standing offered by AID affiliation. More important, the incentive and opportunity to make use of the advice and cultural sensitivity of AID's staff would be lost. This would be an especially severe loss if AID's country missions consisted primarily of people trained for liaison work to promote the best use of technical advice.

Summary

This discussion of two projects to encourage the development of rural electrification in India has not stressed that the funds used were PL-480 surplus rupees. Needless to say, the existence of these funds facilitated the setting up of large-scale programs such as the REC grant. (The co-op program was largely a dollar program.) However, despite the anticipated decline of PL-480 funds the cases studied are interesting both because the organization and methods for initiating and implementing the decisions were typical and because the problems raised by technical assistance are inherent in technical programs everywhere.

I have suggested that the programs were very successful. This success can be attributed to the facts that the agricultural sector was ready for investment and that Indian officials were interested in a program so complementary to India's own development efforts. In addition, the strong morale of the AID mission at the time and its high caliber contributed strongly to the success of these programs and many others that were

undertaken during the same period. These in turn were due in
large part to the excellent reputation of the Mission Director
and his ability to recruit interesting and interested staff. In
discussing personnel and advocating the hiring of a core staff
of country-oriented technically-trained experts, I have in mind
a mission very much like the one in India in the middle 1960's.
If it is necessary to recruit such staff with more prerequisites,
I believe this should be done even at the expense of numbers,
With good liaison people, short-term consultants will be put to
the best use. Insofar as it is possible, the tensions between
generalists and specialists, and between country and function
will be minimized. Furthermore, decentralized implementation
of programs, which is the efficient way to use scarce resources,
is successful only when the personnel are well-trained and
committed. Lewis had advocated this system in 1962 and he
implemented it in his own mission where it did seem to work.
    Coordination both within and outside AID was good.
Washington supported Delhi both in the formulation and
implementation periods. AID staff in Washington were
especially successful in reconciling the needs of Congress and
the needs of India and of AID by educating Congressmen to
the importance of the rural electrification programs and their
relationship to Indian development as well as to their
similarities to earlier U.S. policies. OMB was also provided
with well-documented cases for the release of funds. AID is
an advocate to Congress of the countries in which it has
programs and an advocate in those countries of sound development strategies. It has difficult tasks to perform both in the
U.S. and in host countries, and a small and dedicated staff are
the best insurance that they will be performed well. The two
rural electrification programs are proof that AID has been
equal to its promise.

Summary of Recommendations

A. Organization
1. Present emphasis on area (not functional) bureaus for
policy-making is desirable given the emphasis on AID projects
requested by host governments and the importance of the
recipient government in formulation of proposals.

2. Existing inter-departmental relations are reasonably well-coordinated, although some strengthening of communications with Agriculture may be helpful (they are conspicuous by their absence in this study.) The role of OMB in policy-making must be better defined; its requirements both delayed release of funds, timed releases in ways incompatible with Indian budgets, and imposed instalment release of an approved grant. President Ford's more restrictive view of OMB's role may change this.

3. Increased interaction with embassy personnel would be desirable.

B. Staff

1. It is desirable to build up core staffs of country-oriented experts; they should have enough standing in their fields of expertise to work effectively with other specialists but should also be knowledgeable concerning cultural and political aspects of the country. Their main duties would be as project supervisors and thus as liaisons between short-term consultants and country officials needing those services. To keep them up-to-date in their fields, study leaves should continue to be encouraged. Restrictions on length of stay in one country militate against development of such expertise. Increased employment of nationals may be desirable.

2. Where Mission Directors are persons of high standing in economics or development administration (as John Lewis was), this affects their capacity to recruit first-rate AID personnel. Some previous knowledge of the country and experience in economics is important for success.

3. Evaluation of the long-term impacts of aid programs is presently weak, especially the political impacts of economic programs. Staff as described in (1) should be more sensitive to these questions. There is need for specifically political advice, which might be achieved through increasing the exchanges between embassy political officers and AID staffs, and through consultants.

4. The contract system is inevitable given staff cuts, but it makes the construction of core liaison staffs, as in (1) even more important. More attention needs to be given to expanding the

list of potential contractors, possibly through wider advertising of AID's needs.

5. The proposed new system of allowing recipient governments to recruit their own advisory personnel has numerous disadvantages : lack of insulation from local pressures, lack of prestige appointments, difficulties in assessing qualities of applicants, inability to use AID's expertise on cultural and political implications. These disadvantages make the contract procedure appear wiser.

ional Development

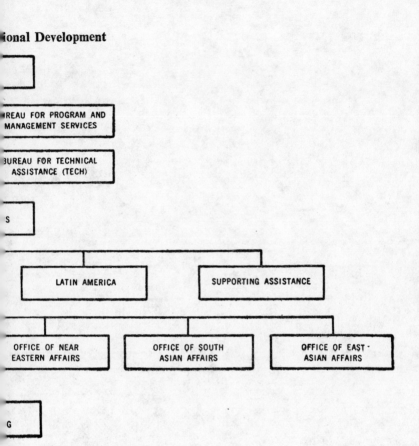

(*Facing Page 282*)

Annex I : Agency for Intern

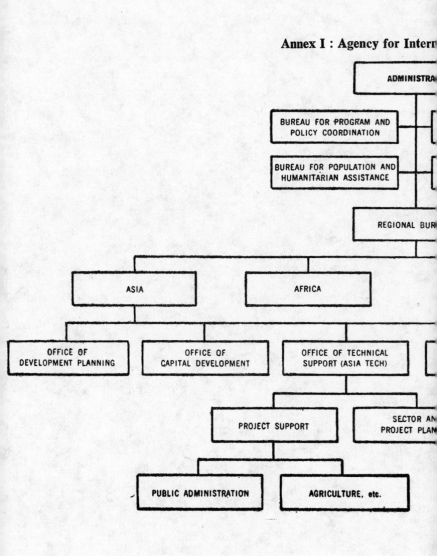

ADMINISTRA...

DIRECTOR OF ... PLANS...
PLANS CONSIDERATIONS

PROGRAM DEVELOPMENT IN AID
HUMANITARIAN ASSISTANCE

REGIONAL BUR...

AFRICA

OFFICE OF TECHNICAL
SUPPORT AGRICULTURE

OFFICE OF
DEVELOPMENT PLANNING

PROJECT SUPPORT

PUBLIC ADMINISTRATION

AGRICULTURE, etc.

CASE STUDIES :
II. ECONOMIC POLICY

C. United States Expropriation Policy and South Asia : A Case Study in Policy Implementation

Stanley A. Kochanek

I. The Decision and Its Background

A. The Issues

Despite massive aid efforts totalling $ 10 billion over the past 20 years, United States economic and commercial interests in South Asia are extremely small in comparison with those in other areas of the world. South Asia has not been an important source of raw materials critical to the United States; except for India, South Asia offers limited potential as an export market; and the major nations of the region—India, Pakistan, and Bangladesh—receive altogether less than 1 percent of total United States overseas investment. Yet as small as United States economic interests in South Asia may be in global terms, attacks on these interests arouse fears that actions in the region, especially in a large and prestigious country such as India, will have serious repercussions in other less developed countries.

In the early 1970's a wave of nationalization swept through the countries of South Asia, engulfing United States insurance companies in India, Pakistan, and Bangladesh. Propelled by domestic political pressures to move in a more socialist direction, faced by demands for redistributive justice, and confronted by the development of strong feelings of economic nationalism, reformist governments in South Asia undertook a series of new economic policies which affected United States business interests in the region. In India the government of Prime Minister Indira Gandhi nationalized all general insurance companies, including six United States firms effective January 1, 1973. In Pakistan the American Life Insurance Company's (ALICO) property was taken by the government of Zulfikar Ali Bhutto on March 19, 1972. Less than a week later, on March 26, 1972, in Bangladesh several small wholly or partially United States owned companies were nationalized by the government of Sheikh Mujibur Rahman. The nationalized companies were subsidiaries of two American insurance groups—the American Foreign Insurance Association (AFIA) and the American International Underwriters (AIU).

In almost all cases involving economic and commercial issues outside the communist bloc, United States policy tends to be global rather than oriented toward a particular region or country. American policy governing nationalization and expropriation had been set forth in a statement issued by President Nixon on January 19, 1972 entitled "Economic Assistance and Investment Security in Developing Nations."[1] The President's statement declared that in future situations of expropriation involving a significant United States interest failure to pay prompt, adequate, and effective compensation would result in a withholding of new bilateral economic aid and a refusal to support loans from multilateral development institutions such as the Inter American Bank, the International Development Association, and the Asian Development Bank, unless major factors affecting American interests require the United States Government to act otherwise. Within a few months this policy was being tested as, for the first time, American economic interests were being nationalized in South Asia.

B. The Major Actors

In order to carry out the policy on expropriation laid down in his January 19,1972 statement, the President had established a special inter-agency group (the Expro Group) under the Council on International Economic Policy (CIEP)[2]. Composed

1. For the text of this statement see Department of State, *United States Foreign Policy 1972 : A Report of the Secretary of State* (Washington : Government Printing Office 1973), pp. 485-487.
2. *Ibid.* p. 15.

of representatives of the White House and the department of State, Treasury, Defense and Commerce[3] and chaired by the Assistant Secretary of State for Economic and Business Affairs, the Expro Group had four functions; first, to review continually all potential and actual expropriation cases and to compile relevant information on current American economic benefits subject to potential United States action such as trade preferences, bilateral aid, multilateral aid, outstanding debt and total foreign investment; second, to make specific findings as to whether an expropriation has occurred and whether reasonable provision has been made for prompt, adequate, and effective compensation; third, to recommend courses of action to the United States Government consistent with the President's January 19, 1972 policy statement; fourth, to coordinate and ensure policy implementation. Any member of the Expro Group had the right to call a meeting to discuss an issue of alleged expropriation. Each member was to make its resources available to obtain information upon which to base a decision. Decisions were made by consensus, or, failing that, the Group chairman was to make a report to the Executive Director of the

3. C.I.E.P. Interagency staff members April 1972 (Expro Group):
   Chairman: Mr. Willis C. Armstrong—Assistant Secretary of State for Economic Affairs (Department of State)
   Alternate Chairman : Mr. Sidney Weintraub—Deputy Assistant Secretary of International Finance and Development (Department of State)
   Department of Treasury : Mr. John Hennessey—Deputy Assistant Secretary for Developmental Finance
   Department of Commerce : Mr. Lawrence Fox—Deputy Assistant Secretary for International Economic Policy
   Department of Defense : Mr. Lawrence S. Eagleburger—Deputy Assistant Secretary for Policy Plans and National Security Council Affairs and Dr. Roger Shields—Assistant to Assistant Secretary of Defence for International Security Affairs (Department of Defence)
   Ex Officio :
   Mr. Dean Hinton—Assistant Director CIEP
   Mr. Moorhead C. Kennedy—Acting Director Office of Investment Affairs (Department of State)
   Mr. J. Dapray Muir—Assistant Legal Adviser for Economic Affairs (Department of State)
   Mr. Lawrence Rosen—Staff Assistant CIEP

C.I.E.P. who could then attempt to resolve interdepartmental differences or submit the issue for a presidential decision. The Expro Group played a role in each of the nationalization cases in South Asia but was particularly active in the settlement of the ALICO case in Pakistan.

Although the Expro Group played an important role at most critical decisional points within the United States Government, day to day activity was the responsibility of the India, Pakistan, and Bangladesh Country Desks in the Bureau of Near East and South Asian Affairs (NEA). The Country Desks monitored daily developments, prepared summary reports and recommendations for the Expro Group, advised the companies on strategy, and verified information. They were also the focal point for pressures from the White House, other executive agencies like Treasury and Commerce, the companies, and Congress. In addition, they drafted and cleared all major instructions to the appropriate embassies.

Although the President's policy statement on expropriation specifically provided for the discretionary application of sanctions in the light of *other* United States foreign policy or security interests, the Executive branch had to consider two Congressional directives dealing with cases of expropriation. These Congressional directives were Section 620(e) of the Foreign Assistance Act of 1961, popularly known as the Hickenlooper Amendment, and Section 12 of the International Development Association Act known as the Gonzalez Amendment. The Hickenlooper Amendment requires the President to suspend bilateral assistance to any country whose government has nationalized, expropriated or seized ownership or control of property owned by any U.S. citizens when such a country fails within a reasonable time (not more than six months after such action) to take steps, which may include arbitration, to discharge its obligations under international law toward such citizen entity, including speedy compensation for the full value of such property in convertible foreign exchange as required by international law.

The Gonzalez Amendment requires the respective Executive Directors to vote against any loan for any country which has nationalized, expropriated or seized ownership or control of property owned by any U.S. citizen or by any corporation owned at least 50 per cent by U.S. citizens, unless the President determines that (a) arrangement for prompt, adequate and effective compensation has been made, (b), the parties have submitted the dispute to arbitration under the rules of the Convention for the Settlement of Investment Disputes, or (c) good faith negotiations are in progress aimed at providing prompt, adequate and effective compensation under the applicable principles of international law. The automatic trigger sanctions of the Hickenlooper and Gonzalez amendments, combined with strong Congressional feelings on issues of expropriation put the insurance companies in a good position to pressure the State Department to assist them in securing their objectives.

Even though the investment involved totalled only approximately eight million dollars, the affected companies were dedicated to the enforcement of the principle of prompt, adequate and effective compensation. The companies acted both individually through company representatives and collectively through the International Insurance Advisory Council of the United States Chamber of Commerce. The most active and vocal of the companies nationalized in South Asia belonged to the American International Underwriters Group, a holding company which conducted business in over 100 countries, including India, Pakistan and Bangladesh. The president of A.I.U was particularly concerned because his affiliates were under attack in many countries and he feared the nationalization actions in South Asia would set an example for other less developed countries. Clearly, expecting strong support from his government, he was both vocal and persistent in taking his case to all levels of the executive branch, including the White House, Treasury, Commerce, State, AID, and the embassies involved, and he frequently threatened and he occasionally carried through on his threats to take the AIU case to Congress.

The final actor of significance in the insurance nationalization cases was the Government of Great Britain. The President's statement of January 19, 1972, directed the United States Government agencies to consult with other governments to work out measures for dealing with expropriation on a multilateral basis. Shortly after it was created, the Expro

Group met with the British and the two agreed on a set of principles for both nations to apply in cases involving expropriation. Since British economic interests in South Asia were far larger than American interests, it seemed appropriate for the two governments to cooperate in dealing with the nationalization of insurance in the area. Differences in diplomatic style, company attitudes, and changing patterns of bilateral relations, however, resulted in an extremely uneven application of the set of global principles of cooperation, despite the existence of what appeared to be an ideal case for mutual action.

C. The Decision Arena

International investments grew rapidly in the sixties, especially investment abroad by United States multinational corporations. United States net foreign investment rose from $45 billion in 1960 to $70 billion at the end of 1970. Meanwhile a strong tide of economic nationalism was sweeping through the less developed countries of the world, bringing with it a wave of nationalization and expropriation of American business interests. By 1971 the Nixon administration had recorded 70 cases in which concerns with United States interests were being subjected to nationalization, expropriation, or a negotiated sale of assets. The estimated book value of these jeopardized assets was about 6-7 per cent of the $20 billion estimated book value of United State's investments in developing countries.[4]

Feelings on issues of expropriation ran high at the White House and on Capitol Hill. The President expressed many of his views about the integrity of private United States economic interests abroad in his January 19, 1972 policy statement on expropriation. Despite the "virtually axiomatic" beneficial role of private foreign capital, he declared, governments had acted against private capital through expropriations which were "wasteful," "shortsighted," and "unfair". "The wisdom of any expropriation," said the President, "is questionable even when adequate compensation is paid."[5]

4. Department of State, *United States Foreign Policy 1971 : A Report of the Secretary of State* (Washington : Government Printing Office, 1972) pp. 215-216

5 *United States Foreign Policy 1972*, p. 486

As the Gonzalez and Hickenlooper amendments indicate, feelings on issues of expropriation were even stronger on Capitol Hill than they were at the White House. The administration had been unable to block the Gonzalez amendment and was even reluctant to request its revision to include some degree of presidential discretion because of a fear that such action would be viewed by Congress as a weakening of the administration's position on expropriation. Such Congressional fears might jeopardize legislative action on aid legislation and on legislative funds for multilateral lending agencies. It might even result in more restrictive congressional directives.

The executive agencies represented in the Expro Group tended to view the expropriation issue less ideologically in terms of their own missions and interests. The departments of State, Defense and Commerce were concerned with how sanctions in cases of expropriation would affect other United States economic, foreign policy and security interests. While the departments were prepared to explain to foreign governments that the Nixon administration was very serious when it came to matters of expropriation, they searched for measures with a less drastic effect than lowering the boom on aid or multilateral loans. Threatened action, they felt, was often more effective than the action itself. In either case, United States Government activity should be used to reinforce the motivations of the parties to reach a compromise solution. Only the Treasury Department was prepared to take a firm stand on demanding prompt, adequate and effective compensation in all cases of expropriation and advocated the use of sanctions to demonstrate American resolve.

The factors of leadership style and domestic political compulsions which shaped United States policy on expropriation pushed the policies of the governments of South Asia in a totally different direction. South Asian leadership in the early 1970's was reformist and socialist. Although the circumstances which led to the nationalization of insurance differed somewhat in the three countries, demands for greater redistributive justice had moved the domestic policies of the governments of India, Pakistan and Bangladesh to the left. Nationalization of the insurance industry was one of the consequences.

On May 12, 1971, shortly after her massive election victory

in March 1971 Prime Minister Indira Gandhi issued an unexpected ordinance establishing government custodianship over all 107 general insurance companies in India. Included were 42 foreign firms. Six of them were American; 30 were British. The Finance Minister assured the foreign insurance companies that the bill as introduced into Parliament would include compensation payable in foreign exchange. The State Department viewed the sudden action as more calculated to dramatize the Congress Party's commitment to its campaign pledges by pacifying the political left while minimizing the impact on the investment climate by choosing the less important general insurance business instead of the more important oil or pharmaceutical industry.

The nationalization of insurance in Pakistan, where American private investment totalled about $100 million, followed the Bangladesh debacle. After the breakup of Pakistan in December 1971, the military government turned power over to a civilian government led by Zulfikar Ali Bhutto, leader of the Peoples Progressive Party (PPP), which was politically committed to the creation of a socialist society in which "all means of production would come under the purview of the state." Shortly after coming to power, the Bhutto regime undertook a number of new economic policies. Some of Bhutto's actions resulted in restricting the operations of several major United States companies, but the only nationalization action that affected foreign investment was the decision to nationalize the life insurance industry. The government promised to pay adequate compensation.

The nationalization of insurance in Bangladesh was announced on March 26, 1972 as part of the Awami League's commitment to the creation of a socialist economy. Nationalization applied to all general insurance and all domestic but not foreign life insurance. Both AIU and AFIA companies were affected by the nationalization, but the companies were small, part of the industry remained in private hands, and the chaotic situation in Bangladesh meant that actual settlement of claims would take a considerable amount of time. Still the companies involved were concerned lest compensation formulas create an unfavorable precedent for negotiation in India.

Although the governments of India, Pakistan and

Bangladesh all promised to pay compensation, disputes over what constituted prompt, adequate and effective compensation generated conflict and resulted in the companies demanding active United States intervention. The tone of negotiations between the host governments of South Asia, the companies, and the United States government depended on the state of bilateral relations and the degree of United States influence.

Despite large-scale American aid and assistance programs, American-Indian relations always appeared strained. India is a large and proud nation, and the government was extremely sensitive about domestic policies involving private foreign capital. These sensibilities were exacerbated by the massive American presence in India and the leverage which the United States could employ either directly or through the sanctions of the Hickenlooper Amendment. After Nixon's decision to tilt toward Pakistan in the Indo-Pakistan war in 1971 and to stop economic aid to India, however, American leverage was further weakened. A wave of anti-Americanism spread throughout India and crept down the corridors of the government ministries in New Delhi.

The situation in Pakistan was quite different. The Government of Pakistan not only enjoyed the benefits of large United States aid programs, but had also succeeded in gaining considerable political support from the United States during the Indo-Pakistan war of 1971. In an effort to preserve its close ties with the Nixon administration and to avoid irritating the Congress, Bhutto's government even went as far as to notify the American Life Insurance Company in advance that it planned to take over the company. Moreover, in late 1972, at a central point in the negotiations with ALICO, President Bhutto said in a CBS interview that the Pakistan government would pay adequate compensation "in accordance with the terms and conditions of U.S. investment which have been approved by Congress. We are going to implement the conditions imposed by Congress in these matters."[6]

The situation in Bangladesh was so chaotic following the December 1971 war that all parties agreed that they would have to be patient. The Bangladesh government faced major

6. For the text of this interview see *Dawn* (Karachi) December 13, 1972, pp. 2-3.

difficulties in its ability to evaluate and pay claims for compensation. Frequent rotation of key personnel, chaotic records, and an acute shortage of foreign exchange would make demands for prompt compensation futile.

D. The Decision Process

The role of the United States Government in the investment disputes in India, Pakistan and Bangladesh was based on decision-makers' perceptions of broad United States interests which included support of American business interests. The timing of many of the decisions, however, was a response to intense and persistent pressures exerted by the insurance industry, especially the AIU group which insisted throughout that it would require the active support of the United States Government in obtaining its objectives. Keenly aware that United States Government leverage varied from country to country, AIU executives tried one tactic after another, but throughout the nationalization crisis in South Asia, at meetings or with telephone calls and letters, the company insisted that the United States Government secure the host government's acceptance of the company's definition of prompt, adequate and effective compensation or invoke executive and legislative sanctions.

Company strategy to protect its interests and secure its objectives in India passed through three distinct phases. The first phase involved a brief, intense effort in May 1971 to get the United States Government to block nationalization. Concerned that nationalization of insurance in India would set a precedent for other less developed countries and encouraged by past efforts to have nationalization plans shelved, AIU executives came to Washington shortly after Mrs. Gandhi had taken over custodianship of their companies. Meeting with members of the Country Directorate, the Deputy Under Secretary of State for Economic Affairs, and AID officials, company executives demanded that the United States Government make strong representations at the highest levels of the Government of India to secure exemption of American companies or face a loss of United States aid. They threatened to alert senators from all the states in which AIU did business if the State Department refused to act.

Although such an appeal would raise a political storm on Capitol Hill and talk of sanctions would harm United States programs in India, the Deputy Under Secretary of State for Economic Affairs accepted recommendations from the Country Director and advised AIU executives that any United States Government intervention at this stage would be unproductive or even counterproductive, especially since the British Government was not expected to make similar representations on behalf of the British companies which formed the bulk of the companies threatened by nationalization. AIU executives were also reminded that United States aid commitments were based on international agreements which the United States could not renounce in cases of nationalization where adequate compensation was to be paid. The company accepted the advice that it concentrate its attention on securing prompt, adequate and effective compensation. A showdown with Capitol Hill was avoided.

During phase two, beginning in early June 1971, the company devoted itself to securing four objectives : prompt repatriation of assets, prompt and adequate compensation, a favored position in insuring AID cargoes, and securing a good share of the re-insurance business in India. The company made it clear that it relied on the help of the United States Government, but rejected State Department advice to cooperate with the British. AIU executives found the British insufficiently aggressive and suspected that the British companies would settle for reduced compensation in return for a larger share of the re-insurance business.

Lack of enthusiastic support at the Department of State led AIU executives to turn to the Treasury Department. Secretary John Connally was known to hold strong views on issues of expropriation, and AIU executives hoped for Treasury support in bringing the insurance nationalization issue to Prime Minister Indira Gandhi's attention during her November 1971 visit to the United States. The company warned Treasury officials that the Indian government had introduced two constitutional amendments which could not only deprive the insurance companies of adequate compensation but also threatened other United States investments in India. Treasury officials pressed the Department of State to place the insurance nationalization issue on the agenda for direct discussion with Mrs. Gandhi, but the Department of State responded that Mrs. Gandhi's visit would be dominated by concern for the political situation in East Pakistan. State further warned Treasury that any discussion with officials in Mrs. Gandhi's party should be based on the general issue of India's attitude toward United States private investment rather than on demands growing from the specific issue of insurance compensation. A compromise approach was worked out. As expected, time prevented the issue from being raised directly with Mrs. Gandhi but the Indian Foreign Minister assured State Department officials that he had no reason to believe that the terms of compensation would be unfair.

During phase three, the almost total loss of United States influence and leverage in India during and after the Indo-Pakistan War placed the American insurance companies in a difficult position. They had little choice but to collaborate with other foreign insurance companies in trying to reach an equitable settlement with the Government of India. Phase three began late in May 1972 when both AIU and AFIA joined in a British led combined effort to influence the nationalization bill as introduced into the Lok Sabha by the Indian Government. The bill, formally nationalizing the Indian insurance industry and specifying the amount of compensation due to each of the 107 nationalized companies, provided a total of $44 million of which the 6 United States companies were to receive $1 million. All foreign companies considered the level of compensation totally inadequate, the American companies estimating they had been offered only 25 per cent of what they deserved. The companies were further incensed on learning that the Government of India considered their compensation subject to tax in the absence of specific exemption by the Indian Parliament.

A delegation of representatives of the nationalized foreign insurance companies sent to India in July 1972, to meet with the Indian Finance Ministry and the Parliamentary Joint Select Committee charged with considering proposed amendments to the government's bill, met with total failure. The Joint Select Committee refused to accept their recommendations for changes in the bill. A British Government aide memoire setting forth the case for higher compensation and a joint approach by several foreign embassies to the Government of India also were rejected. Debates in both the Lok Sabha and Rajya Sabha showed strong support for nationalization and hostility even to the officially proposed amount of compensation. Lobbying by Indian insurance representatives, on the other hand, resulted in an $6.7 million increase in compensation for Indian companies, an increase justified as an attempt to equalize the level of compensation being paid to Indian and foreign firms. The bill as finally passed did not increase the compensation for foreign insurance companies, nor did it exempt that compensation from taxation.

With the battle for higher compensation lost, the foreign insurance companies concentrated on the issue of taxation. A high level British cabinet member discussed the taxation issue with Prime Minister Indira Gandhi as well as with Finance Minister Y.B. Chavan and External Affairs Minister Swaran Singh, the argument being that since the compensation offered by the Government of India was totally inadequate by international standards, it should not be reduced even further by the imposition of a high tax. The Government of India rejected these pleas on the grounds that foreign companies were being compensated so liberally in comparison to Indian companies that a tax was a necessary equalizer. The British government dispatched a special two man delegation of tax experts in late December 1972, to negotiate the details of a taxation agreement : the taxes to be levied on compensation, the base line for calculating the taxes, the taxes due on a variety of other reimbursable funds owed to the companies. In July 1973, after a review of the tax issue by the Government of India and additional representations by the British and other foreign embassies, the Indian Government agreed to a final settlement of the tax issue and by way of an aide memoire to the British Government declared that it would apply a capital gains tax of 35 per cent rather than a 73.5 per cent income tax on the final compensation amount, settle outstanding tax issues according to the British tax mission proposals and treat all foreign insurance companies alike. The British accepted the Indian government's offer but payment of compensation to all foreign companies was delayed pending receipt and auditing of the 1972 balance sheets.

During the stretch of negotiations from May 1972 to July 1973, the general state of Indo-American relations was characterized by the absence of effective leverage by American officials, and concern for the future of American private sector oil and pharmaceutical interests in India seemed to make the joint approach the only viable policy. The United States Government played a minor role and instructed the Embassy in New Delhi to work in cooperation with the British. Though the insurance issue was twice placed on the agenda of the Expro Group, no recommendations were handed down, for there was little, if any bilateral aid to be suspended and to invoke the Gonzalez Amendment to block multilateral loans to India without some foreign support would be difficult. Concerned about the precedent, the American insurance companies wanted at least a clean record that nationalization had not gone unopposed by the United States Government. But on occasions when they sought a legal opinion from the Department of State as to what would happen if they rejected the Indian proposal, the State Department refused to make a judgement. Thus, while the companies continued to believe that they had been offered inadequate compensation, they had no alternative but to accept it.

The joint approach strategy, so frustrating to American insurance interests, also forced the United States Government to become reluctantly but deeply involved in the details of the nationalization process. The United States Government took the position that the parties themselves should decide what constitutes prompt, adequate and effective compensation and that the government should simply devise reasonable steps to ensure compensation. In the Indian situation, however, the United States Government was forced to make representations on detailed questions as part of the process of providing support for the British position.

Several factors played an important role in the actions of the American companies in India. In the first place, they based demands on a realistic appraisal of how much they could expect from the Government of India. Second, they wanted to be sure that they would get a share of the re-insurance business. Third, they realized the United States Government could apply little leverage so long as Indo-American relations remained cool, and thus they accepted negotiations as the only possible vehicle for all terms of settlement.

Throughout the negotiations over nationalization of insurance in India, the machinery for monitoring expropriation cases moved largely in response to pressure from the companies, but the Expro Group itself consistently refused to make a judgement on the substance of the issue. Thus, despite a number of apparently clear presidential and congressional policy directives, the investment disputes which began in May 1971 had still not been settled three years later. The foreign policy establishment concentrated on negotiating a settlement instead of employing sanctions which would harm other United States interests in the area. The official policy provided weapons no one wanted to employ.

The slow resolution of the nationalization issue in India had to be tolerated because the United States Government lacked leverage and because the insurance companies wished to protect other interests. Yet, though the situation in Pakistan was far more favorable—Pakistan-American relations were extremely cordial, the size of its economic programs gave the United States government leverage, and the Government of Pakistan was committed to maintaining good relations with the United States Government and the Congress—the dispute took almost two years to settle, passed through three stages of negotiations, and required direct United States intervention for its resolution.

Direct negotiations between the Pakistan Government and representatives of ALICO, an AIU affiliate, reached a snag shortly following the March 19, 1972 takeover of the company's management. The company contended the Pakistan government had made pre-nationalization commitments which it was not implementing. The Government of Pakistan responded that specific compensation issues could be settled only after a special insurance corporation created under the law came into existence.

The impass in negotiations led the company to shift its focus to Washington. Senior officials in the Bureau of Near East and South Asian Affairs (NEA) counseled patience on

grounds that the Government of Pakistan, having acknowledged
the principle of compensation, was struggling to work out a
formula that would be fair to both foreign and domestic
insurance companies. The Department of State ensured ALICO
representatives that it would instruct the embassy to remind
the Pakistan Government of the President's statement on
expropriation, express disappointment at the delay, and advise
Pakistan government officials that ALICO had requested the
United States government to monitor developments. In direct
discussions with embassy representatives and with John Connally
President Bhutto gave assurances that he desired a quick
settlement. Yet negotiations dragged on into the summer.

In August 1972, ALICO embarked on the first of its two
attempts to secure American Government intervention. The
President of the AIU Group took his case directly to Peter
Flanigan, special advisor to the President on international
economic policy and Executive Director of C.I.E.P. The AIU
demanded that the United States Government take a strong
stand on compensation and enforce the expropriation doctrine
by withholding aid from Pakistan.

The two issues still outstanding after discussion between
AIU and the Government of Pakistan in July were extremely
complex. The first issue was politically sensitive in Pakistan
because it dealt with ALICO's obligations to its policy holders
in Bangladesh. The Government of Pakistan refused to release
ALICO assets in West Pakistan to meet liabilities built up in
former East Pakistan. ALICO demanded, on the other hand,
that the Government of Pakistan include sufficient compensation to cover the companies' obligation to policy holders in
Bangladesh. The second and more critical stumbling block was
the rate of exchange to be used in converting the compensation into dollars. On the date of nationalization on March
19, 1972, the exchange rate was 4.76 rupees to the dollar. On
May 11, 1972, however, Pakistan devalued its currency by
approximately 60 per cent so that the current rate became
11 rupees to the dollar. ALICO insisted on using the exchange
rate in force on the take over date, but the Government of
Pakistan contended that the payment date should determine
the exchange rate.

Flanigan decided to set the case before the Expro Group

and sent his assistant Larry Rosen to review it with the
Pakistan Country Director and his staff. Since ALICO was
expected soon to reach agreement on the rupee figure for
compensation, the key issue was the exchange rate. The State
Department told Rosen that its legal experts and senior officials
basically agreed with ALICO's position on the exchange rate
issue, but no immediate action was taken. In early September,
therefore, ALICO threatened to sue in federal court to trigger
the Hickenlooper Amendment to cut off bilateral aid to
Pakistan. This threat was followed later in the month by a high
level meeting between company officials and State Department representatives.[7] It was decided to convene a meeting of
the Expro Group to consider how to deal with the ALICO
problem as well as other complaints of the unfair treatment
for United States companies in Pakistan.

When the Expro Group met October 18, 1972, the primary
item on the agenda was the ALICO case.[8] The Government of
Pakistan had recently made an initial offer of 11,489,000 rupees
in compensation but since the exchange rate issue had been
left open and other issues also remained in dispute, ALICO
was expected to reject the offer. The consensus of the Expro
Group called for three actions: first, await the formal response
by ALICO to the Pakistan offer; second, sound out the parties
as to the next possible steps, such as further negotiation,
use of Pakistan's legal system, or binding arbitration; third,
continue to let the Government of Pakistan know of the
United States Government's interest in a prompt and equitable
settlement.

7. The September 25, 1972 meeting was attended by two representatives
   from EB/IFD/OIA, a representative from L/E, two representatives
   from NEA/PAB, Larry Rosen of CIEP and a representative from
   Treasury Department, Division of International Affairs.
8. October 18, 1972 Meeting of Expro Group :
   EB/IFD/OIA—Willis C. Armstrong; Sidney Weintraub; Moorhead
   C. Kennedy
   NEA/PAB—Frank Thomas and Bruce Laingen
   WH/CIEP—Dean Hinton
   Commerce—Larry Fox—Deputy Assistant Secretary for Economic
   Policy; Stanley Katz—Director, Office of Investment Affairs
   Treasury—Edward Gordon—Director of Bilateral Relations Defense
   —Captain Joseph Darlin.

Disappointed by the Expro Group's decisions, ALICO took its case to Senator Hugh Scott who found, on inquiry, that the State Department had been so actively seeking a settlement that the issue had been raised directly with President Bhutto through the United States Embassy, the Pakistan Ambassador; and the President's representative John Connally.

The third phase of ALICO's campaign began in mid December 1972. Again the President of AIU went directly to Peter Flanigan and demanded firm United States Government action. He also contacted the chairman of the Expro Group and the Pakistan Country Director in the Department of State. A formal, legal brief prepared by the Department had indicated that contrary to previous assumptions, legal precedents for payment of claims after a currency devaluation showed evidence of support for both positions. The Department of State pressed AIU and the Government of Pakistan to refer the case to binding arbitration as the quickest route to a compromise settlement.

The Department also notified the Pakistan Ambassador of its desire to resolve the matter before it adversely affected United States-Pakistan relations. The Expro Group agreed on December 29, 1972 that since all avenues for negotiations had not been exhausted, the United States Government should simply continue its efforts to arrange further discussions between the parties.

By early February 1973, additional negotiations between ALICO and the Government of Pakistan reached an impasse. Therefore ALICO executives met with the chairman of the Expro Group, Larry Rosen of the White House, and the acting ambassador to Pakistan. It was to take an official United States Government position on the exchange rate issue, the major outstanding issues in dispute and, with the concurrence of AID, Commerce, and Treasury, to dispatch a formal aide memoire at the Cabinet level to the Government of Pakistan. The aide memoire reminded the Pakistan Government of the President's 1972 statement and supported ALICO's position that the effective date of nationalization was March 19, 1972. In delivering the aide memoire, the embassy was to convey to the Pakistan Government the sense of disappointment ALICO officials had expressed to senior officials of the United States Government and Congress.

When no action took place for about two months after submission of the aide memoire, the company began considering legal action and the case was again placed on the agenda of the Expro Group. Following talks at the embassy level in Islamabad and Washington, AIU representatives were invited to hold further negotiations with the Government of Pakistan. A meeting to discuss overall acceptable compensation figures was held in late May. Arguing that the exchange rate was a matter of law, not a matter of negotiation, the Pakistan government representatives nevertheless proposed a series of adjustments in calculating the value of ALICO's claims which brought the total compensation figure very close to an acceptable level. Following the adjustment of additional minor problems as a result of continued United States government involvement, a check for $3 million was delivered to ALICO on December 6, 1973. The case was settled.

ALICO's hard bargaining and its ability to secure United States Government support resulted in its tripling the initial Pakistan Government offer of $1 million. ALICO succeeded in gaining its ends but only after it had succeeded in making the dispute a major irritant to American-Pakistan relations. The importance of United States Government support is demonstrated by the fact that the British companies in Pakistan had to settle for the initial offer when the British Government failed to become involved in the dispute.

Although insurance in Bangladesh was nationalized on March 26, 1972, efforts at securing compensation did not even begin until December, 1973, when the British and AFIA made a joint representation to the Government of Bangladesh. As usual, AIU did not join this joint effort preferring to work independently though with United States Government assistance. AIU also rejected the joint British AFIA proposals because they were so far below the level of its claim in India, that a Bangladesh settlement on such terms might undercut its position in India. AIU submitted its claim in April, 1974 for $125,000. Although it publicly insisted on prompt action, the company realized that administrative chaos and acute shortages of foreign exchange would probably delay compensation for some time to come.

II. Assessment of the Process

A. Formulation Process

On paper, United States policy on expropriation was explicit. Failure to pay prompt, adequate and effective compensation required withholding new bilateral aid and opposing loans in multilateral lending agencies unless there were major factors affecting United States interests which required the continuance of these benefits. Except for the escape clause, the Hickenlooper Amendment and the Gonzalez Amendment were in complete conformity with the President's January 19, 1972 statement.

The policy implementation, however, was obstructed by a number of ambiguities and problems of defining terms, fact finding, and of determining when remedies had been exhausted. In the first instance, what acts of state were encompassed by the term expropriation ? Both the Department of State and the Treasury Department agreed that acts of nationalization, repudiation of debt, or repudiation of a concession contract were clearly covered, but cases of quasi expropriation involving breach of contract, licenses, controls, and tax policies raised substantial problems. Thus, would the Government of India's imposition of a 35 per cent capital gains tax on a full compensation payment constitute expropriation ? How does one classify conflicts over exchange rates ? How does one analyze problems of partition and consequent financial liability between two countries such as Pakistan and Bangladesh ? What happens if, while auditing a company's accounts, the host government deducts from its compensation offer a sum supposed to make up for "unacceptable" financial practices ? In the case of ALICO, for example, Pakistan objected to ALICO's revaluation of its real estate assets shortly before nationalization and to ALICO's failure to transfer back to Pakistan all reserve assets held abroad for re-insurance or co-insurance purposes in conflict with Pakistan laws. Finally, at what point does an expropriation case cease to fall under the expropriation policy of the government ? For example, was a lingering dispute over

$250,000 serious enough to oblige the United States Government to rule that the Government of Pakistan had not offered prompt, adequate, and effective compensation to ALICO?

In addition to problems of definition, there arose problems of evidence. Clearly, any official finding had to be based on realiable facts. While it was easy to obtain decrees and statutes involving nationalization, it was not so easy to prove that compensation negotiations were being conducted in bad faith or even that they had failed. Moreover, how does one evaluate the estimated alleged value of the nationalized property either in terms of the company's claim or the host government's assessment? This was clearly an issue between ALICO and the Government of Pakistan.

A third problem involved how to determine whether remedies had been exhausted before resorting to a *finding* that an expropriation had occurred and that sanctions were required. The Expro Group insisted that the party involved in a dispute must first exhaust all host country internal remedies and the President's 1972 statement urged the use of mechanisms created by international financial institutions such as the International Center for the Settlement of Investment Disputes within the World Bank to settle investment disputes by adjudication or arbitration. Although the Expro Group and the State Department urged ALICO to consider these alternatives, ALICO preferred to conduct direct negotiations at the ministerial level of the Pakistan Government with United States support.

The most important problem facing United States Government decision-makers in expropriation cases, however, was the problem of conflicting United States interests. The President's January 19, 1972 statement provided flexibility for balancing United States interests, but the Hickenlooper and the Gonzalez amendments did not. The Department of State and AID were primarily concerned with maintaining good relations with the countries of South Asia and with continuing United States programs in the area and even the Commerce Department realized that United States insurance interests in South Asia totalled only $8 million. Over-reaction on insurance could trigger responses against the much larger pharmaceutical and petroleum industries, both prime targets for nationalization.

The Department of Defense played only a minor role in the
Expro decision in South Asia but endorsed the position that
other foreign policy and security interests required consideration. The most active supporter of the company's position
was the Treasury Department, yet the Treasury Department
challenged none of the Expro Group decisions on India,
Pakistan, or Bangladesh by taking them to the C.I.E.P.

Both the Department of State and the Expro Group
preferred to try to secure a negotiated settlement without
forcing the United States Government to take a formal position
on the substance of an issue. Except possibly the Treasury
Department officials, no one connected with the Expro Group
even thought in terms of invoking sanctions except as an
extreme last resort. Country desk officers sometimes even
attempted to keep issues outside the expropriation channel.
When the administration was reviewing its policy on nationalization and expropriation in preparation for the release of the
January 19, 1972 policy statement, the Department of State
tried to exclude the nationalization of insurance in India from
consideration by arguing that the Government of India had not
yet actually nationalized the industry.

Both Country Directorates and the Expro Group made
special efforts to ward off triggering the Hickenlooper and
Gonzalez Amendments by refusing either to make a finding or
to acknowledge the possibility of finding that an expropriation
had occurred without prompt, adequate and effective compensation. State Department officials also habitually pleaded that
for the government machinery in the host country to make the
necessary determination takes considerable time and effort.
Thus, when insurance company executives, reconciled to the
prospect of less than adequate compensation in India, nevertheless insisted on an official statement that prospective compensation was inadequate, State Department officials sought
to avoid such a determination pending a final settlement. In
other cases legal experts had problems justifying the Expro
Group's flexibility in administering restrictive Congressional
directives.

In short, there often was a conflict of interest between
United States Government agencies concerned with furthering
overall American policy and the insurance companies which

threatened to invoke the letter of the law to maximize the
compensation they wanted, or if they failed, to make an example
of the government concerned as a lesson to other governments
that might attempt similar actions. Most United States Government decision-makers sought settlement through negotiation,
conciliation, arbitration and adjudication. The United States
had many interests in the area. The companies had only one
interest and it had been confiscated. The American presence
would remain, but the companies would have to cease all
operations in the area.

In all decisions dealing with the nationalization of insurance in South Asia, decision-makers were supplied with more
than adequate information by the embassies, CIA, the companies, the host governments and the British Government.
This information was employed very effectively in clarifying the
perceptions of the parties to the dispute. Such assessments of
host government attitudes and reactions were extremely useful
in briefing the companies and in helping the Expro Group
reach its decisions, and they enabled the Department of State
to deal with misleading statements and claims made by the
insurance companies to members of Congress and other executive agencies. On numerous occasions however, neither the
embassy nor the desk were in a position to evaluate many of
the technical financial and accounting issues.

The decision-making process at all levels of the Department
of State and within the Expro Group was seldom based upon
policy papers outlining various courses of action and their
consequences. Most reports were in the form of background
papers prepared by the economics officer on the country desk.
Whenever an action statement was included by the country
desk, it always recommended only one course of action. Formal
policy analysis setting out a full set of alternatives took place
only in cases where the Expro Group was unable to reconcile
inter-agency differences. Decisions dealing with the expropriation cases in South Asia did not go beyond the Expro Group,
and all actions were based on consensus. Thus since the issues
involved never became major foreign policy problems, they
could be handled largely at the lower levels of the foreign policy
decision-making system. The case of insurance nationalization
in South Asia, therefore, represents an excellent example of the

type of significant foreign policy decisions which never reach the top levels of the United States Government decision-making system.

III. Assessment of the Outcome

The actions taken by the United States Government in response to the nationalization of insurance in South Asian countries were both appropriate and effective. Although the affected companies had both a tangible and a symbolic stake in the outcome and made numerous, forceful and effective representations in an attempt to accomplish their objectives, there is little doubt that the American insurance interests in South Asia did not represent a significant American interest. Unwilling to take actions disproportionate to the size of the investment involved, United States Government decision-makers followed broad policy guidelines and focused upon larger United States interests rather than particularistic pressures. In cases where the companies were clearly being treated unjustly, as in the case of the exchange rate issue in Pakistan, United States Government officials stood firm and consequently ALICO eventually received compensation which even company officials considered adequate and effective. In the Indian case the Department of State's insistence on a joint approach with other foreign governments enabled the companies to take advantage of the British umbrella at a time when the American Government could do little to assist. Even though all foreign insurance companies in India received less than what they considered to be adequate compensation, British Government assistance with the tax threat enabled the American companies to secure a reasonable settlement on that issue at least. More generally, these three instances of nationalization in South Asia demonstrate that the settlement of expropriation disputes is a complex and time consuming activity which may involve not only deep seated ideological differences among nations but also the difficulty of achieving agreement even on the facts of a case.

IV. Assessment of Participating Organizations

The nationalization of insurance in South Asia did not require the creation of high level policy for American decision-makers but the implementation of policy directives set down by the Congress, the National Security Council and the President. The bringing together of the Expro Group was an attempt by the President to establish a specific review mechanism for implementing a policy which in the past had been treated largely on an *ad hoc* basis. Although the primary responsibility for dealing with the insurance nationalization case rested with the Country Desks, the Expro mechanism made it possible for other interested agencies to illuminate issues from points of view somewhat different from the client orientation of the Country Desks and the regional bureaus of the Department of State. Although the Expro Group did not formally convene to deal with all the issues in these nationalization disputes, the existence of the group defined the circle of consultation and clearance. The pattern of concurrence and clearance enabled each agency to present objections or even to block action if State's position was not mutually acceptable.

Regarded from another point of view, the Expro Group mechanism enabled decision-makers to work out an agreement at the lower levels of the bureaucracy while making provisions for channeling conflict up to the C.I.E.P. and the President for final resolution. Unless there was a consensus at the Expro Group level, the Chairman had to file a report with the C.I.E.P. stating the nature of the disagreement. Each agency had the right to communicate its views directly to the C.I.E.P. No such disagreements occurred in the insurance cases. The Expro Group system seemed to work especially well in the settlement of the Pakistan dispute. The effectiveness of the system and the outcome, however, depended very heavily on the state of bilateral relations between the United States and Pakistan at the time. Similar pressures exerted by the British were not as effective in a large, self confident, and institutionally developed country like India.

In dealing with investment disputes in South Asia, United States Government agencies did not need to seek out and consult the economic interests involved. Consultation was forced upon them by the companies themselves. Concerned with preserving good relations with the countries of the area and minimizing the number of irritants in United States-South Asia relations, the State Department tended to respond to company demands either by refusing to act, by delaying

action, or by taking relatively mild action. The companies
sought to force actions through repeated appeals to the
White House, the Congress, and other executive agencies
considered to be more sympathetic.

Domestic economic interests, unhappy with the State
Department response, demanded stronger United States
Government support to accomplish their objectives by taking
the disputed issues directly to the highest levels of the government of the host country. Such demands for high level representations were designed to associate the United States
Government with the issue and so transform unequal disputes
between the host government and the company into a dispute
between the host government and the company backed by the
full force of the United States Government. The result of such
a close identification of American company and American
Government is a practical inability to separate United States
private interests from United States Government interests. The
reaction to this pattern of association varies according to the
domestic political climate in the host country, the size and
impact of American programs, and the state of bilateral
relations. In Pakistan this association was of great value to
the company in securing its objectives. In India, on the other
hand, hostility toward American foreign policy resulted in
hostility toward American insurance companies to such an
extent that the companies were temporarily isolated even from
other foreign companies involved in the disputes. In general,
close identification between the United States Government
and American companies tends to result in a hostility and
suspicion toward all forms of private foreign investment.

To a certain extent, the process of threats and the resort
to multiple points of access used by the companies were
primarily tactical moves to compel action by the agencies most
directly involved. Company threats of action were designed
to provide stronger support to company negotiators when
negotiations had reached a critical point or when they had
stagnated. These threats were not always carried out and were
not always credible to the decision-makers involved. For
example, despite numerous threats of massive congressional
intervention, the actual number of Congressional inquiries was
small and selective.

The insurance companies, in fact, seemed to go out of their way to cultivate contact and rapport with the Department of State. Certain company executives assisted State Department Congressional lobbyists in their campaigning against the Magnuson Bill which would have transferred economic and commercial functions to the Department of Commerce. They were recognized and remembered as men who highly praised the work of the Department of State in economic and commercial fields and who should therefore be supported in a way which would continue to merit their confidence. Moreover, the Assistant Secretary of State for Congressional Relations joined the staff of one of the insurance companies upon his resignation and assisted AIU and the ALICO settlement in Pakistan.

The complexity of private sector and legislative involvement on a purely domestic level within the United States was matched by complexities originating within the countries of South Asia. One of the major obstacles to a satisfactory settlement of the compensation issue in both India and Pakistan was the difficulty of developing a formula to apply to foreign companies which was not disproportionate to that applying to domestic companies. In India, the strength of the Indian private sector lobbying effort was evident when the Joint Select Committee of the Indian Parliament added substantially to the recommended compensation sum by the government. The bulk of the increased amount was very selectively distributed to certain large Indian business houses.[9]

The most delicate aspect of executive-legislative relations in implementing United States expropriation policy in South Asia was not pressure from a flood of Congressional mail, but the automatic trigger characteristics of the Hickenlooper and Gonzalez Amendments. While declaring these Congressional directives to be of little significance, the agencies acted very carefully to prevent them from coming into force. AID was constantly preparing memos on why the Hickenlooper amendment need not be applied. Although Treasury argued that these Congressional directives had a deterrent effect. State, Commerce and Defense responded that they prevented the effective management of foreign policy. Perhaps the most

9. *Capital* (Calcutta) September 14, 1972, p. 453.

serious long range problem raised by these Congressional
directives is the tendency of the bureaucracy to try to evade
or work around them which results in the development of a
credibility gap between the government and the Congress and
between the public and domestic economic elites. A strategy
of trade off would seem more effective than a policy of
sanctions. Nation states may be able to settle some issues at
particular points in time and may have to let others wait. By
maintaining a checklist of outstanding issues which have to be
settled rather than attempting to solve problems in a crisis
atmosphere, the number and level of inter-state conflicts might
be reduced.

V. Performance of Alternate Structures

This case study has been confined to United States expropriation policy as it was applied in the case of the nationalization of insurance in South Asia. Any assessment of
performance therefore has limitations. However, this study
clearly suggests that United States economic and commercial
policies are characterized by a greater complexity than
political-security policy because of the intense interest of
powerful interest groups both within the United States and
within the host countries and because of the active interest in
specific issues taken by the Congress as a result of interest
group or public pressure and internal ideological predispositions.

Nationalization actions in South Asia in the early 1970's
were primarily a response to domestic political compulsions.
The United States Government was not in a position to prevent
these actions. It certainly had no leverage to reverse them.
Powerful domestic economic interests within the area had, in
fact, already failed to block these nationalization actions.
Moreover, the private foreign insurance industry, like other
financial interests and institutions, was under attack throughout
the less developed countries. Governments everywhere were
trying to bring them under public sector control.

In many ways, the application of United States expropriation policy was also based on strong domestic political
compulsions. The Nixon administration and high officials in

the executive had strong ideological commitments against nationalization and expropriation. Within the Congress these commitments were even stronger and led to demands for policies more stringent than those already in existence.

In theory, the principle of prompt, adequate and effective compensation in cases of nationalization and expropriation seemed reasonable. Yet even where the principle of compensation was accepted by the host government, a variety of complex financial, legal, accounting and political issues made implementation difficult. This complexity raised serious questions about the utility of threatening sanctions, especially automatic sanctions, for many of the subsidiary issues were much more amenable to direct negotiations or to arbitration and adjudication than to direct national foreign policy and governmental intervention.

Attempts by the United States Government to deal with expropriation on a bilateral basis have had only limited success. Traditional methods for solving expropriation disputes such as bilateral treaties of friendship, navigation and commerce and bilateral arbitration conventions have failed due to strong commitments in most less developed countries to the principle of economic nationalism and sovereignty which deny a jurisdiction superior to that of national courts. Similarly, bilateral investment guarantee programs and threats to cut off aid or other economic benefits have neither prevented expropriation nor have they always contributed to equitable settlements. It would seem, therefore, that a more promising alternative for the settlement of expropriation disputes is the use of multilateral approaches, such as the development of codes of conduct for capital-importing nations and capital exporting nations, multilateral arbitration conventions such as the International Center for the Settlement of Investment Disputes (ICSID), an affiliate organization of the World Bank, and the proposed International Investment Insurance Agency (IIIA), which would also be affiliated with the World Bank.

Unless nations are prepared to transcend the ideological barriers which have dominated cases of expropriation, investment disputes will never go beyond debates about the use of economic coercion and the sanctity of private property. Investors will not hesitate to invoke the power of the United

States Government in an attempt to gain equitable treatment, and charges of intervention in the domestic affairs of less developed countries will continue.

Yet, as is clear from this case study, expropriation disputes involve more than ideology. They hinge on a variety of disagreements over the facts of the case. One of the major advantages of a multilateral dispute settlement mechanism would be the possibility of establishing over a period of time a body of findings on how to determine factual aspects in dispute as well as bring an end to jurisdictional questions which convert relatively minor disputes into direct conflicts between governments.

CASE STUDIES :
II. ECONOMIC POLICY

D. The U.S., the International Development Association and South Asia

Anthony D. Moulton

I. The International Development Association

The International Development Association (IDA) was created in 1970 as an affiliate of the International Bank for Reconstruction and Development (IBRD) to make concessional development loans (termed "credits") to the poorest developing countries unable to meet the IBRD's commercial lending terms. Only countries with a per capita GNP of less than $375 are eligible for IDA credits. IDA is funded by periodic, non-reimbursable contributions from the U.S. and nineteen other donor countries. Organizationally, IDA is identical with the IBRD, sharing its President, Governors (the U.S. Secretary of the Treasury and other finance ministers), Executive Directors (appointed or elected by the member governments) and staff; IDA is best conceived of as a fund administered by the IBRD and operating under similar articles of agreement.

This paper analyzes the performance of two types of U.S. Government organizations active in the IDA/South Asia arena. The first, oriented toward the routine aspects of lending policy, comprises a formal network of agencies, their interdepartmental council and accompanying communication channels, devoted to routine technical and economic evaluation of proposed IDA projects. The second, oriented more toward political and crisis aspects of lending policy, consists of two components: first, the Nixon-Kissinger foreign policy apparatus

—the National Security Council, the policy levels (Seventh Floor) of the State Department, State's Near East and South Asia Bureau (NEA) and its Economic Bureau, especially as they become active in a crisis such as the Indo-Pakistan war of December, 1971; and, second, Treasury and other members of the routine-oriented inter-departmental council who may articulate viewpoints and interests different from those of the foreign policy bureaucracy.

While the IDA/South Asia arena does not have formal status as such, it nonetheless is a practical reality. From its inception through FY 1974, 55 per cent of all IDA credits went to the six South Asian countries; 40 per cent went to India alone.[1]

II. USG Organization : Routine Project Review[2]

Formal operational contact between the USG and IDA is through the U.S. Executive Director to the World Bank who simultaneously is a paid Bank employee and an unpaid special assistant to the Secretary of the Treasury. The Director is primarily an agent through whom Treasury and other agencies express the position of the USG on IDA projects and policies. Primary responsibility for U.S. participation in IDA (as in the other multilateral development banks) is borne by the Secretary of the Treasury who is empowered to instruct the Director's vote at meetings of the Bank's board of directors. The Secretary formally is autonomous in that function but in practice responds to the recommendations of the National Advisory Council on International Monetary and Financial Policies (the NAC), an interdepartmental body comprising five voting "member" agencies—Treasury (which has the chair), State, Commerce, the Federal Reserve System and the Exim bank—and a number of non-voting "participating" agencies

1. International Development Association, "Statement of Development Credits," June 30, 1974.
2. The single most comprehensive sourc   on USG organizations active in the project review process is : Library of Congress, Congressional Research Service, *The United States and the Multilateral Development Banks* (Washington, D.C. U.S. Government Printing Office, March, 1974.)

including the USDA, AID, OMB, DOD, the Council of Economic Advisors and the Council on International Economic Policy.

The NAC has three levels of organization : its Principals (department secretaries and agency heads), their Alternates (at the Assistant Secretary level) and the Staff Committee. The first two are sharply distinct, by virtue of their policy orientation, from the technically oriented Staff Committee which meets weekly to discuss and exchange agency views on projects proposed by IDA and the other development banks and to recommend to the Principals how the U.S. should vote at IDA Board meetings.[3]

Treasury's nominal preeminence in the NAC and the field of the multilateral banks dates from Reorganization Plan No. 4 of 1965 which, in removing the NAC from its statutory status and placing it under an executive order, shifted authority to instruct the Director's vote from the five member agencies collectively to the Secretary. Reorganization resolved a Treasury-State struggle for formal preeminence but State remains a full co-partner in all substantive respects.

In their scrutiny of proposed IDA projects (Bank officials refer to it as "surveillance") the NAC agencies are concerned most importantly with determining that they correspond to general U.S. foreign policy and that they meet established technical, economic and financial criteria. They accomplish those goals through the most elaborate evaluative process of any IDA member government. Early notification of projects under IDA consideration comes to the NAC agencies through overseas sources (primarily the AID missions which maintain close contact with resident World Bank offices and Bank field teams) and domestic sources. Two components exist domestically, a network of informal contacts between World Bank

---

3. The Staff Committee is composed of technical staff from Treasury's Office of International Development Banks under the Assistant Secretary for International Affairs, State's Office of Development Finance in the Economic Bureau, AID's Office of International Assistance Coordination in the Bureau for Program and Policy Coordination and equivalent offices in the other agencies. The U.S. Executive Directors, their technical assistants and other U.S. representatives to the banks and the IMF attend Committee meetings infrequently.

headquarters and the NAC agencies (mainly Treasury, State and AID) and, second, a parallel formal network through which project information provided by IDA to the U.S. Director passes to the NAC agencies. The Bank's Monthly Operational Report first lists projects about two years before they come before the IDA Board. Detailed project documents are distributed two weeks before Board action.

Publication of a General Accounting Office report in February, 1972, critical of the informal nature of the NAC evaluation process, prompted creation of a Manual of Procedures and Policy Criteria which codified the review. The GAO similarly criticized the skimpy information contained in the monthly Bank report but had little success in its recommendation that the U.S. urge a more detailed report. A follow-up GAO review found that the additional information supplied was "minimal" and insufficiently detailed for adequate assessment of proposed projects.[4]

The contributions of NAC agencies to project review vary greatly in magnitude and outlook. Treasury, State and AID account for the most substantial review efforts, Treasury and AID in economic and technical scrutiny and State in terms of foreign policy. The Federal Reserve's financial review eclipses the efforts of Commerce and the Eximbank whose primary concerns are that IDA projects not displace or preempt U.S. private investment overseas and that they not duplicate Eximbank loans. The agencies' review efforts also reflect their respective orientations toward multilateral aid in general. While Treasury emphasizes relatively close financial monitoring of the multilateral banks and assumes a somewhat skeptical posture toward multilateral aid, State, in a word, is more enthusiastic. State's primary concern is that IDA serve or, at a minimum, not conflict with U.S. foreign policy. State has relatively little interest in the economics of IDA projects, seeing them instead as political resources which solidify cooperative ties among the IBRD/IDA member countries and which thus

4. Comptroller General of the United States, "More Effective United States Participation Needed in World Bank and International Development Association," (Washington, D.C. 1973), Report No. B 161470; Letter from the United States General Accounting Office, International Division, dated July 26, 1974.

can improve U.S. international relations generally. State rarely objects to IDA projects and only in exceptional cases do they receive the attention of Assistant Secretaries. The South Asian country offices virtually always approve proposed projects.

The staff of the NSC, in normal, non-crisis times, shares the State perspective. One NSC respondent referred to IDA's role in "building peace."

A. Evaluation of IDA's Impact on South Asia : The Neglected Function

The NAC and associated machinery focus on project inputs and selection criteria to the almost complete exclusion of the implementation and effects of IDA projects. To supplement that limited focus, Treasury's Inspector General and the NAC Secretary inaugurated in early 1973 an "On-Site Project Visit Program" to evaluate the implementation of the various multilateral banks' projects. Implementation of the visit program itself has been spotty, however, due largely to time and personnel constraints.

Substantial problems afflict implementation analysis, especially in developing countries, but do not prevent more systematic and intensive attention than the topic currently receives or than is intended in the Treasury's visit program. Unconventional dimensions of project impact also must be measured and assessed.

From 1961 through FY 1974, IDA extended credits totalling $3.87 billion to the six South Asian countries, a small amount relative to the immense needs of the region's economies.[5] IDA's impact is enhanced, however. in that it supplies a relatively cheap and predictable source of perennially scarce foreign exchange; in recent years, for example, IDA has provided approximately 30 per cent of India's foreign exchange supply.[6] In that key role, IDA clearly has the potential to affect the South Asian economies beyond that indicated by aggregate credit amounts alone, for example in influencing

5. International Development Association, "Statement of Development Credit," June 30, 1974.
6. IDA credits, although repayable in hard currency, have a grant component of approximately 85 per cent, according to the Office of the U.S. Executive Director.

sectoral allocations of foreign exchange and imports and thus in influencing central government planning dependent on the availability of foreign exchange.

Beyond gross measures of IDA monies expended are other indicators which exist or need to be formulated relating to several impact dimensions. First, of course, is the primary impact on economic development. Beyond that are secondary and usually unanticipated consequences of IDA and other multilateral bank projects for the political and administrative systems of the recipient countries. Too little is known (or known to the U.S. and other member countries) about direct economic effects, in part because the Bank, on grounds of confidentiality, refuses to make public reports on the implementation and operation of IDA projects in South Asia and elsewhere. Even less is known of secondary consequences but it is fair to assume at the minimum that IDA credits serve to buttress the resources of the governments, agencies and individuals through which they are negotiated and administered; those institutions often extend to the village level as is the case in the IDA-supported agricultural credit projects operating in ten Indian states and totalling $319.9 million with which the author has had first-hand field contact. There as in other projects, IDA credits provide external support for a wide network of organizations integral to the recipient economy, for the political, economic and administrative interests which sustain them and for their associated political and administrative cadres.

B. Alternative Organizations

The NAC machinery appears adequate within its narrow mandate of project review. The point at issue thus is the mandate itself. Analysis of NAC activity too lengthy for inclusion in this paper suggests two conclusions : (1) Separate U.S. scrutiny of proposed IDA projects is not essential to U.S. participation and could be performed more effectively in concert with other IDA member nations. (2) There currently is no agency other than the NAC equipped to consider long-range U.S. policy toward economic development and, indeed, the NAC does not perform that function. These conclusions in turn have two organizational implications : first, shifting the project review function from the NAC to an extra-national organization equipped also to redress the lack of attention given to project implementation and impact; second, assigning to a new unit within the USG the goal of formulating broad U.S. policy toward stimulating economic development, another neglected function. An inter-agency group with the potential to perform that function was mandated by the Foreign Assistance Act of 1973.[7] The Development Coordination Committee, to be chaired by AID, is to have a membership of State, Treasury, Commerce, Labor, USDA, the Executive Office of the President and other agencies that the President may designate. The relationship of the DCC to the NAC was unspecified in the legislation and resulting Treasury fears, among other factors, have delayed its formation. Instead of leaving U.S. policy on economic development to be determined by the conflict of two inter-agency groups, Congress should vest that responsibility explicitly in either the NAC or the DCC; the NAC would be less suitable of the two if, as recommended below, its project evaluation function were assigned to an international unit.

A GAO recommendation that a review unit be established within the Bank but independent of management and accountable to the Executive Directors collectively approaches the first of these organizational suggestions. The GAO recommendation was written into the Foreign Assistance Act of 1973, which requires the President to "propose and actively seek" formation of a group to provide "an independent and continuous program of selective examination, review, and evaluation of the [Bank's] programs and activities . . ." with reports to be submitted to Directors and thence to the President, Congress and the Comptroller General.[8] As of September, 1974, the unit was in an intermediate stage of formation.

The GAO's intent behind the review group—to insure Bank adherence to GAO accounting standards—however, is excessively narrow and interventionist; such a group has far more than simple audit potential and a wider multilateral unit is needed for that purpose.

What are the implications for the U.S. of transferring project review to such a group ? Two stand out most clearly.

7. PL 93-189 (December 17, 1973), Section 21.
8. PL 93-189 (December 17, 1973), Section 9.

First, transfer, for better or worse, would not diminish U.S. influence on Bank operations generally (since many other influence and pressure channels exist, as we shall see in the following section) although it probably would do so on individual projects. Second, and more practically, transfer would mean the shifting of a sizeable and increasing volume of work from the NAC and release of the NAC Staff Committee to concentrate on the bilateral aid and international monetary subjects which it now sandwiches in with multilateral project review. Most important, in relinquishing its unparalleled review role and in supporting creation of a review unit accountable to the IDA Executive Directors, the U.S. would help in contributing an important and long-missing element to the relationship between IDA and the member governments. The U.S. simultaneously would adopt a profile comparable to that assumed at present by the other member governments. There *is* need for review and evaluation of IDA projects external to the IBRD/IDA itself, but like IDA it should be multilateral in structure and responsible to all members collectively.

III. USG Organization : The IDA/South Asia Arena During Political Crisis

U.S. policy toward India during and around the Indo Pakistan war of December, 1971, introduced a pronounced antagonism which affected every important aspect of Indo-American relations including that obtaining by virtue of the two countries' membership in IDA. In the remainder of this paper we examine USG organization to evaluate the adequacy of its operation during the period of December, 1971-March, 1972, when the U.S. encountered two successive and potentially disruptive issues : approval of new IDA credits to India following suspension of U.S. bilateral economic aid to India on December 6, 1971, and the proposal to issue an IDA credit to India in March, 1972, for purchase of crude oil tankers. U.S. responses in both cases not only exacerbated Indo-American relations but also seriously jeopardized the U.S.-IDA relationship. While the events escaped public notice, Treasury, State and NSC actors considered IDA/India policy an important, sensitive and integral part of the altered Indo-American relationship and a fundamental issue in U.S.-World Bank relations, a judgment shared by World Bank management.

A. Multilateral Constraints

The political context of U.S. policy-making during the four-month period was the Nixon-Kissinger "tilt" toward Pakistan during 1971-72 (which we know from a variety of sources was believed, in part, to be a posture necessary to preserve the China "opening"), the December war and the bilateral aid cutoff. As the policy process advanced during those months, short-term changes occurred in the decision arena and in the factors weighed by U.S. actors. One key factor that remained unaltered, however, was a set of constraints on U.S. policy deriving directly from IDA membership and the operation of IDA structures, procedures and conventions. Those constraints were as follow :

1. *Structure*

(a) Most important, the U.S. holds 25.65 per cent of the total "voting power" of all IDA members, followed by the United Kingdom (8.74 per cent), West Germany (6.07 per cent), France (4.66 per cent), etc. The minimal winning coalition—a simple majority decides Board action —consists of six members.[9]

2. *Procedure*

(a) IDA's Board of twenty Executive Directors meets weekly or more often to act on proposed credits formally submitted by the Bank President two weeks before they are acted upon.

(b) Board meetings may be postponed and action on scheduled credits deferred for 48 hours at the request of any director; such requests are rare.

3. *Convention*

(a) The Bank President never has been defeated on a

9. The minimal winning coalition of six is possible in two combinations, the U.S., England, West Germany, France and Canada *plus* either Japan (yielding 52.87 per cent) or Sweden (yielding 50.04 per cent.) India has 3.58 per cent of the total voting power, the seventh largest; the six South Asian countries together hold 6.31 per cent. (Library of Congress, *op. cit.*, pp. 204-205.)

Board vote; if he were, it is understood that he would resign.

(b) IDA credits usually are approved by assent; formal Board votes are rare.

(c) Abstentions and votes against IDA credits are extremely rare. In IDA's history (through September, 1974) the U.S. never has abstained and has voted against only one, the Indian tankers credit approved by the Board in March, 1972.

B. Stage I : October —Early December, 1971

Issue : Should the U.S. treat IDA credits to India routinely after the cutoff of bilateral U.S. economic aid ?[10]

Decision : To persuade World Bank management to defer scheduled Indian credits.

Participants : The President

NSC—the National Security Assistant and the Near East and South Asia staff "shop"

State—the Secretary, the Near East and South Asia Bureau (NEA), NEA's India Office (NEA/INC)

Treasury—the Secretary, Office of the Assistant Secretary for International Affairs (OASIA) and OASIA's Multilateral Programs Office

AID—the Deputy Administrator, the NESA Bureau and the Program and Policy Coordination Bureau

It is important in the following two narrative sections to note the sharp distinction which existed between policy-level officials, on one hand, and staff in the NAC and its member agencies, on the other hand. Participants in all stages of what we hereafter call the abstention period were drawn solely from policy levels of the involved agencies; staff below the Office Director level were neither consulted nor aware of policy decisions until late in the second stage.

A second note is in order regarding participants. This

10. IDA signed a total of nearly five hundred credit agreements by June 30, 1974. In the history of the IBRD through FY1973, the U.S. had abstained on six loans, the first two in June, 1971, to Guyana and Bolivia, and had voted against one. (Library of Congress, *op. cit.*, p. 225.)

account of policy-making rests almost entirely on interviews conducted in Washington during the summer of 1974 with officials of Treasury, State, AID, the NSC, the Council on International Economic Policy, the Federal Reserve System and the World Bank. It is known with certainty that U.S. policy toward the Indian projects received the direct attention of Dr. Kissinger, but no respondents could report on the extent to which President Nixon knew of or authorized the abstention policy or the later vote against the tankers credit. We list him as a participant because several respondents believed that he indeed was involved and because his participation and sanction correspond to his close involvement in policy-making as events unfolded in the subcontinent in 1971 and early 1972.

Process : Activity in the early part of the first stage is not completely clear but centered in the NSC. The need for a decision on upcoming IDA credits to India arose from the probability—which grew through October and November—of a bilateral aid cutoff. NSC staff prepared a memo in October detailing implications of aid suspension at various points in the pipeline and the Washington Special Action Group (WSAG, an NSC interdepartmental crisis management forum chaired by the National Security Assistant) discussed at least two scenarios for policy on IDA credits based on alternative World Bank reactions to a war. It was decided by late November to ask Bank management to defer Board action and State and AID officials at the Assistant Secretary level then initiated a series of discussions with the Bank's Director for South Asia to sound out the Bank on deferral of two Indian credits scheduled for Board action on December 21. The National Security Assistant and the Secretary of the Treasury probably made direct contact with the Bank President by early December but, following Bank management discussions, McNamara decided against deferral, reportedly in order to avoid charges that the Bank was a tool of U.S. foreign policy. The outbreak of war on December 3 strengthened the U.S. hand, however, and Treasury representatives, presumably on NSC directions, negotiated with the Bank three provisos governing activation of the Indian credits and written into the loan documents formally distributed to the Executive Directors on December 9. The provisos required that the projects be unrelated to military operations and that their realization be unimpaired by the war. They were unprecedented in IDA's history

Justification for a non-routine stance on IDA credits to India, in the eyes of advocates, followed from the bilateral aid cutoff. While the specific goals were articulated to few of the participants, most took them to be intensifying India's punishment for engaging in the war and preventing IDA credits from counteracting the effects of the bilateral cutoff; the argument was phrased as involving bilateral-multilateral "consistency" or "parallelism."

Two factors were central to the overt U.S. rationale, first a putative Bank rule prohibiting lending to countries at war and second, and more strategically, predictions of the war's duration. Bank management believed the war would last for no more than three weeks. U.S. predictions, as communicated to the Bank, were for two to six months' duration, thus supporting the argument that continued lending might indirectly assist the Indian war effort. That prediction did not jibe with General Westmoreland's private estimate of three weeks to the December 6, WSAG meeting.[11]

Policy-making during the four or five months in question was overlaid by the paramount importance given to Sino-American relations and reflected, of course, the difficulties of dealing with an institution which has as its members many of the closest allies of the U.S. In that context, it is useful to note the absence of an issue which, had it been present, could greatly have exacerbated the USG-World Bank clash over Indian credits: the question of IDA credits to Pakistan during the same period. The Bank had ceased lending to Pakistan in early 1971 in reaction to the new government's reneging on its predecessor's international debts to several Bank member governments (though not to the Bank itself), among them the U.S. The Bank did not resume lending to Pakistan until June, 1972, when the Board approved an industrial imports loan.

C. Stage II : December 9-21, 1971
Issue: Should the U.S. position be expressed more strongly than in the three lending provisos ?

Decision: The U.S. Executive Director was instructed to

11. *New York Times*, January 6, 1972.

abstain from voting for the two Indian credits if they came to a formal vote.

Participants: As in Stage I plus :

Several members of Congress

The U.S. Executive Director to the IBRD/IDA

Process : That the White House and NSC were the driving forces for an emphatic U.S. stance became more apparent after the provisos appeared in print. Nominal though they were, they satisfied State's India Office and Economic Bureau which sent a joint memo (also concurred in by AID's NESA division) to the Secretary of State on about December 14, recommending that the U.S. treat the projects routinely at the Board meeting andthat view be communicated to Kissinger and the Secretary of the Treasury (U.S. Governor of the World Bank) by the Deputy Under Secretary of State (the U.S. Deputy Governor). As drafted, the memo noted precedents for Bank lending to countries at war and listed three alternative U.S. policies together with their liabilities:

1. Attempts to mobilize support for deferral would fail since other countries accepted the provisos as adequate and only one European member favored deferral.

2. Deferral would only delay the need for a definitive policy decision until the following Board meeting in early January.

3. U.S. opposition or abstention would neither "penalize" India (since the credits would be approved anyway) "nor further our longer run foreign policy interests, either in India or in the World Bank".

It is not clear whether the NEA-EB memo was solicited by the Secretary of State or Kissinger or was initiated from below but it was unpalatable to the White House and probably to the Secretary of the Treasury who contacted Kissinger frequently during this period to ascertain the position to be taken on December 21.

The ensuing policy debate proceeded at two levels, that of Kissinger and the Secretaries of State and Treasury and that of the Assistant and Deputy Assistant Secretaries in Treasury, State and AID who consulted with each other and with NSC and World Bank staff to ascertain agency and Bank positions.

Those daily consultations involved contacts among friends and acquaintances and, like much "official" communication in Washington, were conducted in informal but well-established channels, primarily by telephone but also in existing inter-agency forums exclusive of the NAC structure. The NAC was ignored consciously by all participants as irrelevant to political issues. Actors dealt with each other on equal or near-equal terms. By all accounts the information exchange did not involve significant bureaucratic politics within the USG.

Debate occurred also in a third context, between "hard" and "soft" line advocates within the involved departments and agencies. Only AID which considered all the Indian projects well-conceived and important to Indian development and therefore opposed the NSC hard line, was free of internal divisions. Complex lines of dissent were drawn in State where a Seventh Floor hard line prevailed over dissent in NEA (itself divided with the India country director taking a soft line) and the Economic Bureau.

The abstention policy was decided on by Kissinger (presumably with the concurrence of President Nixon) and the NSC between the 16th and 20th of December, that is, either on the day of surrender in East Pakistan or up to three days after the Indo-Pakistan ceasefire on the western front. Without access to NSC documents, the reasons for the choice of abstention from among the range of options available can only be inferred, but the end of the war undoubtedly was the most important consideration militating against a harder line. Others included the lack of precedent for abstention, loss of support among other member countries, dissent within State, Treasury and the NSC staff, unanimous AID support for the Indian credits and the widespread normative conviction that the U.S. should adhere to IDA's prohibition of politically motivated action[12] and to the commitment to multilateral aid which had been expressed most recently in the Senate vote on October 20, which passed the IDA Third Replenishment authorization bill.

Factors pressing toward a harder line included, most importantly, the Pro-Pakistan "tilt" and the activities of

12. International Development Association, *Articles of Agreement of the International Development Association*, (Washington, D.C.) Article V, Section 6.

several members of Congress who allegedly pressed Secretary of the Treasury John Connally (and perhaps Secretary of State William Rogers) for a hard line. Accounts of the friendly and respectful relationship obtaining between McNamara and Kissinger suggest that the tilt applied to IDA was considerably diluted from that directed toward India during the war. Kissinger allegedly had intervened earlier to deflect a Nixon attempt to dislodge McNamara from the Bank presidency.

D. Stage III : December 28-February 29

Issue 1: Should the abstention policy be maintained on an IDA credit to India at the January 11 Board meeting?

Decision 1: As in December, the U.S. Executive Director was instructed to abstain if the credit were voted on formally.

Issue 2: Should the abstention policy be maintained on two credits scheduled for Board action in its February 29 meeting?

Decision 2: No; the policy was dropped and the Executive Director approved the credits by assent.

Participants: The President

NSC—the National Security Adviser and the NESA "shop"

State—the Secretary (Acting Secretary), NEA, NEA/INC and the Economic Bureau

Treasury—OASIA

AID

Process: The duration of the abstention policy was undefined initially and the issue arose in reference to three IDA credits scheduled to appear before the Board on January 11 and February 29. There was a presumption, however, that abstention would apply in January and State's Acting Secretary forwarded a memo (cleared by the Economic Bureau) to the President on January 10, listing three alternatives : approve the credit since the war had ended; insist on the provisos and abstain in the case of a formal vote; and, third, vote against the credit. He recommended abstention. Other agencies apparently accepted abstention as established policy.

The February round was less neat. Two events indicated to USG actors a Bank initiative to have the provisos and abstention policy dropped. First, Robert McNamara visited South Asia in late January and while there promised India 40 per

cent of all IDA credits in a public speech. Second, loan documents for two Indians credits were distributed on February 16
without the three provisos. An additional, complicating factor
was an India credit for oil tankers scheduled for Board action on
March 7, which had aroused intense opposition in most of the
NAC agencies.

In reaction to those changes in the decision environment
and to apparent lack of NSC direction, the third stage displayed the sharpest agency differences of the entire abstention
period. Initiative and responsibility for U.S. policy had been
vested in State after the January Board action and NEA-offi-
cials met with McNamara several days before the February 29
meeting to reiterate U.S. insistence on the provisos but, failing
to move the Bank, informed Treasury's OASIA that the abstention policy would stand. Treasury objected, however, to
the statement which NEA had drafted for the Executive
Director to deliver at the Board meeting and succeeded
through contact with the NEA "shop" in the NSC in getting a
milder version substituted. The emergence of State-Treasury
conflict, combined with McNamara's intent to drop the provisos and the perceived urgency in making strong objections to
the upcoming tanker credit was an important element in the
eventual decision, presumably made by Kissinger, to revoke
abstention.

E. Stage IV: February 28-March 7

Issue: What position should the U.S. take on an IDA
credit to India for the purchase of oil tankers at the March 7
Board meeting?

Decision: To vote against the credit.

Participants: NSC—the National Security Adviser
    State—the Secretary, Deputy Under Secretary for Eco-
nomic Affairs, NEA, NEA/INC, Economic Bureau
    Treasury—the Secretary, OASIA
    AID
    The Federal Reserve System
    Eximbank
    The NAC Staff Committee
    The Ambassador to India
    Members of Congress

Process: An Indian credit which had been termed a "shipping" project in earlier Bank notices was identified in January as enabling India to purchase four tankers to import crude oil from the Persian Gulf. In response to his immediate inquiries the Bank supplied the U.S. Executive Director with detailed information on the project, information which he and his technical assistant found satisfactory.

The tankers project, however, sparked intense concern among U.S. shipping and oil companies whose commercial fears were expressed on the NAC Staff Committee by the Federal Reserve and Eximbank representatives. In addition, all the NAC agencies but AID opposed the project on a number of economic, financial and technical grounds. The issue, in both USG and Bank eyes, was exacerbated by the immediate prologue of U.S. abstention and was treated by all involved as a serious issue in the U.S.-Bank relationship.

NEA/INC learned of U.S. firms' concerns during NAC Staff Committee consultations on the two February projects and learned then also of independent technical criticisms of the project and of Treasury's opposition on the grounds that the tankers might be used to transport petroleum from Iraqi fields nationalized in 1960 without compensation.

As support evaporated from the few other countries which initially had expressed doubts about the project, NEA/INC reported to the Assistant Secretary on March 2, that Treasury, the Eximbank and the Federal Reserve had voiced strong opposition at the March 1 Staff Committee meeting and recommended adoption of the Economic Bureau's proposal that State vote against the project in the NAC telephone poll which precedes the actual issuance of voting instructions to the Executive Director. A rare meeting of the NAC Alternates was contemplated but apparently cancelled due to the near unanimity of opposition. Only AID preferred support for the tankers. At the initiative of its Deputy Administrator and the South Asia division, AID informed the Indian Embassy that it had no economic objections to the project and circulated a memo to State and other agencies on March 2, commenting on each of the objections which had been raised and rebutting several, including the "major argument" that the tankers would hurt U.S. shipping.[13]

As they had done in early December, State and Treasury, the most active agencies, followed two avenues in the week preceding Board action : soundings were taken of the positions of other IDA members and Treasury led attempts, which a Bank official termed "straightforward and brutal," to convince Bank management to postpone Board action. NEA/INC undertook a lobbying effort in AID, informing its South Asia division that State wanted AID's Administrator or Deputy Administrator to persuade the Bank to defer the project or postpone the Board meeting. AID, however, advised in return that McNamara, as he had done in a 1970 Indian agricultural credit project, might threaten to resign if the U.S. opposed the tankers or made serious efforts to mobilize a majority Board decision against the tankers. Given AID's reluctance to participate in the anti-tanker efforts (and consonant with Treasury's traditional preeminence in the multilateral aid field), it was Treasury's OASIA that led attempts to pressure Bank management. Bank officials attended meetings at Treasury where a Congressional defeat of appropriation legislation for the IDA replenishment was threatened if the tankers project were not dropped. OASIA did not suggest, however, that McNamara's presidency was endangered.

The pressures exerted on the Bank were ineffective and it consequently was decided on March 3 or 4, in an unknown forum, that the U.S. would vote against the tankers credit. Attempts at negotiation and compromise continued, however, initiated by a worried Indian government which under the terms of construction orders already placed was required to sign contracts for the tankers on March 9. In New Delhi, the Indian Finance Minister requested the assistance of the U.S. Ambassador. In Washington, the Indian Ambassador having discussed the issue earlier with the Under Secretary of State,

13. The AID memo acknowledged, without comment, that nationalized oil fields might supply the Indian tankers' oil but rebutted three "minor arguments"—that the Bank had inflated the tankers' economic rate of return, that the project would have no employment impact and that prevailing tanker rates were too low for the venture to be remunerative.

apparently raised it again with the Secretary and NEA Assistant Secretary on March 6, but to no avail. When informed by Treasury of the impending, unprecedented vote, the Bank management asked the Indian Executive Director to agree to deferral but failed to win his consent. The U.S. voted against the credit on March 7, following a lengthy statement by the U.S. Director which emphasized the project's alleged economic and financial faults. Only New Zealand abstained. All other Executive Directors voted for the credit and it was approved.

IV. USG Organizational Functioning : Evaluation and Conclusion

On most indices the USG agencies active in the abstention and tanker cases were adequate to the task; the principal faults were procedural rather than organizational. *PLANNING*: In the abstention case, where overriding foreign policy (i. e., the "tilt") was known months in advance, alternative scenarios and policies toward IDA's India credits were investigated weeks before the policy was adopted. Planning, on the other hand, was almost wholly absent from the tankers case due largely to inadequate information in the IDA monthly report. That report still provides only skimpy information on upcoming credits, even after a GAO recommendation that the U.S. urge more detail as a matter of course. The tankers case was also a rare failure of the informal information flow between Bank and USG agency staff. Early supply of more detailed information is preferable to organizational modifications. *AUTHORITY AND CONTROL* : In both cases President and the National Security Adviser were recognized by all USG actors as the definitive policy sources although that did not prevent differences of opinion and judgement from surfacing within and among agencies. AID's reluctance to intervene with Bank management in the tankers case appears to raise a question of the effective control of that agency by State and the NSC, but the moral almost certainly is that State should be encouraged to execute political policy rather than rely on AID officials whose involvement necessarily compromises the agency's at least nominally apolitical status, a lesson of the bilateral aid cutoff as well. *INTER-AGENCY DIVISION OF FUNCTIONS AND*

COORDINATION: Three agencies State, AID and Treasury, and a compact number of their bureaus and offices were assigned clearly defined and usually distinct tasks the result of which were coordinated at the Assistant Secretary and Secretary levels (through both informal consultations and in the NSC forum) and thence fed to the National Security Assistant. That evaluation applies less categorically to the tankers case but only because of short lead time. In neither case was there evidence of conflict or unnecessary duplication of work between the State and Treasury offices assigned responsibility for monitoring the World Bank—the Economic Bureau's Office of Development Finance and OASIA's Multilateral Program Office. *POLICY-STAFF COORDINATION* : Policy-making officials excluded the NAC Staff Committee members from the abstention policy process intentionally. In the tankers case, by contrast, the Staff Committee provided an effective sounding board for agency concerns and positions which were transmitted by the participants to their superiors. Staff Committee representatives understandably show some resentment of their exclusion in the abstention period but in general accept the policy-staff distinction which serves as its rationale. Again organizational modifications are uncalled for. The committee was cut out almost certainly in order that political policy could be made in a delimited and more easily controlled circle. Nor was the content of U.S. policy diminished by exclusion of the Committee's economic and technical expertise since the U.S. stance derived solely from overriding political considerations. *INFORMATION AND COMMUNICATION* : In both cases information on factors relevant to policy appears to have flowed without hindrance among agencies and vertically and horizontally within each agency. The informal policy debate conducted at the Assistant Secretary and office Director levels in December and January prepared a common fund of information which was disseminated throughout the relevant agencies and offices. It also clarified agency and intra-agency policy preferences. In sum, the evidence is that the supply of information which the individuals involved needed was complete, reliable and accurate throughout the period in question. If such qualities are indicative of desirable foreign policy organization, the machinery involved here needs no tinkering. *DISSENT* : Expression of dissent from the dominant political views was permitted at office, bureau and agency levels and, in the abstention case at least, played a part in the policy adopted.

Is the organization of the government with respect to the IDA/South Asia arena therefore optimal ? We would argue that it is not and cite the most striking organizational feature of the four-month policy process—the complete absence of formal Congressional participation. The general disparity in Congressional and Executive roles in foreign policy-making is widely understood, if not condoned, as a product of problems inherent in informing, activating and coordinating 500-odd elected representatives of the people, even leaving aside the wide range of their individual policy views. Redress of the imbalance is perhaps most feasible in the economic field which typically lacks the sudden crises of political-military policy. In the case of the IBRD/IDA and the other multi-lateral banks it is especially important that U.S. participation be regular, predictable in the eyes of the Bank and other member countries and insulated from short-term "tilts," pressures and cross-currents.

It is reasonable to assume that members of Congress—with the exceptions of a few who intervened on their own initiative to support a hard line—were unaware of the U.S. stance as determined by the Executive, particularly since the Senate and House (on October 20, 1971 and February 1, 1972 respectively) passed the IDA Third Replenishment authorization bill by sizable majorities, thereby providing for continued U.S. participation on what most believed would be a routine, non-interventionist basis. It is fair, furthermore, to conclude that Congress is ill-organized to apprehend and act on Executive policy toward the multilateral banks. The lessons of the abstention and tanker cases suggest three changes detailed in the following section : establishing direct Congressional oversight of Executive policy toward IBRD/IDA projects and activities (no such oversight exists at present); multiyear appropriations of the U.S. contributions to the IBRD/IDA corresponding to the successive three-year authorizations voted by Congress; and, finally, transfer of House oversight

from the Committee on Banking and Finance to the Foreign
Affairs Committee.

V. Recommendations for Organizational Change

A. U.S. Policy toward Encouraging Economic Development

1. Congress or the President should formally direct an inter-
agency group to undertake formulation of comprehensive
U.S. policy toward encouraging economic development.

Implications : The issue of department and agency membership and roles is critical to the functioning of such a group.
Treasury and State, the major contenders for the dominant role,
both have legitimate interests in economic development policy.
With equal or near-equal status for State and Treasury as a
precondition, the proposed Development Coordination Committee is more appropriate than the NAC for policy formulation. An alternative, probably acceptable to both State and
Treasury and, furthermore, tending to a more authoritative
policy statement, would be the Council on International
Economic Policy.

B. Review and Evaluation of IDA (and other Multilateral Bank) Projects and Activities

2. Congress and the President should support transfer of
project review and evaluation from the NAC to the multilateral
group conceived in the Foreign Assistance Act of 1973 and
currently in the process of formation.

Implications : Transfer of review to a multilateral unit
independent of Bank management and accountable to the
Executive Directors would reduce U.S. influence in the selection
of individual IDA projects but not in IDA operations as a
whole. It would reduce the NAC's purview and to that extent
would be opposed by all NAC agencies. It would, however,
also reduce the NAC Staff Committee's heavy workload and
allow it to concentrate on other functions now compressed
together with project review. Transfer to a specialized group
would improve the quality and scope of review and, most
important, would place the U.S.-IDA relationship on a basis
corresponding to that of other member governments.

C. Congressional Oversight of Executive Policy Toward IDA Projects

3. Oversight, now vested in the subcommittee on international finance of the House Committee on Banking and Finance and in the Senate Foreign Relations Committee, should focus more on Executive policy toward the IBRD/IDA than toward monitoring the Bank's lending. To that end, Congress should instruct the GAO to report regularly on the circumstances of executive branch opposition to Bank projects and/or assign a staff member of one of the oversight committees to monitor policy toward the Bank through frequent, regular contact with the Assistant Secretaries who act as NAC Alternates.

Implications : The change recommended would be resisted by the White House, NSC and Secretaries of State and Treasury. It would encounter mixed reactions at lower agency levels, reflecting differences in personal convictions about insulation of the Bank from political pressure. Most important, it would keep Congress informed and inhibit the Executive from unwarranted political intervention in the Bank.

4. To further reduce Executive ability to exert political pressure on IDA and the Bank, Congress should consider a formal or informal commitment to three-year IDA appropriations, i.e., for the term of each IDA replenishment. IDA has had successive three-year authorizations and it is reported that key members of the House Appropriations Committee agreed to a *de facto* three-year appropriation for IDA III as a bargaining tool with the Nixon Administration.

Implications : Multi-year appropriations are resisted by appropriations committees regardless of their merits. It should ba noted, hewever, that in the IDA case, multi-year appropriations, contrary to their conventional image, would *increase* Congressional control of U.S. policy toward IDA relative to that of the Executive by reducing its ability to use the annual uncertainty of appropriations as a political lever. Multi-year appropriations would facilitate continuity in IDA operations and demonstrate the U.S. commitment to IDA in a highly tangible manner. Similar treatment for the other development banks probably would be required.

5. To the extent that oversight focuses on IDA and the other banks directly, more attention should be given to evaluation of their projects' developmental effects than to assuring that they meet pre-established financial and economic criteria. An appropriate Congressional change would be to transfer oversight in the House to the Foreign Affairs Committee which has a history of concern with development not found in the Banking and Currency Committee.

Implications : Transfer of oversight was requested by the Foreign Affairs Committee and denied by the Bolling Committee. Transfer would remove the Banking and Currency imprimatur of financial soundness from IDA legislation and thus might cost IDA the votes of some unenthusiastic Representatives who find that commendation persuasive.

THREE

CASE STUDIES :
III. PEOPLE TO PEOPLE DIPLOMACY

A. United States Educational and Cultural Exchange Programs in India

Walter Andersen

U.S. educational programs in India experienced a near moratorium for the two years following the American "tilt" towards Pakistan during the December, 1971 conflict between India and Pakistan. The event which formalized the freeze in academic relations between the United States and India was an announcement from the Ministry of Education and Social Welfare on November 22, 1972, establishing a set of guidelines to govern the academic work of foreign undergraduate and graduate students and Ph.D. candidates. Subsequent guidelines covered senior research scholars and short term group projects.

The November set of guidelines sought to establish greater Indian control over the work carried out by foreign students and research scholars in India. Undergraduate and graduate students could no longer enroll as casual students in Indian colleges and universities, as many Americans participating in special programs had done. They would now have to enroll in an approved certificate, diploma or degree course.[1] Students, consequently, would sit for examinations and abide by attendance rules. Following the model of the University of Wisconsin's junior-year-in-India program, several American

---

1. Certificates (for undergraduate students) and diplomas (for graduate students) are awarded after taking examinations that test for a set of courses in a specific subject. Both require less time to complete than the regular three year undergraduate degree, usually three to nine months.

academic institutions had established six to nine month under-graduate off-campus programs at Indian universities. While utilizing faculty and facilities at the Indian university, these programs were conducted by and largely managed by Americans. In correspondence with the American program directors, the Ministry of Education informed them that all academic work and living arrangements would be assumed by the Indian university with which the programs were affiliated. The Ministry also noted that no American academic personnel could be associated with either the academic or the welfare aspects of the Indian program. Vice-Chancellors at the affiliated Indian institutions were informed by the Ministry to make the necessary welfare arrangements for foreign students. The November announcement also required that American institutions award grades that conformed with the results of the Indian examination.[2]

From the American perspective, the requirements placed on Ph.D. candidates carrying out research in India posed a serious problem. Most American Ph.D. students in India were there to collect data for their dissertations, generally in the social sciences and humanities. The guidelines required that foreign students working for their Ph.D. in Indian Studies enroll as Ph.D candidates in an Indian university. In effect, this created a double jeopardy requirement for the Ph.D. candidates. They would not only have to satisfy the Ph.D. requirements of their American university, but the Ph.D. requirements of an Indian university as well.[3] Ph.D. students in comparative fields, whose research focused on an aspect of Indian society or culture, were not required to enroll for another degree; but they were required to continue their research work for as long as their Indian supervisor felt was necessary. In both cases, the evaluation of the Indian supervisor

2. Because grading systems in the United States and India are different, American colleges and universities had to work out their own rules of conversion.

3. As in the case of undergraduate students, most Ph.D. candidates in India had formerly enrolled as casual students. While many had Indian advisors, the supervision was often minimal and the students were generally free to pursue their research on their own.

was to be given equal weight with the evaluation of the American supervisor.

Table 1.—Number of American and Indian Scholars Funded by the U.S. Government

FY	Americans	Indians
1960	41	181
1961	134	242
1962	130	290
1963	319	386
1964	344	481
1965	419	342
1966	340	383
1967	419	409
1968	270	266
1969	232	194
1970	205	110
1971	305	116
1972	547	113
1973	284	76
1974	360	32

On January 12, 1973, the Ministry of Education announced another set of guidelines for post-doctoral research fellows. They too would need to affiliate with an Indian university and work with a project supervisor or consultant.[4] Research scholars were informed that they ought not to carry out research on a list of topics. These topics fell into two categories: (1) those that involved India's security (i.e., border areas, tribal areas, defense and security matters); (2) those that could result in an unfavorable interpretation of Indian society (i.e., questions involving "sensitive" political, regional, communal or religious themes). Moreover, it was stated that the list might

4. For research scholars in health, engineering and the natural sciences, this regulation did not pose a problem since most were funded by American agencies which had collaboration agreements with their Indian counterpart agencies. This had not been general among scholars in the social sciences and the humanities.

be extended to "Any other field in which special restrictions may be imposed by Govt. (sic) from time to time."[5]

Besides the concern for parity and security that runs through the guidelines, there is also some reference to the size of the American academic presence in India.

The presence of American scholars and students, particularly in the social sciences and humanities, increased rather dramatically during the mid-1960's, as the figures in Table 1 demonstrate.[6]

These figures represent recipients of grants funded at least in part by the office of Education, Institute of International Studies, the Bureau of Educational and Cultural Affairs, the United States Information Agency and a number of agencies dealing in the physical and biological sciences, notably the National Science Foundation.

The number of science students has always been considerably less than students in the social sciences and humanities, primarily because most Indian universities do not have the facilities or the same sequence of courses required by American schools. Research by senior science scholars has been less controversial than social science research for several reasons. It represents a "product" with a high demand in India (unlike the social sciences). Projects in health, engineering and the natural sciences have usually involved very close collaboration with Indian institutions.[7] These collaborative efforts can be more easily justified in the name of national development than

5. These topic restrictions were als applied to undergraduate, graduate and Ph.D. candidates. The Ministry of Education had, as early as 1969, been reluctant to grant visas to scholars who wanted to study border areas or defense matters. The sequence of events that led to this decision will be described on the following page.

6. Compiled from records at United States Information Service, New Delhi.

7. While the number of scholars in the natural sciences has been less than in the social sciences and humanities, the expenditures have tended to be higher. In 1973, 5 American agencies involved with health and environmental studies had 71 projects with a budgeted expenditure of $10.71 million. Six other agencies, concerned primarily with research in the physical sciences, had 66 projects in India, with a budgeted expenditure of $2.60 million. Figures supplied by the Office of the Science Attache, Embassy of the United States, New Delhi.

can work in the social sciences and humanities. Yet, despite its less controversial nature, there was also a near-moratorium on new science and technology projects during the 1972-73 freeze period.

Up to 1967, there was a rather steady increase in the number of American students funded by government agencies. Between 1968 and 1970, there was a sharp decline. It picked up again in 1971, largely because of the increased number of short term summer programs funded by the Institute of International Studies. The decline in the number of Americans studying in India, after 1967, and certainly the decline in the number of Indian students going to the United States resulted from a reduction in the funds allocated to the United States Educational Foundation in India by the Bureau of Educational and Cultural Affairs, as reflected in Table 2.[8]

The large drop in the rupee allocation between 1966 and 1967 is due, at least in part, to the Indian devaluation of the rupee. There was another significant decline in Fiscal Year 1969, resulting from the general budget cut for the Bureau of Educational and Cultural Affairs.* The next major cut came in Fiscal Year 1973, during the educational freeze, when the Bureau placed India on a "back-burner". It remained there in Fiscal Year 1974.

While the constraint was never stated formally, various American funding agencies were advised that India could not accept more than 20 research scholars from any one country, on the grounds that Indian academic and research facilities were limited. The concern for numbers also showed up in the informal guidelines that the Ministry of Education set down for short-term study programs, most of which are funded by the Institute of International Studies. These programs had become increasingly popular and, in 1973, almost one half of the 547 Americans funded by the State Department's Bureau of Educational and Cultural Affairs and by the Institute of International Studies were participants in these short-term

---

8. Figures recorded in a publication of USEFI. *The Fulbright Program of Educational Exchanges between the United States and India,* Appendix I.

* Ed. Note : Probably related to Vietnam War budget cuts:

study programs.[9] The Ministry stipulated that no more than 10 such programs could be accepted in any single year, each program not to exceed 25 participants.[10]

Table 2.—Funds Allocated to U.S. Educational Foundation in India by the Bureau of Educational and Cultural Affairs

FY	Rupee Allocation (*Expressed in $*)	Dollar Allocation	Total
1962	1,000,000	185,290	2,185,290
1963	1,185,191	275,450	1,461,641
1964	1,174,307	236,480	1,410,787
1965	1,347,419	252,069	1,599,488
1966	1,211,909	262,884	1,474,793
1967	811,828	272,051	1,083,879
1968	757,813	244,689	1,002,502
1969	369,241	202,065	571,306
1970	372,032	193,587	565,619
1971	638,275	137,694	775,969
1972	675,242	137,775	813,017
1973	349,371	87,920	437,291
1974	302,338	99,575	401,913

The Ministry of Education's guidelines for the short-term study projects are interesting because they represent an approach to education that differs from the views of some of the American institutions that draw up short-term study proposals. According to the guidelines, every group must affiliate with an Indian university. Each group must have an Indian director, appointed by the Ministry of Education. Faculty members at the affiliating university, drawn largely from the social sciences and humanities, would be utilized to deliver lectures on a set of topics. The Ministry itself would pay for the Indian director and the lecturers. Groups could

9. Since Fiscal Year 1973, these programs have been administered by the United States Educational Foundation in India.
10. In 1973, the limit was exceeded because the Prime Minister herself interceded on behalf of one short-term study program.

supplement their academic work with a certain amount of travel and all did so.[11]

The Ministry tended to view as "valuable" educational experience in terms of lectures, required readings and reports. Many of the American administrators and participants in these programs, as well as in undergraduate programs, felt that as much, if not more, can be learned from a more unstructured experiential encounter with Indian society and culture. Many of the complaints about Office of Education funded short-term study programs, as well as about American students generally, can be traced to this disagreement on educational philosophy.

The restrictive content of the various guidelines was not entirely unexpected. At least since the mid-1960's, there had been a growing self-assertiveness by Indian academics, particularly in the social sciences and humanities. At one time American assistance and scholarly effort in the social sciences and humanities might have been welcomed. More recently, however, prominent academic and political leaders had expressed the opinion that the American influence on Indian scholarship, particularly in the social sciences, created an academic dependency complex which prevented Indian scholars from developing concepts and techniques relevant to the country's needs. Moreover, there were frequent charges that American social science represented a value system not necessarily applicable to India. Coupled with this was the concern that American academic influence was undermining values required for national development.

The complaints about the influence of American scholarship in India were catalogued in the December 1968 issue of *Seminar*, a prestigious monthly devoted to public affairs. A major theme of the articles was the proposal that American influence on the Indian academic system created the aforementioned dependency complex, labeled "servitude of the mind" by one of the writers. One writer suggested that "Academic autarky is the most appropriate slogan for the present genera-

11. In late spring, 1974, the Ministry of Education informed USEFI that the short term study groups must spend two-thirds of the program time at an Indian university. The Ministry had previously stipulated that one-half the program time could be used for travel.

tion of academics."[12] Another theme related to the alleged subversive uses of much American academic research in India. The lead article, defining the problem of the issue, claimed that American academics collected information which was utilized by the CIA, the Pentagon and other agencies to enable the United States to dominate Afro-Asian countries. American social scientists were identified as the major suppliers of this subversive information. Rajni Kothari, one of India's most prominent political scientists, suggested several solutions to the problems raised in the articles. He proposed the creation of a semi-autonomous academic body, funded by the government, to screen foreign research proposals "from the standpoint of national interest".[13] In order to free Indian social scientists from dependence on foreign funding agencies, he proposed that this body have sufficient resources to support research projects.

Not long after this issue of *Seminar* appeared, the Government of India did create a new agency within the Ministry of Education to carry out what Kothari had proposed. The Indian Council of Social Science Research both funds Indian social science research and also reviews all foreign social science research proposals before visas are issued by the Government of India.

The potential security risks of American social science research had become a public issue during the summer of 1968 when it was discovered that the Himalayan Border Study Project, a large-scale research project carried out by American social scientists, had received funds from an Agency of the United States Department of Defense. The source of the project's funding was discovered during hearings before the Senate Foreign Relations Committee on May 28, 1968, when Vice-Admiral Rickover made a critical reference to Defence Department spending on behavioral and social science projects outside the United States. Senator William Fulbright, Chairman of the Committee, revealed that he had a letter from Dr. Gerald Berreman at the University of California, Berkeley, criticizing the use of Defense Department funds on the Himalayan Border Study Project in which Dr. Berreman was one of

12. Girja Kumar, "Servitude of the Mind", *Seminar* (Dec. 1968), page 24.
13. Rajni Kothari, "The Tasks Within," *Seminar* (Dec. 1968), page 18.

the chief researchers.[14] Indian newspapers and politicians picked up the information and it was debated on the floor of the Lok Sabha.[15] On December 4, 1968, the Prime Minister informed the Lok Sabha that the Government of India had investigated the project and that it was terminated.[16]

One result of the investigation of the Himalayan Border Study Project was the requirement of the Ministry of Education that all foreign scholars must associate with an Indian university or institute.[17] The ministries which investigated visa applications (Education, External and Home) began more closely to scrutinize the research proposals of graduate students and research scholars, often causing extensive delays in the issuance of visas. Funding agencies were informally told that projects relating to border areas, tribal areas and defense were not likely to receive government clearance. Because of the new regulations, the Office of Education delegated to the United States Educational Foundation in India the responsibility for securing visa clearance on research projects for those graduate students and research fellows who had received grants authorized under the Mutual Educational and Cultural Exchange Act of 1961 (sometimes referred to as the Fulbright-Hayes Act).[18]

14. This project had been established at the University of California, Berkeley in 1960 to study social groups living in the Himalayan region. Beginning in 1967, the Advanced Research Project Agency, a branch of the Department of Defense, provided the Himalayan Project with funds that would have financed some 60 per cent of its costs up to 1970.
15. *Lok Sabha Debates*, August 5, 1968, page 236.
16. *Lok Sabha Debates*, December 4, 1968, page 120.
17. Previously some U.S. funding agencies had arranged such affiliation but it had not been a condition for receiving a visa.
18. These grants are sometimes confused with other grants funded under the authorization of the Mutual and Educational and Cultural Exchange Act of 1961, P.L., 87-256, which are granted by the Bureau of Educational and Cultural Affairs of the Department of State. Its grants are administered by the United States Educational Foundation in India. The approval procedures for the two sets of grants are different. The State Department grants are screened by the Council for International Exchange of Scholars (for senior researchers) and the Institute of International Education (for pre-doctoral researchers). In 1962, an executive order of President Kennedy delegated to the Office of Education the responsibility for administering projects

The American Institute of Indian Studies, a private academic association which receives funds from both the Institute of International Studies and the Bureau of Educational and Cultural Affairs, continued to use its own organization to secure visas and administer its grants. In 1972, the Institute of International Studies proposed that AIIS administer its Fulbright-Hayes doctoral dissertation grants. However, the Ministry of Education suggested that the Institute utilize the services of USEFI, primarily because of the binational character of USEFI's commission.[19]

In September 1970, representatives from the Ministry of Education and the External Affairs Ministry began a general review of all foreign cultural and educational programs in India.[20] The investigation was set in motion by the unauthorized construction of a cultural mission of the U.S.S.R. at Trivandrum. The roof of the building collapsed, killing several laborers. The event received a great deal of publicity and it was debated on the floor of the Lok Sabha. On January 26, the Minister for External Affairs announced the policy that foreign cultural centers would be permitted only in cities in which governments had consular offices.[21]

The Minister also announced that negotiations would be held with the concerned embassies on alternate arrangements for managing the cultural centers. On February 18, the External Affairs Ministry ordered the embassies to close their cultural

---

authorized by section 102(b) (6), of P.L. 87-256. Initial applications for these grants go through an American university for both dissertation research and post-doctoral grants.

19. The University of Wisconsin, on behalf of the undergraduate programs it managed in India, suggested in 1973 that AIIS disburse the rupee counterpart funds which had been allocated to it by the Institute of International Studies. The Ministry suggested that the funds be disbursed through the Office of the Cultural Attache.

20. There is a widely held misconception that the review of foreign educational programs began after the December 1971 war with Pakistan.

21. Most of the cultural missions outside consular cities were run by the U.S.S.R., the U.S.A. and cultural organizations managed by the embassies of Great Britain (British Council Library), the German Federal Republic (Max Mueller Bhavan), and France (Alliance Francaise).

centers in non-consular cities within three months.[22] Meanwhile, contacts were made with the embassies to work out some arrangement which would give the Government of India greater control over programming and the selection of books. With the exception of the United States, agreements were worked out with all other foreign governments. The cultural centers in non-consular cities would now operate as autonomous agencies. The Indian Council of Cultural Relations, a branch of the External Affairs Ministry, would have representation on their managing boards. The United States Information Agency refused to consider any alternative to exclusive U.S. management. Its director did not want to establish a precedent that would permit foreign control over its information activities. The argument was that the American libraries had operated with the full knowledge of the Government of India and that the Government had sanctioned their continued operation in 1954-55 and again in 1965-66. It was further argued that the United States was being made to suffer the consequences of the bad publicity caused by the unauthorized Soviet cultural mission at Trivandrum. The U.S. Secretary of State stated that the Indian decision was an "unfriendly act."[23] The Government of India extended the closure date of the libraries by one month, in part to give it more time to work out a negotiated agreement for the continued operation of the foreign cultural centers. However, on May 6, 12 days before the original date for the scheduled closure of the cultural centers, Ambassador Keating announced that the libraries would be closed on May 18, 1970.[24] The libraries were closed on May 16, two days before the scheduled closure. Flowing from this whole affair, the Education Ministry, in September, 1970, began a comprehensive review of cultural and educational relations with foreign countries.

Between 1970 and 1972, no decisions were arrived at by the high-level review. The war with Pakistan in December, 1971, introduced specifically political elements into the evaluation, since any decisions taken would affect relations with the United

22. The United States had centers in Bangalore, Hyderabad, Lucknow, Patna and Trivandrum.
23. Statement reported in *Times of India* (Delhi), March 4, 1970.
24. Reported in *The Times* (London), May 8, 1970.

States, the country with the biggest educational presence in India.[25]

By March, 1972, it had become clear that group programs and individual scholars might experience long delays before their visas would be granted by the Government of India. For those who inquired, the answer from the Education Ministry was that visas would not be granted until the deliberations on educational exchange were completed. It was obvious that the government was in no mood to make a decision quickly. Few new science and technical exchange agreements were negotiated during 1972. The Education Ministry called a moratorium on approving new textbooks for the PL-480 funded Textbook Program, under which American textbooks are printed in India at about one-third their cost in the United States.

Several events in 1972 served to keep Indo-American relations frigid. One specifically involved the American academic community. After the breakup of Pakistan, President Nixon, in his State of the World Message, spoke of communal conflict and ethnic feud in India. The External Affairs Ministry responded sharply and stated, among other things, that American South Asian area centers had done an inadequate job presenting India to the American public. Some editorial writers saw a British colonial mentality in American scholarship while others noted that, despite the protest of individual American scholars over the "tilt" towards Pakistan, the American scholarly community seemed to have very little influence on the decisions of their government.

Prior to 1972, very few visas had been rejected by the various reviewing agencies of the Government of India, though it was not uncommon for visa applications to take two to three months for final approval. During 1972, 62 American scholars, mainly in the social sciences and humanities, applied for visas. By the end of the year, only 36 had been approved, 14 were refused, 10 had withdrawn because of long delays and 1 was still pending.[26] All American

25. The Political Affairs Committee of the Union Cabinet had Indo-American relations under on-going review in 1972 and 1973; questions of educational and cultural exchange were an element in its deliberations.
26. Based on information at USIS, New Delhi.

undergraduate programs, most of which were scheduled to begin during the summer, were cancelled since none had received visa clearance. However, the short-term study groups did receive visas. In late November, 1972, the first formal announcements on the long anticipated guidelines were released. The Cultural Attache advised American funding agencies to work out new programs based on the guidelines.

During much of 1972, there was no U.S. ambassador in New Delhi. Ambassador Kenneth Keating left for the United States on July 26, 1972 and Ambassador Daniel P. Moynihan did not arrive in India until February 20, 1973. On the issue of educational exchange, this vacancy did not really matter, as it had been decided that the educational freeze would not be elevated to an issue of diplomatic disagreement. No official negotiations on the issue were attempted nor were any official protests lodged. Easwar Sagar, the Washington correspondent for *The Hindu*, wrote that while officials in the State Department were not pleased with the educational restrictions, "They take the view that this is a matter purely between the Indian Government and the members of the American academic community affected by the restrictions."[27] Sagar's information was correct.

Educational relations began to thaw after the arrival of the new American Ambassador, who brought with him plans for solving the problem of the huge accumulation of PL-480 rupee counterpart funds. The new American proposals would, in effect, write off about two-thirds of this Indian debt and were a tangible sign to the Indians that the United States was no longer in "tilt".

One of the first signs of better relations was informal communications from the Ministry of Education to American funding agencies that many of the restrictions would be very liberally interpreted. For example, the double jeopardy requirement for Ph.D. candidates was not enforced. With a few exceptions, the Government of India showed considerable liberality in approving research topics, some of which came very close to the subjects that had earlier been placed on the "off-limits" list. By the end of 1973, 59 of 68 applications, in graduate student, lecturer and senior research categories, had

27. *The Hindu* (Madras), September 6, 1973.

been accepted. Only 7 were refused, 1 withdrew and 1 was still under consideration.[28]

After some indirect pressure from the U.S. Embassy the Government of India decided to lift its restriction on the number of senior research scholars who could receive visas in a single year. On September 3, 1973, an article appeared in the *New York Times* which drew attention to the Government of India's informal restriction that no more than 20 research scholars from any country could come in a single calendar year.[29] The writer claimed that U.S. Embassy officials felt that the restrictions were an indication of "blatant hostility to Americans". The article received wide publicity in both the United States and in India. At an interview on September 16, Ambassador Moynihan stated that South Asian studies would suffer if restrictions were applied to scholarly activities.[30] The issue of restrictions was taken up by the Political Affairs Committee of the Union Cabinet. On September 28, the Education Minister, at an open news conference, stated that there would be no restrictions on the number of American senior scholars who could be granted visas in any year. He also stated that post-doctoral fellows need not register at an Indian University.[31] In late 1973, the Ministry also unofficially informed U.S. funding agencies that no restrictions would be placed either on the number of short-term study programs or the number of undergraduate scholars who could come to study at Indian universities.

Between January 7-10, 1974, a summit conference of American and Indian scholars met at New Delhi, to discuss educational collaboration between the two countries. The proposal of a summit had been floated within the Ministry of Education and discussed by the Bureau of Educational and Cultural Affairs well over a year before it was finally held. It was not until late 1973 that the Ministry gave its formal appro-

28. Based on information at USIS, New Delhi.
29. The number of American senior research scholars had not exceeded 20 by very much in previous years, but the restrictions did create the impression that senior American research scholars in South Asian studies might have difficulty getting visas for their field work.
30. Reported in *Indian Express* (Delhi) September 19, 1973.
31. Reported in *The Hindu* (Madras), September 29, 1973

val for the summit and the director of USEFI arranged the meeting for January, 1974. Originally, the meeting was supposed to discuss the implementation of the guidelines. It ended up discussing programs for joint educational collaboration. The Bureau appointed twelve American delegates, only two who could be said to represent the interests of South Asian Studies, despite the fact that American scholarly interest in India is mainly in this area. Its inaugural session was attended by both the American Ambassador and the Indian Minister of Education. While it could be debated how much was substantively achieved, the meeting was a public sign that the educational freeze was over and that the two sides were ready to discuss each other's needs and interest. The conference drew up a set of topics in (1) sciences and technology, (2) social sciences and humanities, that both sides considered important for future research. The suggestions for the social sciences were sufficiently broad to permit research on almost any topic. Its vagueness also means that the Ministry is not committed to support any specific research proposals.

It is clear from the proceedings that the issue of parity in academic relations was a prominent theme, particularly in relation to the social sciences and humanities. It was suggested that the two countries establish binational seminars to identify specific collaborative projects, that academic institutions set up collaborative research agreements and that both sides identify potential sources of funding.[32] The double jeopardy requirement was omitted for doctoral candidates. Instead, it was simply stated that a Ph.D. candidate be attached to a university and work under the guidance of a supervisor, whose evaluation should be considered in the final evaluation of the research work. The Education Minister's statement in September that senior scholars need not be attached to a university was incorporated into the general recommendations.

Perhaps the most interesting recommendation was the suggestion that an Advisory Group of American scholars be constituted "to inform the academic community there on areas of fruitful academic cooperation arising out of these recommendations."[33] The University Grants Commission quickly

32. Page 6 of the *Joint Statement* of the Conference.
33. Page 7 of the *Joint Statement*.

established an Advisory Group in India, composed largely of scholars who had attended the summit. The American and Indian groups were charged with assisting "scholars in choosing areas of research and training beneficial to them and relevant to the needs of their country."[34] No Advisory Group was formed in the United States because there was no organization within the Government that could bring together scholars representing the broad spectrum of American academic interest in India. Subsequently, the Advisory Group concept was abandoned. The Secretary of State informed the Bureau that he wanted to bring to India a proposal for establishing a joint commission with three sub-commissions to deal with three areas of potential collaboration: (1) trade and commerce, (2) science and technology and (3) educational and cultural exchange. The agreement to set up these sub-commissions was signed by the Secretary of State in India on October 28, 1974. Another high-level educational meeting was scheduled for early 1975 to discuss the implementation of this agreement. The suggestions drawn up at the 1974 meeting served as a guide for identifying areas of joint educational and cultural collaboration.

Assessment of the Decision-Making Process

Educational and cultural exchange between India and the United States began in the nineteenth century primarily under the sponsorship of missionary societies. It has since expanded enormously and today includes foundations, universities and colleges, educational associations, international agencies as well as government agencies, which have increasingly become the major funding source for American educational and cultural exchange. Very little coordination exists between these agencies. Most of them, particularly the private agencies, would prefer to keep it that way, since they do not want to subordinate their own goals to those of another organization. Private funding agencies are particularly concerned that cultural diplomatic policies of government agencies not influence their own programs. However, American scholars and students, whatever the source of their funds, are affected by the political relations between the two countries and the form of future exchange will be determined by the educational

34. Page 8 of the *Joint Statement*.

and cultural agreements which are worked out between this country and India.

It is important for the continuance of scholarly exchange with India that serious attention is given to Indian private and official opinion on the type of educational and cultural exchange they will permit within their own country. The State Department has been accommodating to the official Indian view-point, as evidenced by its reaction to the Ministry of Education's guidelines, by the composition of the American delegation to the academic summit and by the issues discussed at the summit. The American academic community is concerned that any decision arrived at not overlook the needs of American scholarship. Those involved in international education in India, as elsewhere, are interested in the development of technical and intellectual skills, in the establishment of links of communication between people engaged in similar intellectual and cultural activities, in the creation of a sympathetic understanding of beliefs, attitudes and cultural forms. For these goals to be realized, effective lines of communication must exist between the educational and cultural communities and the State Department. Otherwise short range political issues are likely to inform the United States' educational and cultural exchange policies.

Educational and cultural exchange has not received a high priority within the State Department and perhaps, for that reason, the educational and cultural communities have had very little influence on its policies. The low priority of education and cultural exchange is demonstrated by the way the United States organizes the exchange in India, as elsewhere. The exchange is managed overseas by the United States Information Agency (USIA),* an organization whose major goals are to create support for U.S. foreign policy objectives and to develop a favorable image of American society. Within the United States Information Service, the overseas post of USIA, the Cultural Affairs Officer (CAO) is supposed to coordinate and plan government funded educa-

---

* Editor's Note : This agency was superseded by the International Communications Agency (ICA) in 1979. Most of the issues Anderson discusses remain live.

tional and cultural exchange.[35] The CAO, who reports back to the area desks of both CU and USIA, is located within USIA's promotional system.[36] The CAO is appointed by USIA, with the approval of the Bureau of Educational and Cultural Affairs (CU), and is charged with supervising CU's programs, as well as those USIA programs that involve scholars and books, including USIA libraries.[37]

There is no clear-cut boundary between programs funded by USIS and CU. Generally, CU funds the exchange of persons while USIS funds things—books, magazines, audio-visual material, exhibits. Each organization prepares a separate annual country plan, which is jointly administered in the overseas USIA post. Since 1971, the USIA budget for India has been between five and six million dollars, about seven times larger than CU's Indian budget. The emphasis on information as a total part of USIS operations is demonstrated by the fact that the press and publications allocation is twice that of the entire CU budget.

The CAO is administratively subordinate to the Country Public Affairs Officer (CPAO), who is chief of the USIA post in India. Because India has recently had a series of distinguished CAOs who have been recruited from academic life, the CPAOs have given them considerable freedom to define their tasks. While this has enhanced the importance of educational goals within USIS, it means that the chief cultural officer is not likely to know the people or the operating procedures

35. While some science projects are now being considered by the United States Educational Foundation in India, most science projects are coordinated through the Office of the Science Attache, which reports back to the State Department's Office of International Scientific Affairs.

36. This dual arrangement is a result of John Foster Dulles' decision in 1953 to remove educational, cultural and informational activities from the Department of State and place them in a separate informational agency, the USIA. The Senate feared that educational and cultural exchange would receive a very low priority in an informational agency and a Senate resolution proposed that such programs remain within the State Department. The Senate's intent to separate information and education is negated by combining the two activities in the field.

37. The Information Officer at USIA directs the "fast" media activities, such as radio, television, films, publications and press releases.

in the Washington offices of CU and USIA. This has inevitably weakened their ability to exert pressure on the people who must draw up the final country plans and who must negotiate for the funds needed to implement the plans. Perhaps the major limitation on the CAOs ability to aggressively pursue educational goals is the environment in which they must work. USIA activities are basically informational, with an emphasis on the "fast" media such as radio, television and press releases. Educational and cultural activities tend to be considered support for the informational goals.

The linkage of education to a propaganda agency of the United States Government has, in the opinion of a former USEFI director, created the impression that U.S. scholarly effort is related to propaganda, a particularly damaging association in a country where there is already considerable suspicion about the goals and funding sources of U.S. scholarship. The State Department's most recent reorganizational study suggested eliminating USIA and placing all cultural and informational activities within a single branch of the State Department.[38] This suggestion overlooks the need to remove education from the pressures of public relations. To achieve the required separation, the CAOs need greater independence and a back-up agency in Washington which can effectively plan and negotiate for funds. As presently organized, the State Department is not a congenial atmosphere for educational goals to receive a serious hearing. Charles Frankel, in his study of the State Department's educational program, points out that the Department's "career service does not consist of men whose central interest lies in education, scholarship, or the arts."[39]

The existing planning process makes it difficult to consider seriously long range educational goals. Because of the necessity to submit yearly budgets to Congress, CU must draw up annual country plans that focus on short range objective.s The commingling of CU's plan with that of USIA in the field accentuates the short range perspective of its plans. CU plans are the result

38. *Diplomacy for the 70's : A Program of Management Reform for the State Department*, page 478—481.

39. Charles Frankel, *The Neglected Aspect of Foreign Affairs* (Washington: 1966), page 140. See his discussion of the difficult circumstances under which CAOs operate to carry out their educational tasks. *Ibid,*. pages 9 — 23.

of negotiations between USEFI, chaired by the CAO, the CAO and CU in Washington. The advice of American academics (usually through the Conference Board of Associated Research Councils and the Institute of International Education)[40] is sought only when the plans are already in a well advanced stage. In effect, their major responsibility is to select participants for programs over which they had only marginal influence.

The Institute of International Studies' planning is entirely separate from CU, even though USEFI now provides services for most of the Institute's programs in India. While there is regular communication between CU and the Institute, it is on an *ad hoc* basis and no mechanism exists that would bring the two sides together to systematically plan their long range objectives. Perhaps because no consultative mechanism exists, the Institute was not involved in planning for the January 1974 summit. It was not consulted on the educational agreement signed with India and it was not consulted on the 1975 meeting. It had no representatives at the 1974 summit.

The Institute does consult the CAO on the political sensitivity and feasibility of specific project proposals. The CAO and CU do influence the Institute's final decisions on specific projects; however, some in the Institute question the reliability of CU's interpretation of the Government of India's views on political sensitivity. Spokesmen within the Institute recognize that they do need a clearer picture of the political situation in India, and that it would be helpful to have their own representatives in the field to supply them with information relating to political sensitivity and feasibility.[41] Even if the Institute could arrange to send a representative to India, it does not have the funds to support an overseas representative. Its present staff is inadequate to properly plan and implement its present responsibilities. Despite an increased work load, the Institute operates with fewer than one-half the staff it had

40. These are private academic associations which have contractual agreements with both the State Department and the Institute of International Education to provide advice on planning and to review applications for specific grant categories.

41. The International Education Act passed in 1966, but never funded, would have permitted OE to have representatives abroad. The Institute is a unit of the Office of Education (OE), Department of Health, Education and Welfare.

five years ago. The low priority of international education within the Office of Education is demonstrated by the fact that OE proposed a budget in 1974 which allocated zero funding for NDEA—Title VI grants, which fund about ten per cent of the total operating costs for the area studies centers in the United States.[42] The congressional appropriations sub-committees restored the allocation, in large part due to the pressure exerted by individual American scholars and by educational associations. Since World War II, Congress has proved to be more consistently sensitive to the needs of educational exchange than either the State Department or the administration. It has also, on several occasions, expressed its opinion that educational exchange should not be closely tied to the activities of United States Information Agency.

The Institute has received considerable criticism from both CU and USIS over the number of programs it finances and the types of people it selects to participate in its programs. While it does listen to CU's advice on the political sensitivity and the feasibility of projects, it is reluctant to abandon its freedom to judge the academic worth of projects. The distinction between political sensitivity, feasibility and academic worth is not a clear cut one. When there is a conflict between these two sets of criteria, academic worth receives a higher priority. Institute spokesmen claim that CU and the Institute tend to direct their attention to different American academic audiences. According to those spokesmen, CU funds programs which will create a good impression of American scholarship and society in India and hence, show a partiality towards senior scholars from recognized centers of international education. The institute, on the other hand, is more interested in funding younger scholars

42. In 1973, the administration considered impounding $13.3 million appropriated for NDEA-Title VI. After considerable pressure on OMB and HEW from the academic community and Congress, $12.67 million was released. Several academic associations interested in international education have vigorously protested against the amount ($8.6 million) which the administrations proposed for funding NDEA—Title VI in 1975. The House Appropriations Sub-Committee on Labor-HEW added two million to the administration request. The Senate reported out a somewhat higher figure and the final House Senate Conference figure for both NDEA—Title VI and Fulbright Hayes was $14.3 million, about $3 million more than the House sub-committee recommended for both funding categories.

and in providing an international experience to teachers from schools which are in the process of developing international programs, precisely the kinds of people one often hears complaints about from CU and USIS.

The educational freeze and the guidelines were the result of basically political causes. When Indo-American relations began to improve in 1973, particularly with the solutions of the PL-480 issue, educational relations also improved. The State Department's policy of accommodation was probably the only response that would not have jeopardized the continuation of educational exchange. Had the State Department decided to vigorously protest the guidelines or to implement retaliative measures, it would have been politically difficult for the Ministry to liberally interpret the guidelines or to consent to an academic summit to discuss the future development of educational and cultural relations.[43] Nevertheless it still remains that the government agencies funding education had no long range plans to serve as a guide in responding to the freeze, or more importantly, no planning mechanism to bring together a broad spectrum of American academic interest in India to consider proposals to submit at the 1974 academic summit. The State Department, which will negotiate the terms under which educational and cultural exchange will continue, operates without a clear understanding of the needs of the American academic community. It is not surprising that American academics are concerned that short range political concerns might be accorded a higher priority than educational goals in new exchange agreements.

Recommendations

The Indian and American academic systems differ considerably, both in terms of local autonomy and in terms of financial independence. On the Indian side, curriculum control and

43. None of the guidelines have been formally revoked by the Government of India, which means they could be more literally interpreted should Indo-American relations deteriorate again. During the summer of 1974, the Ministry added another guideline to its list. The heads of departments at Delhi University and principals of its constituent colleges were informed by the Ministry of Education that no foreign scholar could be invited to deliver a lecture without the prior permission of the Ministry. This decision was vigorously protested by teachers at Delhi University.

funding are highly centralized, whereas educational institutions in the United States operate with considerable autonomy in determining their educational objectives and in finding financial resources. These different systems have led to different conceptions of what educational and cultural exchange between the two countries should be. The Ministry of Education would like a cultural agreement between the two countries, on the model of cultural agreements it has negotiated with countries in Western Europe and elsewhere. In these agreements, binational commissions have been created, composed of representatives from the ministries of finance, education, and foreign affairs of the two countries. The commissions meet a few times each year to establish broad policies governing the cultural agreement for the year. Subcommittees composed of representatives from both countries identify the areas of need, available facilities and then arrange for the exchange of students, research scholars, lecturers and various kinds of cultural groups.[44]

Once the needs and available facilities have been identified specific cultural programs are decided upon by the two countries. The Bureau of Educational and Cultural Affairs opposes the proposal for a cultural agreement between the United States and India. The Institute of International Studies opposes it even more strongly.

The major argument against a cultural agreement is that the United States has a pluralist system of education. The various units in the American educational system would reluctantly abandon the freedom they now have to define their own goals and to supervise their own programs. Undoubtedly, the

44. Very few American groups in the performing arts have come to India, since CU has not had sufficient funding to pay the high transportation costs involved in bringing groups to India. CU has funded 6 to 7 Short Term American Grantees (STAG program) each year for the past several years to participate in seminars and deliver a few lectures. It also funds the International Visitors Program (IV Program) in which prominent Indians come to the United States for a month or so. During the academic freeze, the Government of India did not permit any Indians to participate in this program. During 1973-74, Ambassador Moynihan took a direct interest in bringing prominent American intellectuals to India to deliver lectures in a program funded by USIA.

State Department would also not want to get embroiled in the controversies that might develop between American academic institutions, American scholars and the governing body which would have to implement the cultural agreement.

The Ministry of Education would like a single point of contact with some educational agency representing American academic interests. At the least, they seek an agency which could identify what topics or subjects Americans are studying, the subject matter of research projects and the sources of funding. Such a reporting agency might provide certain pay-offs to American scholars as well. If the agency were one in which the Ministry of Education had confidence, it could speed up visa approval on proposals which were delayed, by clarifying to the Ministry the source of funds and the nature of the proposals.

An agency now exists, which, with some changes, could discharge the reporting and coordinating functions mentioned above. The United States Educational Foundation in India seems the most likely candidate for these tasks. It was established in 1950 through an agreement between the Governments of the U.S.A. and India to facilitate exchange of knowledge and professional talents through educational contacts. However, most American academic work in India has been carried on outside its jurisdiction (though the Institute of International Studies has recently delegated to it the administration of its grants to American students, research scholars and group programs). The Foundation has developed valuable contacts inside the Government of India and with Indian scholars. It would be accepted as a legitimate contact point by the Ministry of Education. The Ministry of Education has already suggested to CU that USEFI become the Ministry's contact agency for American scholarship.

If named as the coordinating agency, USEFI could create program sub-committees with representatives from the various funding agencies which operate programs in India, as well as representatives from the Ministry of Education. These program sub-committees could advise American funding agencies on specific topics or program formats which might be accepted by the various Indian ministries which review grant proposals. This proposal would provide for the minimum reporting and coordinating functions sought by the Ministry of Education without imposing controls which would not be acceptable to the various American institutions and scholars interested in South Asian Studies.

USEFI could also serve as the secretariat for the Cultural Affairs Officer. This assumes the separation of education from public relations. USIS has a legitimate informational task to perform, but it is not the agency to manage the overseas educational and cultural programs of the United States Government. The present arrangement weakens the credibility of American scholarship in India. More importantly, this arrangement tends to make educational exchange a support for short range informational goals.

The CAO's position within the Embassy hierarchy should be equal to that of the CPAO. The CAO should have a separate organization, in this case USEFI, to manage all educational and cultural programs funded by CU, USIS and the Institute of International Education. This would include U.S. libraries, book programs, the STAG and IV programs, as well as all faculty and student grants funded by CU and the Institute of International Studies. The CAO would continue to serve as chairman of USEFI's board of directors. The board would also continue to serve as one element in the planning process, along with the CAO, and the agency in Washington responsible for funding the exchange program.

Up to now, USIA has not been willing to permit any foreign control over any of its activities. This policy resulted in the closure of the U.S. libraries in non-consular cities. This proposal would permit, through USEFI's binational board of directors, foreign involvement in the planning and the operation of U.S. libraries and other government funded exchange programs. One criticism of foreign involvement is that it would deprive American government funding agencies of the freedom to formulate their own goals. However, this has not been considered a serious problem with the exchange programs now planned and administered by USEFI. Moreover, the issues of political sensitivity and feasibility would be more accurately assessed if there were informed opinion from the Indian side during the early stages of the planning process. For the continuance of educational and cultural programs within India, it would be prudent to construct an organizational strategy that considers long range educational needs within the limits of what is politically possible and feasible.

It still remains to consider what organizational entity within the United States should be responsible for planning and funding the government's educational and cultural exchange programs, if, in fact, there should be a single agency. Both CU and the Institute of International Studies have low priority within their respective departments. Because of this, neither CU nor the Institute has been conspicuously successful in upholding the interests of international education. It would make sense to create a single semi-autonomous foundation with a governing board composed of members drawn from concerned government departments (i.e. the State Department, the Office of Education, the Library of Congress, the National Endowment for the Humanities, and other agencies involved with international education), as well as representatives from various private educational and cultural associations. Such an agency would be analogous to the National Endowment for the Humanities, which has both private and official representation on its governing board and which receives financial support from both public and private sources. This foundation should have a full time staff of career officials who would periodically serve in the field. The American representatives on the new joint sub-commission for educational and cultural exchange should be appointed by and receive their instructions from the foundation's governing board.

The major advantage of such a foundation is that it provides an organizational framework within which long range educational and cultural goals would have top priority consideration. Such a foundation could do a more effective job of representing the needs of international education to Congress than the agencies now responsible for planning international education. Presently the task is divided between several departments and agencies, many of which consider international education a rather unimportant part of their total effort. Because of the broad spectrum of educational and cultural interests represented on its governing board, the foundation would be responsive to American scholarly and cultural interests.

Even with the proposed foundation, a large part of over-seas educational and cultural activities in India will remain outside its jurisdiction. The American educational system is not unified and its diverse parts will surely continue to pursue their own interests in their own way.

CASE STUDIES :
III. PEOPLE TO PEOPLE DIPLOMACY

B. The Role of the Peace Corps in U.S. Relations with South Asia

Charles S. Lenth

The Peace Corps Act of 1961 established a new and unconventional government agency of American diplomacy and international involvement. The new agency was directed to recruit, train and support American "volunteers" in programs which would, as was suggested in the Act, assist in meeting the middle-level manpower needs of nations who requested such aid, contribute to a fuller understanding of the United States by those nations, and increase the understanding of foreign nations among Americans. The Peace Corps was established as an assistance program, but it could not claim to offer direct economic, material or political benefits. The agency at best could offer the assistance of the modest talents, the different outlook and the oftentimes considerable dedication of individual Americans who sought the challenge of learning, adapting and contributing to different and less "developed" societies. With the retrospect of fifteen years, it seems clear that the framers of the Peace Corps Act underestimated the difficulties and ambiguities of human resource development and the costs inherent in their notion of development.

The Peace Corps was also meant to promote educational and cultural exchange and, through it, mutual understanding and appreciation between peoples and nations. However, to the degree that the agency was intended as an exchange program, it was limited by the one-way flow of personnel and by preconceived notions about the requirements and direction of "development." Finally, and permeating its other purposes, the new agency was intended to give a new orientation to U.S. foreign policy and to improve the American image in the Third World. The Peace Corps was the Kennedy's administration's opening to the world, its initial, most visible proposal in response to anti-American attitudes and perceptions within the neutral and developing nations.

The Peace Corps objectives were multiple and sometimes inconsistent. The new agency entered the foreign policy arena as the "benign and benevolent" American presence abroad. Yet it was unavoidably political, despite disclaimers by the agency, and explicit in its dependence on U.S. and host-country government support for its activities. Often individual country Peace Corps programs were used by the U.S.G. as a part of its foreign policy objectives or accepted by host governments for reasons which were external to the agency's stated goals. At times the agency itself took advantage of its ambiguous and unconventional role in foreign policy to pursue, sometimes at the expense of overextending its real capabilities, its own organizational and ideological goals. The agency cultivated a style of crusading idealism hospitable to ambitious undertakings; at times it was this claim to be altruistic, non-political and uncompromising that fed criticisms of its naivete at home and accusations of imperialistic and surreptitious operations abroad.

This case study characterizes the role of the Peace Corps in U.S. relations with the states of South Asia. India is the main focus; unfortunately, there is no consideration of the relatively successful and continuous Peace Corps program in Nepal. It is not the intention of this study to recount or assess the effectiveness of specific volunteer projects within South Asia, which would be a much different, interesting and more substantial undertaking. Evaluation is included only to the degree that the strengths or weaknesses of particular projects appeared significantly to influence the role of the Peace Corps within bilateral relations. On the one hand, this study focuses on the overall role which the agency attempted to play in U.S. foreign policy; on the other it attempts to identify the political significance which was given to the agency's programs within the host nations and by the host government.

The most general conclusion of this study is that when the Peace Corps as an agency, or separate country programs in particular, became too closely identified with conventional U.S. policy abroad or too closely controlled by actors or contingencies external to the agency, it was unable to pursue its stated objectives with respect to volunteer assistance projects; cultural-educational exchange; and the promotion of international understanding. "Success" depended upon some degree of insulation from political and policy considerations, and a difficult mix of support and independence from the context of bilateral relations within which the Peace Corps programs operated. Thus, on a general level, this study attempts to examine the conditions and organizational requirements for a government agency to pursue effectively non-strategic, non-economic people-to-people goals in foreign policy.

A brief outline of the establishment and organizational status of the Peace Corps might be helpful. The agency appeared as one of the first major initiatives of the Kennedy administration on March 1, 1961, after a few intensive weeks of planning by a group gathered together by Sargent Shriver. The agency was initially established by executive order, using the authority and contingency funds provided to the President under the Mutual Security Act of 1954. This strategy avoided immediate congressional challenges, and along with the appointment of Sargent Shriver as Director, helped the agency to establish its independence, to build a base of support, and to overcome the controversies which its establishment inspired.

However, as overall plans for the new foreign assistance organization began to take shape, David Bell, director designate of the AID program, wanted the Peace Corps to be integrated into a single structure of American programs abroad. In an April meeting in which neither the President nor Shriver were present, a decision was made to make the volunteer program part of AID and a chapter within the foreign assistance bill. Shriver and his staff were already committed to building an independent agency. They sought to avoid identification with the bureaucracy and reputation of the old International Cooperation Administration and conventional assistance programs. Through the intercession of Shriver's associates with Vice-President Johnson and Johnson with Kennedy, the AID association was reversed.

The Peace Corps Act as passed by Congress several months later gave the Secretary of State authority to oversee the operations of the agency, and to provide a degree of integration with U.S. foreign policy and assistance commitments. Vaguely defined supervision over individual country programs was extended to the chiefs of U.S. diplomatic missions abroad. In practice, the authority retained within the State Department was not as important in determining the operations of the agency as Secretary Rusk's cordial view of the Corps, on one hand, and Shriver's leadership, stress on independence, and White House connections on the other. Peace Corps saw itself as representing a "new" America abroad; it sought to be a people-to-people program and attempted to maintain its autonomy, both organizationally and philosophically, from the routines and national self-interest presumed to be the basis of conventional foreign policy.[1]

Programs with Unstable Political Support : Pakistan and Ceylon

The difficulties encountered by the short-lived and politically manipulated Peace Corps programs in Pakistan and Ceylon highlight some of the problems faced by the agency. It attempted to establish projects under the constraints of volatile host country political conditions and unstable bilateral relations. As one of the nations which appeared to be most sympathetic to its initial overtures for program requests, the Peace Corps early in 1961 proposed several projects to the Government of Pakistan. Pakistan accepted, no doubt pleased to be able to demonstrate its cooperation and close ties with the U.S. during that period. The program in Pakistan expanded to nearly 200 Peace Corps Volunteers (PCVs) by the end of 1963, but then leveled off and began to decline in size as the military government recognized that a large contingent of

---

1. There are several good accounts of the establishment and early months of the Peace Corps. See for example : David Hapgood and Meridan Bennett, *Agents of Change* : *A Close Look at the Peace Corps* (Boston : Little Brown, 1968), and Robert G. Carey, *The Peace Corps* (New York : Praeger, 1970), p. 46.

volunteers was no assurance of American support in other
areas and was detrimental to establishing a neutral international
status. The program in East Pakistan proved to be troublesome
as the PCVs made known their support of the Bengali region
against the government in the West. The volunteers were
finally withdrawn from the East on the insistence of the
military government during the 1965 Indo-Pakistan war. In
short, the failure of the program to serve the interests of the
Government of Pakistan led to the decision not to accept any
additional groups after 1965. Moreover, it was understood
that this decision was also intended as a response to the withholding of weapons and supplies by the U.S. to Pakistan during
that period. The Peace Corps program in Pakistan was dominated by the existing conditions within U.S.-Pakistani relations
and the narrowly defined interests of the military government.
The exaggerated initial support, the emerging constraints, and
the final rejection attempted to use the Peace Corps program
for purposes unrelated to its own objectives as a volunteer
agency.

In contrast to Pakistan, the initial acceptance of a Peace
Corps program in Ceylon (now Sri Lanka) in 1962 was not
enthusiastic. The left-leaning government of Madame Bandaranaike avoided any appearance of close ties with the U.S. and
the agreement for a small group of PCVs was the result of the
agency's hard-sell approach and determination to exploit whatever opening it could find.[2] The difficulties of this lack of firm
support within the host government soon became apparent.
One week before their arrival, the Parliamentary Secretary to
the Prime Minister would not admit to Parliament that the
government had agreed to allow PCVs into Ceylon. The lack
of public and private support continued in the refusal of the
Bandaranaike government to defend the Peace Corps against
the severe attacks by leftist and nationalistic politicians. As a
result, the program remained a totally American effort and
accomplished little towards improving bilateral relations.

Within this oftentimes inhospitable political atmosphere, a
series of initial mistakes by the inexperienced Peace Corps
administrators made the agency's program in Ceylon even

2. *Peace Corps Country Evaluation—Ceylon*, Peace Corps, Washington,
   1964.

more difficult to defend. Seemingly unaware of the growing number of educated unemployed within Ceylon (including teachers) the program placed PCVs as teachers in secondary schools. The agreement with the Ministry of Education had unrealistically anticipated that after a short training period the PCVs would be capable of teaching in Sinhalese or Tamil. Adding to the difficulties, they arrived during the mid-term of the last semester of the school year, facing months with no work. Finally, the PC staff in Ceylon had flush toilets installed in all of the schools where volunteers were stationed, providing physical convenience at the cost of personal embarrassment and a fueling of political commentary by the opposition. After other forms of American assistance in Ceylon were suspended under the Hickenlooper Amendment in 1963, the Bandaranaike government refused to renew the agreement with Peace Corps when the initial group terminated in 1964.

Following a change in government, a second Peace Corps program in Ceylon began in 1967 through an agreement with the more pro-Western government of Dudley Senanayake. Senanayake evidently requested the program as a means of initiating a more friendly posture towards the U.S. In reality, however, it did not appear that the political environment or the degree of government support for the Peace Corps had improved. The first announcement of the agreement for eighty-one PCVs first reached Ceylon through a USIA bulletin from Washington, which put the government and the program on the defensive. An opposition book, *The Peace Corps Again : A New Invasion of Ceylon*, made a contention to which both the program and Senanayake's government were vulnerable : "Ceylon does not need the help of any Peace Corps, but the United States has made it imperative that countries like Ceylon should accept a contingent of the Peace Corps as a gesture of good will and prove our *bona fides* that we are not anti-American."[3] Control of the government returned to the more leftist and nationalistic parties, and no new volunteer groups were approved after 1969.

In Ceylon and Pakistan, the Peace Corps programs suffered from unstable or unsympathetic host government support for

3. *The Peace Corps Again : A New Invasion of Ceylon* (Ceylon: Tribune Publications, 1967), p. 1.

the agency's projects. It seems apparent that the volunteer projects were accepted not because of an understanding of or commitment to the agency's purposes, but because a token gesture of cooperation towards this relatively inconsequential U.S. program seemed appropriate at the moment. Given this conception of U.S. policy and this type of host government support it is understandable that the Peace Corps was unable to establish viable and independent volunteer programs. These two examples point out the underlying dependence of country programs on the prevailing condition of bilateral relations. Without some insulation from both American and host country politics, programs aimed at softer, longterm objectives easily become little more than instrumentalities manipulated for short-term effects.

The Peace Corps in India

Similarly, but to a lesser degree than in Pakistan and Ceylon, the attitude towards the Peace Corps program in India and the role which the agency was allowed to play in U.S policy was influenced by the underlying conditions of bilateral relations between the two nations. The difference was that the attitude of the Government of India (GOI) was never simplistically opportunistic or openly hostile to the agency. GOI generally respected the intentions of the agency, and showed a good deal of understanding of its requirements and capabilities. This general understanding and acceptance of an American volunteer program in India was supported by the similarities between it and the philosophy and projects of the Gandhian "sarvodaya" tradition for social service and village uplift. Both GOI and U.S. government allowed the Peace Corps/India (PC/I) to develop, to build a base of support, and to demonstrate the potential for low-level assistance and exchange programs. The two important factors appear to have been the maintenance of open and friendly bilateral relations and some degree of insulation from the other agencies and issues involved in bilateral relations. Unfortunately, both insulation and good bilateral relations were strained and damaged during the mid and later 1960s.

The activities and program size of Peace Corps/India were subject to broad guidelines set by GOI, which in turn reflected domestic political interests and the success and leverage of the agency itself, as well as the conditions of the Indo-U.S. relations. The decisions and determinations regarding general policy and specific projects were shared and manipulated by many actors and affected by subtle shifts in the nature and enforcement of the guidelines. Separate political decisions on the acceptance or rejection of PC/I projects represented a way by which the individual states could establish an identity and position towards the U.S. presence in India.

Within the agency, decisions on the size and role of PC/I projects revealed competing views and the working out of organizational and policy questions. What was to be the relationship between the PC/I program and foreign policy objectives as viewed from Washington? Between Washington and field determined policy within the agency itself? Between PC/I and the American country-team in India? The underlying questions involved the degree of autonomy on one hand, and coordination on the other, necessary for PC/I to be able to pursue its own objectives within the political and social context of India.

The Difficulties of Program Formulation and Expansion

In spite of the general receptiveness for the Peace Corps idea in India, for practical and political reasons the Indian leadership was not anxious to see a very large contingent of young Americans become involved in the complex problems of rural India. The national leadership had initiated ambitious developmental programs in the 1950s, and was well aware of the complexities, the need for careful planning and reformulation, and the uncertainty of results. There was justifiable skepticism of the raw idealism, untested approaches and the foreign involvement which the Peace Corps represented. In addition, Nehru's policy of non-alignment sought to avoid too close identification with the U.S. Direct responsibility within GOI for overseeing the Peace Corps and other national volunteer programs was given to the Planning Commission, which was controlled by the Prime Minister and committed to development through its own brand of democratic socialism. Among GOI bureaucracies, it was one of the organizations least receptive to U.S. proposals. The Peace Corps represented a very different outlook. The directness of its approach, the idealism and boldness of its objectives, and its inclination to attribute resistance to its initiatives to the conservative, unimaginative nature of government bureaucracies resulted in a clash of attitudes.

The underlying difficulty for PC/I and a reason for the cautious GOI position was that India had no obvious middle-level manpower needs which volunteers could fill. With underemployment already a problem among Indians with education and skills comparable to American volunteers, it was unacceptable to bring in Americans who might displace or appear to threaten Indian counterparts. PC/I had several broad options for justifying and placing volunteers, none of which were free of dangers and limitations. Peace Corps Volunteers could be placed in positions alongside and rivaling Indian counterparts with the intention that they act as agents of attitude change. Another alternative was to develop new positions within projects, types, and areas of work which Indians were unwilling or culturally unprepared to undertake. But role definition and project formulation were continuing problems within PC/I. For example, the agents of change approach created difficulties in the recruitment and training of volunteers for unspecified roles in India. Both attitude change and the establishment of new types of work raised issues which were culturally and politically sensitive.

The understanding in principle but lack of cooperation in practice which characterized PC/I relations to counterpart Indian agencies also influenced its relations with other U.S. government organizations. In the early years the agency was shaped by the leadership of Sargent Shriver and the direct connections he had with the White House of both Kennedy and Johnson. He instructed his country directors that they had an importance equivalent to ambassadors, and that they were to remain separate from the conventional foreign policy institutions and objectives. While the PC/I Director sat on the embassy's country-team in Delhi, he did not actively participate or take part in cooperative agency projects. To do so, he felt, would have been out of line with Shriver's directives.[4] Under these arrangements coordination between U.S. agencies

4. Personal correspondence with Charles S. Houston, August 8, 1974.

was minimal and relations took on the appearance of competition. A photo essay put out by PC/I ("This People India") was well received by GOI; its success so upset rival American agency officials that the press run was confiscated from Washington and the booklet was republished in nearly identical form under the USIS imprimatur. As another example, shortly after his return to New Delhi as Ambassador in 1964, Chester Bowles cabled USDA in Washington to locate an expert who would be able to help a PC/I project on a particular poultry problem. The reply from USDA informed the Ambassador that the foremost American expert in the field was already working in an AID project within the same state as the volunteers.[5]

In spite of these initial difficulties in formulating acceptable volunteer projects and the incompleteness of working relationships with related Indian and U.S. agencies, PC/I projected a very considerable expansion of the size of the program. The level of 200 to 400 volunteers which had been maintained in the 1962-64 period was considered a pilot stage. A PC/I projection made in 1964 foresaw an expansion from the 400 level to over 1000 PCVs by 1966, 1700 by 1967, and over 2700 by 1969.[6] These projections were in line with the anticipation of the growth of Peace Corps around the world.

The process of "indenting" the granting of final approval for new groups by the Planning Commission, was seen as the main obstacle to expansion in India. PC/I administrators complained of difficulties in dealing with the official liaison at Planning, and accused him of self-serving and irrational treatment of indenting requests. Within the discretionary guidelines agreed to by GOI, this official preferred to keep the program at a size and in activities which he could personally oversee. From the PC/I point of view, he sought to run the program from his turban. His authority over the approval and distribution of volunteers and projects created a log-jam in the efforts to expand. PC/I disregarded the possibility that the official's

---

5. Chester Bowles, *Promises to Keep: My Years in Public Life 1941—68* (New York: Harper & Row, 1971).
6. "Five-Year Projection." Peace Corps India Memorandum, New Delhi, March 27, 1965.

attitude might signal an underlying political determination by GOI to limit the size of the volunteer program in India. The situation also showed the limits of the agency's independence. In this situation it required embassy level support in the coordination of country programs. GOI control over the PC/I program had been captured by Planning partially as a result of the agency's own modes of operation.

Pressures from Washington and the Expansion in 1965

PC/I administrators sought support for expansion of the program in India by appealing up the ladder, even as far as the Prime Minister. While they received sympathy, they did not achieve results. Finally in 1965, Peace Corps in Washington wrote to Asoka Mehta, Deputy Chairman of the Planning Commission, suggesting a high level visit to the U.S. in order to discuss the agency's proposals for expansion in India. The trip was made by Mahmood Butt, Joint Secretary to Government in the Planning Commission and one step above the Delhi liaison. His report back to the Commission relayed Washington's concern over the unimpressive size of the program.[7] He was assured by Washington that the Peace Corps could supply 2000 to 2500 volunteers to help meet the manpower needs of India's development programs. His report stressed that India competed with other nations for a limited number of high-quality PCV's, with program size and official cooperation constituting important factors. The report implied that large national programs had more leverage in Washington, and urged increased support from the Indian government at all levels.

Following Butt's return from Washington, the log-jam in the indenting of program requests gave way. Ten new groups of volunteers were brought into India in the last months of 1965 and early 1966. In contrast to the impression which was apparently given to Butt in Washington and conveyed to Delhi through his report, the new projects were not more technical in nature than those of the past, nor were the volunteers more specialized or better trained for their work. Quite the opposite was probably the case. The quick expansion of the program

7. Mahmood Butt, "Report to the Planning Commission on Trip to the United States," Planning Commission, Government of India, New Delhi, June, 1965.

brought in younger and less skilled volunteers who might not have been accepted if the quota for recruitment had not been so large. Several of the new groups did expand the relatively successful efforts of the Peace Corps in projects for the development of poultry raising in India. But other large groups were assigned to experimental and hastily formulated projects in community development, applied nutrition, and family planning. Many of these were noticeably unsuccessful. Thus the first wave of real program expansion in India demonstrated the weaknesses rather than the strengths of existing arrangements for project formulation and approval by both Indian and PC/I administrators. The Planning Commission had little information or appreciation for the needs and preferences of the States which were to receive the volunteers, or for the problems of project implementation and administration at lower levels. Peace Corps was not sufficiently aware of the training, selection criteria, and degree of support necessary to make the projects viable.

The Requests for Food Grains and the Rapid Expansion of the Peace Corps into Agricultural Programs in India

The March, 1966, meeting between President Johnson and Prime Minister Indira Gandhi in Washington seemed to indicate changing conditions in Indo-U.S. relations. With respect to the Peace Corps, it demonstrated again how the agency was influenced and itself could exploit the conditions of the bilateral relationship within which it operated. The Prime Minister had come to Washington to seek assurances of increased grain shipments to meet the needs of India during the mid-decade droughts. In the joint communique of March 29, the President indicated that, Congress willing, the U.S. would aid India in meeting the immediate grain needs and would continue to participate in long-range programs to help India achieve self-sufficiency in food grain production. The Prime Minister agreed with these objectives, and expressed India's gratitude for the support of the President and the American people.[8]

The following day the President sent a special message to Congress urging quick recognition and approval of the

8. President Lyndon Johnson and Prime Minister Indira Gandhi, Joint Communique, Washington, March 29, 1966.

necessary measures to fulfil the agreements of the communique. Following a statement in which he praised India's own efforts to increase agricultural production, he stated his belief that Americans could participate in these efforts. "If they can be used", the President's message read, "I feel certain that American agricultural experts would respond to an appeal to serve in India as part of an Agricultural Training Corps or through an expanded Peace Corps."[9] He was optimistic about the Peace Corps's ability to attract and use agricultural experts and of the contribution they could make to the Indian programs.

The next day, March 31, in a speech to business and cultural groups in New York, the Prime Minister talked briefly about her impression of the Peace Corps. She seemed to view it primarily as a people-to-people educational exchange and was more reserved than the President about the contributions which Americans might be able to make to India's developmental efforts. Yet, her remarks gave the impression that changing Indo-U.S. governmental relations might facilitate cultural and cooperative programs between the two nations.

Probably neither the President nor the Prime Minister gave much thought to their mention of the Peace Corps program in India. In comparison with ten million tons of food grains, the size of the volunteer program was of minor importance, and the two leaders did not appear to share a common view of its nature and purposes. Yet, following the March meetings, the remarks of the leaders and the changing conditions within bilateral relations took on a logic and direction of their own. India was in need of grain shipments from the U.S. and was willing to play the role of a cooperative friend, accepting American involvement in India as a part of this friendship. From the U.S. perspective, increased grain shipments would be more likely to get support, especially in Congress, with demonstrations of Indian friendship. As an agency of both friendship and assistance, the Peace Corps was a suitable means of indicating and accepting American involvement in India. Pressure built up

9. President Lyndon Johnson, Special Message to Congress, March 30, 1966. See also, Brent Ashabranner, *A Moment in History* : *The First Ten Years of the Peace Corps* (Garden City, New York : Doubleday, 1971).

within the agency to exploit the opportunities of changing bilateral relations and to pursue greater expansion.

On the day of the President's message to Congress and Mrs. Gandhi's address in New York, a cable arrived in the PC/I office in New Delhi from Warren Wiggens. At that time the Deputy Director and in charge in Washington, Wiggens had a reputation within the agency as the foremost proponent of expansion and large-size volunteer programs. His cable to the programs office in Delhi read, in part :

> Message appears to be direct challenge to PC to consider dramatic and meaningful contribution. . . . (Situation) in India as dramatized by Prime Minister's visit and President's message offers unique opportunity to respond in full to need for agricultural experts and Cropsmen through dramatic expansion in size and emphasis (of) PC/I program . . .[10]

Wiggens spoke of 1000 additional PCVs for India, including specially recruited agricultural specialists, and anticipated that GOI would be ready to cooperate at all levels.

The PC/I Director at this time was Brent Ashabranner. His reply to the cable argued against the proposed expansion, pointing out that the program in India was already in line with the President's message. New groups with 480 volunteers were scheduled to arrive to replace those terminating and to boost the size of the program to over 1000 by the end of the year. But Ashabranner was a lame duck administrator, scheduled to return to Washington to take up another position. Jack Vaughn, who had been confirmed as Director of the Peace Corps only the previous month, was also in New Delhi at this time. His position on expansion in India seems to have been between that of Wiggens and Ashabranner. In a speech to the National Press Club in Delhi he foresaw a more modest 50 percent increase in the volunteer program in India as a result of the improved bilateral relations, and was less certain than either President Johnson or Wiggens about the potential of the Peace Corps to provide real "agricultural expertise" to India.[11]

10. Allan Bradford, David Hapgood and J. Richard Starkey, "Overseas Evaluation : India," The Peace Corps, Washington. July 28, 1967.
11. *Ibid.*

Several days later Vaughn and Ashabranner met in Delhi with the GOI Secretary for Agriculture, C. Subramaniam. The meeting had apparently taken place on the advice of the Ministry of External Affairs, though the Secretary did not say so. In the meeting no agreement was reached on the number of PCVs to be taken into agricultural projects, but there was clearly a new receptiveness to PC/I proposals for expansion.[12]

The potential for placing PCVs within expanded agricultural development programs in India had been debated for some time. Beyond the immediate conditions of the 1965-66 droughts, both Indian officials and foreign observers looked forward to rapid rural development through the introduction of new varieties of seeds, different crops, fertilizers, and improved practices. Government programs were expanding and it appeared that PCVs could be useful as extension agents. However, whether volunteers commanded the technical background and skills necessary for such a program was uncertain. In early 1965, a series of communications from Chester Bowles to Shriver proposed a joint AID-PC/I program in Indian agriculture combining the technical resources of the former with the volunteer approach to rural extension.[13] Bowles strongly supported the joint agency approach. Many in PC/I, including volunteers from the field, supported higher levels of technical competence for volunteers, so they could play a useful and significant role in Indian agriculture. But the proposal was discouraged by Shriver because of a fear that any identification with AID and the use of technical criteria for the selection and placement of volunteers would damage the established approach of the agency. It was this unwillingness and inability of the Peace Corps to accept the field evaluations of the needs of Indian agriculture and meet the requirements of viable volunteer programming which had delayed expansion for agriculture.

Chester Bowles returned to Washington in July, 1966, in order to clear up difficulties which had arisen over the food grain shipments. Again the question of an expansion of American programs in Indian agriculture came up. Bowles was

12. Correspondence with Brent Ashabranner, August 2, 1974.
13. Judy Mudd, "India : Peace Corps' Stumbling Block," Interns Report, Peace Corps, Washington, September 15, 1967.

a firm supporter of the PC/I program. While doubtful of its
present technical capabilities, he saw it as having an advantage
over high-level assistance programs because of the ability of
volunteers to adapt and fit into Indian conditions. As
his personal account of his ambassadorship makes clear,
however, Washington was not often sensitive to the Indian
point of view. While in Washington Bowles learned that without consultation with Delhi, USDA had proposed and the President seemed inclined to support a delegation of one thousand
American experts to help India remake its backward agriculture. Bowles was appalled by the one-sidedness of this proposal,
the lack of consultation, and the potential disruption caused by
such a mass migration of experts. He cabled his staff in India,
"asking them to meet immediately with Indian officials and
persuade them to make a formal request for five hundred
Peace Corps Volunteers to work especially on agricultural
problems." The arrangements were made, and while still in
Washington Bowles was able to get approval for the Peace
Corps program in place of that of the USDA. While skeptical
about the technical capabilities of PCVs, Bowles saw that an
expansion of the Peace Corps could probably be handled without causing a great deal of reaction or disruption within the
ongoing GOI programs and the improving climate of Indo-U.S.
relations.[14]

The program indents expedited by the maneuvers directed
by Bowles from Washington committed PC/I to rapid and
extensive expansion into a largely untested program area. It
had previously undertaken agriculture programs; nine of the
twenty-seven programs prior to mid 1966 had been involved
with some area of rural extension. But these had been loosely
structured volunteer placements, and no additional agriculture
programs had been approved during the previous year. PC/I
had no proven pattern to draw upon in this expansion—no
standards of selection, training, placement, or support. The
issue of the degree of technical skill and support needed for
productive work in Indian agriculture extension had never been
satisfactorily resolved. This contributed to the misunderstanding and exaggerated expectations of the programs among Indian
officials. In the opinion of PC/I Director Ashabranner, who left

14. Bowles, *op. cit.*, p. 524.

just prior to this period, the big build-up in what were called "agriculture" volunteers would never have occurred had it not been for the unusual conditions surrounding the supply of needed food grains to India.[15]

The new groups which arrived in India were under projects called Village Level Food Production. As extension agents in villages and local government centers the PCVs conducted demonstrations and worked with individual cultivators in the pattern established by Indian village-level workers, and as part of the extensive efforts by GOI and the Indian states to bring new inputs and techniques to village agriculture. PC/I planning and training of the first groups for VLFP began before the July indents initiated from Washington by Bowles. However, in quick succession from September to the following February eight of ten programs which arrived in India came under the same description, bringing over 400 volunteers to eleven Indian states. Another three programs, one state, and 120 volunteers were added by September, 1967. Agriculture extension at the village level became the backbone of the PC/I program. Mainly as a result of the expansion into agriculture extension projects, the size of the PC/I program, which had doubled from 1964 to 1965 to nearly 600 volunteers, more than doubled again to 1,439 volunteers and trainees in India at the end of 1966. It remained above the 1000 level until the end of 1967.

Smaller Size and Decentralization of the Program in India
The results of this rapid expansion were very mixed. An early 1968 Peace Corps evaluation concluded that the "great haste of that build-up accounts for most of what went wrong in the 1966 programs—a hazy conception of what Volunteers would actually do in the field, weak and irrelevant training and speedy, sloppy site selection."[16] The poorly prepared and quickly placed PCVs were nearly as likely to disrupt as aid in the slow-moving but constructive Indian government programs in the rural areas. One state received a group which was one-third female volunteers, although the request had specified only males. The promised quotas of those with agriculture skills

15. Correspondence with Brent Ashabranner, August 2, 1974.
16. Peggy Anderson and Walter Arenberg, "*Overseas Evaluation* : *Indian Agriculture Program*, Peace Corps, Washington, April 8, 1968.

were inevitably undercut. One group had two weeks of agriculture "experience" before their arrival. In a report commissioned by PC/I, Kusum Nair, the well known journalist and student of rural development, severely citicized the training and technical deficiencies of the volunteers, their unstructured role and their often antagonistic attitude toward India's agriculture programs.[17] This was a confusion wrought by poorly defined goals and a lack of understanding of the needs and conditions of rural India.

On the other hand, there were good volunteers and well received programs during the expansion into agriculture. The more understanding and sympathetic Indian officials and observers accepted the PCVs not as skilled technical resources, but for their ability to bring "fresh air" into some areas of rural India and the often unresponsive Indian bureaucracies. From several of the more successful programs, guidelines were developed for better training, programming, and more adequate support of VLFP volunteers. Through more conscientious programming and support PCVs without agricultural expertise continued to be requested for village level agriculture programs into the 1970s.

In the aftermath of the period of expansion the number of PCVs in India declined as sharply and rapidly as it had risen. Many of the groups from the 1965-66 expansion completed their terms and were not replaced. The total program fell to below 600 volunteers by the end of 1968, and remained below 500 thereafter. The lower level was not the result of a single policy decision or agreement on the size of the program by GOI, Washington, or the Peace Corps. It was the result of new operational guidelines drawn up by different decision makers, more thorough consultation with officials in the states and at lower levels, and the changing political climates in which these decisions were reached.

Feedback into the decision making process was a major factor in determining the changes which occurred. The volunteers, unlike unused equipment or wasted dollars, did not sit idly by as symbols of American friendship when they felt their purposes had been betrayed and their intentions unfulfilled.[18]

17. This study by Kusum Nair is referred to in the Anderson evaluation.
18. This theme is developed by Hapgood and Bennett.

A forum in New Delhi in 1967 of representatives of all the PC/I groups in India demonstrated the volunteers' concern and disappointment. In a questionnaire sent by the Forum to all volunteers in India, only 60 per cent replied that they felt they had made some sort of significant contribution in their positions, 54 per cent thought that their co-workers and supervisors had not been advised or prepared for their arrival, and 58 per cent did not feel that their programs should be followed by another.[19] The negative responses, however, were skewed between programs, revealing the weaknesses of certain programs which had been undertaken during expansion.

.During 1966 and concomitantly with the expansion period the staff in India went through a nearly complete turnover. The first issues and problems which the new administrators faced were those resulting from the expansion, and they were determined not to let it happen again. They emphasized a decentralization of operations, both in programming and support. New programs had to be worked out with the cooperation of the state ministries and district level officials. Several new regional offices were established along with smaller offices in several of the state capitals which brought the number of full-time PC/I staff to over forty. An increasing number of these were Indians, and most were fully involved with the preparations and support of volunteer programs. Although there was a five-year limitation on service within Peace Corps imposed by Congress and generally supported within the agency, PC/I built up a group of administrators with valuable program experience. This degree of professionalism, binationalism, and organizational support greatly improved the volunteer projects.

During early 1967, PC/I solicited the aid of Ambassador Bowles to have GOI responsibility for the program moved from the Planning Commission to the Department of Economic Affairs in the Ministry of Finance. PC/I was freed from dealing with the official who for years had assiduously exercised his personal prerogatives at the expense of a good working relationship. In DEA the Peace Corps found officials with whom they could deal frankly and constructively, and who were in agree-

19. "Forum : Peace Corps India," Peace Corps India, New Delhi, April 5, 1967.

ment with the plans to decentralize programming responsibilities and require more involvement from the states. The Finance Ministry seemed more aware of the complexities of center-state relationships and less prone to dictating projects and volunteer placements to the states, as had often been the case with Planning.

DEA arranged for the appointment of state level coordinators for volunteer programs, each with authority to carry out negotiations for new projects with the regional staff of PC/I. Such a delegation of responsibility had never been possible under Planning. The PC/I staff did the necessary legwork involved in the preparation of project proposals and volunteer placements. The proposal went first to the state level coordinator for consultation and approval to approach the appropriate lower-level officials in the state departments or district offices. With his permission to pursue the project, details of volunteer qualifications, placement and support were worked out with the Indian agencies or departments. The final proposal went from the department officials back to the state level coordinator for his approval and submission to a political screen—usually the Chief Minister of the state or the minister of the concerned department. Proposals approved at the state level proceeded to DEA for indenting. At any of these three levels a new project could be blocked without explanation. After indenting, the project proposal was sent to PC/I in Delhi for approval and forwarding to Washington to initiate recruitment and training of volunteers.

The new process located primary authority for approval or rejection with those most directly concerned. More informal procedures resulting from the close working relationships which developed (especially between DEA and PC/I in Delhi, and between the regional offices and the state level coordinators and departmental officials) often speeded up this complicated process. But the existence of these procedures and the involvement of officials at many levels improved the preparation for new projects and helped to assure support once the volunteers had arrived.

Along with the adoption of better programming procedures, changing political configurations within the states contributed

to a decrease in the requests for volunteer groups coming to
PC/I by the end of 1967. Kerala, under a CPI (Marxist) led
government after the 1967 general election was among the first
state governments to change policy towards the Peace Corps
programs. The initial announcement of expulsion of the Peace
Corps from Kerala received considerable publicity. As it
worked out, one of the four groups was never asked to leave,
two groups peacefully finished their two year stint two months
after the decision was issued, and the final group had sufficient
support from the All Kerala Poultry Producers Association
that the Kerala government was led to reverse its decision
after arrangements had already been made to move the PCVs
to Mysore State. The rise of anti-American political parties in
West Bengal created a situation similar to Kerala. The difficult
working environment and lack of state government support
finally led to the withdrawal of the PCV groups. The governments of Andhra Pradesh, Maharashtra, and Uttar Pradesh
reacted to the excessively large and unproductive groups which
had been brought in during the expansion period. While groups
were not removed from these states, the requests were reduced
and the number of volunteers in the states became a sensitive
political issue. The increased coolness towards Peace Corps
demonstrated broader changes in the attitudes and political
climate within India in regard to all foreign assistance and
developmental programs. There was a reaction to the mid-
sixties period of pride-wounding dependency on foreign grain
shipments and the influx of Western experts and efforts in developmental programs. Rising national pride and some encouraging results after 1967, especially in the field of agriculture
development, supported the belief that India would be able to
achieve self-sufficiency without extensive foreign participation.

This change of attitude within India was taking place at
the same time as a change of attitude and approach within
Peace Corps. Disillusionment on the American campuses with a
government program claiming to achieve peace in the world
and some frank revaluations of the whole Peace Corps idea led
to a decline in applications in 1967-68. Director Vaughn sought
a lower profile for the agency; from a policy of enthusiastic
expansion, Peace Corps moved towards steady size and consoli-
dation of support.

The relations between PC/I and DEA over program approval and requirements were extremely open and constructive during the 1967-70 period. The regional and state offices of PC were given a good deal of freedom to work out proposals and agreements with state and district officials, while these were sorted through and given approval in Delhi. Encouraged by DEA, PC/I concentrated its programs in areas where it would not be controversial. Though the working agreement between DEA and PC/I allowed a volunteer program of from 500 to 1000 PCVs, in fact it remained near or below the minimum after 1968. This was due to the low-profile which GOI and PC/I deliberately sought and the efforts which were made to assure good programming and support.

In mid-1970, the Ministry of Finance announced a review of all volunteer programs in India and approval of new groups was postponed. New size guidelines were finally announced in September, 1971. The total number of foreign volunteers in India was not to exceed 600; the maximum allowed Peace Corps was 400. Approval of several new groups within the new guidelines was anticipated by PC/I in December 1971.[20] With the outbreak of war between India and Pakistan on December 3rd, GOI placed an immediate freeze on all foreign volunteer programs. In mid-1972 it was announced that all programs in India would be limited to fifty volunteers each after January, 1974. Though this limitation applied to all foreign volunteer programs, its effect was felt by the Peace Corps most directly. There is little doubt that the GOI decision was influenced by the coolness of Indo-U.S. relations.

By early 1974 the number of PCVs had fallen to less than twenty, and permission to bring in more volunteers in small groups was granted by DEA. PC/Washington appointed a new Country Director, indicating a willingness to continue even at the level which GOI imposed. Most of the other foreign volunteer programs either withdrew from India as a result of the new guidelines or had not received any new requests from the states. Although other U.S. assistance agencies had not been asked to remain in India, PC/I was approached by four states with requests for over a hundred volunteers—more than would be approved by GOI. Two factors clearly contributed to

20. Correspondence with David Rogers, August 6, 1974.

this. PC had established a base of support within several of the states, and had developed a reputation for useful work and little disruption. Second, as the DEA Deputy Secretary told a former Country Director in India, the Peace Corps had been allowed to stay because of the understanding they had shown in dealing with the Government of India.[21]

The Peace Corps in U.S. Relations With South Asia : Limitations and Recommendations

The programs in South Asia illustrate that the Peace Corps was not effective in achieving short-term objectives in foreign policy. When used as an instrumentality, the agency realized neither its own goals nor those of its manipulators. Many of the difficulties of the programs in Ceylon and Pakistan, of the expansion period in India in 1966-67, and the atrophy of the program after 1971 were the result of the dependence of country programs on good bilateral relations with the U.S. Manpower assistance and educational exchange programs are aimed at long-term objectives: results are difficult to evaluate and cannot be expected to have immediate impact. Programs which are intended to be of a people to people nature require a degree of insulation from the politics of bilateral relations.

Peace Corps programs also suffered when they failed to achieve integration into the foreign political environment. The agency's program in India suggests that integration demands a great deal of organizational and operational decentralization. Country programs must be based upon mutual understanding and involvement between Peace Corps personnel and host country nationals at all levels. Specific projects must fit into the priorities and politics of their environment, and the program must be sufficiently useful and accepted to build up local support. On a higher level, country programs are dependent upon the establishment of good working relationships with the host country liaison and continuing back-up support by the host government.

The agency's own ideological and organizational rigidities often contributed to the inability of the Peace Corps to be accepted within foreign political contexts. The ideology was not overtly political, but stemmed from the roles and rubric

21. Correspondence with David Rogers, August 6, 1974.

under which the agency operated. For many years Peace Corps represented an extreme can-do attitude which was little more than a simplistic faith in the ability of Americans with strong hands, stout hearts and an idealistic outlook to work miracles abroad. As the horse of this rejuvenated American frontiersman, the Peace Corps was ridden to death. Exaggerated idealism was eventually out of place, and good intentions had to be accompanied by the ability to produce. In the late 1960s the Peace Corps adopted a policy of "new-dimensions", attempting to make up for lost innocence by emphasizing the technical nature of small programs and specially recruited volunteers. This approach was also a simplification of the agency's purposes and strengths. Both approaches confused and antagonized host countries when the Peace Corps could not live up to its public image.

In organization and program structures Peace Corps was overly attached to the patterns adopted at its establishment. For instance, selection and training criteria were reshuffled to emphasize different mixes of technical skill, language ability, and cultural adaptability. Always the same basic structures and need for uniformity were maintained. The programs in South Asia suggest that these narrowly defined constraints and organizational rigidities should have been reexamined and more attention given to fitting the volunteers, their training, and the projects to the multiple purposes of the Peace Corps and the needs of the host nations. Flexible and, if necessary, longer training periods were needed in order to promote the multiple purposes of volunteer programs.

Finally, the Peace Corps in South Asia was limited by its identification with a particular historical period and outlook. Established with the zeal and idealism of new American leadership in the early 1960s, the agency first exploited and then suffered from changing social and political moods. By defining its role too ambitiously, Peace Corps obscured its more modest purposes. In attempting to be conspicuous in its uniqueness, the agency overextended itself, and cut itself off from necessary cooperation with other agencies.

Programs with a people-to-people and humanitarian orientation draw support from a lasting constituency within the United States. The idea of a Peace Corps caught on and, despite difficulties, continued to be alive in America as in no other nation. Its constituency can continue to participate, contributing its spirit and moral conception of the U.S. role in the world to the composite of U.S. foreign policy. Peace Corps adds an alternative, an element of pluralism in the definition of foreign policy goals which has an integrity at home and abroad.

Annex : A Chronology of Events in South Asia Bearing on the Conduct of Foreign Policy

Joan Landy Erdman

1965

February

Supplies of U.S. wheat to India were again delayed by a prolonged dockers' strike in ports on the Gulf of Mexico, which held up 60 ships loaded with wheat and rice for India. The failure of the 1965 monsoon led to a sharp fall in the 1965-66 crop; emergency aid from the U.S. and other countries alleviated fears of wide-spread famine.

19 An agreement for a loan of U.S. $60,000,000 by China to Pakistan was signed in Karachi. This interest-free loan was to be used for Pakistani imports of commodities from China and for financing projects in Pakistan.

March

6 In response to an appeal by the U.S. Ambassador to India, Mr. Chester Bowles, the U.S. dockers decided to load food ships for India, while continuing their strike as far as other shipping was concerned.

19 The International Monetary Fund (IMF) announced that it had approved a stand-by arrangement authorizing India to draw up to the equivalent of $200 million over the following 12 months, since "increased foreign exchange outlays had been necessary for imports of foodgrains, as domestic output during the recent past had failed to meet the substantial increase in consumption which had resulted from the rapidly rising population and an accelerated monetary expansion."

April

2 The Chinese Prime Minister, Mr. Chou-en-Lai, arrived in Karachi and had a two-hour meeting with President Ayub Khan, leaving the following day for Peking.

9 Fighting between India and Pakistan broke out in the Rann of

Kutch, on the frontier between Indian Gujarat and West Pakistan, and continued until the end of the month, when *de facto* ceasefires came into effect. On June 30 a formal ceasefire was signed, through the mediation of the British Government. India protested to the U.S. use of American arms against India, and on May 22 U.S. Embassy sources in New Delhi confirmed that the U.S. Government had lodged a strong protest with Pakistan, which had not been made public because of on-going cease-fire negotiations.

16 The White House announced that State visits to the United States by President Ayub Khan of Pakistan and the Prime Minister of India Lal Bahadur Shastri, which were scheduled to take place on April 25-26 and June 2-3 respectively, had been postponed.

April

20 In a Lok Sabha discussion the postponement of Mr. Shastri's visit to the U.S. was attacked, and it was suspected that it was a reaction to Indian criticisms of U.S. policy in Vietnam. On 4/21 the White House said that the invitation to Mr. Shastri still stood, and that President Johnson hoped that the Prime Minister of India would visit Washington in the late summer.

June

22 A formal agreement covering compensation payments to Shell, Caltex and Esso, to be spread over five years, covering assets largely taken over in 1962 by the State-owned Ceylon Petroleum Corporation, was signed in Colombo. On May 11, a Ceylon government spokesman said that the Government's offer for compensation had taken into consideration the need for the resumption of U.S. aid, suspended in Feb. 1963 as a result of the compensation dispute.

July

3 The U.S. Agency for International Development announced that Ceylon had again become eligible to receive U.S. economic assistance under the Foreign Assistance Act.

August

Fighting broke out between India and Pakistan on the Indian side of Kashmir between infiltrators from the Pakistan side and Indian security forces, and subsequent occupation by Indian forces of posts on the Pakistan side of the ceasefire line. On Sept. 3 the Indian Ambassador in Washington, Mr. B.K. Nehru, lodged a strong protest with Secretary of State Dean Rusk, against the use of U.S. equipment by Pakistan in Kashmir, and pointed out that this violated assurances given to the Indian Government in 1954, that the equipment supplied to Pakistan would not be used against India.

September

3 The British Prime Minister, Mr. Wilson, sent a personal message to Mr. Shastri and President Ayub Khan expressing concern over the fighting in Kashmir, which had broken out in August.

3 Mr. B.K. Nehru, Indian Ambassador in Washington, lodged a

strong protest with Mr. Dean Rusk, the Secretary of State, against the use of U.S. equipment, including Patton tanks, F-86 Sabre jets, and F-104 supersonic fighters, by Pakistan in Kashmir, and pointed out that this violated assurance given to the Indian Government by President Eisenhower in 1954 that equipment supplied to Pakistan would not be used against India.

6 U.S. officials in Delhi informed Washington, after visiting the Indian side of the Jammu front, that Pakistan was using American equipment against India.

September

7 Mr. Bhutto announced that Pakistan had invoked the CENTO agreement in the face of "Indian aggression." No request for aid under the pact was made to Britain, however, as the British Government had repeatedly informed Pakistan in the past of its view that the pact would not cover a dispute between the two Commonwealth countries.

8 The British Government imposed a ban on shipments of arms to India; Pakistan had not been receiving arms from Britain, and was therefore not affected.

8 U.S. Secretary of State Dean Rusk informed Congress that all U.S. military aid to India and Pakistan had been stopped, and no further economic aid would be granted until Congress had been consulted. Throughout the war the Chinese Government repeated its full support for Pakistan. Great Britain, Canada, the Soviet Union, and the U.S. made mediation attempts.

10 In a communique, after talks between the Persian Prime Minister and the Turkish Premier, the Persian and Turkish Governments declared themselves ready to support their brother and ally, Pakistan, and supported international initiatives to end the conflict. Reportedly they rejected a request from Pakistan for 24 jet aircraft, with pilots and instructors, on the grounds that they could not send Pakistan arms supplied by NATO or as part of U.S. military aid.

13 The Indian Government requested the U.S. to ensure that American arms did not reach Pakistan through Turkey and Persia. A similar request by the Indian Government was made to the Soviet Union to ensure that Indonesia did not supply Soviet arms to Pakistan.

23 Cease-fire between India and Pakistan, in accordance with resolution of the Security Council of the U.N.

November

8 Both Prime Minister of India Lal Bahadur Shastri and Pakistan's President Ayub Khan agreed to meet in Tashkent in January 1966, accepting the Soviet offer of good offices in their Kashmir border dispute. It was expected that the Soviet's Kosygin would take part in the meeting.

December

15 President Ayub Khan of Pakistan addressed the U.N. General Assembly regarding the Kashmir problem.

16 The Government's Bill giving legal effect to the agreements reached with the Shell, Caltex and Esso oil companies on the payment of compensation for their properties taken over by the former Government of Mrs. Bandaranaike, passed the Ceylon Senate, having been approved in the Ceylon House of Representatives on October 7, and received the Government's assent.

16 After talks between President Johnson of the U.S. and Pakistan President Ayub Khan in Washington, a joint communique was issued, in which they reaffirmed their Governments' support for the U.N. Security Council resolution of Sept. 20, 1965, in all its parts, as well as the resolutions adopted on Sept. 27, and Nov. 5, 1965. Subjects discussed also included the upcoming Tashkent meeting between President Ayub Khan and Indian Prime Minister Mr. Shastri, and a projected visit to Washington by Mr. Shastri in February for talks with President Johnson.

1966

January

4-10 Meeting in Tashkent, the President of Pakistan Ayub Khan and the Prime Minister of India Lal Bahadur Shastri, with the mediation of Soviet Prime Minister Kosygin, signed on January 10 a declaration under which India and Pakistan agreed to renounce force in the settlement of their disputes and to withdraw their troops to the positions existing on August 5, 1965, before the outbreak of hostilities between the two countries.

11 In the early hours of the morning Indian Prime Minister Shastri suffered a heart attack and died shortly thereafter. Midst military honors and world-wide tributes, the body of Mr. Shastri was flown, over Pakistan, to Delhi, where it was cremated on January 12.

February

12 Sheikh Mujibur Rehman, President of the East Pakistani Awami League, issued a six-point programme for regional autonomy.

15 An agreement between Ceylon and the U.S. Agency for International Development was signed, providing for a loan of $7,500,000 to help Ceylon finance the import of essential commodities for its industrial and agricultural development from the U.S.A.

March

2 U.S. Government agreed to resume the sale of "non-lethal" military equipment to India and Pakistan, the distinction between "lethal" and "non-lethal" military supplies depending on political considerations and being the subject of discussions between the U.S. and the two Asian countries.

12 A Food-for-Peace agreement under U.S. Public Law 480 was signed in Colombo by the Governments of Ceylon and the United

States. Under the agreement the U.S.A. was to provide Ceylon with 50,000 metric tons of wheat flour and 5,000 metric tons of corn-gram sorghum, together worth $4,100,000. Payment was to be made by Ceylon in rupees and 70 per cent of these counterpart funds were to be made available to Ceylon in the form of long term loans for economic development projects.

20 President of Pakistan Ayub Khan denounced the autonomist movement in East Pakistan as aimed at the disruption of Pakistan and the unification of East Pakistan and West Bengal as an independent state, and declared that the country would accept the challenge of civil war if one were forced upon it.

21 The U.K. Commonwealth Relations Office announced that Britain would resume the sale of arms to India and Pakistan, which had been suspended on Sept. 8, 1965.

27-31 The Prime Minister of India, Mrs. Indira Gandhi paid an official visit to the United States, at the invitation of President Johnson. En route Mrs. Gandhi paid a 3-day private visit to Paris, and met with President de Gaulle on March 25, and with Prime Minister Pompidou. In Washington March 27-29, Prime Minister Gandhi met with President Johnson, met U.S. Administration leaders and addressed the National Press Club. In New York March 30-31, Prime Minister Gandhi met Mayor Lindsay, addressed U.S. economists and industrialists at the Economic Club, visited the U.N. and had a meeting with U Thant. On her return journey to India Prime Minister Gandhi met with Prime Minister Harold Wilson in London, and with Soviet Prime Minister Kosygin in Moscow, on April 2 and 3 respectively.

28-29 At a White House dinner on March 28, and in a communique issued March 29, President Johnson proposed, and Prime Minister Gandhi welcomed, the establishment of an Indo-American Foundation to be set up in India and endowed with $300,000,000 of counterpart funds, i.e., U.S. owned Indian currency accumulated in payments made by India to the U.S A. for PL-480 wheat etc. Its aims should be to "promote progress in all fields of learning, to advance science, to encourage research, to develop new teaching techniques in farm and factory, and to stimulate new ways to meet age-old problems."

29-30 Within two hours of the Indian Prime Minister's departure from Washington for N.Y., President Johnson asked Congress for approval for emergency shipment to India of a further 3,500,000 tons of American grain in addition to the 6.5 million tons which the U.S. was already providing in the financial year ending June 30, 1966. Shipment of vegetable oils and milk powder was also proposed to Congress.

April

19 By voice vote and without opposition, both Houses of U.S. Congress approved a resolution which endorsed and supported President Johnson in organizing substantial American participation

in an urgent international effort to combat malnutrition in India, to encourage the expansion of Indian food production, and to send food to Indians in dire need.

May

14 The Government of India signed an agreement with the American International Oil Company (AMOCO) for the construction at Madras of India's largest fertilizer plant. To be known as Madras Fertilizers, the new plant was to be a joint Indo-American venture, with 4 American and 4 Indian directors, one of the latter being Board Chairman, and having a tie-breaking vote. Managing Director of the company was to be an American. Of the equity capital, 51 per cent will be held by the Indian Government and 49 per cent by AMOCO.

27 An amendment to the U.S. food aid agreement of Sept. 24, 1965 with India was signed in New Delhi, providing for the shipment of an additional 3.5 million tons of food grains to India to supplement the 6.5 million tons allocated since July 1965.

June

5 It was announced in New Delhi that the Indian Government had decided to devalue the Indian rupee by $36\frac{1}{2}$ per cent and that the new official exchange rate would be 7.50 rupees to the dollar. The previous rate had been 4.76190 rupees to the dollar. Confirming the new par value of the Indian rupee on June 5 in Washington, the International Monetary Fund said it had concurred in the change.

1967

February

15 An agreement was signed in New Delhi by Dr. Atma Ram, Director General of the Indian Council of Scientific and Industrial Research, and Mr. Chester Bowles, the U.S. Ambassador, providing for an exchange of scientists and engineers between the two countries.

15 Chairman of the Indian Atomic Energy Commission, Dr. Vikram Sarabhai, announced in Moscow that the USSR would help India to send rockets into space in the next few weeks in order to check the chemical composition of the atmosphere at very high altitudes. Dr. Sarabhai and Mr. L.K. Jha, Secretary to the Prime Minister, also had successful discussions with Soviet scientists on cooperation between the two countries in the field of utilizing atomic energy for peaceful purposes.

April

12 The U.S. State Department announced that the U.S. would not resume military assistance to either India or Pakistan and did not contemplate selling combat equipment to either country, suspended since Sept. 1965. "Lethal end items" (i.e. finished products for combat) would not be sold by the U.S. to either India or Pakistan, i.e. such equipment as armoured vehicles, combat

aircraft, infantry weapons, and artillery. Restrictions of the U.S. Government on the kinds of spare parts which might be sold to India and Pakistan were removed.

December

1 Mr. Zulfiqar Ali Bhutto, the former Foreign Minister of Pakistan, formed the People's Party, its policy being described as one of Islamic Socialism, democracy, and an independent foreign policy.

1968

January

23 On a round-the-world journey, President Johnson stopped at Karachi airport for an hour's meeting with President Ayub Khan. Their joint statement said that Johnson had congratulated Ayub Khan on Pakistan's continued economic progress, and that the two Presidents had agreed that everything possible should be done towards achieving a rapid peace in Vietnam.

February

1 The U.S. Defence Secretary, Mr. Robert McNamara, said in Washington that the U.S.A. was continuing to refrain from sales of "lethal weapons" to India and Pakistan.

9 In his message to the U.S. Congress on foreign aid, President Johnson predicted a dramatic recovery in India's ability to meet its food needs, but pledged continued U.S. help.

May

13 Mr. B.R. Bhagat, Indian Minister of State for External Affairs, announced in the Rajya Sabha that India had sent strong protests to both Pakistan and China against the construction of the Gilgit-Sinkiang Road, stating that the building of the road sought to interfere with Indian sovereignty in Kashmir, and that Pakistan-China agreements concerning "Pakistan occupied Kashmir" were "illegal, invalid, and totally unacceptable to us."

20 Mr. Arshad Husain, Foreign Minister of Pakistan, announced in the Pakistan National Assembly that Pakistan had given notice to the U.S. to close its communications base near Peshawar, which had been handed over to the U.S. in 1959 under a bilateral agreement to expire on July 1, 1969. The *New York Times* stated that the U.S. communications unit in Pakistan had been used by the U.S. for 9 years for surveillance on the Soviet Union and Communist China.

June

19 The trial in the "Agartala Conspiracy" case opened in Dacca. The defendants, including Sheikh Mujibur Rehman, were accused of "plotting to deprive Pakistan of its sovereignty over a part of its territory by an armed revolt with weapons, ammunitions and funds provided by India." All the accused pleaded "not guilty."

August

8 Strong opposition was expressed in the Indian Lok Sabha against the continuation of the University of California sociological

research project underway since September 1960 in the Himalayan border regions of India. Concerned that the U.S. Defense Department might use the results of the project, the Minister of State for External Affairs, Mr. B.R. Bhagat, stated in reply to questions that the Government of India was reviewing the advisability of permitting the continuance of the U.S. programme.

12 Yielding to the pressure of opinion against the University of California sociology project in the Himalayan border regions, and despite the denial of Mr. Ivan Vallier, Acting Director of the Institute for International Studies of connections between the project and U.S. espionage, the Government of India was reported to have decided not to allow the University of California to continue its project.

September

28 Vice-Admiral A.R. Khan, Pakistan Minister for Kashmir Affairs, opened the first all-weather road linking Gilgit, in Azad Kashmir, with Skardu, in Chinese Sinkiang. An agreement for construction of the road, which was to be usable throughout the year by jeeps, was signed on October 21, 1967.

1969

January

24 The Jawaharlal Nehru Award for International Understanding for 1966, posthumously conferred on the American Negro civil rights leader, Rev. Dr. Martin Luther King, was presented to Mrs. Coretta King, by the President of India, Dr. Zakir Hussain in New Delhi.

February

19 The third major Economic Agreement between the U.S.A. and Ceylon was signed in Colombo, providing for the supply of about 150,000 metric tons of wheat flour at an estimated cost of $17.5 million.

21 President of Pakistan Ayub Khan announced his "final and irrevocable" decision not to seek re-election as President. The next day the Government withdrew all charges against Sheikh Rehman and the 33 other accused in the Agartala Conspiracy Case, who were released on the same day. On Feb. 23 Mr. Bhutto flew to Dacca for talks with Sheikh Rehman.

March

25 President of Pakistan Ayub Khan resigned, following mass strikes and revolt in East and West Pakistan, and martial law was proclaimed, with the result that order was restored without difficulty. The Commander-in-Chief of the Army General Yahya Khan, who had been appointed Chief Martial Law Administrator and dissolved the National and Provincial Assemblies, assumed the Presidency on March 31. On April 10 he gave an assurance that elections to a Constituent Assembly would be held on the basis of direct adult franchise.

April

   3 Mr. Kenneth Keating, currently serving as Associate Justice of the New York State Court of Appeal, was nominated as the next Ambassador of the U.S. to India.

July

  12 It was learned in London that India had protested to Russia and the U.S.A. against what it believed were Soviet and U.S. moves to build rival military bases in the Indian Ocean.

  25 President Nixon, on a round-the-world tour, visited five Asian countries : the Philippines, Indonesia, Thailand, India, and Pakistan, and also Rumania in Eastern Europe. Among those accompanying him were Secretary of State William Rogers, Presidential Foreign Affairs Adviser Henry Kissinger, and White House Press Secretary Ronald Ziegler. Included in the trip was a previously-unannounced stop in Saigon, where Nixon met with President Thieu of South Vietnam.

  25 At an informal news conference at Guam with press correspondents accompanying him on his round-the-world tour, President Nixon said that the time had come when the United States should be emphatic in telling its Asian allies that, except for a threat by a major power involving nuclear weapons, the United States had the right to expect that the problem would be increasingly handled by the Asian nations themselves. If the U.S.A. just continued on the road of responding to requests for assistance, of assuming the primary responsibility for defending these countries when they had international or external problems, they were never going to take care of themselves.

October

  13 In an agreement signed in New Delhi, the U.S.A. agreed to supply to India 3 million tons of wheat, 100,000 bales of cotton, and 95,000 tons of vegetable oil under a new PL-480 agreement.

1970

June

  14 The Governor-General called upon members of the Ceylon House of Representatives to draft and adopt a new Constitution declaring Ceylon to be a free sovereign and independent Republic pledged to realize the objectives of a socialist democracy.

July

  12 It was announced that the Government of Ceylon had decided to extend full diplomatic recognition to the Democratic People's Republic of Korea (North Korea) with effect from June 25, 1970.

  15 It was announced that the Government of Ceylon had decided to extend full diplomatic recognition to the Democratic Republic of Vietnam (North Vietnam) with effect from June 24, 1970.

  19 In a speech to members of the Ceylon House of Representatives, Ceylonese Prime Minister Mrs. Bandaranaike moved the following resolution : We the Members of the House of Representatives,

in pursuance of the mandate given by the people of Sri Lanka at the general election held on May 27, 1970, do hereby resolve to constitute, declare, and proclaim ourselves the Constituent Assembly of the people of Sri Lanka for the purpose of adopting, enacting and establishing a Constitution for Sri Lanka which will declare Sri Lanka to be a free, sovereign and independent Republic pledged to realize the objectives of a socialist democracy including the fundamental rights and freedoms of all citizens, and which will become the fundamental law of Sri Lanka deriving its authority from the people of Sri Lanka and not from the power and authority assumed and exercised by the British Crown and the Parliament of the United Kingdom in the grant of the present Constitution of Ceylon nor from the said Constitution . . ."

29 The Ministry of Defense and External Affairs announced that Ceylon had decided to suspend diplomatic relations with Israel with immediate effect. Furthermore it was announced that in accordance with the election manifesto of the United Front, the Cabinet had decided that the American-sponsored Asia Foundation should wind up its activities in Ceylon by October 31, 1970.

August

Chairman of the Pakistan Atomic Energy Commission Dr. I.H. Usmani, visited the United States, and finalized the draft of a bilateral agreement between the U.S.A. and Pakistan on mutual cooperation in the peaceful uses of atomic energy, under which the U.S.A. will supply to Pakistan enriched uranium fuel for the Rooppur station for a period of 30 years.

October

9 Final agreement for the supply of the entire equipment of a nuclear power station at Rooppur in East Pakistan between the Pakistan Atomic Energy Commission and the Belgian firms of Cockerill and Ateliers de Construction Electrique de Charleroi was announced in Brussels. ACEC is a subsidiary of the American Westinghouse Company, and the plant was to be based on American technology (the Karachi nuclear plant now nearing completion is based on Canadian designs).

November

10-15 The President of Pakistan, Gen. Yahya Khan, paid a State visit to China.

December

7 Elections in Pakistan to the National Assembly were completed, with Sheikh Mujibur Rehman's party emerging victorious. Mr. Z.A. Bhutto's People's Party was second.

10 While Pakistani political parties discussed Constitution-making, Maulana Bhashani called for an independent and sovereign East Pakistan. On December 12, three more parties joined the independence demand. On December 17 in Provincial Assembly elections, the Awami League won an overwhelming majority in East Pakistan. On December 28 Mr. Bhutto voiced disagreement

with Mr. Rehman's call for provincial autonomy. On December 29, Gen. Yahya Khan conceded Mr. Rehman's demand for holding the National Assembly session in Dacca.

15 The British and U.S. Governments announced that the building of a naval communications centre at Diego Garcia in the Indian Ocean would begin in March. The U.S. Congress approved President Nixon's request for $5.4 million to begin construction, to counter what the Administration claims to be a growing Soviet naval presence in the area.

1971

February

13 Gen. Yahya Khan fixed March 3 for National Assembly session, but on March 1 postponed it on Mr. Bhutto's request. Mr. Rehman called for general strike in Dacca to protest the postponement. March 8, civil disobedience movement was launched in East Pakistan. Meetings on March 19-22 in Dacca with Gen. Yahya Khan, Mr. Bhutto, and Mr. Rehman to discuss Constitution were deadlocked.

March

6 A carefully planned armed attack was made on the U.S. Embassy in Colombo, Sri Lanka involving damage to property and the death of a police inspector.

15 The U.S. State Department announced that the last remaining restrictions on travel by American nationals to the People's Republic of China had been lifted, and U.S. citizens would no longer need special permission to visit mainland China.

17 Ceylon (Sri Lanka) proclaimed a state of emergency following a number of incidents: the Government assumed sweeping emergency powers, and on March 23 disclosed a plot to overthrow the Government by an armed left-wing organization calling itself the People's Liberation Front (JVP).

21 Following the discovery of a large arms cache on the campus of the University of Ceylon, the Ceylon Government authorized, under its emergency powers, the death penalty for arson, looting, trespassing and damage by explosives.

26 Civil war broke out in East Pakistan, and the Awami League leader, Sheikh Mujibur Rehman, declared a sovereign independent People's Republic of Bangla Desh, even as the President, General Yahya Khan, ordered the Army to "fully restore the authority" of his Government in the turbulent East Wing.

26 In a broadcast to the Pakistan nation, General Yahya Khan charged Sheikh Mujibur Rehman with committing an act of treason and insulting the National Flag.

25-26 Sheikh Mujibur Rehman arrested at his residence in the evening; subsequently it was reported that Sheikh Mujibur had been taken to West Pakistan, where he was detained.

31 Both Houses of the Indian Parliament passed resolutions express-

ing solidarity with the people of East Bengal following the arrest of Sheikh Mujibur Rehman on March 25, 1971 and Pakistan's crackdown.

April

1 India told the U.N. that "the scale of human suffering in East Bengal is such that it ceases to be a matter of domestic concern of Pakistan alone."

6 Prime Minister of Sri Lanka Mrs. Sirimavo Bandaranaike announced in a radio broadcast that the Janatha Vimukthi Peramuna (JVP) had been banned, a nationwide dusk to dawn curfew imposed, and the closure of all universities, schools and other educational institutions following a series of attacks the previous day by JVP insurgents on 25 police stations, security patrols and Government buildings.

6 China accused India of "interfering" in Pakistan's internal affairs and "conniving at provocation" against the Chinese Embassy in New Delhi. The next day India rejected China's protest, and the Note was returned to the Chinese Charge d' Affaires.

10 A team of American table tennis players and accompanying journalists visited China at the invitation of the Chinese Table Tennis Association. At a reception held in Peking on April 14, the Prime Minister, Mr. Chou-en-Lai, said that the visit by the U.S. team had "opened a new page in the relations between the Chinese and American peoples."

14 President Nixon of the U.S. announced a relaxation of American restrictions on travel and trade with China.

15 The U.S. Ambassador to India, Mr. Kenneth Keating, said in Bombay that his Government did not view the current tragic events in East Bengal as an internal affair of Pakistan. The international community could not remain indifferent to the events in East Bengal under the cover of "internal affair."

15 The Government of Ceylon reported that it had been successful in combating the threat posed by the insurgents, "despite attempts by the so-called People's Liberation Front to unleash terrorism against the people and public property," Prime Minister Mrs. Bandaranaike said.

15 India protested to Pakistan against the "wanton and unprovoked firing" along the East Bengal border.

18-24 Pakistan Deputy High Commission in Calcutta declared its allegiance to Bangla Desh; Pakistan withdrew its Deputy High Commission from Calcutta and asked India to withdraw its mission from Dacca from April 26, 1971.

23 Prime Minister Mrs. Bandaranaike announced that the Army was in full control of the situation in Sri Lanka, and that 3,000 insurgents were in custody, and an amnesty was being offered to the rebels.

May

6 India appealed to the U.N. to take up direct responsibility for

relief of the refugees from Bangla Desh as it had done in other places. On May 18, Indian Prime Minister Indira Gandhi warned Pakistan that India was undeterred by any of her threats and said : "If a situation is forced on us, we are fully prepared to fight."

June

9 India and the Soviet Union called for immediate measures by Pakistan to create conditions in East Bengal which would stop the flight of people to India.

15 Speaking in the Rajya Sabha, Prime Minister Indira Gandhi of India said that the developments in Bangla Desh created for India a challenging situation, and that India would never endorse any political settlement "which meant the death of Bangla Desh."

22 After the *New York Times* reported that two Pakistani ships had sailed from New York in May 1970 with cargoes of U.S. military equipment, the Indian Ambassador in Washington raised the matter with the U.S. State Department. In reply the U.S. Administration stated that no fresh foreign military sales to Pakistan had been authorized or approved and no export licenses for commercial purchases issued or renewed since March 25, when the civil war in East Pakistan began; the ships might have been carrying items licensed for export before that date.

24 Mr. Swaran Singh, Indian External Affairs Minister, told the Rajya Sabha that besides the U.S. shipments China was the only country which had given military assistance to Pakistan after the crisis developed. Both the French and Soviet governments, he announced on July 6th, assured that they had not delivered arms to Pakistan since March 25.

28 In a broadcast President Yahya Khan barred Sheikh Mujibur Rehman and the Awami League from any role in his scheme of transfer of power to elected representatives of the people. On June 29 the Pakistan People's Party Chairman, Mr. Z.A. Bhutto, demanded the lifting of the Martial Law ban on political activity and asked for a smooth transition to civilian government.

July

7 Dr. Henry Kissinger, Presidential Adviser on Security Affairs, visited New Delhi, and the Indian Government raised the question of U.S. military aid to Pakistan, but failed to obtain an assurance that it would end.

9-11 Dr. Henry Kissinger held secret talks in Peking with the Chinese Premier, Mr. Chou-en-Lai, while on a fact-finding mission, which took Kissinger to the Republic of Vietnam, India and Pakistan. In Pakistan he was said to be indisposed, and his appearance in Paris was delayed a day, allowing time for the Peking visit.

12 Mr. Swaran Singh, Indian External Affairs Minister, told the Lok Sabha that "our view of the subject" of U.S. arms to Pakistan "has been conveyed in unequivocal terms to the U.S. Government," but rejected demands for the recall of the Indian Ambassador in Washington.

15 The U.S. President, Mr. Richard Nixon, announced in a televised broadcast that he would visit China some time before May 1972. In announcing his plans, he disclosed that Kissinger had held secret talks with the Chinese Premier, Mr. Chou-en-Lai, from July 9 to 11, 1971.

(Last week in July)

In an interview President Yahya Khan refused to give an assurance that Sheikh Mujibur Rehman would not be executed after he had been tried by a military court for "high treason." The secret proceedings began, according to informed Government sources, on August 11th. On that day Prime Minister of India Indira Gandhi appealed to the leaders of several nations to exercise their influence with General Yahya Khan and save the life of Sheikh Mujibur Rehman.

August

8 President Yahya Khan of Pakistan threatened to unleash a war on India.

9 India and the Soviet Union signed a 20-year Treaty of Peace, Friendship and Cooperation, effective from August 18, 1971.

16 American Senator Edward Kennedy, who had earlier visited refugee camps in India, accused Pakistan of perpetuating genocide in East Bengal. He demanded the release of Sheikh Mujibur Rehman.

16 At a press conference in New Delhi, Senator Edward Kennedy said that the reasons given by the Administration in the U.S. for its continued support to Pakistan were difficult to understand, and that he would make every effort in the Senate to stop not only further arms supplies but those in the pipeline.

22 Indian Minister of State for Food and Agriculture, Mr. A.P. Shinde, stated that the Indian Government proposed to stop all foodgrain imports by December 1971, and had decided not to enter into any fresh commitment for the import of foodgrains from the U.S. under the PL-480 scheme after the existing agreement expired in June 1972.

September

27 Prime Minister of India Indira Gandhi arrived in Moscow on a State visit to the USSR.

October

12 In a broadcast to the nation, President Yahya Khan promised his people a new Central Government by the beginning of the new year, but gave no indication about its likely composition and character.

20-26 Dr. Henry Kissinger paid a second visit to Peking to prepare the groundwork for the U.S. President's visit.

Oct. 24-Nov. 13

Prime Minister Indira Gandhi left New Delhi on October 24 for a tour of six Western capitals : Brussels, Vienna, London, Washington, Paris, and Bonn—and in each held meetings with heads of state, discussing the situation in East Bengal, the refugee repatriation problem for India, international support for refugee relief, etc. These issues were also discussed in press conferences and public meetings.

November

4 Prime Minister Gandhi arrived in Washington for talks with President Nixon. After their meeting the White House stated that the President supported the withdrawal of their troops from the frontiers by both sides—Pakistan and India. Mrs. Gandhi spoke at a White House dinner the same day, referring to the magnitude of the refugee problem, and the strains on a country already battling with the problems of huge population and poverty.

8 The U.S. Administration announced that it had revoked export licenses for military equipment for the Pakistan Army valued at more than $3 million, although spare parts to the value of $16,000 would be allowed.

13 In statements to both Houses of Parliament in India, Prime Minister Gandhi said that she thought that international opinion had shifted from a "tragic indifference" to a growing sense of the urgency of seeking a political solution of the Bangla Desh issue with the elected leaders. She stated that most countries also realized that the release of Sheikh Mujibur Rehman was essential, and intended to impress this fact on the Pakistani military regime. She had been told of the U.S. decision to stop further arms shipments to Pakistan.

14 The Chinese Premier, Mr. Chou-en-Lai, in a message to the Prime Minister of India Indira Gandhi, expressed the hope that the friendship between the Indian and Chinese peoples would "grow and develop daily". The message, the first to be exchanged between the heads of the two Governments in many years, was in reply to the felicitations cabled by Mrs. Gandhi from Vienna on China's admission to the U.N.

30 Prime Minister of India Indira Gandhi called for the withdrawal of West Pakistani troops from East Bengal to prove that General Yahya Khan wanted a peaceful solution of the crisis.

December

1 The United States announced the suspension of all future licenses for arms shipments to India, and cancelled licenses for arms and ammunition valued at about $2 million which had already been approved. Licenses for communications and other non-lethal military equipment worth about $11.5 million were "under review."

3 The U.S. announced cancellation of all outstanding licenses for shipment of military equipment to India, covering communications and electronic equipment and aircraft spare parts to the value of $11.5 million.

3 Pakistan declared war against India. President Giri of India declared a state of emergency in India following Pakistan's attack on Indian air bases in the eastern and western sectors. On

December 4, Indian forces entered East Bengal in support of Mukti Bahini, the Bangla Desh freedom fighters. India informed the U.N. of Pakistan aggression on India, and on December 6, India recognized the People's Republic of Bangla Desh. On the same day, Pakistan broke diplomatic ties with India.

4 A senior official in the U.S. State Department asserted that India bore "a major responsibility" for the war between India and Pakistan. Admitting that the beginning of the crisis can be fairly said to be the use of force by Pakistan, the official maintained that "Indian policy, in a systematic way has led to the perpetuation of the crisis, a deepening of the crisis, and India bears a major responsibility for the broader hostilities which have ensued."

5 In a statement issued by the official Tass Agency the Soviet Government attributed responsibility for the Indo-Pakistani War to Pakistan and warned other Governments to avoid becoming involved in the conflict.

5 Two resolutions in the U.N. Security Council calling for a cease-fire in the Indo-Pakistani War were vetoed by the Soviet Union.

6 Chinese official statements attributed entire responsibility for the Indo-Pakistan War to India, and accused the Soviet Union of encouraging Indian "aggression."

6 United States economic aid to India to the value of $87.6 million was suspended. A State Department spokesman said that "the U.S. will not make a contribution to the Indian economy which will make it easier for the Indian Government to sustain its military effort, and that the question of similar action against Pakistan did not arise because all the aid in the pipeline was earmarked for humanitarian relief in East Pakistan.

7 Dr. Henry Kissinger said at a news conference that the Administration had felt it necessary publicly to blame India for the outbreak of the war because the United States had an obligation to make it clear that it did not favour military solutions to political problems.

7 The U.S. Seventh Fleet moved from the Gulf of Tonkin to the Bay of Bengal.

16 The unconditional surrender of Pakistan forces was accepted by Lt. Gen. Arora, General Officer Commander-in-Chief of the Indian Eastern Command, in Dacca. Prime Minister Indira Gandhi announced unilateral cease-fire on the western front with effect from December 17, 1971. On that day General Yahya Khan accepted India's unilateral cease-fire, and the 14 Day Indo-Pakistan War ended.

18 The discovery of the mutilated bodies of a score of leading Bengali intellectuals in Dacca was made. They had disappeared from their homes over the preceding week.

21 The World Bank's International Development Association (IDA) approved two new loans to India totalling $50 million.

29 The Central Minister of State for Agriculture in India, Mr. A.P. Shinde, disclosed in Chandigarh that India had stopped wheat imports from the U.S. under PL-480, and decided to stop with immediate effect the import of rice for domestic requirements.

1972

January

5 It was announced that the U.S. Government had been informed by the Indian Government that the remaining 400,000 tons of the 1,750,000 tons of wheat to be imported under the last PL-480 agreement, signed in April 1971, would not be required in view of the excellent rabi (spring) crop.

7 It was officially stated in New Delhi that India's diplomatic representation in North Vietnam had been upgraded to the level of an Embassy from this date. A protest regarding this move was lodged by the U.S. Ambassador in India, Mr. Kenneth Keating, when he called on Mr. S.K. Banerji, Secretary (East) in the External Affairs Ministry. On January 8 India firmly rejected the U.S. protest.

8 Sheikh Mujibur Rehman was released from detention in West Pakistan and taken to London in a PIA plane; he proclaimed in London that Bangla Desh was "an unchallenged reality" and called for world recognition and the admission of his country to the United Nations.

9 According to a joint statement issued in Calcutta after talks between Prime Minister of India Indira Gandhi and Prime Minister of Bangla Desh Sheikh Mujibur Rehman, Indian armed forces would withdraw from Bangla Desh by March 25, and every means would be adopted to ensure the return of all refugees from India.

9 President Nixon notified Congress in a message that in the light of the more normal situation in Pakistan, the fact that the Pakistan authorities were no longer in control of Bangla Desh, and the return of most of the refugees to Bangla Desh from India, the restrictions imposed by Congress in 1971 on U.S. military and economic aid to Pakistan no longer applied.

February

14 The Bangla Desh Government statement in which it stated that Bangla Desh would remain a sovereign state and that "there is no question" of existing within the framework of Pakistan, was made a U.N. Security Council document.

March

4 The Prime Minister of Ceylon Mrs. Bandaranaike, sent a message to Sheikh Mujibur Rehman announcing Ceylon's recognition of Bangla Desh and expressing the wish for "close relations and friendly cooperation" between the two countries.

16 President of Pakistan Z.A. Bhutto arrived in Moscow for a three day official visit.

17 Indian Prime Minister Indira Gandhi arrived in Dacca to a tumultuous welcome by a vast crowd, where she was greeted by Sheikh Mujibur Rehman.

April

4 U.S. Secretary of State William Rogers announced diplomatic recognition of Bangla Desh by the United States. He said that the principal U.S. officer in Dacca, Mr. Herbert D. Spivak, was on his way back to Bangla Desh following consultations in Washington, and was carrying a message from President Nixon to Sheikh Mujibur Rehman "informing him of our recognition and avowed desire to establish diplomatic relations at the embassy level."

20 The U.S. Defense Department declassified its records, revealing for the first time that it gave Pakistan eight times as much military aid as India prior to the 1965 war. Following the war, the U.S. greatly curtailed its aid programs to both Governments, and subsequently Pakistan received most of its arms from China.

May

11 It was announced that Pakistan had devalued its rupee; now 11 Pakistani rupees would equal one U.S. dollar. The parity value before devaluation was Rs. 4.75 (Pakistani) to the U.S. dollar.

11 The official par value of the Pakistan rupee was reduced from 0.186621 grams of fine gold per rupee to 0.0744103 grams; in terms of dollars the devaluation was from 4.7619 to 11 rupees.

13 In Washington President Nixon welcomed the prospect of direct talks between the leaders of India and Pakistan on the problems of South Asia. The occasion was the acceptance of the credentials of the new Ambassador of Pakistan to the U.S. Mr. Sultan Mohammed Khan.

17 The International Monetary Fund announced its approval of a stand-by arrangement with the Government of Pakistan authorizing purchases of foreign exchange up to the equivalent of 100 million special drawing rights over the succeeding 12 months. The new par value of the Pakistan rupee corresponded to a rate of 11.9428 rupees per special drawing right.

26 Under the chairmanship of the World Bank, representatives of the Governments of Belgium, Canada, France, Western Germany, Italy, Japan, the Netherlands, Norway, Sweden, the U.K. and the U.S.A., as well as the IMF, the Asian Development Bank, the Development Assistance Committee of the Organization for Economic Cooperation and Development, and Switzerland, met in Paris, with a view to concluding an agreement on debt relief and to considering Pakistan's request for new commodity assistance in support of its efforts to increase the pace of development.

June

2 In a dispatch the *New York Times* said that China had delivered to Pakistan substantial quantities of new military equipment, including jet fighter-bombers and tanks, as part of an economic

and military aid agreement worked out in early February when Pakistan President Z.A. Bhutto visited Peking.

8 The U.S. General Accounting Office (GAO) reported to Congress that most of a grant of about $10 million made to Pakistan last autumn for humanitarian relief was diverted by Islamabad for the construction of military defenses on what was then the East Pakistani border with India.

13 The United States Senate voted by 44 to 41 to cut off military aid to Pakistan, India, Bangla Desh, Nepal, Ceylon, and other areas. The Senate voted the full $100 million requested for economic aid to Bangla Desh.

July

4 President Nixon's personal envoy, John Connally, arrived in New Delhi from Dacca to hold talks with Government officials on Indo-U.S. relations.

6 The American Ambassador to India, Mr. Kenneth Keating, announced his resignation from the post and his intention to "campaign actively" for the re-election of President R. Nixon.

29 The International Development Association (IDA) approved a $50 million credit for Pakistan.

August

1 Sri Lanka's Deputy Defense Minister, Mr. Lakshman Jayakodi, told Parliament that Chinese arms and gunboats gifted to Sri Lanka recently were meant for the island's internal and external security.

10 The U.S. Security Council members, striving to avert a Chinese veto, agreed to defer further consideration of Bangla Desh's application for U.N. membership.

September

14 The Prime Minister of Bangla Desh, Seikh Mujibur Rehman, returned to Dacca to a large welcome after a 49 day stay abroad for medical treatment. On the way to Dacca he had stopped in New Delhi for three hours and talked with Prime Minister of India Indira Gandhi.

27 Speaking at a National Press Club luncheon in Washington, the Finance Minister of India, Mr. Y.B. Chavan, referred to the state of Indo-U.S. relations and what was being done by both sides to repair them. Both countries should make an effort to "understand deeply" the views of the other.

October

2 India and the Soviet Union signed in Moscow an agreement for cooperation in the fields of applied science and technology.

2 The Government of India banned the landing in India of U.S. military airlift command flights without prior clearance, pursuant to the Government's policy to follow a uniform policy and discourage flights of military aircraft for purposes that could be served by commercial aircraft.

November

19 President Nixon, in a message to Prime Minister Indira Gandhi of India on her 55th birthday, said that he shared her "desire that the relations between India and the United States be further strengthened," and thanked her for her "very thoughtful message on my re-election as President of the United States."

27 The President of Bangla Desh, Mr. Abu Sayeed Chowdhury, arrived in New Delhi on a 10 day state visit.

28 President Z.A. Bhutto of Pakistan inaugurated the Karachi nuclear power plant with a pledge to use nuclear energy for peaceful purposes only.

November-December

As a result of the failure of the monsoon, the Indian Government's buffer grain stock fell from 9 million to 5 million tons between July and October 1972, and was expected to be exhausted by March 1973. The Government in consequence was compelled to abandon its policy of self-sufficiency, and entered into contracts in November and December 1972 for the purchase of 2 million tons of grain from the U.S., Canada, Argentina, and Australia.

December

11 It was officially announced in New Delhi that Mr. Patrick Daniel Moynihan had been appointed U.S. Ambassador to India, succeeding Mr. Kenneth Keating.

14 The Constitution of the People's Republic of Bangla Desh was signed by members of the Constituent Assembly in Dacca. Prime Minister Sheikh Mujibur Rehman was the first to sign the master copies written in Bengali and English. On December 16, 1972 the Constitution came into force, to mark the first anniversary of the liberation of Bangla Desh.

16 The Foreign Office of Bangla Desh announced that Mr. Hossain Ali, High Commissioner in Australia, had been appointed Ambassador to the U.S.A.

19 Addressing a news conference at Colombo, Sri Lanka, the Deputy Minister for Defense and External Affairs, Mr. Lakshman Jayakodi, said that no foreign power had facilities on the east coast and, "even if asked, we will definitely not accede to such a request." Sri Lanka at that time had a proposal before the United Nations to declare the Indian Ocean region a peace zone.

20 India and Pakistan announced completion of the withdrawal of their troops to the international border in conformity with the Simla Agreement, in a joint statement, issued in Islamabad and New Delhi.

31 On this date the Government of the U.S. had rupee funds in India totalling Rs. 687 crores, resulting from PL-480 transactions for the import of foodgrains since 1956, and non-PL 480 credits from development assistance under PL-665, repayments and interest payments.

1973

January

20 The Pakistan Government announced that it was setting up an inquiry commission to investigate alleged cases of atomic spying by Pakistan International Airlines flying over China. The affair came to light on April 11, 1972 when the Karachi newspaper *Morning News* reported that a special commission was investigating the use of instruments and tapes for top level espionage missions on the Dacca-Shanghai route.

February

5-11 In the current quarterly issue of scholarly journal published by the Far Eastern Institute of the USSR Academy of Sciences *Problemi Dalnevo Vostoka*, Soviet scholars discarded their sympathetic reserve in favour of a frank exposition of Chinese cunning and full support to the Indian position on its territorial problems with China and Pakistan. Official maps of the Sino-Indian border remained to be changed, however.

February, first week

Pakistan's Law Minister, Mr. Abdul Hafex Pirzada, paid a three-day visit to Moscow, during which he signed a Cultural Agreement with the Soviet Government and continued talks on improving economic and trade ties. Mr. Pirzada's principal mission, however was political—to secure Soviet help in getting the release of prisoners of war in India. As a special envoy to Moscow of Pakistan President Bhutto, he discussed this question with the Soviet Foreign Minister Mr. Andrei Gromyko.

February

18 The Finance Minister of Bangla Desh, Mr. Tajuddin Ahmed, said in Dacca that Bangla Desh had formally become a member of the Asian Development Bank (ADB), an affiliated body of the World Bank.

February

19 The Indian Charge d'Affaires Mr. Brajesh Mishra, walked out of a banquet in Peking, China, during a speech by Begum Bhutto, wife of the Pakistan President, who had arrived on the inaugural Pakistan International Airlines flight to Peking. Mr. Mishra left when Begum Bhutto said, "We are still in the process of recovery from the traumatic events of December 1971, when by use of naked force efforts were made to destroy the very existence of our State."

February

27 Pakistan's Ambassador to the USA, Mr. Sultan Mohammed Khan, told an Overseas Writers Luncheon in Washington that his country welcomed the arms it had been able to obtain from China and France, but it still would like to see a renewal of its traditional arms supply from the United States. He also accused India of pressuring USA to recognize her "dominant position" in South

Asia and to refrain permanently from any further arms shipments to Pakistan.

February

27 Asked what was Pakistan's real role in the visit of Dr. Kissinger to Peking in the fall of 1971 and the subsequent groundwork for President Nixon's visit in February 1972, Mr. Khan said that it was very limited. He explained that Pakistan merely communicated certain views, presumably the feelers from President Nixon, that he was interested in a detente—and provided certain communication facilities—presumably the PIA plane and crew which secretly flew Dr. Kissinger and his aides to Peking.

February

27 Although officially opened in a ceremony on February 1971, the Karakoram Highway which connects Gilgit and Hunza with Kashgar in Sinkiang China, had not yet been opened to full traffic, Pakistan's Ambassador to the USA noted in a speech.

February

28 The United States Ambassador, Mr. Daniel Patrick Moynihan, presented his credentials to President V.V. Giri of India, at Rashtrapati Bhavan in New Delhi.

March

1 Pakistan and the United States signed agreements for three separate development loans amounting to $64 million; $40 million for import of industrial commodities, $20 million for import of fertilizers, and $4 million for completion of the Tarbela Dam.

March

10 The Soviet Union and Pakistan signed an Agreement which would have the effect of taking away from Pakistan the debt payment liabilities for the State credits utilized in East Pakistan before December 1971.

March

14 It was officially announced in Washington that the United States had resumed sales of non-lethal military equipment plus spare parts to Pakistan and India. State Department spokesman Charles Bray said that the USA had no intention of entering into an arms race in South Asia, and that both Pakistan and India had been informed of the US decision. Through Ambassador Daniel Moynihan, the Indian Government said that any resumption of American arms supply to Pakistan would be a negative factor in normalizing India's relations with both of them.

March

14 It was announced in Washington that the U.S. had lifted the embargo on arms supplies to India and Pakistan imposed in December 1971 at the time of the Indo-Pakistan War. That is, the State Department explained, the U.S. could sell "non-lethal" equipment and spare parts to either Pakistan or India.

March

15 The United States announced the release of a $87.6 million

development loan to India—which had remained suspended since December 1971—for priority imports. The announcement was made by Mr. D.G. McDonald, Assistant Administrator of the AID, in testimony before a House Foreign Affairs sub-committee. The release of the funds was timed to follow the State Department's announcement that Pakistan had been given over $14 million worth of military equipment, including reconditioned aircraft engines.

March

15 At a news conference President Nixon stressed that the military sales to Pakistan would not affect the balance of power in the subcontinent, where "India's superiority is so enormous that the possibility of Pakistan being a threat to India is absurd."

March

23 Press reports quoted official sources as saying that the Soviet Union had offered to assist Sri Lanka develop in a big way key sectors of the economy, including oil, fertilizers and petro-chemical industries. The Soviet Union signed an agreement on March 26, 1973 to provide Sri Lanka with aid worth ĸs. 1.9 million for expansion of a Government-owned State flour mill, and equipment and machinery required for production of components for pre-fabricated housing.

April

1 Following the failure of the 1972 monsoon in most states of India, and with the continuation of drought conditions into summer 1973, a plan under which the Government took over wholesale trade in foodgrains was implemented in the wheat-growing states of Punjab, Haryana, Madhya Pradesh, Uttar Pradesh, Maharashtra and Gujarat.

April

2-8 Mr. Triloki Nath Kaul, former Foreign Secretary, was appointed India's Ambassador, to the USA, succeeding Mr. L.K. Jha.

April

10 A bilateral Aid Agreement between Bangla Desh and the United States for $30 million was signed in Dacca, for supply of vital agricultural input, such as fertilizers, insecticides and vegetable seeds from the USA.

April

19 In his annual report on US foreign policy issued in Washington, the Secretary of State, Mr. William Rogers pledged "to continue our strong support for the viability and cohesion of Pakistan," justified by "our long-standing relationship and its importance to the stability of the entire region." Turning to India, Mr. Rogers said that in recent months India had expressed a desire to improve the relations with the USA. "We reciprocate that desire. We will look to India as South Asia's largest nation to play a leading role in building a climate for peace in South Asia ..."

April

23 The UN General Assembly adopted a formal declaration making
the Indian Ocean a zone of peace. While granting the unimpeded
use of the Indian Ocean for peaceful navigation, the declaration
stated that "warships and military aircraft may not use the Indian
Ocean for any threat or use of force against the sovereignty,
territorial integrity and independence of any littoral or hinterland
States of the Indian Ocean in contravention of the purposes and
the principles of the UN Charter."

April

26 The Dacca newspaper, *Bangla Bani*, quoting responsible sources,
said on April 26 that Bangladesh had received 10 MIG-21 fighter
planes from the Soviet Union and would establish its first fighter
squadron in the next few weeks. The planes were given following
Soviet assurances of military assistance to the Prime Minister,
Sheikh Mujibur Rehman, on his visit to Moscow in March 1972.

April

27 Pakistan and the Soviet Union signed in Islamabad a three-year
Trade Agreement, providing for Soviet import a number of
manufactured goods, including cotton textile, hosiery, towels and
sheets, machine-made carpets. footwear and surgical instruments.
The Soviet Union would export, among other things, dyes and
chemicals, pharmaceuticals and tractors.

May

3 President Richard Nixon asserted that U.S.A will not join any
groupings or pursue any politics directed against India, in his
annual State of the World message. Stressing India's stature as
a "major country", he said that while India's relationship with
the major Powers was for it to decide, "We have a natural concern
that India not be locked into exclusive ties with major countries
directed against us or against other countries with whom we have
relationships which we value." In regard to aid, he said where
"our economic assistance does not serve mutual interests, it should
not be provided," but added that "where it does, ways must be
found to assure that the form of aid is consistent with the dignity
of both the donor and recipient", with the donor not expecting
"special influence in return." ...In short, he said. "USA wants to
see a subcontinent that is independent, progressive and peaceful.
We believe India shares these objectives, and this can be the firm
basis of a constructive relationship."

May

5 The Director of the Stockholm International Peace Research Institute (SIPRI), Mr. Frank Barnaby of Britain, said that of the
several countries with the capability, "India is probably closest
to acquiring nuclear armaments. There is an influential group
of politicians in India lobbying for the development of a peaceful
nuclear programme, and it is only a matter of time before India

may decide to develop nuclear weapons. . . . ", in order to "keep her prestige and leading role in Asia."

May

5 It was disclosed in a news dispatch that China was supplying TU-16 jet bomber aircraft to Pakistan, and Chinese advisers, and pilots and aircraft maintenance technicians had arrived in large numbers in Pakistan to train Pakistan Air Force personnel on the use of the TU-16 aircraft.

May

29 The International Development Association (IDA) an affiliate of the World Bank, announced that it had granted $71 million in two credits for agriculture in India, financing farmers in Madhya Pradesh and Uttar Pradesh in a three-year programme designed to increase agricultural production.

June

8 The International Development Association (IDA) the soft loan affiliate of the World Bank, announced a loan of $100 million to India for import of industrial raw materials, components and spares for medium and large-scale enterprises in selected priority industries.

June

15 The Aid Consortium announced at the end of its meeting in Paris that member-States and institutions had agreed to commit for the current year non-project assistance including debt relief of $70 million and project assistance of about $500 million to India.

June

17 During an official visit to Canada, Prime Minister of India Mrs. Gandhi had discussed the possibility of importing wheat with the Canadian Prime Minister, Mr. Trudeau, and in New Delhi in June Mr. Ahmed had raised this subject with Mr. Daniel Moynihan, the U.S. Ambassador.

June

18 The US Navy put into operation a communication station on the British-held island of Diego Garcia in the Indian Ocean. The station will help in controlling movements of American ships and planes in the area. The station was commissioned on March 20, but there was no public announcement. USA is therefore the first of the super-Powers to establish a military base on foreign territory in the Indian Ocean. Indian protests went unheeded in both Washington and London.

June

18 President Richard Nixon of the USA and Soviet Communist Party Secretary Mr. Leonid Brezhnev, met in a marathon summit session in Washington, and signed agreements (1) committing their nations to negotiate before the end of next year a Treaty calling for mutual reduction of nuclear weapons; (2) undertaking to do everything possible to avoid a nuclear war not only between their two nations;

but also with third nations; and (3) to increase commercial ties between their nations, and to lay plans for establishing a joint "chamber of commerce."

June

18-19   The Chinese Foreign Minister, Mr. Chi Peng-fei, visited Karachi for talks with President Z.A. Bhutto. Topics discussed included the Pakistan prisoners of war, and the situation on the sub-continent.

June

26   The Pakistan Government appointed Mr. Mumtaj Ali Alvie, the Foreign Secretary as the new Ambassador to China to replace Mr. Agha Shahi.

July

10   The National Assembly of Pakistan approved a resolution giving President Z. A. Bhutto authority to recognize Bangla Desh.

July

13   Mr. Munir Ahmed, Chairman of the Pakistan Atomic Energy Commission said that plans had been finalized for setting up a giant nuclear power station in the northern part of the country, to be completed in two and one half years.

July

26   The Minister of Agriculture Mr. Fakhruddin Ali Ahmed announced in the Lok Sabha that the Government proposed to make further purchases from the United States, Canada, Argentina and Australia.

August

8   Bangladesh signed the first Agreement with USA for the purchase of 80,000 tons of wheat under the amended PL-480 Food for Peace Act which provides for payment in dollars.

August

28   In an agreement signed in New Delhi by India and Pakistan, the repatriation of prisoners, from Pakistan and India and Bangla Desh, as well as other humanitarian problems left over from the 1971 war were dealt with. Addressing a news conference at Rawalpindi the next day, the Pakistan Minister of State for Defence and Foreign Affairs, Mr. Aziz Ahmed, indicated that Pakistan would recognize Bangla Desh soon.

August

30   Pakistan's Minister of State for Foreign Affairs and Defence, Mr. Aziz Ahmed, paid a visit to Peking, after returning from successful talks with India in New Delhi. In Peking he met with Foreign Minister Chi P'eng-fei, and Premier Chou-en-Lai. At a banquet in honor of Mr. Ahmed, Mr. Chi P'eng-fei reiterated Chinese support for the Pakistan Government in combating "foreign interference and defending State sovereignty."

September

10   Pakistan to get 60,000 tons of wheat from the USA on an urgent

basis under an agreement signed in Islamabad. USA's President Nixon would also authorize supply of an additional 30,000 tons through the World Food Programme.

September

18 Meeting in Washington, President Nixon and Pakistan's Prime Minister Mr. Zulfikar Ali Bhutto reviewed plans for future long-term US assistance to Pakistan. Mr. Nixon assured Mr. Bhutto of "strong US support for Pakistan's independence and territorial integrity," which he considered a guiding principle of US foreign policy.

September

18 President Nixon of the USA announced that he intended to nominate the veteran diplomat Mr. Henry Byroade, to be U.S. Ambassador to Pakistan.

September

28 The Soviet Union offered India 2 million tons of food grains, including some rice, on a loan basis. The offer came personally from Mr. Leonid Brezhnev, General Secretary of the Communist Party of the Soviet Union, and it was accepted by the Government of India.

September

28 The U.S. Senate voted to prevent the Administration from agreeing to settle an Indian debt of $3,000 million worth of rupees (arising out of the wheat sales under PL-480) for less than the full amount unless Congress agreed to such a step. The measure, attached as an amendment to a Military Procurement Bill, was introduced by Senator Harry Byrd. who said the step was taken because Mr. Daniel Moynihan, US Ambassador to India, had recommended that the Indian debt be settled at a substantial discount.

September, 3rd week

During the visit of Pakistan Prime Minister Bhutto to Washington it was decided to let Pakistan keep six helicopters sent there to fight floods in August despite an embargo on the delivery of military weapons to South Asia. State Department officials said on September 26 that the helicopters were unarmed, and therefore, the action was not contrary to present US policy.

October, 1st week

India repatriated 1680 more Pakistani prisoners of war as Pakistan and Bangla Desh mutually decided to continue the air-lift of stranded citizens beyond the original deadline of Sept. 30.

October

8 A Colombo report said that China had agreed to provide Sri Lanka with an advance supply of 40,000 tons of rice immediately, to be set off against what Sri Lanka would buy next year under the Sino-Lanka bilateral trade pact now due for renewal.

November

26 The Soviet Communist Party chief, Mr. Leonid Illyich Brezhnev, received an enthusiastic welcome when he arrived in New Delhi for a five-day visit. Mr. Brezhnev and Mrs. Gandhi highlighted the common ideal of peaceful co-existence shared by their countries at a State banquet on November 26. At a civic reception in Delhi on November 27, Mr. Brezhnev said "We shall stand by you in the future, in times of trial, test and triumph." The need for long-term cooperation was stressed. A number of agreements were signed on November 29.

December

12 An agreement was reached in New Delhi for resolving the problem of US rupee holdings amounting to Rs. 2,497 crores either already standing in USA's name with the Reserve Bank of India or which would be due to it in coming years.

December

26 According to an official communique issued in Colombo, China will supply to Sri Lanka 200,000 tons of rice by the end of 1974 including a gift of 40,000.

December

27 India and the Soviet Union signed in New Delhi a Protocol providing for Soviet aid for the coal industry including development of two or more large open cast mines in the Singrauli coalfield in UP and MP.

December

29 Bangla Desh and India agreed in New Delhi on long-term bilateral cooperation in regard to the production of raw jute and export of jute goods.

December

31 In another initiative to facilitate the process of normalization in the subcontinent, India proposed to Pakistan to exchange delegations to start negotiations in terms of the Simla Agreements.

1974

January

20 A French news agency, quoting authoritative sources in Islamabad, reported that China would collaborate in production of ground-to-air missiles in Pakistan. The plan had been initiated when General Tikka Khan, Army Chief of Staff for Pakistan, had visited Peking in January 1973.

January

22 Prime Minister of Sri Lanka Mrs. Bandaranaike arrived in New Delhi to a warm welcome on a week's official visit.

February

18 India and USA formally signed the agreement on the disposal of the USA-held PL-480 rupees. The agreement was signed in New Delhi by American Ambassador Daniel Moynihan and Mr. M.G.

Kaul, Secretary, Department of Economic Affairs, Finance Ministry.

February

22 Pakistan and Bangla Desh recognized each other, 26 months after the erstwhile East Pakistan wrenched itself away to become a sovereign nation.

May

12-16 The Prime Minister of Bangladesh, Sheikh Mujibur Rehman, paid a state visit to New Delhi, during which he had talks with the Indian Prime Minister, Mrs. Indira Gandhi, on a wide range of political and economic questions.

May

18 India became the sixth nuclear power when she carried out her first nuclear test, involving the detonation of a plutonium device in the 10-15 kiloton range at a depth of over 100 metres in the Rajasthan desert. Responding to foreign criticisms of India's nuclear test on May 25, Prime Minister Gandhi said: "The same argument (i.e., that such a poor country such as India could afford the luxury of peaceful nuclear experiment) was advanced when we established our steel mills and machine-building plants. They are necessary for development, for it is only through acquisition of higher technology that you can overcome poverty and economic backwardness. Is it the contention that it is all right for the rich to use nuclear energy for destructive purposes but not right for a poor country to find out whether it can be used for construction ? . . ."

June

7 An application by Bangladesh for admission to the United Nations was unanimously approved by the Security Council, will go before the UN General Assembly at its 29th session in the autumn Bangladesh's first application for membership had been vetoed by China in August 1972.

June

18 The Chinese Government announced that it had successfully conducted a new nuclear test "over the western region" on the previous day. The communique declared that "the conducting of necessary and limited nuclear tests by China is entirely for the purpose of defence and for breaking the nuclear monopoly of the super-Powers and for ultimately abolishing nuclear weapons", and that "at no time and in no circumstances" would China be the first to use nuclear weapons."

June

27 The Prime Minister of Pakistan, Mr. Bhutto, arrived in Dacca for the first official visit to Bangladesh by a Pakistani leader since the country became independent. Talks between Sheikh Mujibur Rehman and Mr.Bhutto produced no agreement on the issues discussed, which included the repatriation of refugees to Pakistan from Bangladesh, the exchange of diplomatic missions, assets and liabilities, etc.

July

25 President of the U.S., Richard Nixon, accompanied, among others, by Dr. Henry Kissinger, Secretary of State, visited the Soviet Union, where on July 8 President Nixon and Soviet leader Brezhnev signed several statements including a Soviet-American treaty on the limitation of underground nuclear weapon tests, effective March 31, 1976.

EPILOGUE

The Tilt Policy Revisited :
Nixon-Kissinger Geopolitics
and South Asia

Christopher Van Hollen

THE WORD "Tilt," now part of the common parlance, was introduced into the American political lexicon just over eight years
ago, compliments of columnist Jack Anderson. During the
Indo-Pakistan war over Bangladesh, Anderson's columns carried
excerpts from secret White House meetings at one of which
an exasperated Henry Kissinger warned government officials
that he was "getting hell every half hour from the President
that we are not being tough enough on India." The President
"does not believe we are carrying out his wishes," Kissinger
complained. "He wants to tilt in favor of Pakistan."[1] Although

© 1980 by The Regents of the University of California, Reprinted from
   Asian Survey, Vol. 20, No. 4, pp. 339-361 by permission of The
   Regents.
 1. Excerpts from the secret meetings of the Washington Special
   Action Group (WSAG) began to appear in Jack Anderson's
   syndicated columns in mid-December 1971. On January 4, 1972,
   Kissinger charged that Anderson's quotations were "out of
   context," whereupon Anderson released to the press the full texts
   of the minutes of the WSAG meetings of December 3, 5, 6, and 8.
   These, and other secret documents, became known as "The
   Anderson Papers." The WSAG minutes are contained in Marta
   R. Nicholas and Philip Oldenburg, comps. *Bangladesh : The Birth
   of a Nation—A Handbook of Background Information and Document-
   ary Sources* (Madras : M. Seshachalam and Company, 1972),
   Appendix 10.

Anderson won a Pulitzer Prize for his journalistic coup, his revelations were politically damaging to Richard Nixon, and personally embarrassing to Nixon's Assistant for National Security Affairs. A few days before, Kissinger had assured a background press conference that the White House was evenhanded, and that charges of an anti-India bias were "totally inaccurate."[2]

In *White House Years*, Kissinger provides an aggressive defense of the Nixon administration's controversial handling of the nine-month Bangladesh crisis in 1971, characterizing it as "perhaps the most complex issue of Nixon's first term."[3] Across 76 pages of a chapter appropriately titled, "The Tilt," he paints the South Asia scene with broad and vigorous rhetorical strokes, portraying it as only one part of a much larger geopolitical canvas. Just as the work of an accomplished muralist depends for total effect upon the foundation strokes, an acceptance of Kissinger's claim that the White House's geopolitical design succeeded in South Asia depends upon an acceptance of his basic assumptions.

The thesis of this essay is that many of Kissinger's assumptions and conclusions are incorrect. Contrary to his claims, the United States did not need to remain mute to the Pakistan army's repressions in East Pakistan to protect the White House opening to China. Washington could have pressed President Yahya Khan harder to make political concessions in East Pakistan. India did not have a grand design to dismember West Pakistan; nor was the Soviet Union urging Indira Gandhi's government in that direction. It was both unnecessary and unwise to raise the Bangladesh regional crisis to the level of global geopolitics. Kissinger is wrong in concluding that Nixon's willingness to risk war with the Soviet Union, including the deployment of a U.S. aircraft carrier to South Asia, saved West Pakistan and preserved the structure of world peace. In sum, the White House policies, so spiritedly defended in Kissinger's

---

2. Believing he was helping the administration, Senator Barry Goldwater inserted Kissinger's background remarks in the *Congressional Record*, December 9, 1971, pp. S21012-S21016.

3. Unless otherwise indicated, all quotations from Kissinger are from chapter XXI of his *White House Years* (Boston : Little, Brown and Company, 1979), pp. 842-918.

memoirs, were badly flawed and ill served the interests of the United States.

White House Perceptions

As *White House Years* makes clear, the secret opening to China was the most important factor shaping Nixon's and Kissinger's reactions to the 1971 events in East Pakistan—an area of no strategic importance to the United States. Nixon had first broached the idea of an American overture to China to President Yahya when he visited Lahore in July 1969; he later used Pakistan, as well as Romania, as a secret channel through which to pass several exploratory messages to China. Although they were unaware of these overtures at the time, members of the National Security Council's Senior Review Group (SRG) were exposed to the White House's sensitivity toward China on March 6, three weeks before the Pakistan civil war broke out. Kissinger convened the SRG meeting, attended by senior representatives from State, Defense, and CIA, to review U.S. options in face of mounting tensions between the two West Pakistani leaders, Yahya Khan and Zulfikar Ali Bhutto, and the East Pakistani leader, Mujibur Rahman (Mujib). At this first SRG meeting on South Asia, Under Secretary of State for Political Affairs Alexis Johnson expressed the State Department view that the crisis was neither an issue between the major powers nor a matter of U.S.-Indian confrontation. The Soviets, Indians and Americans, Johnson asserted, all considered that their interests were served by continuation of a united Pakistan.[4]

Johnson suggested that one option for the U.S. was to try to discourage President Yahya from using force in East Pakistan against Mujib and his Awami League followers. But he did not press the point after Kissinger cautioned SRG members to keep in mind President Nixon's "special relationship" with

4. Informal Notes, Senior Review Group (SRG) meeting, March 6, 1971. There were no formal agreed minutes of either the SRG or the WSAG meetings. Representatives of individual departments took their own notes. The Anderson Papers, for example, were based on Defense Department notes. In this article, similar notes, recorded by one or more members of the State Department, are referred to as "Informal Notes."

Yahya—a relationship that surprised and perplexed the participants. The President, he said, would be reluctant to suggest that Yahya exercise restraint in East Pakistan, adding that the Pakistanis, "wouldn't give a damn" if the U.S. Ambassador were instructed to weigh in with Yahya. Following this cautionary note, and further discussion of various alternatives, the SRG members concluded that "massive inaction" was the best policy for the United States.[5]

In addition to the China initiative, Nixon's reaction to South Asia was influenced by his long-standing dislike for India and the Indians, and his warm feelings toward Pakistan. Because these feelings were evident to anyone who had close association with Nixon, Kissinger was not credible when he told the press in December 1971 that he was unaware of the President's "preferences for Pakistani leaders over Indian leaders."[6] Discounting the stereotypes, he is more accurate in his memoirs in explaining that the "bluff, direct military chiefs of Pakistan" were more congenial to Nixon than "the complex and apparently haughty Brahmin leaders of India." When Yahya visited Washington in October 1970, Nixon assured him that "nobody has occupied the White House who is friendlier to Pakistan."[7] When Mrs. Gandhi's actions ran counter to White House desires, Nixon's customary sobriquet was replaced by more unprintable epithets. Despite disclaimers, Richard Nixon's contrasting feelings toward the Indian and Pakistani leaders undoubtedly colored his judgments in 1971.

5. *Ibid.*
6. *Congressional Record*, December 9, 1971, p. S21104. See also Marvin Kalb and Bernard Kalb, *Kissinger* (Boston : Little, Brown and Company, 1974), p. 258, and interviews with Marvin Kalb and two State Department officials in Lawrence Lifschultz, *Bangladesh* : *The Unfinished Revolution* (London : Zed Press, 1979), pp. 159-161. These interviews are reproduced in the appendix of the Lifschultz book; this author disagrees with some of Lifschultz's interpretations of the 1971 events.
7. G. W. Choudhury, "Reflections on Sino-Pakistan Relations," *Pacific Community*, 7 : 2, January 1976, p. 266.

The Humanitarian Issue

Kissinger's comments that there was "justified outrage" when reports began to come in of the Pakistani "atrocities" in Bengal are the words of the elder statesman-author, viewing events retrospectively ; they were not the words of the Assistant to the President in March-April 1971. At no time during that period is Kissinger on record as voicing outrage or humanitarian concern as the Pakistani armed forces obeyed Yahya's crackdown orders with a vengeance. To escape the repression, millions of the frightened Bengalis, mostly Hindus, poured across the borders into India while the Awami League leaders who were left behind were arrested and, in the case of Mujib, sent to to prison in West Pakistan. Outside the confines of the White House Situation Room, substantial parts of the American public, media, and Congress were indeed expressing outrage.

Because the Awami League, which favored greater autonomy for East Pakistan, had won an overwhelming victory in the December 1970 elections—capturing 167 out of 169 seats— the strong emotions in the U.S. reflected a belief that a free political movement was being brutally liquidated by Pakistani military forces.[8] Of particular concern to Congress, the Pakistan military used American-supplied equipment, M-24 tanks and F-86 aircraft, to suppress the Bengalis.

Outrage at the Pakistani atrocities was also felt within the bureaucracy—especially at middle levels in State and AID—but most directly by members of the American Consulate General in Dacca. The Dacca Americans were already offended by Washington's insistence that the airlift of dependents from Dacca be officially characterized as a "thinout" rather than an "evacuation" so as not to offend Yahya. As the carnage continued and the White House failed to issue a statement of condemnation, Consul General Archer Blood sent a telegram to Washington, signed by nineteen members of the Consulate-General, registering "strong dissent" with a policy that "serves neither our moral interests, broadly defined, nor our national interests,

---

8. In a White Paper issued in August 1971, the Government of Pakistan stated it had been compelled to take military action because of the "atrocities and acts of lawlessness committed by the Awami League militants prior to 25 March, 1971." Nichoals and Oldenburg, *Bangladesh : The Birth of a Nation*, p. 84.

narrowly defined." It was an eloquent expression of concern, transmitted through the State Department "Dissent Channel" specifically designed for such purposes. But Kissinger denigrates the message, claiming that it was deliberately given low classification to assure that it would be leaked. However, in noting that Nixon ordered the transfer of the Consul General, he acknowledges "there was some merit to the charge of moral insensitivity."[9]

In defending their stance, Kissinger explains that he and Nixon faced a dilemma : "The United States could not condone a brutal military repression in which thousands of civilians were killed and from which millions fled to India for safety," but the East Pakistan crisis "burst upon us while Pakistan was our only channel to China; we had no other means of communication with Peking." On the first point, Kissinger is insensitive to the fact that the administration's official silence was interpreted as condoning the atrocities in East Pakistan, and that the administration's subsequent problems with American public opinion stemmed largely from this perception. It is most unlikely that a statement of U.S. disapprobation would have caused President Yahya to back out of his intermediary role ; he was honored to have been tapped by Nixon as a communications link with China and desperately wanted to retain the goodwill of both Washington and Beijing.[10] The second point is factually incorrect. When the fighting broke out in East Pakistan, on March 25, there were two channels to Beijing, one through the Pakistanis, the other through the Romanians. Of the two, the White House had a "slight preference for the Pakistani channel."[11] Not until a month later, when Pakistani Ambassador Agha Hilaly delivered a reply to Nixon from Chou-en-Lai, did the White House opt for the Islamabad link.

9. The text is in Lifschultz, *Bangladesh : The Unfinished Revolution*, p. 158. Consul General Blood later received the American Foreign Service Association's Herter Award, which is awarded for "intellectual courage and creative dissent."

10. As G. W. Choudhury, formerly a member of Yahya's cabinet, noted : "Pakistan was delighted to have this opportunity . . . it was almost a God-sent gift for Pakistan," *Pacific Community*, 7 : 2, January 1976, p. 264.

11. Kissinger, *White House Years*, p. 704.

Arms and Economic Assistance

Kissinger is highly critical of the State Department's initial reaction to the crisis, which took the form of actions to stop U.S. military supply to Pakistan and to hold up U.S. economic assistance. He attributes both actions, which he says were taken without White House clearance, to the Department's ignorance of the China initiative and its "traditional Indian bias." On one aspect there is full agreement : the State Department was totally ignorant of the China initiative. Not until three months later, when Kissinger was in Islamabad about to board a Pakistani aircraft for Beijing was the Department's hapless leader, Secretary of State William P. Rogers, informed of Kissinger's secret China trip—the most important foreign policy initiative of the Nixon years. On the other point there is also agreement : the State Department did have an "Indian bias." This was not because, as Nixon was fond of saying, it was staffed with soft-headed "Indian lovers" but because there were hard-headed reasons for the priority attached to U.S. relations with India.

After the Pakistan military crackdown, an Interdepartmental Group consisting of Harold Saunders from Kissinger's NSC staff, and representatives of State, Defense, AID, CIA, and USIA, met to reassess U.S.-Pakistan relations and review policy options. The group's unanimous conclusion, forwarded to the White House for the April 19 Senior Review Group meeting, was that the Pakistan army's action in East Pakistan had reinforced the relative priority of U.S. interest in India, which had already been apparent because of India's greater size, resources, and political, strategic, and economic potential. In contrast to the deteriorating situation in Pakistan, the group judged that India seemed to be moving into a period of new political stability and was demonstrating a renewed willingness to develop a cooperative relationship with the United States. Thus, on the basis of an objective assessment of the power equation in South Asia, there was government-wide agreement that India merited greater attention in the terms of U.S. interests.

The Department of State did not move toward a new arms embargo against Pakistan because it had any emotional bias toward India ; instead, in light of clear evidence that U.S.-

supplied tanks and aircraft were being used against the Bengalis, and strong media and Congressional reaction to such use, the Department imposed a "hold" on military equipment for Pakistan pending a formal White House decision. But in a textbook example of a bureaucratic snafu, although the State Department thought it had stopped all military supplies to Pakistan—and had conveyed that impression to the Congress and the Indians—small amounts of arms, most of which were outside U.S. government control, were shipped after March 25; this equipment had been purchased under licenses issued before the hold action. When the *New York Times* reported in late June that Pakistani freighters had sailed, or were about to sail from U.S. ports with arms, a credibility gap was created with Congress and with the Indian government; Indian Foreign Minister Swaran Singh had just returned to New Delhi from Washington with what he thought were assurances no arms were being shipped.[12]

These State Department actions on military and economic assistance were reported to the White House with the statement that they were "interim decisions which will require formal ratification," and the interim actions were discussed with Kissinger at the April 19 SRG meeting.[13] General guidance from the President was needed, Kissinger agreed, and promised to talk to the President and Secretary Rogers to determine how to proceed. Unfortunately, the promised guidance in such cases seldom materialized in a form helpful to the bureaucracy, either then or at other times during the nine-month Indo-Pakistan crisis.

Kissinger sought to exercise close White House control throughout the crisis, but there was no real Presidential leader-

---

12. The amount of arms shipped to Pakistan after March 25, 1971 was not large, although the exact amount may never be known. Senator Edward Kennedy of Massachusetts used the figure of $50 million on several occasions, and this figure was given prominence by the Indian press. But a General Accounting Office study, undertaken at Kennedy's request, later reported that $3.8 million in military supplies were exported between March 25 and September 30, 1971 on licenses issued before March 25; it is unlikely that arms shipped after March 25 exceeded $5 million. *New York Times*, February 5, 1972.

13. Informal Notes, SRG meeting April 19, 1971.

ship through the National Security Council (NSC), which met only twice, on an ad hoc basis. There was little direct communication by the President with top officials other than Kissinger.[14] As Kissinger suggests in describing one of the NSC meetings, the problem was that the President's efforts to express his wishes "as usual" were "so ambiguous that they made things worse." Similarly, little coherent policy direction was conveyed by Kissinger through the two NSC committees he chaired : the Senior Review Group (SRG) and the Washington Special Action Group (WSAG).[15] Many of the staff studies and option papers sent from the bureaucracy to the White House were often either ignored or considered irrelevant to the larger, unexplained, Nixon-Kissinger game plan. The essentially technical guidelines transmitted back to the bureaucracy were hardly helpful in providing senior departmental officials with a conceptual appreciation of the broader geopolitical principles, which, one now learns, were the mainsprings of White House policy.

White House vs. The Bureaucracy

By the summer of 1971, Henry Kissinger writes, on "no other issue—except perhaps Cambodia—was the split between the White House and the Departments so profound as on the Indo-Pakistan crisis." Yet he seems unaware of the fundamental nature of the differences, dismissing them as "trivial issues, any one of which would seem too lightweight or technical to raise to the President." A central issue, and certainly not a trivial one, was that of political accommodation in East Pakistan. State Department officials were convinced it would be impossible to resolve the crisis short of war unless Yahya was encouraged through private diplomatic channels to make

14. The first NSC meeting was held in San Clemente on July 16, the day after the China announcement; the second was in Washington on December 6, after India and Pakistan had gone to war. Both were essentially ad hoc discussions that did not deserve the label "NSC meetings." In addition, Nixon met briefly with senior officials dealing with South Asia on August 11 and December 9, 1971.

15. The membership of the SRG and WSAG was essentially the same : State, Defense, JCS, CIA, AID, and NSC staff. The SRG was converted into the WSAG when there was need for "crisis management."

genuine political concessions looking toward greater autonomy for East Pakistan.

Earlier White House reluctance to press Yahya harder
became more comprehensible with the dramatic July 15
announcement of the secret Kissinger trip to China via
Islamabad. Hopes rose among some officials that U.S. policy
toward South Asia would no longer be held hostage to the
China opening (a direct link to Beijing through Paris was
established the day after the announcement), but these hopes
were dashed by the new strategy that grew out of Kissinger's
visit to the subcontinent. Kissinger returned from Islamabad
convinced that Yahya would accept advice on such questions
as relief assistance for East Pakistan, but he would not be
amenable to U.S. suggestions for political accommodation;
specifically, Yahya would not deal with members of the out-
lawed Awami League—which had won 98% of the seats in the
East Pakistan elections.[16]

Therefore, the new Nixon-Kissinger strategy was to
separate the humanitarian aspects of the policy from
the political, a strategy that had a double purpose. By expend-
ing large sums of money for the refugees in India, the
White House hoped to reduce the barrage of criticism it was
receiving from the media and the Congress, led by Senator
Edward Kennedy as Chairman of the Judiciary Committee's
Subcommittee on Refugees. More to the point, it hoped that
this strategy would defuse pressures upon the White House to
exert influence on Yahya to make meaningful political concessions.

Almost to a person, the officials working on South Asia
were convinced that the White House strategy would not work.
They recognized the limited influence the U.S. could bring to
bear on Yahya; the Pakistani President's flexibility was circum-
scribed by important West Pakistani political and military
leaders who, understandably, were reluctant to countenance the
break up of their country. Nonetheless, Under Secretary of
State John Irwin and other senior U.S. officials believed a
greater effort should be made to persuade Yahya to face up to
the helplessness of his army's military position in East Pakistan,
and to encourage Yahya to deal realistically with some of the

16. Informal Notes, SRG meetings, July 23, 1971 and July 31, 1971.

more moderate elements of the Awami League. Unless there was genuine progress on the political front, the refugees would not return to East Pakistan, India would not stop supporting the guerrillas, it would be impossible to administer humanitarian relief in East Pakistan—and the prospects of war would mount.[17] This belief that the United States should make a greater effort to awaken Yahya to political realities was reinforced by the Pakistan president's sudden decision to hold a secret treason trial for Mujibur Rahman.

The First Tilt

Another difference between the White House and the bureaucracy was their midsummer assessments of Indian and Soviet intentions. In building his case in *White House Years*, Kissinger indicates that by the middle of 1971 Indian leaders had made a decision to launch an attack on East Pakistan; he believes they were also considering the destruction of West Pakistan as well, and were being encouraged by the Soviet Union, which "played a highly inflammatory role. . . acting throughout like a pyromaniac." Although the Indians were engaged in military contingency planning, and Mrs. Gandhi was under strong political pressure to act more decisively, there is no firm evidence that India by midsummer had made a definite decision to go to war or that the Soviets wanted war. In fact, contrary assessments were put forward by CIA Director Richard Helms and Assistant Secretary of State Joseph Sisco at the two Senior Review Group (SRG) meetings in late July.[18]

Against a background of these CIA/State Department assessments, Kissinger's remarks at the July 31 SRG meeting are particularly revealing. They belie his later statement that his celebrated instructions to tilt were taken "out of context," and that the White House had been pursuing an evenhanded policy. When Deputy AID Administrator Maurice Williams made the modest suggestion that the U.S. recommend to Yahya that he remove the army from civilian-type administration in East Pakistan so that relief assistance could go forward, Kissinger snapped back : "Why is it our business how they govern themselves ?," adding, in the first use of the word "tilt,"

17. Informal Notes, SRG meetings, July 23, 1971 and July 31, 1971.
18. *Ibid.*

that "the President always says to tilt toward Pakistan, but every proposal I get is in the opposite direction. Sometimes I think I am in a nut house."[19] In short, after the China announcement had presumably lessened U.S. obligations toward Yahya, and before the Indo-Soviet Treaty was signed, and at a time when both State and CIA judged war not imminent, Henry Kissinger was exhorting the bureaucracy to tilt toward Pakistan and discouraging any serious efforts to move Yahya toward political accommodation—the only route that gave any hope of avoiding war.

Kissinger's treatment of the Soviet-Indian Friendship Treaty of August 9, 1971, illustrates his technique of reinterpreting history in order to develop a dramatic geopolitical scenario against which to explain the White House's tilt policy. At the time, the treaty did not create a significant stir in Washington, either inside or outside the White House. Kissinger now describes it as a "bomb shell," charging that "Moscow threw a lighted match into the powder keg." He dismisses as "fatuous" a CIA intelligence report at the time that suggested that the Soviets may have regarded the treaty as an instrument through which they could exercise restraint over the Indians; he also contends that the treaty was not a reaction to American policy.[20]

It is true that a treaty between the Soviet Union and India had been under consideration for more than a year, but if there was any "bomb shell" that converted discussions into a formal text, it was undoubtedly the surprise announcement of Nixon's forthcoming visit to Beijing. The treaty gave Mrs. Gandhi, who was being attacked at home for a weak-kneed policy toward Pakistan, a diplomatic triumph by providing India with an offset to what many Indians perceived to be an emerging Washington-Islamabad-Beijing axis. Against the background of continuing U.S. arms supply to Pakistan, however small, and evidence that Islamabad was seeking a Chinese commitment to intervene militarily should India

19. Informal Notes, SRG Meeting, July 31, 1971.
20. The CIA report was leaked to the press, causing considerable consternation in the CIA. See *New York Times*, August 13, 1971 and Thomas Powers, *The Man Who Kept the Secrets : Richard Helms and the CIA* (New York: Alfred A. Knopf, 1979), p. 206.

attack, the treaty provided the Gandhi government the reassurance it needed—a warning to Beijing that any Chinese military moves against India might lead to a Soviet response. Furthermore, the limited increase in Soviet arms that followed the signing strengthened India's military position at a time when Kissinger had made it clear to the Indian government that, unlike 1962, India would not receive support from Washington in case of Chinese intervention.

The treaty did not mean unequivocal Soviet support for India nor a cessation of Moscow's efforts to encourage a political settlement. The Soviets continued to provide economic assistance to Pakistan, referred to "East Pakistan" rather than "Bangladesh," and called for a solution agreeable to "the entire people of Pakistan." To the displeasure of the Indian government, these general themes were reiterated by the Soviets in an exchange of top-level visits between New Delhi and Moscow during September and October as Moscow continued to counsel against use of force. Continued Soviet military supply to India was not inconsistent with this objective; in the Soviets' eyes, it enhanced India's sense of security—psychologically as well as militarily—and strengthened Moscow's ability to influence New Delhi.[21]

The Drift Toward War

Although Nixon in August told a rump NSC meeting in San Clemente that there could be no war between India and Pakistan, by early fall it was clear that the prospects of war were increasing. Kissinger's thesis is that while U.S. diplomacy worked actively during this period to urge restraint on all parties, and persuaded Yahya to make significant political concessions, Mrs. Gandhi, despite professions of peace, had already made a decision to go to war to establish Indian supremacy on the subcontinent.

When she came to Washington on November 4—5 for "the two most unfortunate meetings Nixon had with any foreign leader," Mrs. Gandhi was told by the President what the

21. On the Indo-Soviet treaty, see William J. Barnds, "Moscow and South Asia," *Problems of Communism*, Vol. 21, May—June 1972, pp. 24-25; also Robert Jackson, *South Asia Crisis : India, Pakistan, and Bangladesh* (New York: Praeger, 1975), pp. 72-73; and pp. 84-87.

United States had accomplished "through persuasion" with
Yahya, including appointment of a civilian governor for East
Pakistan, proclamation of an amnesty, the promise not to
execute Mujib, and Yahya's willingness to talk to some Bengali
leaders. Mrs. Gandhi and her senior advisers also were assured
that Yahya had a clear timetable for a political solution:
civilian government would be established in Pakistan by March,
with independence shortly thereafter.[22] But according to
Kissinger, Mrs. Gandhi listened to this presentation with
"aloof indifference." Yahya's mounting concessions "aggravated" her problem because of the "near certainty" they
would lead to a favorable outcome. "Mrs. Gandhi was going
to war," he says, "not because she was convinced of our failure,
but because she feared our success."

This is an extraordinary claim. The President's February
1972 Foreign Policy Report to the Congress, written by
Kissinger and his staff, candidly admitted that the "United
States cannot be certain that the steps it proposed would have
brought about a negotiation, or that such a negotiation would
have produced a settlement."[23] Kissinger, the Revisionist, now
asserts emphatically that the "near certainty" of "our success"
drove Mrs. Gandhi to war. In fact, it is most improbable that
any negotiations—which had not even begun at the time—
would have succeeded, even if the imprisoned Mujib had been
brought into the picture. Earlier contacts between the U.S.
Consulate General in Calcutta and some Bengali representatives had proved abortive; the controlling elements within the
Bangladesh government-in-exile apparently backed off from
these discussions because they did not have an independent Bangladesh as their objective, and because the

22. In his book, Kissinger gives the impression that the President did
most of the talking in "one of Nixon's better presentations." Mrs
Gandhi reports otherwise : " . . . it was not so much Mr. Nixon
talking as Mr. Kissinger, because Mr. Nixon would talk a
few minutes and would then say, 'Isn't that right, Henry?' and
from then on . . . I would talk with Henry rather than Nixon."
Gandhi interview with Jonathan Power of the *International Herald
Tribune*, reprinted in the *Washington Post*, December 30, 1979.

23. *U.S. Foreign Policy for the 1970's : The Emerging Structure of Power*,
A Report by Richard Nixon to the Congress, February 9, 1972,
p. 145.

Indians discouraged contacts with the Americans. Since Mujib by late 1971 would not have settled for less than independence, a demand Yahya could not meet, any negotiations were doomed to failure—which helps explain why they never occurred.

Similarly, it is highly unlikely that Yahya's timetable for political evolution would have succeeded. There was, first of all, no assurance that the civilian government he planned for late December would have included any Awami Leaguers who reflected the views of Mujibur Rahman. Since the Awami League had been banned, the most likely prospect would have been some type of puppet representation, unreflective of the political aspirations of the Bengalis. Given the unlikely prospect of any concession by Yahya on this point, there is no basis for Kissinger's anticipation of early autonomy for East Pakistan. The judgment he expressed to the press in December 1971 was closer to reality : "The U.S. recognized," Kissinger said in a prepared statement, "that the time required to bring about a political evolution . . . might be longer than the Indian capacity to withstand the pressures generated by the refugees."[24]

Nixon believes that Mrs. Gandhi purposely deceived him and that while they were talking in the White House she knew that her generals and advisers were planning to intervene in East Pakistan and were considering contingency plans for the West.[25] On her part, Mrs. Gandhi returned to New Delhi unconvinced that there was any prospect for a viable political settlement. By that time, a combination of factors combined to make the military option increasingly attractive to India: unrelieved pressure of the refugees, a perceived lack of progress toward political accommodation, assurances derived from the Indo-Soviet Treaty, and the probability that the Chinese would not intervene.

Most detached accounts of the Indo-Pakistan conflict set December 3 as the date the war formally began. On that day, Pakistani aircraft launched a surprise attack on eight Indian airfields in northern and western India, and Pakistani army

24. *Congressional Record*, December 9, 1971, p. S21015.
25. Richard Nixon, *RN : The Memoirs of Richard Nixon* (New York : Grosset and Dunlap, 1978), pp. 525-526.

units made limited strikes across the West Pakistan-Indian border. India retaliated with an all-out invasion of East Pakistan,
with air strikes in the west, and with an essentially holding
action on the ground in the west.

In Kissinger's book, the war begins on November 22 when
Washington received reports that regular Indian army units
had crossed into East Pakistan in support of the Mukti Bahini
guerrilla forces. Despite denials, Indian forces did make cross-
border forays—ostensibly to quell the shelling of Indian territory from East Pakistan, but undoubtedly also to tighten the
screws on the Pakistan army. Some troops remained in East
Pakistan until December 3.[26] However, the situation in late
November was ambiguous at best, as Kissinger acknowledges
in explaining that he successfully dissuaded Nixon from terminating U.S. aid to India until the provocation "was unambigu-
ous and the facts uncontestable."

Between November 23 and December 3, despite bureaucratic clashes between the White House and the State Department, the Nixon administration undertook a number of even-
handed moves in a final effort to prevent hostilities. Nixon sent
messages urging restraint to India, the Soviet Union, and
Pakistan, and the Chinese were kept informed of these actions
by Kissinger, who held his first secret meeting in New York
with Huang Hua, the new PRC Permanent Representative to
the United Nations. But these actions were of no avail.
Although Nixon's message to Yahya tried to dissuade him from
attacking India in the west to relieve the pressures in the east,
the Pakistani president, in a desperate, suicidal move, ordered
military attacks against western India that were doomed to
failure. These actions gave India the *causus belli* it needed to
move openly against East Pakistan.

A CIA Report That Counted

Shortly after war broke out on December 3, rapid Indian
military successes in East Pakistan rekindled White House
suspicions that this might be only the first step in India's
grand design to dismember West Pakistan and convert it into
a "vassal state." The origins of these suspicions were unclear.

26. Lachhman Singh, *Indian Sword Strikes in East Pakistan* (New
Delhi : Vikas, 1979), pp. 66-81.

They probably stem from Nixon and Kissinger's earlier conversations with Pakistani leaders, who had always questioned India's acceptance of the creation of Pakistan, from Kissinger's discussions in China, and from Mrs. Gandhi's remarks at the White House in November about the fragility and artificiality of the Pakistan state. Whatever the origin, the "dismemberment" thesis became an *idee fixe* for both Nixon and Kissinger. It helps explain their reflex reaction to a CIA intelligence Report, received in Washington a few days after the fighting began, which Nixon considered "one of the few really timely pieces of intelligence the CIA had ever given him."[27]

On the basis of information purportedly obtained from within Prime Minister Indira Gandhi's cabinet, CIA Director Richard Helms told a December 8 WSAG meeting that "before heeding a UN call for cease-fire, she intends to straighten out the southern border of Azad Kashmir. It is reported that prior to terminating present hostilities, Mrs. Gandhi intends to attempt to eliminate Pakistan's armor and air force capabilities."[28] Kissinger interpreted the report ominously; to him it meant that Mrs. Gandhi planned to reduce West Pakistan to impotence; it was to be "dismembered and rendered defenseless."

Two points should be made : first, regardless of the intelligence report's authenticity, it is quite possible that the substance of the report accurately reflected Indian contingency planning for a post-East -Pakistan phase of the fighting; second, Nixon and Kissinger were virtually alone in the U.S. government in interpreting the report as they did.[29]

27. Powers, *The Man Who Kept the Secrets*, p. 206. The Powers book revived the long standing controversy that has surrounded this CIA report. (The source was also the source of the report in August—which Kissinger labeled as "fatuous"—that said that the Soviets viewed the Indo-Soviet treaty as an instrument of restraint on India.) Indira Gandhi injected the report into the last Indian election campaign, alleging that some of her political opponents might have provided information to the CIA. *New York Times*, November 20 and 21, 1979.

28. Nicholas and Oldenburg, *Bangladesh : The Birth of a Nation*, p. 128.

29. *Ibid*. For example, in the December 8 WSAG meeting, Assistant Secretary Sisco expressed doubts that India planned to convert West Pakistan into a "client state."

Entirely separate from West Pakistan, Kashmir had been the object of bitter dispute between India and Pakistan since their independence and had been fought over in two wars—in 1948 and 1965. India claimed all of the area, including the Pakistan-held "Azad Kashmir"; Pakistan claimed "Indian-occupied Kashmir." Pakistani military forces had advanced across the Kashmir cease-fire line on December 3 and occupied parts of Indian Kashmir in the Chhamb region. Thus an Indian objective to "straighten out the southern border of Azad Kashmir" was a logical military and political goal, just as the Pakistanis undoubtedly hoped to dislodge the Indians from areas they occupied in Azad Kashmir. Similarly, the Indian military objective of trying to destroy Pakistani aircraft and armor capabilities (Kissinger incorrectly substitutes "army" for armor) was not illiogical, because planes and tanks had spearheaded the Pakistan attack on December 3.

There is no evidence for Kissinger's claim that India had a definite war aim to dismember West Pakistan. The Indian government shifted from support for a united Pakistan before the civil war to support for an independent Bangladesh because it judged that the uncertainties about the political orientation of a new nation on its flank would be offset by the restoration of stability in Eastern India through the return of the refugees. In the process, India could attain unquestioned supremacy in the subcontinent. Having achieved these objectives, there would be no clear Indian interest in dismembering West Pakistan. The breakup of West Pakistan into four separate states would pose threats to the integrity of the Indian Union, already facing fissiparous tendencies.

The White House nonetheless persisted in its conviction that India sought the destruction of West Pakistan, despite bilateral assurances to the contrary from Indian Ambassador L.K. Jha and Foreign Minister Swaran Singh, and a public statement by Mrs. Gandhi in New Delhi on December 12 denying any territorial ambitions in West Pakistan. Aside from the questions of West Pakistan, Kissinger emphasizes that Indian officials would not deny that India had aspirations in Kashmir. But the reasons should have been obvious. Because India had always claimed all of Kashmir as Indian territory, just as the Pakistanis made the reverse claim, no Indian official would be likely to give such assurances—nor would any Pakistani. He fails to mention that the State Department did not reply to Ambassador Jha's request for assurances that Pakistan would vacate those areas of Indian Kashmir its forces had occupied.[30]

Pakistan As An "Ally"

The CIA report also caused Kissinger to try to promote a close U.S. alliance relationship with Pakistan suggesting that, if India attacked West Pakistan, the United States was committed by prior agreements to come to its defense. But he misunderstands the evolution—and the devolution—of the U.S.-Pakistan alliance relationship and its inapplicability to the situation in 1971.

Describing the establishment of the U.S-Pakistan military supply relationship in the 1950s, and Pakistan's decision to join CENTO and SEATO, he makes the surprising judgment that there "was no recognition that most Pakistanis considered their real security threat to be India," and that India "viewed our arming of Pakistan as a challenge undermining our attempt to nurture its favor." Anyone who dealt with South Asia during the 1950s clearly recognized that there was a dual perception, tacitly accepted by both sides : the U.S. supplied Pakistan with military equipment as part of the Dulles era effort to contain the monolithic Sino-Soviet threat; in receiving the arms, Pakistan endorsed this anti-Communist theme, but regarded the arms primarily as a security shield against India. U.S. policy-makers later faced serious dilemmas when Pakistan moved toward a close relationship with China, when the U.S. supported India against China in 1962, and when Washington cut off military supply to both India and Pakistan during their 1965 war.

A limited arms supply relationship with Pakistan was resumed after that war, but by 1971 Pakistan—unhappy over the U.S. failure to support it in 1965—was playing only a passive role in CENTO and SEATO. Kissinger is wrong in suggesting that the 1959 U.S.-Pakistan Bilateral Agreement

30. L.K. Jha, "Kissinger and I," *India Today*, November 1—15, 1979, p. 55. See also Jha's interview in *The Hindustan Times*, November 26, 1979.

committed the United States to assist Pakistan in the case of an Indo-Pakistan war (during the 1965 war, the agreement did not come into force). The language of the 1959 bilateral agreement was carefully drafted so that the U.S. would not automatically undertake any such obligation; rather, it called for the U.S. to provide assistance "as is envisaged" in the Middle East Resolution—a resolution that was directed against attacks by Communist countries.[31] Even if one were to accept Kissinger's view, who would have decided which country was the aggressor in late 1971 ? And would such a finding, and the purported U.S. commitment, have been supported by the U.S. Congress ?

In keeping with his trans-Himalayan geopolitical vision, Kissinger had another reason for promoting the alliance with Pakistan : he wanted to demonstrate to Beijing that the United States stood by its "ally" in time of need. During his preparatory briefings on China, and his conversations in Beijing in July and October, Kissinger became convinced that the Chinese placed a premium on the "reliability" of another country's actions.[32] Consequently, White House policy toward Asia was strongly influenced by a sensitivity as to how the American actions would be viewed through the Chinese prism. However, Nixon and Kissinger seemed to have overemphasized the impact of American actions in the subcontinent on the prospective Nixon visit and on the broader Washington-Beijing relationship. In his December 1971 backgrounder, Kissinger said that he did not have the impression that China considered agreement with the United States on other issues as "a prerequisite for a successful visit," a judgment based on the observation that preparation for the Nixon trip had not been jeopardized by U.S. policies in Vietnam, nor UN issues on which the U.S. and China differed.[33] The Chinese had a strong independent interest in forging the U.S. connection as an offset

31. For the text, see *Congressional Quarterly*, January 26, 1980, p. 176.
32. On the importance of assuring China that the United States was "reliable," see the interview with Winston Lord, a member of the NSC staff who accompanied Kissinger on his trips to Beijing. Lifschultz, *Bangladesh : The Unfinished Revolution*, p. 156.
33. *Congressional Record*, December 9, 1971, pp. S21013-S21014; *White House Years*, pp. 704, 710.

to the Soviet Union, and it seems unlikely that a more distant
U.S.-Pakistan relationship would have significantly affected the
evolving U.S.-Chinese ties.

Geopolitics Risks War

Persistent suspicions of Indian and Soviet intentions, the belief
the U.S. was somehow formally committed to Pakistan, and the
ultrasensitivity toward China, set the stage for the most dramatic and disturbing episode described in Kissinger's memoirs :
the December 12 White House meeting between Nixon,
Kissinger, and General Alexander Haig before Nixon and
Kissinger left for the Azores to meet French President Pompidou. By that date, India had given several assurances that it
had no territorial ambitions in West Pakistan but it had not
provided assurances regarding Kashmir. On the basis of earlier
hard line remarks by Huang Hua, the Chinese Ambassador to
the United Nations, Nixon and Kissinger expected that China
would "increase its assistance" to Pakistan ; if the Chinese
moved militarily, they thought the Soviet Union would use
force against China. The President decided that the United
States would not stand by if the Soviet Union threatened
China ; and Nixon therefore decided "to risk war in the trian-
gular Soviet-China-America relationship."

The President did not work out the precise nature of the
"significant assistance" he planned to extend to China but, to
give effect to his strategy, he ordered an eight-ship U.S. Navy
task force, headed by the carrier *Enterprise*, to proceed through
the Straits of Malacca to the Bay of Bengal. Kissinger sums up
the geopolitical rationale for the decision to risk war to save
West Pakistan in the following rhetoric-laden passage in *White
House Years* :

> The naked recourse to force by a partner of the Soviet
> Union backed by Soviet arms and buttressed by Soviet
> assurances threatened the very structure of international
> order just when our whole Middle East strategy depended
> on proving the inefficacy of such tactics and when
> America's weight as a factor in the world was already
> being undercut by our divisions over Indochina. The assault
> on Pakistan was in our view a most dangerous precedent

for Soviet behavior, which had to be resisted if we were not to tempt escalating upheavals. Had we acquiesced in such a power play, we would have sent a wrong signal to Moscow and unnerved all our allies, China and the forces for restraint in other volatile areas of the world. This was, indeed, why the Soviets had made the Indian assault on Pakistan possible in the first place.

As it turned out, there was no need to implement any high risk decisions. When the Chinese UN Ambassador next contacted the White House, he made no reference to any military move ; instead, he agreed to the proposed solution through the United Nations already accepted by the Soviet Union and Pakistan—a resolution calling for a cease-fire and withdrawal, but with a fallback willingness to accept a cease-fire in place. Nonetheless, as a precaution in case the U.S. initiative in the UN failed, the *Enterprise* task force, which had been held up temporarily, was ordered to continue toward the Bay of Bengal to create "precisely the margin of uncertainty needed to force a decision by New Delhi and Moscow." When Mrs. Gandhi offered unconditional cease-fire in the west on December 16, Kissinger was convinced that it was a "reluctant decision" resulting from Soviet pressure that resulted from American insistence, including the fleet movement and the willingness to risk the Moscow summit.

Geopolitics Misapplied

In claiming that the White House actions saved West Pakistan, and were undertaken "to preserve the world balance of power for the ultimate safety of all free people," Henry Kissinger laments that this "essentially geopolitical point of view found no understanding among those who conducted the public discourse on foreign policy in our country." But perhaps this lack of understanding was for the greater good "of all free people." The Nixon-Kissinger geopolitical approach to South Asia was flawed both in conception and implementation. By attempting to resolve an essentially regional dispute through global geopolitics, the President and his National Security Adviser de-emphasized or misinterpreted the political dynamics in the subcontinent and exaggerated the role and influence of the major external powers. They unnecessarily elevated the local crisis into one of U.S-Soviet confrontation in keeping with their thesis that the U.S.-Soviet contest must be fought out at all levels and in all regions, and that the Soviets should be held responsible for the actions of their "allies." In this case, the Soviet Union should be held responsible for its "client" India, which was fighting a "proxy war" for the USSR.

Among the defects in this type of geopolitical theorem was the failure to perceive the unique features in the South Asia situation—including the failure fully to comprehend the political-economic impact of the millions of refugees in India, the essential requirements for a political settlement in East Pakistan, the nuances of the Kashmir issue, and the nature of U.S. commitments to Pakistan. Kissinger's "client state" philosophy caused him to misjudge the more balanced character of the Soviet-Indian relationship and to ignore or dismiss Soviet assurances to Washington that Moscow was counselling restraint on India. There is no support for the claim that India had decided upon an allout assault on West Pakistan; there is certainly no support for the contention that the two countries were working in tandem toward that goal. The apocalyptic warning that such an attack would "threaten the structure of international order" and upset "the forces for restraint in other volatile areas of the world" represents the domino theory raised to global heights—and to the heights of incredulity.

Despite Kissinger's conclusion that skilled White House geopolitical diplomacy forced Mrs. Gandhi reluctantly to agree to a cease-fire, he produces no evidence to support this claim. All indications suggest that she reached her decision on the basis of several complex considerations, internal and external, but not as a result of pressure exerted by the Soviet Union at the U.S. behest. At the time of the cease-fire, Indian forces had achieved total military success in East Pakistan, they occupied about 2,500 square miles in the Sind and Punjab provinces of West Pakistan, and they held small parts of Azad Kashmir. But these military successes were at substantial external political cost. Two Soviet vetoes were required to block UN Security Council resolutions calling for Indian withdrawal from East Pakistan, and India was isolated when a similar resolution passed the General Assembly by a 104 to 11 vote, with 10 abstentions. Sensitive to the potential for outside intervention in dissident regions, no Third World country except Bhutan supported the Indian government nor did any other country outside the Soviet bloc. Having achieved India's war aims in the east, the Gandhi government's decision to declare a unilateral cease-fire was probably influenced largely by the strong international climate favoring the cessation of hostilities.[34]

Once the military issue in East Pakistan was resolved, the Soviet Union was also counselling India in the direction of a cease-fire in the west ; at that point, Soviet and American aims were generally similar.[35] But the Soviets were not significantly influenced by American pressure nor by a potential Chinese military move. They were motivated by independent Soviet interests, in South Asia and elsewhere. Moscow, which had sought to mediate the affairs of the subcontinent at Tashkent after the 1965 India-Pakistan war, was anxious to prevent further military conflict and to retain its political relationship with Pakistan ; it was also sensitive to its negative image in the Middle East as a result of its support of India during the East Pakistan phase of the fighting.

There is no indication that the *Enterprise* deployment had any immediate political or military impact on events in South Asia, although, as noted below, it may have had adverse longer-term repercussions in terms of U.S. interests. The eight ships comprising Task Force 74 did not arrive in the Bay of Bengal until December 15, the day before the fall of Dacca to Indian and Mukti Bahini guerrilla forces ; they arrived with the transparently false cover story of helping to evacuate the less than 50 Americans still in Dacca. Since the task force was some 1,300 miles from West Pakistan, and the U.S. had not clearly signalled New Delhi that its deployment had any relationship to events in the west, the Indians apparently concluded that the United States was trying to inject itself into the military picture in East Pakistan at a time when Indian arms had clearly prevailed. Although the Soviet Union was aware of the task force's movements, through press reports and

---

34. Pran Chopra, *India's Second Liberation* (Cambridge : MIT Press, 1974), pp. 212-213.

35. *Ibid.* See also Nixon interview with *Time* magazine editors. *Time*, January 3, 1972, p. 14.

"warnings" conveyed through Kissinger's deputy Haig, there is no indication that the task force had any impact on Moscow's decision-making. As part of a 1978 Brookings Institution study of U.S. armed forces as a political instrument, a careful examination of the *Enterprise* deployment concludes that "it is important to emphasize that Soviet and Indian support for a cease-fire was *not* the result of U.S. military pressure generated by Task Force 74."[36] Kissinger offers no evidence to refute the Brookings' conclusion.

In addition to misreading Indian and Soviet intentions, Kissinger also misjudged the Chinese, believing, as late as December 12, that Beijing might take military action in support of Pakistan. Despite the seemingly hard-line remarks of the Chinese Permanent Representative, there was little to support this belief. Still embroiled in the Cultural Revolution, Beijing in mid-December showed no serious intention to become militarily involved; it limited itself to exercising its weather net communications system in Tibet and protesting an Indian border violation in the Sikkim area.[37] Even if the Chinese internal political tensions had not acted as a restraint, any government in Beijing would have thought carefully before attacking across the Himalayas in winter.

The Closed White House System

While many of these miscalculations stemmed from a misapplication of a global philosophy to regional disputes, the process of foreign policy-making under the closed Nixon-Kissinger system compounded the problem. In the context of the early 1970s, this essentially two-man system may have worked reasonably well on bilateral issues between the major powers, such as those between the United States and the Soviet Union and China. But the White House-centered system was ill-equipped to handle a multifaceted regional crisis, especially one that had not been on the regular White House agenda, extended over many months, and required a

36. Barry M. Blechman and Stephen S. Kaplan, *Force Without War* (Washington : The Brookings Institution, 1978), p. 200.

37. *Ibid.*, pp. 203—206. See also G.W. Choudhury, *India, Pakistan, Bangladesh, and the Major Powers* (New York : The Free Press, 1974). pp. 213—214.

number of operational decisions on such issues as arms supply, aid levels, and executive-congressional relationships.[38]

Over a period of nine months, there were some twenty Senior Review Group (SRG) and Washington Special Action Group (WSAG) meetings, most of them in the November-December period when war seemed imminent or was underway. During the early period, as much as two months elapsed between meetings, and even those sessions that occurred were often devoted to tactics, such as decisions to instruct American ambassadors to urge restraint on host governments, or efforts to determine how much U.S. economic assistance was in the pipeline. Much of the earlier difficulty stemmed from the intersection of the China opening with the Pakistan civil war and President Yahya's role as an intermediary between Washington and Beijing. However, even after the China initiative became public in midsummer, Kissinger failed to explain to senior officials the White House geopolitical approach to the Bangladesh crisis or the rationale for some of the White House decisions.[39]

This lack of effective dialogue, and the cumulative effect of the White House suspicions of the bureaucracy, led to the December 12 meeting at which the beleaguered President and his two associates, Kissinger and Haig, reportedly risked war, isolated from the rest of the Executive Branch and the Congress. The self-induced isolation and failure to consult the Secretaries of State and Defence, and the Director of the CIA, and their staffs, contributed to misjudgements of military intentions. It also caused Nixon and Kissinger to overestimate the effectiveness of U.S. actions—such as the cutoff of aid to India and the deployment of the *Enterprise*—and to rely excessively or unnecessarily on secret personal negotiations and the use of the Hot Line. The secretive, inward-looking Nixon-Kissinger system alienated the White House from the Con-

---

38. See I.M. Destler, "The Nixon System, A Further Look," *Foreign Service Journal*, February 1974, pp. 9–14, 28–29.

39. For a review of some of the key policy decisions, and observations on the failure of the White House to communicate with the bureaucracy, see Philip Oldenburg. "The Breakup of Pakistan," in the Present Volume.

gress on the Bangladesh issue and enhanced prospects of Executive Branch leaks, which proved so damaging to the White House image.

Legacies of the Bangladesh Crisis

Richard Nixon, who apparently expected to receive credit for Mrs. Gandhi's cease-fire, was unprepared for the mounting postwar criticism of his policies, fueled by Jack Anderson's exposure of Kissinger's handling of the secret White House meetings. Most commentators charged that the U.S. had badly blundered. It had placed itself on the wrong moral side of a civil war and on the losing side of the international war; the Soviet Union had achieved a major diplomatic triumph by supporting India, now the unquestioned dominant power in south Asia, and by aligning itself with the Bangladesh independence cause.

The President attempted to shift blame to the coauthor of the tilt policy, who for several weeks was denied access to the Oval Office and allowed to "twist slowly, slowly in the wind." However, in Kissinger's perception, the South Asia crisis soon disappeared; he patched up his relations with the President, and a "string of spectacular foreign policy successes"— notably the Beijing and Moscow summits—soon wiped out the Bangladesh episode and gained popular support. But Kissinger misjudges the longer-term repercussions of the Bangladesh crisis in brushing it aside as an "episode" analogous to a storm at sea—rough at the time, but without lasting damage to the vessel. In fact, there were three adverse legacies of the tilt policy, two affecting the domestic political climate, the third affecting U.S. global security interests.

The first legacy was the further erosion of the credibility of the Nixon administration in the eyes of the Congress, the media, and the foreign affairs community. With its image already tarnished by the secret military actions in Indochina, the administration's professed neutrality in the Indo-Pakistan crisis was held up to public ridicule by the Anderson Papers' revelations of pro-Pakistan bias. Coming on top of the earlier impressions that the administration had dissembled in claiming that the U.S. arms supply to Pakistan had been terminated, the public exposure of Kissinger's efforts to tilt American

policy in a less than-evenhanded direction opened the administration to the charges that its public statements and private
actions were in conflict. Other leaks, including Ambassador
Kenneth Keating's telegram from New Delhi questioning a
number of Kissinger's assertions to the press, reinforced the
impression of White House dissimulation. This loss of credibility undoubtedly contributed to later Congressional actions
to curb the powers of the White House and to enhance the
role of the Congress in formulating foreign policy.

Failure of the Nixon administration to condemn the
Pakistani military excesses in the east, while simultaneously
supporting what was considered to be an authoritarian dicta-
tor, contributed to a second legacy : the mounting criticism
of Nixon and Kissinger for their failure to take account of
the human equation in international affairs. Despite Kissinger's contention that the civil war in East Pakistan was
essentially an internal affair, many Americans regarded the
Pakistan army's actions as a brutal effort to suppress the
political aspirations the Bengalis had expressed in free
elections. The Nixon administration's expenditure of millions
of dollars for refugee relief carried little weight, either with the
Congress or with the media; both viewed it as "conscience
money" to atone for the White House's failure to speak out
against the human suffering in East Pakistan. Evidence that
the Nixon administrations put a higher premium on "geopolitics" than "humanitarianism" during the Bangladesh
crisis was one of the strands leading to the emergence of
human rights as an issue in the 1976 presidential campaign.

Perhaps the most serious longer-term legacy of the U.S.
tilt policy was its effect on the foreign and defense policies
of the Indian government, including the question of the
nuclear weapons option. Since the mid-1960s there had been
a sharp debate in India as to whether the country should take
the nuclear weapons route, particularly in view of China's
nuclear capability. No firm decisions had been made by 1971,
but the events of that year proved a turning point in terms of
Indian policy.

In the Indian perception, the U.S.-Pakistan-Chinese
alignment that emerged during the Bangladesh crisis was
designed to interject super-power influences into South Asia

for the purpose of thwarting Indian aspirations in the sub-continent. The decision to send a task force into the Bay of Bengal—headed by the nuclear-powered aircraft carrier *Enterprise*, which many Indians believed had nuclear weapons aboard—represented the first threat by the United States to use military force against India. As the discussions of the defence budget in the Indian parliament in 1972 attest, this action greatly intensified the Indian debate on the nuclear issue and increased pressures for the development of a military nuclear capability. Proponents of nuclear weapons for India repeatedly pointed to the American carrier as the reason such a capability was needed. They advanced the argument, suggested by Indian defense analyst K. Subrahmanyam, that "had India possessed nuclear weapons the *Enterprise* would not have steamed into the Bay of Bengal during the Indian-Pakistan war in what appeared from New Delhi to constitute atomic gunboat diplomacy."[40] India might have gone nuclear in any event but the Nixon administration's tilt toward Pakistan, including the decision to deploy the *Enterprise*, strengthened the hands of the nuclear advocates. It may have tipped the scales toward India's decision to explode a nuclear device in May 1974.

Needed : A More Upright Policy
American interests would have been better advanced in 1971 if Nixon and Kissinger had curbed their penchant to cast the Indo-Pakistan conflict in superpower geopolitical terms and, instead, had adopted the more realistic goal of trying to resolve the dispute in the South Asian regional context. The U.S. should have issued an early public statement deploring the military repression in East Pakistan and followed with cessation of all U.S. military supply, quickly closing any loop-holes that later developed. If these actions had been explained to President Yahya in advance through diplomatic channels—as reflecting the strong humanitarian and human rights concerns of the American public and Congress—they would not have jeopardized the China initiative, which was intrinsi-

---

40. K. Subrahmanyam, "India : Keeping the Option Open", in Robert M. Lawrence and Joel Larus, eds., *Nuclear Proliferation : Phase II* (Lawrence : University of Kansas Press, 1974), p. 122.

cally very much in Pakistan's and China's interest. U.S. influence was limited in both India and Pakistan but such an initial public position would have increased the *bona fides* of the Nixon administration in urging restraint upon India; because there were few external options open to Yahya, such a stance should not have reduced U.S. leverage over the Pakistani president in encouraging him to reach a political settlement in East Pakistan.

When the war broke out, a policy of working primarily through the United Nations would have been the preferred course. By placing greater emphasis on the UN., and less public blame-laying—including charges of aggression—the Nixon administration could have reduced the allegations of bias that so badly eroded its credibility. And by relying on the U.S. intelligence community, rather than their own intuitive judgments, Nixon and Kissinger probably could have avoided misassessments of Indian, Soviet and Chinese military intentions. They could also have avoided the potentially high-risk geopolitical posturing, including the imprudent decision to intervene in South Asia with the *Enterprise*. In short, a more upright and less tilted policy would have better served the interests of the United States.

Index

Abshire, David, Assistant Secretary for Congressional Relations, 153
Academic autarky, 343; community, American, 348, 353; institutions, American, 338; research, American, 344
Academic systems, Indian, 343
Academics, advice of, 356
Acts, Appropriations, 1953, 245ff; Agricultural, 1954, 202; Criminal, 177; Elementary and Secondary Education, 1965, 243; Food for Peace, 416; Foreign Assistance, 1961, 132, 188ff, 286, 319, 334, 392; Fulbright-Hayes, 345; Higher Education, 1965, 243; International Development, 286; International Education, 1966, 242ff; Merchant Marine, 1936, 205; Mutual Educational and Cultural Exchange, 1961, 242, 345; Mutual Security, 1954, 367; National Defense Education, 1961, 242; National Foundation on Arts and Humanities, 1965, 243; Peace Corps, 1961, 365, 368; Public Broadcasting, 1967, 243
Administration and conventional assistance programs, 367
Administrative cadres, 318
Administrative committee, 32; hierarchy, 13,15; management, 4; market control, 236; offices, 64; procedures, 274; reform, 3, 5, 8, 98
Advanced Research Projects Agency, Defense Department, (USG) 84

Advisory Committee, 245, 254; group, 352
Afghanistan, 31
Afro-Asian countries, 344
Agartala conspiracy, 397
Agency for International Development, 76, 206, 213ff, 272, 315, 379, 427; agency, 250; association, 367; country mission, 277; Foreign Aid, 147, 236, 274ff, 397; mission, 268, 277; officials, 292; project, 374; strategy, 222
Agreement process, 211-14
Agricultural assistance activities, planning of, 223
Agricultural committees, 212, 216ff; commodities, 204, 221, 252; commodities, distribution of, 248, 255; credit, 256; credit projects, 318; development, 221, 225, 237ff, 250, 256, 273; development efforts, 222; development policy, 222; economies of less developed countries, 214; exports, 209; investment, 237; market development, 241; policy, 228, 240; production, 264, 271; production and distribution system, 201; production capacity, 209; production team, 270; Programs in India, 376; projects, 379; reforms, 39; Research, Council of (GOI), 217; strategy, 238; technocrats, 217; trade development, 202; training corps, 377
Agriculture, United States Department of, 32, 205 see reference